THE
SPIRAL
STAIRWAY

THE SYSTEM TO BUILD
A HOLISTIC COMPANY

JOHN OOMMEN

The Spiral Stairway: The System to Build a Holistic Company, First Edition.

Copyright © 2022 John Oommen. All rights reserved.

This book may not be reproduced in whole or in part, or transmitted in any form, without written permission from the publisher, except by a reviewer who may quote brief passages in a review; nor may any part of this book be reproduced, stored in a retrieval system, or transmitted in any form or by any means electronic, mechanical, photocopying, recording, or other, without written permission from the publisher.

The information contained within this book is strictly for educational purposes. The author has made every effort to ensure the accuracy of the information within this book at the time of publication. If you wish to apply the ideas in this book, you take full responsibility for your actions, and the author does not guarantee any results. The author does not assume and hereby disclaims any liability to any party for any loss, damage, or disruption caused by errors or omissions, whether such errors or omissions result from accident, negligence, or any other cause.

ACUMES

Published by Acumes LLC, in the United States of America.
Editing by J. Austin Lee
Cover design & layout by Wayne Kehoe

First printing edition April 2022.
ISBN: 979-8-9860012-0-3
Library of Congress Cataloging-in-Publication Data has been applied for.

Inquiries: **info@acumes.com**

Table of Contents

How Must We Build And Manage A Company? ... 9

A Holistic Company Focuses On Fundamentals. ... 14

The Path To Intrinsic Value. ... 32

PART A
Management Approach Articulates The System In Which People Work. ... 47

    A.1 Let Leaders Lead. ... 54

    A.2 Set Core Values As Behavioral Guardrails. ... 63

    A.3 Design Organization To Map Skills To Growth Stage. ... 74

    A.4 Hire For Skills And Incentives To Enable Organization Design. ... 92

    A.5 Build Objective And Transparent Performance Management. ... 105

    A.6 Deploy Performance-Based Compensation To Instill Meritocracy. ... 127

PART B
Value Engine Synergistically Creates Customer Value. ... 145

    B.1 Enable Sustainable Value Creation Via Productization. ... 157

    B.2 Scale Operations With Effective Processes. ... 192

    B.3 Micro-Evolve Using Objective Data, Analysis, And Reporting. ... 221

PART C
Corporate Strategy Is The North Star For Macro-Evolution. ... 251

    C.1 Internalize The Essence Of Strategy. ... 259

    C.2 Analyze The Market Problem To Trigger Macro-Evolution. ... 273

    C.3 Pin Down Optimal Customer To Initiate Strategic Choices. ... 298

    C.4 Triangulate Towards What-To-Offer And How-To-Deliver Strategic Choices. 326

PART D
Strategic Planning Charts The Path To Corporate Strategy. 363

    D.1 Build A Strategy-Led, Operations-Focused Plan To Enable Execution. 370

    D.2 Translate Strategy Into Operations With Enablement Planning. 390

    D.3 Predict Unit-Level Performance Via Operations Planning. 410

    D.4 Optimize Scale And Outcomes Through Investment Planning. 435

PART E
Execution Management Dictates Outcomes From Operations. 474

    E.1 Optimize Execution Using Decision-Making Frameworks. 481

    E.2 Empower Macro-Evolution With Effective Change Management. 494

    E.3 Connect Strategy To Operations Via Enablement Execution. 511

    E.4 Achieve Peak Performance Via Transparent And Predictive Operations Execution. 538

Align Holistic Purpose With Methods. 566

Definitions of Fundamental Concepts. 568

Infographics

1 – Holistic companies balance incentives of all stakeholders 21
2 – Sustainable growth demands recurring evolution 28
3 – A company fundamentals self-assessment 31
4 – The Spiral Stairway™ evolutionary growth methodology 42
5 – Organizational roles & responsibilities matrix 45
A.1 – Management Approach Maturity Model 52
A.2 – Purpose dictates strategy and operations 56
A.3 – Values Funnel Framework to develop core values 65
A.4 – Core hiring principles to balance incentives 93
A.5 – Objective and transparent performance management framework 111
A.6 – Role-specific compensation design framework 138
B.1 – Value engine builds on management approach to create value 148
B.2 – What does low labor market productivity growth imply? 150
B.3 – Optimizing value engine enables sustainable growth curve 152
B.4 – Value Engine Maturity Model 155
B.5 – Repeatability and reproducibility enable productization 162
B.6 – Capability mindset enables net positive customer value 174
B.7 – Capabilities are multi-dimensional 181
B.8 – Sustainable scale demands a strong process mindset 198
B.9 – Effective process design focuses on performers' journey 201
B.10 – Six elements of effective process design 203
B.11 – Operations technology always follows process design 212
B.12 – Process-Data Symbiosis 224

B.13 – Divergent applications of analysis and reporting	**237**
B.14 – Setting reporting targets & limits	**240**
C.1 – Corporate Strategy Maturity Model	**256**
C.2 – Three legs of a market problem	**274**
C.3 – Player groups in a market ecosystem	**284**
C.4 – Journeys of player groups in the market	**288**
C.5 – Value flows render three legs of the market problem	**291**
C.6 – The sweet spot and three customer roles	**302**
C.7 – Top customer groups with aligned journeys prescribe sweet spot	**311**
C.8 – Who-to-Serve Trade-offs Decision Framework	**324**
C.9 – Single viable strategic zone to create sustainable value	**326**
C.10 – Operations baseline and who-how-what decision cycle	**328**
C.11 – How-to-Deliver Trade-offs Decision Framework	**337**
C.12 – Each capability dimension spans four effectiveness vectors	**345**
C.13 – Build vs. Buy vs. Borrow vs. Avoid Decision Matrix	**350**
C.14 – Capability Levers Framework inform what-to-offer trade-offs	**354**
C.15 – What-to-Offer Trade-offs Decision Framework	**357**
C.16 – Comprehensive and cohesive corporate strategy trade-off decision	**360**
D.1 – Strategic Planning Maturity Model	**367**
D.2 – Input-Process-Output Strategic Planning Model	**379**
D.3 – Three-Phased Strategic Planning Approach	**386**
D.4 – Operations gap assessment for enablement planning	**393**
D.5 – Strategic Initiatives Map enables effective enablement planning	**401**
D.6 – Strategic Initiative Prioritization Framework	**408**
D.7 – Chain of Controllability enables predictive and actionable plan	**412**

D.8 – The power of leading indicators	**417**
D.9 – Leading indicators vs. lagging indicators	**419**
D.10 – Impact timeline of leading and lagging indicators	**425**
D.11 – Operations plan forecasts unit performance	**430**
D.12 – Importance of strategic initiative steady state	**441**
D.13 – Strategic initiatives' steady state trigger investment decisions	**445**
D.14 – Tiered investment prioritization of strategic initiatives	**450**
D.15 – Initiative Investment Map prescribes enablement investment	**454**
D.16 – Operations Investment Map enables scale optimization	**459**
E.1 – Execution Management in The Spiral Stairway™ context	**475**
E.2 – Execution Management Maturity Model	**478**
E.3 – Four decision management tools enable execution	**489**
E.4 – Pressure Valve Framework empowers change management	**499**
E.5 – Effective strategic initiative execution principles	**526**
E.6 – Operations execution is predicated on a mature operations baseline	**547**

How Must We Build And Manage A Company?

Have you ever seen a single cohesive and comprehensive articulation of what a 'good' and holistic company looks like? I searched for two decades and came up short. So, I framed an answer based on my twenty years of hands-on experience for everyone out there asking the same question.

The fundamental idea of capitalism is that companies compete, and the best ones win. Unfortunately, through decades of competition with weak referees, the holistic parameters of a 'good' company are still inadequately defined, and the qualifiers for 'winning' are often interpretive.

There are over 1.3 million firms with ten or more employees in the United States. Yet, we focus on a handful of success stories without considering that their outstanding success could be happenstance. Many unsung companies in the 1.3 million exist happily, with their obscurity, creating balanced value for those involved. But as we increasingly glorify outsized victories without considering the cost, every company is tempted to jump in the race to become one of those beacons of success.

This creates a problem if we don't define a 'good' company in a game with often contrived rules. Not everyone can wake up one day and just choose to be a Jeff Bezos or a Serena Williams. But when the definition of 'good' is unclear, many try with basic information, resulting in a dysfunctional path to achieve glory.

Dysfunction for a company doesn't refer to growth rate or profit. Instead, dysfunction is the collateral damage along the path in an attempt to achieve such outcomes. A dysfunctional company can be traumatic for employees. It can fail to deliver value for customers and promised returns to investors or lenders. A company can force society to pay for its mistakes. We have all experienced such dysfunction as consumers or active participants in a company, whether we recognized it or not.

A single event early in my career altered my decision about the role I wanted to play in the market economy. A large, poorly run company lured me away from my first job at General Electric, the largest company in the world at the time. After living through a comical series of blunders, the company laid me off in less than six months, along with many others. Armed with this new awareness of cause-and-effect, I dove into companies under challenging circumstances to understand why bad things happen and how we can avoid them.

I am not an investor, an academic, or someone who skipped all the middle ranks in a company. Instead, I am an electrical engineer turned business engineer who spent my entire career rolling up my sleeves to fix every potential problem for companies to answer a simple question – **how must we build and manage a company?**

It is a straightforward question, but I have never found an unbiased, informative, and convincing answer. Search and see for yourself.

We treat adults like children and water down complex topics to 140 characters and bite-sized opinions. We are inundated with click-bait headers and search optimized articles packed with trivial and tactical information intended to do one of two things – get us to look at something we should buy or share subjective information to move us as societal herds. Simplifying complex and nuanced topics leave us with an illusion that we understand them, which is more dangerous than knowing we need to dig deeper.

Business books and classrooms often tackle niche topics and cover only a tiny fraction of a company's operations. But every company is a complex array of dependent issues. Thinking in a single dimension while ignoring the multitudes of other dependent dimensions is like trying to solve a Rubik's cube if we are color blind. Running a business is not a single-dimensional game.

The alternative is to connect the dots ourselves across the vast array of complex and intertwined topics that make a company run. Even a six-color Rubik's cube can have 43 Quintilian combinations. So, how are we supposed to take the various opinions on each aspect of a company's operation and combine them into an optimal prescription for its holistic performance? It's nearly impossible.

Now we are in between a rock and a hard place to guess and hope that piece-meal answers will suffice. Such a systemic challenge blocks our efforts to answer our question – *how must we build and manage a company?*

No wonder dysfunction in companies is prevalent.

I grew up tinkering with electronic and mechanical projects in my little home lab, enjoyed physics, chemistry, and mathematics in school, and ended up becoming an electrical engineer. Because of these formative experiences, I firmly believe in concepts that offer repeatability and reproducibility.

It doesn't matter what field we are involved in; we mustn't keep reinventing the wheel in our daily lives. Instead, we should find commonalities between situations to simplify problem-solving. Firm grounding through generalities and theories allows us to move forward to create problem-solving formulae for more significant problems.

Creating such formulae is complicated because companies are full of people and people are complex. Corporate environments include a wide range of personality types based on profiling factors, including different nationalities, religions, cultures, genders, prior work experiences, and even personal upbringing. Such diversity in backgrounds and thoughts leads to significant behavioral and interpretational skews around companies.

However, let's think about the variations caused by individuals in companies as noise in the data and look for patterns. Then, we can develop an objective and structured methodology as our business formula.

The Spiral Stairway™ is my answer to the question – *how must we build and manage a company?*

> **We must focus on fundamentals and intrinsic properties to build and manage holistic companies that can maintain an equilibrium between the incentives of all stakeholders – customers, investors, employees, partners, and society – and are self-sufficient.**

We all deserve an operating model where the incentives of all stakeholders are purposefully aligned, and our companies are managed and operated in a manner that aligns with that purpose.

For close to twenty years, I have been a business operator and leader, researching and gathering information on how companies succeed or fail. In addition, I have worked in the bowels of several companies, solving strategic and operational problems. These experiences span a variety of sectors, including large public companies, early-stage start-ups, and highly successful and profitable companies. And, of course, I've also worked with those that filed for bankruptcy.

I have helped very young companies scale up and develop their offerings and commercial strategy to become market leaders. I have assisted companies in pivoting from legacy business models to embrace market shifts and become competitive again. Finally, I have worked with companies to rebuild their operations to reignite growth.

Even if he's losing, a good poker player stays in the game long enough to understand the cards other players hold and how they play them. Likewise, if you are a climate researcher, the most valuable data exists in storm systems, not exclusive beach resorts.

I've worked with several companies facing challenges. I have seen miscalculated hiring frenzies and mass layoffs, rational business decisions that didn't stick, completed business acquisitions that failed to live up to promises, companies that drove the best employees to quit, companies filing for bankruptcy... you get the idea.

These hands-on experiences led me to create *The Spiral Stairway*™. It offers growth-phase companies, which include sub-divisions of large entities, a cohesive path to balance the incentives of all stakeholders – customers, owners, employees, partners, and society at large – while sustainably growing profitably.

This book isn't about creating an Apple, Google, or a Meta. There has always been a Carnegie, a Rockefeller, or a Jobs. They are successful freaks of nature aided by time and place. So, our conversations here will not focus on a single success story; one or two data points don't make a trend. Instead, I've based it on my hands-on work performed for over three dozen companies.

The Spiral Stairway™ is for folks interested in rolling up their sleeves and getting to work on creating and running better companies. It's an end-to-end methodology to build a holistic company organically, and it works.

You may be a CEO or senior executive trying to create or reassess your approach to manage your company optimally; this methodology is your checklist to ensure that you cover all the bases. It offers a comprehensive set of frameworks and concepts to guide you through structuring organizational problem solving cohesively. If you want to be a critical thinker and an influencer, these components and principles offer you a how-to and what-not-to-do guide. *The Spiral Stairway*™ is a comprehensive handbook that can be your companion as you solve problems at your companies.

All of us can influence the behaviors and outcomes of our companies if we ask critical and challenging questions and focus on balancing incentives optimally.

A Holistic Company Focuses On Fundamentals.

WHEN economic growth prospects darken, governments act by spending more taxpayer money to encourage trade in their country or by pushing down the interest rates, hoping that increased borrowing will lead to more trade.

Such economic busts happen when risk taking goes too far in the economy, and economic history tells us they are unavoidable. There are one or two very popular pockets of economic activity during a perceived 'boom,' and risk takers rush into these pockets until they are exhausted.

Every decade or so, this results in a bust where investors place too many bad bets. The most recent snag was the financial crisis of the late 2000s, where risk taking focused on the real estate market. When the real estate crisis hit in 2008/09, it affected trade across all sectors and in most countries worldwide. That was a particularly devastating downturn as it shook the global financial system to its core for an extended time.

Predictably, governments decided to lubricate their economies to catapult themselves out of economic doldrums. So, just like any other downturn, one way to stimulate the market was to find a way to engage risk takers.

One of those paths is low-interest rates on lending by governments which nudges everyone to place their bet on riskier endeavors that might grow the economy. Another path is for governments to buy their own debt back in exchange for creating new money that didn't exist before. In theory, these paths work. But human nature often tends to take things too far.

Since the financial crisis of 2009, we have been living in an era of easy money with low interest rates and governments printing more money for most of that time. People started businesses on the back of easy money, forming rapidly escalating bubbles. We were due for a correction when I began writing this book in 2019.

Then came Covid-19 in early 2020. It cataclysmically decimated economies around the world and destroyed all normal rules. However, the economic devastation of Covid-19 had a counter-intuitive impact. It masked the evidence of risk-taking gone too far since 2009.

Governments doled out economic stimulus packages with figures that are hard to comprehend, reduced interest rates down to zero, and printed even more new money. Only time will tell the long-term ramifications of governments' further loosening of monetary policies because nothing in life is free.

The punchline is that unintended economic cycles are an unavoidable reality that every company has to operate within.

Economic cycles form a noisy, unintended backdrop for companies.

Drilling into our most recent economic cycle, we have been living in an era of easy money since 2009. It has extended for such a long time that methods and frequency with which companies are created, grown, and managed have changed systemically.

Large companies such as Google, Amazon, and Salesforce had become highly valued companies just before we embarked on this easy money era. These companies started and became behemoths in a short time. What if investment professionals could replicate such behemoths and show outsized returns on investment to attract money from those who have it? This has been the pocket of risk since 2009.

Enter the meteoric rise of private investment firms. The last two decades have given way to the disproportionate increase in venture capital firms and private equity firms. Such private investment firms have existed for decades. They provide a robust economic purpose of investing in companies too risky for traditional investors since they haven't proved themselves or have been facing growth or existential challenges.

Venture capital and private equity firms gather money from wealthy people and other institutions that manage people's wealth to create investment funds. However, there is a small but critical difference between private equity firms and venture capital firms. Private equity firms own the companies, often larger ones with a track record. They invest in the company and generally take it over, intending to fix it up. This scenario incentivizes them to actively manage the companies to grow them and make them more profitable.

On the contrary, venture capital firms tend to place significantly more small bets across many companies, with usually smaller ownership shares. Moreover, the distributed ownership structure of these smaller companies means that management of the companies continues to sit with the company leaders, who are often the founders.

If we get past all the jargon, it is pretty simple. Private investment firms promise a significant return on investment to the people and institutions they collect money from by the time they close each investment fund within a previously agreed time horizon. They have become astronomically more popular in the last two decades because anyone with enough money is looking for a better return on investment in the easy money era. According to data published by Preqin, a financial data provider, the number of such private investment firms has more than quadrupled between 2012 and 2021. That's staggering, by any measure.

The problem is that creating or owning companies isn't enough for private investment firms to give money back to their investors. Someone else has to buy their ownership share. The traditional path for private investors to offload companies is through a public market listing called Initial Public Offering (IPO), where everyone can buy shares.

Such ownership hand-offs are always the risk spiking points in any economic cycle. I spent my time at Capital One, a large US bank, analyzing and reversing the complex pass-the-hot-potato game we created with mortgages and related securities prior to the financial crisis. Replace packages of mortgages in the last economic cycle with companies in this one, and the similarities are uncanny.

We live in an investment ecosystem that always encourages risks. During this cycle, they come in the form of 'start-ups.' The popularity of these investment vehicles and exponentially greater available amounts of money have allowed many more entrepreneurs to take their ideas to market. Their capital-infused, accelerated early growth often dominates their market and displaces traditional players. As a result, start-ups have quickly risen to reach consumers and companies faster than ever before. Uber's fast rise and displacement of taxis is a prime example of how access to significant amounts of funding can help upstarts topple weak and antiquated competitors quickly.

What is a holistic company?

A conducive ecosystem offers a reduced threshold for starting a new company and growing it early on. For example, companies can hire sales teams and engineers very quickly because they have easier access to funding; they can spend money to market their products via search and social media advertising, such as Google and Meta.

This is a great part of the story, since small and mid-sized businesses are the bedrock of a thriving economy. However, life is a zero-sum game. One person's victory is another person's loss.

These enablers aren't unique to any particular start-up, and any entrepreneur who can sell an idea can get funded. That means there are a lot of companies taking advantage of this ecosystem, which creates competition between young companies with a wide range of effectiveness with which they solve each market problem. The market economy then works its magic over time.

The market economy's magic is that a company has to reach a sustainable growth phase to be a viable entity long-term. It could be a standalone or subsidiary of another company that acquires the start-up. Either way, market economics demands that companies are profitable within a reasonable period.

> **Things to Remember: Sustainable Growth Mindset**
>
> **A sustainable growth mindset implies that a company exists to achieve profitability and continue to grow and create increasing value for customers without perpetually borrowing funds from financial institutions or raising funding from investors by giving away shares.**

All companies germinate as start-ups. This life cycle involves high-risk investment during the early days of operation, where investors support the company as it seeks a significant market share. Unfortunately, the failure rate during this stage is very high, and few companies progress to sustainable growth. *So, what is the incentive to do this?* Focus on extrinsic value to pass the company to someone else and cash out.

Extrinsic value is the worth of a thing strictly based on how someone else might value it. One of my finance professors used to say, "What is something worth? One cent less than whatever the next idiot is willing to pay for it!" That's extrinsic value. Sheer focus on extrinsic value hides the reality of what something is worth or might be worth in the future.

The notion of calling 'mission accomplished' by handing over unprofitable companies with questionable prospects to large companies listed on the stock market or letting the public buy up its shares through stock market listings has broader societal implications. Such hand-offs of unprofitable companies with questionable intrinsic value to the public at large raise ethical considerations.

An extreme historical example of this pass-the-hot-potato game is the story of Broadcast.com. During the height of the dot-com bubble, Yahoo!, one of the earliest internet companies, bought the unprofitable Broadcast.com for $5.7B. Yahoo! was a public company, and it was the largest acquisition Yahoo! ever made. Yet, Yahoo! gave up and shut down the Broadcast.com service within three years of buying the company. In other words, Yahoo!'s public shareholders got very little value from this acquisition. In this transaction, Yahoo! gave away most of the $5.7B of value to the handful of shareholders of Broadcast.com. 30% went to the CEO and founder of Broadcast.com for creating an unsustainable company that Yahoo! shut down soon after. This CEO has since been considered a model investor and a start-up advisor on Shark Tank, a popular TV show highlighting investors and want-to-be entrepreneurs. Go figure!

We talked about the private investment model, where each fund places many bets. Here is why it works easily when money is cheap. These investment models follow a Power Law Curve, a mathematical distribution where very few funds succeed beyond expectations, and the vast majority have limited or no success. Nevertheless, the investment funds operate, hoping they will be on the winning team if they place the right bet.

This works only because of inflated extrinsic valuations of companies. Many privately funded companies are valued at incredibly high numbers with little relevant substantiation. These valuations exist only because of cheap money.

What else follows a Power Law distribution? Lotteries. People buy lottery tickets because of the minuscule probability of an outsized victory.

What happens when cheap money dries up as interest rates rise and excessive government spending stops? What happens when public markets and other private investors, which are the only paths for any fund to exit their investments, put downward pressure on artificially high valuations? It is inevitable. When these things happen, the opportunity to exit companies with outsized valuations is gone.

So, the only ethical path for investors to achieve their return on investment is to associate with companies created and managed with a sustainable growth mindset.

Additionally, playing the economic cycle roulette wheel is an investor's game. We are more interested in creating and managing 'good' companies. While investors index heavily on maximizing their potential upside from the extrinsic value of companies, it forces the customers, partners, employees, and the society at large to live with the risk without benefiting from the outsized return.

In other words, Power Law doesn't work for any other company stakeholders. Employees only get to invest their careers in one company at a time and aren't privy to outsized returns, even if it happens. A friend at a start-up reflected on this and reacted, "people forget how important it is to be stable."

Customers and partners invest in young companies with a long-term, value-creating partnership in mind. We don't have a business if our customers and partners aren't comfortable with our survival prospects.

Companies without a sustainable growth mindset often instigate poor customer behaviors or the destruction of competitors. Unfortunately, such companies leave others to deal with their negative externalities once their artificially inflated growth cycles flame out.

Sustainably profitable growth is only possible if a company understands and objectively balances the needs of customers, employees, investors, partners, and society at large throughout its existence. An equilibrium between these two sides frames a **Holistic Company**.

> **Things to Remember: A Holistic Company**
>
> **A holistic company satisfies two symbiotic conditions. First, holistic companies originate and exist with a sustainable growth mindset. Second, they balance the incentives of all stakeholders throughout their existence.**

We are all collectively better off if we keep our focus on building holistic companies. When either condition – sustainable growth mindset or balancing stakeholder incentives – fails, a company is no longer holistic. Then, we must ask ourselves – *whose unbalanced benefit does such a company exist to serve?*

A holistic company does not focus on extrinsic value.

Easy access to financing due to a very accommodative ecosystem is the equivalent of booster rockets attached to a young company. But these boosters are not enough to launch a company into a sustainable growth phase. Rockets need extraordinary structural integrity, a long-lasting propulsion system, and guidance systems to take their payload to outer space.

The ease of availability of capital has created a tendency to add more and more expensive boosters and try to propel start-ups, often prematurely. Such a tactic to brute force a company's growth is called rapid scaling. i.e.,

A HOLISTIC COMPANY FOCUSES ON FUNDAMENTALS

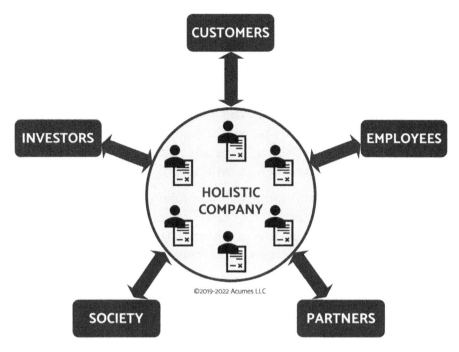

Infographic 1 – Holistic companies balance incentives of all stakeholders

an effort to apply steroids to create a large company quickly. Unfortunately, even in the best of scenarios, it hasn't proved effective long-term.

If a company has quickly perfected its offering to solve the market problem and built a perfectly scalable organization, rapid scaling makes sense in theory. But this is inevitably not the case. Instead, creating a company's culture and optimizing market fit usually takes years.

Oyo is an India-based hotel chain backed by the largest venture capital fund in the world today. The hotel chain was founded in 2013 and had aspirations of becoming the largest hotel chain in the world by 2023. Imagine the challenges behind getting one stand-alone hotel to run more effectively. In any rational sense, how is it humanly possible to go from zero to the top in such a complex business worldwide with differing consumer tastes, hotel ownership structures, and local rules and regulations in ten years?

Hotel owners who signed up for the brand began complaining that Oyo didn't meet their agreements. In early 2020, even before Covid-19 impacted us, the company downsized its plans by laying off 2000 employees and pulling out of 200 cities. The company's CEO said, "I have no hesitation in saying that maybe we were accelerating towards [#1 spot] too fast for us to be balanced."

By March 2021, Oyo had retreated from Europe, China, and South America. The interim UK executive of the company stated, "There are global issues for Oyo in a very big way, but they will use the pandemic to put the blame on Covid and not take a body blow." The same report included feedback from past employees – "Oyo had regularly added unviable hotels while attempting to demonstrate high growth rates."

Even companies such as Peloton, a fitness solutions provider, with early success through an effective offering can regress. As 2800 employees were being laid off in 2022, the departing founder and CEO said, "To meet market demand, we scaled our operations too rapidly, and we over-invested in some areas of our business."

These very public stories are well-documented, but the same challenges exist with companies that are not household names that I have seen first-hand.

Rapid scaling a half-baked business model and blitzing through massive hiring phases are essentially building up a house of cards that is significantly more likely to crumble over time than one built up with a sustainable growth mindset with a bit more patience.

A "house of cards" is exactly how an introspective CEO I worked with described his company's 25% revenue loss in a single year. I interviewed many customers that discontinued services with this mid-sized company. The themes that came through loud and clear were that the customers' value needs had grown beyond the value offered by the company, and the quality of the company's offering deteriorated over time because of its inability to scale its original offerings to a more extensive customer base. Unfortunately, this is a common situation that I have seen where companies struggle to take a market validated offering to a sustainable growth phase.

Even the companies known as recent beacons of quick success grew organically. Amazon didn't start in its current form; it was an online bookseller that caught the first eCommerce wave in the mid-1990s when its only competition was brick and mortar stores; the company listed on the stock market within two years of its inception. Meta's success was not because it scaled by spending money; it just caught fire because the world was ready for social media, and it was profitable within five years. Google became profitable within three years. But these are very rare market disruptive stories that easy money has incentivized many artificial replications.

A thirteen-year veteran founder CEO's reaction to the exit valuation of the company he founded was "...Not a positive outcome... Many lessons learned I may write about." An extremely popular yellow journalism website published an article about this deal that was inflated by 25%, compared to the actual merger valuation that I corroborated through multiple internal sources, with the caveat "in what we understand to be a $100M deal." Compared to such careless reporting about extrinsic value, employees who had exercised their stock options and spent years at the company received 30% below the price they bought those options. That means employees lost money on their time investment in the company and real money they invested in buying those options.

The reality is often far different from what's externally observable.

Why is rapid scaling not as effective as it is propped up to be?

Every Marathon trainer will tell you ad nauseam to plan your race meticulously down to how fast you will run each mile, what you will wear, and your hydration method. They will also tell you that it's not how quickly you start your race, it's about the pace you can maintain for a long time. I am no expert marathoner; I completely screwed up on my first marathon when I barely stumbled across the finish line after clocking some excellent times in the first 20 miles. My first marathon time would have been significantly better if I had taken some good advice. Growing companies sustainably is not so different.

The concept of rapid scaling implies that a company will invest significantly into the business model very early on. But too much investment too early often creates problems. Throwing too much wood onto a fire has the counterintuitive effect of dampening the fire because not enough oxygen flows in.

Rapid scaling implies decreasing organizational productivity with scale. We measure productivity as the output created by an investment. i.e., what is the most the company can produce in customer value and related revenue by holding the investment in people, technology, and other assets constant?

If a company continues to invest in areas that are not as productive as they should be, each additional dollar invested creates less value. The larger such a company gets, the average productivity continues to decrease until it hits a stall point. This is why many start-ups with significant investment and valued at over $1B, a threshold that entitles them to the term 'unicorns,' end up regressing and shrinking.

When assessing any start-up's potential success or failure, we come across an interesting question: *what is failure?* An accurate measurement is incredibly spurious because one could argue what constitutes success or failure.

Did the We Company, a shared workspace solution provider that owns the WeWork brand, fail or succeed as a start-up? The founder might say it was a success because he walked away with $1.7B when investors finally took over the company from the management team in 2019. Would the 8000+ employees laid off that same year share similar sentiments? Would the biggest investor, SoftBank, whose investment in We Company dropped in value by 80% during the second half of 2019 alone, say that the start-up is a success? We could consider other stakeholders, including real estate owners that partner with the company. Note that this part of the WeWork story played out in 2019 before the Covid-19 pandemic. In 2021, WeWork became a public company. Would the public shareholders who now hold the company's stock consider it a success? Who won? Who lost? You be the judge.

So, when approaching companies, tags of success and failure are often prejudiced and heavily depend on the person's vantage point. However, we will take a rational, objective, and analytical stance.

A HOLISTIC COMPANY FOCUSES ON FUNDAMENTALS

Our definition of success for a start-up will be creating a holistic company that focuses on creating intrinsic value. Intrinsic value relies on tangible and lasting solutions to market problems that can be delivered with profitability. Such a company is also a value-creating machine that can stay relevant and continue to create more value over time through its own people and methods.

Symptomatically, a holistic company moves away from the need for external investment to survive and to a phase where they are profitable. That is not to preclude investment for future growth, but the business foundations are such that on a day-to-day basis, the business is self-sufficient.

Think about a holistic company seeking sustainable growth as a seedling growing into a tree that can survive and thrive on its own with the sun, water, soil, and air.

As we already discussed, there is no proof that growth at any cost will work in the long term. Barring a few exceptions, almost all artificially rapid-scaled companies from the past decade remain unprofitable. The only possible path to profitability is to be the last company standing in their market in a war of attrition. But this is not a value-creating path. For example, suppose only one ride-sharing company survives after years of unprofitable competition. That company ends up charging consumers as much or more than taxi cabs, and ride-share customer service mirrors historic taxi driver attitudes. What was the gain in this exercise other than easier access using mobile phones and GPS, which is prevalent in everything we do today anyway? Funny enough, I had written that question in 2019. By the time of the publication of this book, the cost of ride-sharing options had become so outlandish that consumers were reverting to hailing traditional cabs using a simple app or using their feet to walk acceptable distances.

Holistic companies focus on intrinsic value and fundamentals.

When a company has the cash to invest, a few tactics can be quickly and easily implemented.

- *The company can lease office space.*

- Money can go into digital and social marketing to drive some leads.
- Early sales team members can be hired to do selling activities focused on those marketing leads.
- A few engineers can help spiff up the bells and whistles of the company's offering.
- Marketing automation and customer relationship management (CRM) technologies can be purchased and booted up in a standard format.
- The team can conduct off-sites for sales kick-offs.
- The marketing team can offer promotions to get early customers on board.
- A roadmap with features that customers request can be the company's north star.
- Senior executives can create a financial projection for potential revenue and expenses.

At an elementary level, these are all important. But is that it? If every company had some investment dollars to spend and some basic awareness, what stops them all from being a winning team?

Creating intrinsic value in our company is like internalizing the principles behind a complex math problem. We can copy a classmate's answers or from the internet to get points on our exam. These points are extrinsic value. But we have gained zero intrinsic value because we still don't know how to do the math problem.

Dr. Daniel Kahneman is a Nobel prize-winning psychologist and economist. He postulated that our human mind operates in two modes. First is a fast-thinking, reactive, intuitive, and emotional mode. The vast majority of our thoughts and problem-solving fall in this category. The second is an intentional, energy-consuming, and objective thinking process necessary for unbiased problem-solving. I categorize the obvious and everyone-else-is-doing-it items into the first category. But that isn't enough. Dr. Kahneman's advice to businesses is exactly that – don't be led astray by only relying on the first type of thinking.

Companies that grow long-term continuously improve the value created for customers and organizational productivity. They focus on investing in aspects that evolve both these interim outcomes. Such evolution is intentional, methodical, and objective, and it takes much more energy and depth of thinking than acting on our instincts alone.

Dr. Kahneman frames that 98% of human thinking falls in the first 'fast' category. Creating intrinsic value requires a lot of slow thinking. This second category of purposeful thinking and decision-making focuses on building and evolving our company's fundamentals. It is a necessary investment to ensure that we don't operate in an unsustainable environment where we bring together a large number of people where 98% of their thoughts are instinctive.

The evolution of fundamentals is the bedrock of sustainable growth.

Imagine a sports team trying to meet its expectations, whether to win the championship or get to the playoffs. But maintaining a sustainable, long winning streak comes down to fundamentals. How well does the head coach, the coaching team, and the players gel together? Can they play cohesively as a team in almost every game throughout the season? How do they react as a group when they fall behind or lose one or two games?

A company, too, has fundamentals that make it a winning entity. They focus on the essence of its strategy to win its market and dovetail day-to-day operations. Sales kick-offs are only effective in driving growth if the details align with how the company's customers buy. Roadmaps to build solutions only lead to market leadership if they entail cohesive descriptions of what customers will need in the future.

The company's growth from the early stages when founders are working to acquire the first few customers and validating the company's offering to reaching a sustainable growth phase is not a linear path.

It is a multi-phased journey.

Each growth phase requires the company to evolve and operate at a higher maturity level than during the previous phase.

People launch companies to solve niche problems, and even with early success, a company will have a small group of customers that greatly appreciate the company's offerings. Those early customers feel the pain of the problem significantly or have a high-risk tolerance for trying new solutions. Favorable pricing incentivizes some other early customers. There is a low bar on the fundamentals required to gain these early customers.

As a company grows, there are fewer and fewer such easy customers. Beyond the early few, customers will become increasingly demanding as the company will sell to prospects with differing needs. Suppose a company continues to operate with its early-stage maturity level and just throws more money at it. In that case, the growth will stall, and even the early customers' needs will no longer be met effectively.

I think about a company's entire market opportunity, often described as addressable market, as a normal distribution as shown in the figure below.

> **Things to Remember: The Addressable Market**
>
> **The addressable market is the universe of customers that the company can realistically serve, given its current offerings and abilities.**

Unfortunately, capturing a larger share of the addressable market is increasingly more challenging.

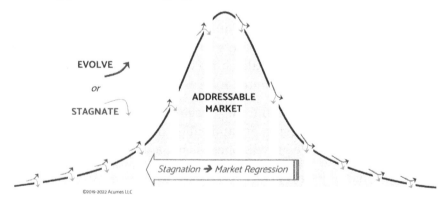

Infographic 2 – Sustainable growth demands recurring evolution

First, every customer demands more value over time. Imagine that the normal distribution is like a treadmill that's moving forward. It means a company must continuously evolve and reinvent itself even to keep its current customers.

Second, the value demanded per dollar by the whole addressable market is extremely divergent. Early customers are willing to accept a lower value than later customers. This means the company will have to evolve its offerings and create more value to acquire more significant portions of the addressable market.

Third, the cost to acquire and serve customers that are further to the right of the addressable market is intrinsically higher because they are more demanding and more reluctant to buy. As a result, a company will have to evolve its commercial efforts to be incrementally more effective to move further to the right of the addressable market curve.

Lastly, serving an increasing portion of the addressable market implies that the company is getting bigger. Running a larger company requires a greater level of sophistication and maturity, without which the company will crumble under its own weight.

A company must evolve its fundamentals to address all four reasons above to jump from the first group of customers to the second group, and so on. Once a company evolves and is ready to acquire and serve the second group of customers, the next necessary cycle of evolution is around the corner for the company to be able to serve the following and more demanding group of customers.

Naturally, it is daunting to feel that we are constantly climbing a mountain. But that is the reality of growing a company beyond the market validation stage. For that same reason, many companies fall prey to the tendency to think – "if it ain't broke, why fix it?" That fallacy only applies if the whole world is standing still, time is constant, and every customer in the market is exactly the same.

I think about the growth journey across the spectrum of the addressable market as having large crevasses that we have to jump across to reach the next level of growth. Each of these jumps is an evolution of the company's fundamentals. Each growth phase ends with a stall point. Evolution or stagnation is inevitable at the end of each growth phase.

Throwing money at scaling without evolving fundamentals as each growth phase draws to a close will essentially stall the company's maturity growth. If a company doesn't evolve, customers and competitors will pass the company by. Future customers in the addressable market will be further out of reach.

From the days of Thomas Edison's light bulb, General Electric set a gold standard for over a century until the 2000s, when the focus shifted to growth through financial engineering that left the company with almost 50% of the company's value in an artificially bloated GE Capital business that triggered its regression. Even mature companies can fall back.

So, our conversation throughout will focus on this iterative, evolutionary journey that continuously improves fundamentals, which creates intrinsic value and drives sustainable growth. A few paragraphs earlier, we listed some of the items a company can readily take on with the availability of financing. Fundamentals ensure that the intrinsic quality and value of those tactics are high. With our self-sufficient tree in mind, we will talk about the importance of soil, water, air, and sun. Without getting the basics right, there is no organic growth.

Strong fundamentals imply several observable behaviors. As a high-level diagnostic, consider the statements in Infographic 3 and assess your company's fundamentals. Throughout this book, you will see maturity models, components, and principles that take you deeper into what makes each of these desirable behaviors possible. I encourage you to reconsider your assessment of the current maturity level as you go through our methodology, identify opportunities to improve, and take that back to your teams.

It is important to note that these concepts do not just apply to young companies. Upstarts are disrupting every segment of every market, and that means even established companies will need to have an evolutionary mindset about their fundamentals. So, let's fight against our tendency to think instinctively and emotionally and build structures around us to inject more intentional and objective thinking into our holistic company.

A HOLISTIC COMPANY FOCUSES ON FUNDAMENTALS

WHAT DO STRONG FUNDAMENTALS LOOK LIKE?	RATING
Leadership & People	
The company's day-to-day operations are fully aligned with the path to customer value creation and are not an imitation of other successful companies.	**How would you critically and objectively rate current state?**
Executives hire increasingly experienced and skilled employees and ensure personnel backgrounds and personalities are diverse to limit groupthink.	
The most skilled and hardworking employees stay with the company long-term, while mid-tier performers strive to improve performance to match top players and low performers leave.	
The company has a balanced focus on all internal value chain functions and does not disparately attribute success or failure to specific functions, especially during hard times.	Strongly Agree
	Agree
Objectivity & Use of Information	Unsure
Experienced, customer-first, strategic thinkers with strong analytical backgrounds are in core functions and focus on customer needs instead of tactical internal dynamics.	Disagree
	Strongly Disagree
Problem-solving at all levels focuses on root causes instead of individuals and supports a genuinely objective and collaborative mindset.	
Executives and employees have a strong objective and analytical approach to problem-solving and decision-making and ensure that information biases don't blindside the company.	
Decisions are delegated to topical experts without dependence on organizational hierarchy or reversal to democratic tactics.	
Cohesive & Comprehensive Strategy	
Company focuses on core offering(s) without being distracted by longtail of unprofitable frills.	
Design and development of offerings is diligent and can meet customers' future needs and is not focused on reactively giving customers what they want.	
A comprehensive and cohesive strategy leads the revenue-generating transactions as opposed to being reactive to a wide range of customers.	
Existing customers are happy and can be profitably served perpetually.	
Relationships with partners and vendors are equitable and do not hinge on unsustainable short-term agreements.	
Planning & Execution	
Investment decisions on people, technology, and other assets are highly efficient, avoid waste, and limit organizational 'fat.'	
Investment decisions are based on objective and measurable criteria and market knowledge without reliance on 'Hail Mary' tactics.	
Strategy is reevaluated and refined on a cadence and dictates all investment decisions and revenue and expense projections without relying on history or mimicking other companies.	
'What good looks like' for all major projects and day-to-day efforts are clearly articulated, adopted by the whole organization, and executed effectively.	©2019-2022 Acumes LLC

Infographic 3 – A company fundamentals self-assessment

The Path To Intrinsic Value.

Let's build our holistic company brick by brick.

From a timing perspective, business problems are similar to dangerous late-onset diseases that allow us to live with negligible symptoms for a significant period before the situation becomes acute. I've worked with many companies over the years, and most do not believe that challenges that cripple other companies will ever happen to them.

It is a natural psychological response.

I have taken a few long road trips. A day or two before the trip, I consider the risks of falling asleep at the wheel or having a flat tire, and I plan to create playlists for the road and check my spare beforehand. But I have always been fascinated by how little such thoughts bother me once I start driving, even if I failed to act on my precautionary plans. I have an irrational sense of control with a very different perspective about the probability of any risks I acknowledged just the day before.

The same difference in perspective takes over when a team focuses on solving day-to-day challenges within a company.

Predicting business challenges is more about observing intrinsic behaviors of employees, customers, partners, and investors rather than focusing on major company-level outcomes or revenue numbers. By the time challenges become observable, the root causes have likely already metastasized into something far worse. At that point, the company is no longer in a growth environment. Instead, it is in a turnaround one, and at that stage, it is a far more complicated task to perform surgery on the fundamentals.

The time to focus on fundamentals is yesterday, not tomorrow when the causes behind observable challenges have taken root.

My methodology to drive sustainable growth by focusing on intrinsic value creation through fundamentals is called *The Spiral Stairway*™. As we begin exploring these ideas that senior executives, supervisors, and employees can embrace to build a holistic company focused on sustainable growth, we need to start with two overarching philosophical concepts.

The intrinsic value philosophies.

Philosophy is an underlying school of thought that dictates all the structures we build on top. *The Spiral Stairway*™ methodology has many components, and every aspect of it will embrace two philosophies.

Philosophy 1: Solve problems with a 'String of Pearls' mindset.

Replicating bits and pieces of successful companies is tempting because it's easy, but it is unlikely to render good results. No two people, companies, or industries are alike. Nor are the problems they need to solve. One company's ideas, however bright, won't help grow another company sustainably unless they are harmonious with all the other parts of the company. All concepts have to fit seamlessly with each other and function in a symbiotic manner.

Understanding the fundamentals necessary to win isn't about standalone tactics; it is about stringing together a set of logical, cohesive concepts and executing them to perfection… or at least better than the next best contender.

Consider this – would we ever buy one pearl or a random assortment of different pearls? Highly unlikely!

The reasons are simple. As beautiful as one pearl might be, it is practically useless on its own. Even with several dissimilar pearls, it is hard to do anything with them. Additionally, finding more pearls that exactly match the others will be extremely difficult.

In this analogy, a single pearl is a specific corporate tactic. Applying the same thinking, we should never get too excited about one-off tactical ideas. Standalone ideas are often mistaken for game-changing answers and result in significant distractions. Such ideas are valuable inputs for brainstorming exercises but not solutions to major organizational issues or customer problems.

How much more valuable is it if we can string together a set of matching pearls into a beautiful necklace? We immediately know that the creator took the time to find and put together pearls that match and ensure that the whole is more than the sum of its parts.

Corporate tactics are very much the same. This is a critical foundational concept in our digital age because we live in a time of information abundance and access.

Disinformation, a tactic where information is purposely shared to mislead, is prevalent throughout search engines and social media. As a result, it is increasingly difficult to discern between marketing and objective information.

For example, companies invest in sending employees to all sorts of conferences to generate leads and market the company. In itself, any single event can be a good idea. But the return on investment is only likely to be high if the chosen conference aligns perfectly with the company's overall strategy and its operational prowess to generate leads and close deals from those conference leads. Unfortunately, as obvious as this might seem, most companies I have worked with have made this mistake.

Attempting to solve big overarching organizational problems with one-off tactical ideas can not only be ineffective, but it can also come at a high price due to wasted investment. It also often results in a period of paralysis where more cohesive ideas could have driven the organization in a better direction.

One typical example of standalone tactics gone wrong is a penchant for buying technology and expecting challenging problems to go away. Customer Relationship Management (CRM) and Enterprise Resource Planning (ERP) technologies are compelling and, when used well, can create significant value. Years ago, I oversaw parts of the implementation of ERP technology at a large distribution client. The overall project was budgeted to cost over $100M a year. But the project didn't dovetail with the overarching company-level strategy. Implementation didn't include employee training and upskilling, and many oversight and governance steps were skipped. As a result, despite the enormous investment, the company saw a minimal positive impact on operational effectiveness, let alone revenue or profitability. This scenario occurs even more often at growth-phase companies.

All efforts in an organization should dovetail with each other to ensure those efforts, collectively, solve small and large problems. We can apply this thinking to practically any organizational problem we solve.

> **Things to Remember: Philosophy 1 - Solve problems with a String of Pearls Mindset**
>
> **Build the company's fundamentals as though we are creating a cohesive string of pearls instead of hoping to win with one or two silver bullets.**

This is the first foundational philosophy that we will carry forward for the rest of our conversation – always think about organizational problem solving as creating a cohesive and well-matched string of pearls.

Philosophy 2: Operate with a 'Systems First' mantra.

Over the years, I have asked many folks the same question: *What is a company?* I admit that it is a tricky question to spring on someone. I usually get these long, drawn-out explanations with complex words that make a company sound like a mythical creature with a mind of its own. Is it, though?

I have a simple definition.

> **Things to Remember: Company**
>
> **A company is a set of people who have created a contract with each other to conduct trade. The people involved 'write' the complex agreement to satisfy their particular agendas. So, a company is nothing more than the sum of the people involved and their agendas.**

So, how should we think about root causes when companies face problems?

Often when a company faces challenges, heads roll. For example, at a macro level, nearly every major corporate scandal or persistent performance challenge culminates in the replacement of the CEO. Sometimes these are rational decisions because the head of a company is responsible for ensuring positive outcomes, and they have the authority to control their destiny. But such sensationalized macro incidents create a tendency to replicate the same decision-making mindset at all company levels, which is suboptimal.

There are differing opinions and perspectives where several people are involved, not to mention human biases. Just like a country requires a constitution, laws, regulations, and law enforcement, a company needs well-articulated and well-understood rules of engagement to help its people operate. The term 'culture' has become an overused buzzword that has lost its meaning. So, I call this tangible structure a company's **System**.

> **Things to Remember: System**
>
> **A company's system is a predefined, agreed-upon set of constructs that every individual involved in a company internalizes and is committed to executing.**

Let's consider sports teams again. There is a massive difference between winning consistently for multiple seasons and collecting trophies instead of winning a handful of entertaining matches celebrated by fans. Certain aspects are common among consistent top-performing teams.

What are the common traits of top-tier teams?

- *They often win even when their top players are injured or sitting out games.*
- *Many players excel and contribute to winning any given game instead of only the top few players.*
- *The scoreboard does not heavily influence their style of play because they believe in their approach.*
- *They don't elaborately celebrate regular-season wins or look for excuses in losses.*

- *Everyone knows their contribution, which allows the team to win together or lose together.*

If a company was a sports team, great individual employees and their standalone performances can win a few customer deals or build one exceptional portion of an offering. But seasons are not won by individuals; teams with robust systems are more effective over extended periods. So, root causes for organizational challenges should always be attributed to the system, not the individuals.

For example, Mercedes AMG Petronas is a Formula 1 racing team with the most consecutive championship wins of all time. Their team principal frames their approach as "we blame the problem rather than the person."

From a business perspective, this translates into a cohesive approach to running the entire business that the senior executives, employees, board, analysts, regulators, partners, and even customers understand and believe. The cohesiveness, comprehensiveness, and transparency of the system determine its effectiveness. Each part of our methodology will help you build a unique system that works for your company.

Why is this philosophy critical in a holistic company focused on sustainable growth?

As discussed above, a company is just a collection of people with agendas. Most of us are not heroes who can single-handedly save the day. We will all make mistakes. However, we cannot allow our justifications for these mistakes to overshadow actual performance and root causes. Individual players must become commodities in a highly organized team to succeed over the long haul.

Many organizations fall into the trap of blaming individuals for systemic organizational problems. Sometimes, they blame lack of talent or experience within their ranks for poor results. Other times, individuals may be considered misfits in the organization. However, these gaps aren't caused by those individuals.

They are often caused by a flawed system that allowed ineffective managers to hold senior positions or the wrong senior executives to make hiring decisions. Possibly their hiring practices stay underdeveloped or have people management practices that didn't align individual skills with the requirements of roles, or training and coaching to be overlooked, and so on. Focusing on individuals perpetuates the same mistakes without addressing underlying causes.

A strong system brings together people with the right skills and experience to perform at their best. The reverse is rarely true. Focusing on finding heroes that can save the day will not serve the best interest of all the company's stakeholders or the company's long-term future. Additionally, heroes effective in one growth phase are unlikely to help the company evolve into the next growth phase.

Conversely, when a company faces challenges, replacing individuals is very easy and provides a quick fix that merely kicks the can down the road. Not too long ago, I was leading turnaround efforts at a mid-sized company with revenue growth challenges, and the root cause was an ineffective system that the CEO had failed to improve. Unfortunately, instead of addressing the root cause, the company had replaced three successive sales executives and the sales reps and supervisors those executives hired in three years with no change in prospects.

Creating an effective system takes patience and discipline, which is why short-term tactics around individuals often displace it. The lack of an effective system is a breakdown in fundamentals and a precursor to growth challenges.

However, we must not confuse focusing on developing a strong system with filling up the company with poor talent or moderate willingness to perform at a high level. A strong system attracts and retains people with optimal skills and extracts the most value from those people. So, always start with the presupposition that building a strong system is a foundational outcome of evolving the company's fundamentals through each growth phase.

As we go through the growth methodology, think of our mission as improving the company's system without getting distracted by individual personalities and agendas. On the contrary, a strong system moderates personalities and agendas to achieve collective success.

> **Things to Remember: Philosophy 2 – Operate with a Systems First Mantra**
>
> **Design fundamental components to drive towards building a strong system for the company as opposed to putting a microscope on people.**

Let's embrace these two overarching philosophies to ensure that we apply the components of the methodology with the right frame of mind.

Now, let's superimpose these two philosophies onto our methodology.

The Spiral Stairway™

Did you know that in the last ten Tour de France, the world's most prestigious cycling championship, the overall winner only won an average of 2 out of the 21 stages each year? A couple of those years, the overall winner didn't even win one of the 21 stages. The Tour attributes significantly more value to being extremely competitive across all 21 stages than winning a few and performing poorly among the rest.

Developing intrinsic value to grow a company is similar. I didn't create the sustainable growth methodology because I am the foremost expert across all components covered in five parts. But through many positive and negative experiences, I realized that creating a holistic company with sustainable intrinsic value demands that we operate with high maturity across all these components. Ignoring one important part allows the rot to start there and spread to the rest of our system.

The Spiral Stairway™ is a playbook for executives and critical thinkers at growth-phase companies with a market-validated offering. Based on practical lessons, I have evolved and improved the details and composition of this methodology to help companies quickly and effectively. Now it's your turn to apply it with a critical-thinking mindset.

The methodology starts with two assumptions that further refine our definition of a company.

First, we will assume that the company has already performed very early-stage market validation of its offerings and is ready to grow. If you are an entrepreneur without an offering and a small customer base, *The Spiral Stairway*™ can give you foundational principles to consider. Although its holistic application will be premature, it will prepare you for effective leadership once you have a market-validated offering.

Second, we won't address topics around financial leverage, which means borrowing money as a financial strategy, or mergers and acquisitions (M&A) as a path to growth because these don't create intrinsic value.

A growth-phase company must first figure out how to organically grow profitably before buying another company that is an unknown entity. Any relationship expert would say that we should be mentally and physically ready for a relationship before finding a significant other. Expecting someone else to solve our internal problems through an alliance is an unsustainable tie-up.

We will also keep any notion of financial engineering out of scope. Quite simply, banks and investors will always be available to support companies with strong fundamentals. Inversely, why should any rational financial institution risk loaning money to companies with poor fundamentals unless they plan to sell the company for parts when it folds?

Remember, our company is a group of individuals that have entered into a mutually beneficial contract to create value for external stakeholders by deploying the group's unique set of strengths.

This definition implies that our company can be a start-up with a market-validated offering just as much as an organically growing sub-division of a large company. It holds true as long as it operates as a self-sustaining entity.

Infographic 4 introduces *The Spiral Stairway*™, which is our five-part methodology. The five parts are:

A. *Management Approach.*

B. *Value Engine.*

C. *Corporate Strategy.*

D. *Strategic Planning.*

E. *Execution Management.*

As you go through each part, I will present you with what 'good' looks like and a path to achieve it. Each section will give you a five-level maturity model that summarizes underlying components. We will also discuss common pitfalls that you can avoid because they often derail most honest and best intentions. I suggest you work through each of the five parts and underlying components sequentially because the concepts build on each other.

The journey from market validation to sustainable growth is like climbing a lighthouse to the lantern room at the top. We must take that spiral stairway to reach our goal at the top.

I know what you are thinking.

No! Lighthouses do not have elevators.

The first two parts of the methodology, **Part A: Management Approach** and **Part B: Value Engine**, are our company's present-day snapshot. Collectively, this includes the people agenda of our company, our offering to the market, and how we deliver it. If we sold our company today, these two parts would form its intrinsic value. These two parts, collectively, create what I call our **Operations Baseline**.

> **Things to Remember: Operations Baseline**
>
> **If we do a bottom-up valuation of a company, the components under the first two parts, management approach and value engine, contribute to all the considerations we would add up to the intrinsic value of our company, which we will call the operations baseline.**

All components under these two parts are ongoing efforts that our company stays focused on throughout the year. At the beginning of each year of our company's existence, our operations baseline covers the fundamentals we have built up over the years since the company's inception.

Our operations baseline can and must make ongoing tactical improvements if we have good information to act upon. These improvements tweak specific parts of our company. I call these improvements **Micro-evolutions**. Micro-evolutions include basic process improvements or

THE SPIRAL STAIRWAY™ – THE SYSTEM TO BUILD A HOLISTIC COMPANY

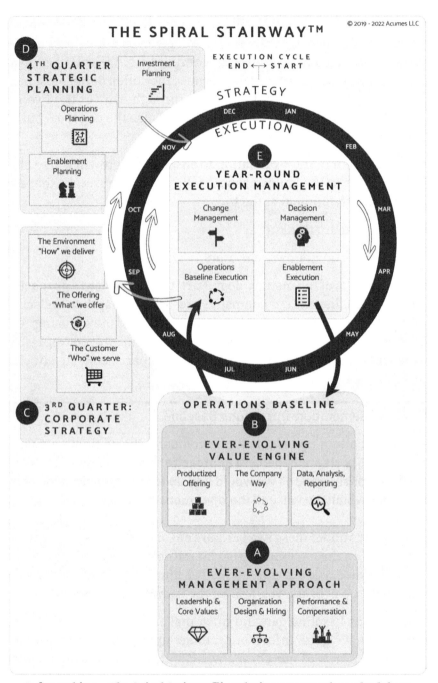

Infographic 4 – The Spiral Stairway™ evolutionary growth methodology

tactical improvements of our offerings that stay within our overarching company's direction.

> **Things to Remember: Micro-evolutions**
>
> **Micro-evolutions are continuous and tactical optimizations of our operations baseline at its current maturity level to enable our sustainable growth mindset.**

However, these will not be enough for us to grow through the various stages of our addressable market and keep up with the world around us. The remaining three parts, **Part C: Corporate Strategy**, **Part D: Strategic Planning**, and **Part E: Execution Management**, form the **Macro-evolution** cycle of our operations baseline. The top portion of Infographic 4 reflects how a company must operate as an evolving machine sitting on top of the two foundational parts that form our current state. They compose a cycle that enables the company to make major forward-looking decisions, act on those decisions, learn from those actions, and improve on past decisions to take *The Spiral Stairway*™ up to a sustainable growth stage.

Think about a micro-evolution in each part of our operations baseline as a rotation of each planet in the solar system, while the overarching macro-evolution of our whole company is a complete revolution of all those planets around the sun. They both always need to happen.

> **Things to Remember: Macro-evolutions**
>
> **Macro-evolution cycles identify and inject comprehensively higher maturity into the operations baseline to create and deliver increasing customer value and operational effectiveness to support that value creation.**

I consider one year as a reasonable timeframe to go up that one level of macro-evolutionary growth. What worked last year may not work the next for a scaling company because the market and competitors are fast evolving. The company's scale is getting larger, requiring a different set, not necessarily more of the same, of skills to help the company climb to the next level of growth.

I prefer to use the start and end of a company's fiscal year as the pivotal reference point of the annual growth cycle, which I call the Annual Strategy & Operations Cycle.

Many myths have originated from the world of start-ups about the death of analysis and planning. Having worked in the bellies of several sectors, the sources of these myths are not interested in building sustainable or holistic companies or don't have experience beyond their own ecosystem. Most start-ups create software solutions, and they don't experience any greater uncertainty or risk than a traditional restaurant concept. It's arrogant to think so. Software solutions solve real-world problems just like any other solution. The only difference is that an empty restaurant is much harder to explain than unused software, even though both mistakes can cost the same. The future of any market-validated company can be analyzed, planned, and methodically managed.

Even Google search was not a novel idea. LexisNexis and similar companies have cataloged public content and made them searchable since the 1970s. Google was aided by the disruptive proliferation of the internet, internet advertising, and hardware, while stalwarts of content management didn't evolve to keep new competition at bay. Saying that Google didn't evolve from the history of the content management ecosystem is rubbish.

Additionally, one notable and purposeful exclusion in my methodology is the mission and vision of a company. In my experience, these two concepts together are a re-articulation of a company's corporate strategy. If a company doesn't have an effective corporate strategy, its mission and vision are merely distracting wall decoration.

Each part of the methodology will require different executives and functions to take ownership and execute. Infographic 5 breaks down the roles that senior executive positions must play in each part of the methodology. It is never too early for us to discuss the importance of roles and responsibilities. Every component requires appropriate ownership, the ability and willingness to execute, and a support structure to empower accountable and responsible parties.

ROLES AND RESPONSIBILITIES MATRIX

	Accountability	Responsibility	Enablement	Impacted
Part A: Management Approach	Chief Executive Officer	Human Resources Executive	Strategy & Operations Executive	All Employees
Part B: Value Engine	Chief Executive Officer	Functional Executives	Strategy & Operations Executive	All Employees
Part C: Corporate Strategy	Chief Executive Officer	Strategy & Operations Executive	Functional Executives	All Employees
Part D: Strategic Planning	Chief Executive Officer	Strategy & Operations Executive	Functional Executives	All Employees
Part E: Execution Management	Chief Executive Officer	Functional Executives	Strategy & Operations Executive	All Employees

©2019-2022 Acumes LLC

Infographic 5 – Organizational roles & responsibilities matrix

First, the components under management approach are generally owned by the CEO and executed by human resources, with the evolutionary support of the strategy & operations executive. These components dictate the company's overall modus operandi, including definitions of roles and responsibilities, performance assessment, incentives and rewards, and day-to-day behaviors of all employees.

The **second** part, value engine, enables our company to build a scalable offering and predictable, transparent, and data-driven environment that enables our employees to perform their job optimally. It covers the constructs that constitute a compelling offering for customers and the foundational processes and tools to take it to customers. The CEO must empower a strong, hands-on strategy & operations executive to enable functional executives on these responsibilities.

We will start the macro-evolution cycle in the **third** part with recommendations around building a cohesive and comprehensive strategy based on a deep understanding of the market and the company's strengths. We will cover how such an articulation will dictate all company-wide efforts.

Much of this effort will be the responsibility of the strategy & operations executive, while the CEO owns and oversees the outcomes.

In the **fourth** part, we will explore how the CEO and the strategy & operations executive can use the company-level strategy to build a strategic plan that quantifies and qualifies all execution efforts. We will learn that creating a company-wide plan is a lot less complex and more effective if we follow a structured framework.

Lastly, senior executives, supervisors, and individual contributors will have to play their respective parts laid out in the strategic plan and execute effectively. Our senior executives and supervisors will have to develop a path to plan, manage, and track day-to-day execution and course-correct where necessary. We will discuss this in the **fifth** part of our methodology.

The five parts of the methodology give every executive and employee clarity on what every player in the company is doing and how it will all add up to the desired overarching outcomes.

All five parts are symbiotic and interlocked. They support each other, and the whole is exponentially more valuable than the sum of its parts. They are not standalone topics, and without effective implementation of key components, other related components will likely prove ineffective. As you go through each one, notice how it incrementally creates a domino effect of improving other components in our holistic company.

PART A

Management Approach Articulates The System In Which People Work.

IMAGINE holding a dart and looking towards the bullseye you intend to hit. You have tuned out the surroundings and have a good idea of how you will hit the bullseye. You are ready, and you throw the dart towards that bullseye in perfect form. What could go wrong, right?

The dart hits the bullseye perfectly but then falls on the floor with a broken tip. You walk up and check the dartboard and realize that the board isn't cork or any fungible material. It is just cloth covering a brick wall. Would you continue playing the game?

An effective **Management Approach** is akin to a corkboard. It is a foundational people agenda that can absorb the evolutionary demands of sustainable growth. Without such a foundation, it will be impossible to develop an optimal offering. We will be unable to design scalable operations, a winning corporate strategy, a related strategic plan, and an effective execution approach. In other words, an ineffective management approach will leave our company in a position where it cannot absorb any of the other fundamentals.

Management approach is our CEO's most significant contribution. It doesn't matter how knowledgeable the CEO is about the market and customer or how well their sales acumen can close deals or market the company to investors. The CEO's primary value is building the management approach. No one else can do this.

We can look back in history and find a few unique examples where the CEO is a visionary, a strong salesperson, or a company marketer who defied the odds and led their company to long-term success. But these types of people tend to be outliers. So, do we really want to bet the company's future on the hope that the head of the company can emulate Steve Jobs or Elon Musk?

For mere mortals, a management approach is necessary to ensure that the company has the stable groundwork to support the increasing weight built above it.

> **Things to Remember: Management Approach**
>
> **Management approach is a set of levers that dictates 'company culture.' Management approach is not culture. Culture is the nebulous outcome that we cannot directly control.**

A strong management approach correlates with solid growth and a corporate culture that supports fundamentals necessary for growth; a weak management approach renders toxic work cultures that send a company spiraling down even if externalities are favorable. Culture is a result.

Management approach is a tangible path to develop a productive system that attracts top players.

"Culture eats strategy for breakfast" has been a fan favorite phrase for a few decades, and it is debatably attributed to Peter Drucker, a management guru. Whenever problems arise in a company, the pundits retrospectively assassinate its culture and find correlations between the CEO and behavioral issues at the company.

But if we say that a CEO is just a mere mortal, how is one person supposed to magically get all the employees to behave optimally? The path is not what we have come to blanketly call company culture.

The concept of company campus perks was a product of work environments. For example, if a successful company builds a sprawling campus, providing free lunches allow employees to grab food without leaving their work. Likewise, a free gymnasium encourages employees to come to the work campus earlier in the day or stay longer in the evening.

These were all fringe benefits associated with successful companies. But, more importantly, these companies attracted productive, high-performing employees due to company fundamentals, and the perks were simply fringe benefits intended to make their life a little bit better.

Mistaking these fringe benefits for success factors is a fallacy. As the share of employees that performs their work remotely increases in the years to come, these fringe benefits will continue to become less relevant. In 2022, the revised form of such conformity is promotions of remote work or flexible hours. However, these aren't drivers of culture either.

The 2019 study *Effect of a Workplace Wellness Program on Employee Health and Economic Outcomes* published in the Journal of American Medical Association revealed wellness programs offered by US companies had limited return on investment. To quote a summary from the study, "…but there were no significant differences in other self-reported health and behaviors; clinical markers of health; health care spending or utilization; or absenteeism, tenure, or job performance after 18 months."

Regardless of the amount of time employees spend in the office compared to working from home in the post-Covid world, in-office and virtual perks are just that – perks.

With the help of the human resources executive, the CEO's purpose is to create an environment that attracts the best talent and extracts the most value out of them. A 2012 McKinsey Global Survey, called *War for Talent,* shows that in very complex job roles, such as management and software development, the job productivity of high performers is a staggering 800% higher than average performers.

The CEO must balance the incentives of employees with external stakeholders. The CEO's **first** priority is creating high employee satisfaction to attract and retain top players, improve the performance of mid-tier players, and allow bottom players to improve or move on to other things.

Second is to continuously improve employee productivity and maturity to create the best possible offering for customers while generating a high return for investors, owners, and employees.

Management Approach Maturity Model.

The maturity model in Infographic A.1 articulates our evolutionary pathway, where we must strive towards the right side of the maturity model. As we move from the left side to the right, the CEO increasingly focuses on fundamentals that optimally serve a growing number of customers and external stakeholders while building a top-tier team that embraces micro-evolution and macro-evolution cycles.

Towards the model's left side, we are operating as a family business and at the whims of a few people where most others are considered a means to an end.

On the furthest left end of the maturity model, *Level 1: Biased*, the company's management approach is in tatters. The CEO and human resources have failed to develop an objective approach to manage the organization. Aspects such as likability and homogeneity are likely to rise to the top as factors that keep employees around. Top performers who push for the company's evolution will likely not feel equitably rewarded for their contributions.

These top performers who prefer to work at a winning, meritocratic company will likely leave quickly. Low performers who are satisfied with the status quo and are personally close to other tenured employees will probably feel at home. Loyalty and groupthink are highly valued. Hiring, terminations, performance, and compensation management decisions are likely to feel personal and subjective. A company stagnant at Level 1 of the management approach will find it impossible to evolve and mature on any of the other four parts of our growth methodology.

At *Level 2: Informal* and *Level 3: Democratic*, the organization is struggling to string together the essential components of the management approach. Attracting, hiring, and retaining top talent will be difficult. The maturity of the organizational design is unlikely to improve. As a result, it will struggle to keep top talent.

As we move further to the right of the maturity model, the CEO and human resources executive are more disciplined and objective about creating a structured approach to people, behaviors, and related decisions.

We must at least operate at *Level 4: Objective* to have any sustainable growth prospects. This maturity level allows us to hire and retain highly skilled employees and align their incentives with company values and goals. In addition, this floor enables that company to work towards evolving organizational design and related alignment of employee skills to deliver greater value to customers.

Our desired state is on the model's right side – *Level 5: Systemic*, where the company operates at a maturity level that supports growth. This level is a fully transparent environment where all employees know what is expected and what it takes to succeed. The components of the management approach systemically ensure that employee incentives fully align with company values and are designed to meet the needs of customers and partners. Personnel decisions will not cause surprises, and it will ensure that the highest performers stay while the rest strive to catch up to them. Customers will look at the company as a cohesive unit and a trusted partner where most employees can consistently deliver on their actual needs.

As a self-assessment, use this Management Approach Maturity Model and consider where your organization is today before going into the components that can help improve its current state. Taking each step to the right towards greater maturity is no easy feat, and this shift will prove increasingly hard as the organization gets older and habits and behaviors are entrenched.

Put that preventative care hat on. I worked with an early-stage technology company with six employees that has now blossomed into a unicorn, and I am confident about their sustainability. The CEO focused on the components in this management approach before the company scaled beyond ten employees.

Conversely, I worked with a 200-employee technology company that prioritized this mission after it experienced persistent growth challenges. Unfortunately, this delayed effort to improve the company's talent pool, work ethic, and productivity rendered limited success. Changing a subpar

THE SPIRAL STAIRWAY™ – THE SYSTEM TO BUILD A HOLISTIC COMPANY

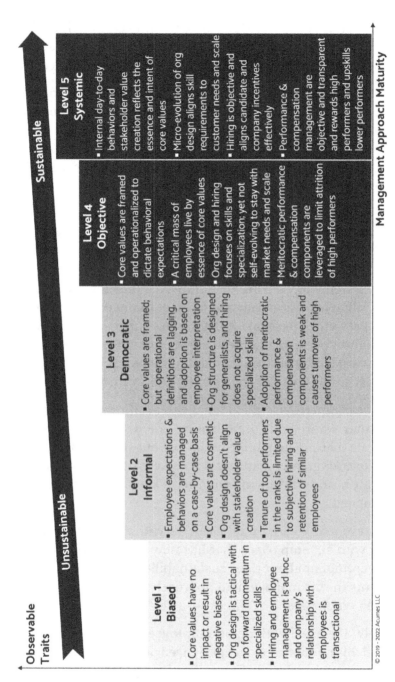

Infographic A.1 – Management Approach Maturity Model

environment is exponentially more complicated than thinking ahead and laying out the right foundational management approach.

The six components of the management approach will create a transparent, objective, disciplined, and efficient organizational environment to achieve a fair balance between the satisfaction of top performers and a system focused on creating intrinsic value for all stakeholders. No amount of employee perks can substitute the impact of our management approach components.

A.1
LET LEADERS LEAD.

LEADERSHIP is a nebulous concept. Many famous authors have different perspectives on what qualifies a good leader and one we are willing to follow. I'm not going to redefine leadership here. But beyond the theories laid out in management books, there are a few practical principles of leadership that a growing company needs to demonstrate to enable the rest of our methodology.

In all my experience trying to drive evolutionary change in companies, the one area that I found uncompromisable has always been the intrinsic behaviors, experience, and motivations of people in the senior-most executive seats. So, it is important to start here because even if we have put the best efforts into all the other components that we discuss, we are likely to have a near-zero impact if our company lacks effective leadership in these top few seats.

It is easy to confuse popularity with leadership, especially because strong leaders tend to be popular – positively or negatively. Many leaders are revered posthumously after they are vilified during their lifetime. Leadership is about understanding the needs of all stakeholders and taking a stand that balances those needs. Leadership isn't about making popular choices. Likability and social media following are not effective measurements of leadership if it's just repeating popular views.

We can look back at the 2020 Covid-19 pandemic and assess the decision-making approach of various country heads, state governors, and city mayors. It doesn't matter your belief system about the choices or political parties we align with; we will find decisions made by many elected officials that were either copycat or pandering decisions that allowed them to reduce their career or popularity risk. A leader's role is to understand the situation, get hold of information that constituents do not have, and make the right choice on their behalf. Leadership comes with risk. But these individuals also have the power to run the entity into the ground.

So, not every person in charge is made equal. History has made it clear that good leaders are far rarer than poor ones in their positions because of luck or sheer will and self-belief.

Companies are no different. This component will discuss the importance of good leaders overseeing a growing company.

Principle 1: Leaders align purpose with strategy and operations.

The owners of every company are different with different incentives. So, the purpose of existence of every company must be different. I don't mean an altruistic mission or vision statement. Rather, it is brass tacks – *why do the owners keep the company running?* The answer to this question must be selfish and true-to-self. A company must have leaders in senior executive seats who can answer these questions objectively and explicitly in collaboration with owners, whether external investors or employees. Then, leaders must build the answer's implications into all the growth components.

We live in a growth-or-nothing ecosystem that nudges everyone to want to grow at 100% each year or at least pretend to do so. Some successful companies have created a thin veil that purports that high growth and evolution can come without hard choices and long nights. It is just a tactic to meet recruitment goals. You don't get something for nothing.

I asked five senior executives of a venture-backed company with low employee morale, retention, and growth, "do you want to be a high-growth company or a lifestyle company?" The team struggled with the question. The challenges in the company were reflective of the confounded responses of four of the five executives. The CEO understood the relevance; the remaining executives did not. The company's wishful purpose created marketing, hiring, and fundraising perceptions aligned with a high-growth environment. But actual hiring, performance management, compensation, the effectiveness of offerings, processes, and continuous improvement reflected a company that was happy to be a lifestyle-focused, cash-flow business. This incongruity caused chaos.

> **Things to Remember: Company Purpose**
>
> **Company purpose is the honest and selfish incentives of the company owners, and it objectively answers the question – *why does the company exist?***

Infographic A.2 – Purpose dictates strategy and operations

So, throughout the rest of this book, 'sustainable growth' implies the growth rate and the market impact that the company owners are happy with. A 5% growth rate is just as fine as a 100% growth rate. The same methodology applies to divergent strategy and operations. We will assume that the leaders internalize the purpose and have the mettle to engrain its ramifications into company fundamentals.

Consider the following question:

Do the most senior executives objectively internalize and align on the purpose of the company, beyond externally focused altruistic slogans, to align the company's strategy and every element of operations with that purpose?

Principle 2: Leaders create systems to follow.

Many aspects such as fundraising and marketing and selling the company's offerings often dominate executives' mindshare. Of course, these are unavoidable and important, but building a strong system, especially the components under the management approach, is something that only the CEO and top few senior executives can own.

The complexion of companies changes very quickly through the growth phase, and the number of employees increases exponentially from single figures to hundreds in a few years. Every new employee in such a quickly changing environment is looking around for guidance on the daily behaviors to demonstrate and the values that they should uphold. Therefore, the CEO and senior executives must be strong leaders who can show a path for every new employee to follow. This is even more important at smaller companies because the ecosystem changes with the addition of every new employee.

> *Consider the following question:*
>
> *Are the CEO's role and the executive team staffed with strong leaders who prioritize the maturity of the management approach?*

Focusing on building a system aligns every existing and new employee's expectations and skills with company operations and its path to intrinsic value creation.

Conversely, a weak senior executive team allows democracy to take over. A company should never be a democracy. The last thing a fast-growth company needs is for the system to be defined as an average of the behaviors of all employees. This eventually leads to a senior executive team with limited influence beyond dictatorial actions or democratic vote counting.

Principle 3: Corporate leaders require business acumen and experience.

This sounds obvious, but real-world observations don't seem to align with its obvious nature. Leadership is often misunderstood for motivational speaking. The world has seen very charismatic influencers who have led their followers astray. So, leadership isn't just about banding a crowd together. We don't need a Pied Piper trying to start a revolution or a mass exodus in corporate settings.

Several years ago, I was thinking about how to utilize my Jack-of-many-trades background in my next opportunity. Then, along came a 100-person start-up that became a short-term strategic planning client. This two-week period in a conference room at the company opened my eyes to the great opportunity of supporting growth-phase companies on my own.

Here is the image – a capable and experienced CEO, who is also the company's best salesperson, wanted help to organize his team for the following year. He was visibly frustrated and stretched thin. Here's the rest of the room – a technology executive who is a glorified programmer who shared almost no business-level insights in the two weeks that I was in the room, a sales executive who was a likable ex-sales representative with no experience leading a sales organization, and a marketing executive, whose previous job was as a digital marketer at an agency. I did not doubt that these were all talented and capable people. But experience and ability are necessary for executive-level roles, and there is no way to substitute that.

Fast forward, within 18 months, that CEO was gone. Over time, the company has fizzled and is a dying entity.

> **Consider the following question:**
>
> *Do the most senior roles in the company demonstrate a solid experiential foundation covering business acumen, the importance of serving customers effectively, and the ability to operate beyond one's own needs to have a well-calibrated compass to lead people with?*

Starting a company is different from running one. A founding CEO or executive must consider handing over the reins to someone experienced with a business operator's mind. Cherry-picking data points from a few successful companies is not an objective use of data. For every successful founding CEO, there are several forcefully removed from their position. Google founders recognized their limitations and wisely brought on Eric Schmidt as a CEO early on. Unfortunately, such self-awareness is less common than you would imagine.

Senior executives must have the experiential depth to internalize and operate the business with a cross-functional strategic mindset than a tactical day-to-day operations mindset. In our Systems First philosophy, odds are long for our desire to grow sustainably if senior executives do not hold the experience and insight to think and operate strategically and objectively.

Principle 4: Strong leaders understand their strengths and when to follow.

No human being can be a trailblazer at everything they get involved in. Everyone has areas they are passionate about and has behavioral and topical spikes, which are their unique strengths. Unfortunately, it also means everyone has areas of weakness.

Effective leaders embody two facets around abilities. **First,** they have tangible world-class talents that are directly pertinent to their responsibilities. They embrace and lean into these abilities. **Second,** they have the humility to follow and take help in areas that are not their strength.

For example, a creative founder executive should know that there are many operational areas, such as sales, strategy, operations, etc., that they will have to follow in an educated and objective manner. An effective leader will let others show the path based on their know-how without becoming an organizational drag in their weakness areas.

At the 100-person company mentioned above, a potential root cause of scoring low on Principle 3 could be that the CEO felt too confident in his ability to bring all the relevant spikes across the whole company. Optimally, the CEO would have internalized his own weaknesses across multiple functions and recruited executives with favorable spikes in other areas.

> ***Consider the following questions:***
>
> *Do senior executives have tangible superpowers? Have they mastered these spikes in abilities?*
>
> *Have senior executives understood their weaknesses, and proactively chosen to depend on others in their areas of weakness?*

If a person always appears fully in control in a senior role, they are more likely not to know how and when to follow. Following is just as important a leader's trait as showing the path for others to follow. Senior executives focusing on their own superpowers and demonstrating the ability to follow experts illustrate the importance of skills to the rest of the organization.

Principle 5: Leadership is taken, not given.

My upbringing involved a lot of churchgoing, and habits stick. When I moved to a small town for my first post-college job, the only way I knew how to make friends was to go to church youth groups. Before we had cell phones, I created email lists of people I met at church and started inviting folks to do fun things around town, primarily to keep myself busy. People came to these things because they had nothing else to do either.

One day, the youth pastor called me and asked me to lunch. After some polite back and forth, he asked me – "do you think leadership is given or taken?" I was a little confused by the pop quiz, and I can't remember my initial response. But I remember his response very well. He said, "God picks leaders like Paul to lead people!" Suddenly, it dawned on me where he was going with this. It turns out my random invitations to do fun events made him feel like I was stepping on his feet because he had just started his role as a lead youth pastor.

Guess who 'gave' him the leadership role? His dad found this megachurch and was the lead pastor. His mom was up on stage every weekend leading choir. So, should he have been 'given' a leadership role right after college? I still think about this story when I think about leadership.

Consider the following question:

Who around us has earned their senior positions compared to others sitting in chairs because they were 'given' leadership?

Paul, the apostle, was a strong Roman leader in his own right before he was 'given' a different role. Leadership isn't about titles or hierarchy; it is the ability to show others an optimal path and make hard and unpopular decisions to enable that path, even if it implies personal risk.

A common mistake is to confuse seniority or elevated positions with leadership. The truth is that we meet leaders at all levels of a company, and we may meet tactical managers with senior job titles. A leader simply focuses on how they can help the world around them, and their approach, ability, and passion flow into their actions and decisions.

These decisions often show the difference between leaders and senior job titles. Tough decisions imply risk. The CEO and senior executives must internalize the importance of taking a stand based on objective information.

Being right is not a measurement of leadership. Having a backbone is.

Principle 6: Leaders are trustworthy.

How many good leaders do you personally know? I am not talking about popularity or seniority. Who do you really trust? Often, it takes time for the difference between popularity and leadership to reveal itself.

Leaders demonstrate their commitment; tactical managers talk about their commitment. It's hard to know the difference unless you observe it over time.

Making lofty statements that one cannot live by daily does not evoke trust or confidence among employees, and an organization must ensure that senior executives can demonstrate their commitment to every idea they support. Good leaders own up to their mistakes and admit when they are wrong.

An organization has to develop a genuinely objective system that can support the evolution of fundamentals to attract top talent from various backgrounds. An objective system starts with senior executives being able to demonstrate trustworthiness. Executives must ensure that every statement they make is backed by actions to evoke such trust.

> *Consider the following question:*
>
> *Do senior executives pass the simple litmus test of following the age-old saying, "actions speak louder than words?"*

One example of trustworthiness is a demonstration of accountability. We discussed that good leaders search for people they can follow in areas where they are weak. A follow-on requirement is that they coach and mentor them to succeed and put themselves at risk with such personnel choices and decisions. This creates a positive ripple effect in an organization where leaders respect and learn from each other for their spikes while supporting each other to succeed.

Conversely, poor leaders tend to look for personnel they can manage and stay above. It results in the poor leader blaming others for problems instead of taking accountability themselves. It degrades trust.

In summary, leaders embrace the risk associated with their actions and decisions. They align purpose with reality, implement the management approach components, focus on their strengths and value creation, and are trustworthy in the long term. Tactical managerial skills are optimal for supervisory positions but not ideal for senior executive roles to whom employees look for behavioral and moral guidance.

I can tell you that long-term retention of one influential executive who privately believes that "let's hire someone quickly and we can let them go after we need them" will be ineffective because the organization will be at ground zero on its management approach maturity.

Leadership is our warmup component. But one that's absolutely necessary for us to get through the rest of our evolutionary growth journey. So, the first act of the board and the CEO should be to ensure that effective leaders occupy senior executive roles.

A.2
SET CORE VALUES AS BEHAVIORAL GUARDRAILS.

IF the CEO's effort to build the management approach is analogous to creating an organized religion, then core values are the actionable commandments that convey expected day-to-day behaviors.

It is hard to find companies without an altruistic-sounding set of core values displayed on their walls. Most scaling companies talk about their core values as their path to future success. However, there are core values that look and sound good, and then there are core values that work and are lived by. A successful growth-phase company introduces its equivalent core values with, "we don't have core values; we have core behaviors!" This is the right frame of mind.

> **Consider the following question:**
>
> *When quizzed by surprise, what percentage of employees get at least 80% of core values and the essence of its meaning correct? A low score implies ineffective core values.*

Each employee has their own personal value system. Expecting an individual to override it with a company's value system requires their understanding of the core values and how they can best implement them.

The goal of a company is to serve its market. Conversely, a company must not attempt to accommodate every potential hire or employee's value system into the company.

> **Things to Remember: Core Values**
>
> **Core values articulate the company's DNA necessary to serve its market and allow the company to attract and retain the right people to serve its market.**

First, core values articulate the company's expected operational behaviors. Developing them, operationalizing them, and consistently ensuring adoption is the most critical task of the CEO and the human resources team. It is a vaccine formulated, tested, iterated, and prescribed by the CEO based on market knowledge. Human resources must inoculate it as prescribed.

Second, the process to define core values should not be democratic. The CEO's decision and articulation are based on an adequate set of market and internal assessments. Unfortunately, the most common pitfall that companies fall into is to start with asking the democratic question – *What do you think our core values should be?*

Core values are not meant to be an average of any internal stakeholders' opinions or desires – not the senior executives or other employees. If we create a perception that opinions matter, we open the door to potential downfall in adoption.

Understandably, taking the pulse of all employees is a much easier path to defining core values. But this path is unlikely to lead to the right behaviors that will help win the market. Core values must lead employees, not follow employees.

Simplistically, core values define the desired behaviors that impact internal and external stakeholders. Core values dictate the day-to-day behaviors of all employees. The behaviors articulated by the core value should balance the value created for customers, vendors, partners, investors, senior executives, and employees.

However, core values are not meant to market a company's intent to customers, partners, or vendors. External stakeholders only care about the behaviors demonstrated by the company; they don't read the core values before they decide to do business.

A.2 SET CORE VALUES AS BEHAVIORAL GUARDRAILS

Core values must do two things. **First**, companies must focus on identifying the right behaviors that meet the real needs of key stakeholders. Although it is tempting to worry about the optics of core values, the only optic that matters is the ultimate impact it drives. **Second**, core values are effective when they become the operational and behavioral DNA of the company. In other words, every employee must adopt and live by the intent of the core values when they are within the company walls.

Core values must score well on adoption and impact. If our core values feel ineffective, we must be bold and change them. Forget all the rules about how often we are supposed to change them and what everyone else thinks. Corporate strategy development is an optimal pathway for the macro-evolution of core values.

Infographic A.3 – Values Funnel Framework to develop core values

I recommend leveraging a Values Funnel Framework to arrive at the correct core values. Infographic A.3 illustrates my Values Funnel Framework. The funnel has three levels that result in effective core values that can dictate the company's operations.

Principle 1: Core values align with external stakeholder needs.

It is tempting to think that a management approach is all about a company's internal dynamics. Ultimately, a business exists to trade with customers, vendors, and other partners. It is the only path to revenue or profitability. Even if a company has highly productive, top talent firing on all cylinders, the direction that energy is expended is important. Such a group can spend its efforts in a direction that doesn't serve its external stakeholders well on the tepid end to misdirect stakeholders on the unethical end.

There are two essential aspects that we must address to identify the needs of external stakeholders. **First** is a clear articulation of our key stakeholders. This may comprise any combination of customers, suppliers, partners, members on two-sided offerings, etc. Of course, this choice entirely depends on the company's business model. But ignoring a key stakeholder group can have dire consequences.

The **second** is the importance of understanding the stakeholders' *real needs* instead of *perceived needs*. Think about real needs as root causes of problems they are trying to solve and perceived needs as symptoms. We need to design our organizational behaviors that meet stakeholders' real needs. We will discuss both factors further in Part C: Corporate Strategy.

For example, I worked with a *software-as-a-service* (SaaS) company that took great pride in 'responsiveness' as a value. Their responsiveness scores approached ten out of ten for years. But they found customer loyalty elusive. My work with them revealed that the correct measure for customers' real needs was the average number of hours customers spent each month with its offering. Essentially, customers wanted to take the results of the offering without wasting time to troubleshoot or extract the results.

The company mistakenly used a narrow measurement of answering customer phone calls politely and chasing down problems quickly as success criteria. The customers' actual need was that they didn't want to spend any time on the offering in the first place. The company should have focused on taking the onus of using the offering away from the customer entirely. Instead, a core value of 'turnkey' was more apt.

In the first layer of the funnel, all the preferences of external stakeholders become the superset of all values that a company should consider and narrow it down to a manageable set of values based on the company's chosen market and the real needs of key stakeholders.

No company can be good at everything. Senior executives must choose the employees' specific traits when executing operational processes or owning and implementing major initiatives. This alignment between behavioral expectations and operational needs is critical to ensure that all key stakeholders' needs are being met, which is the only path to sustainable growth.

Consider the following questions:

Who are the company's key external stakeholders?

What are the behaviors that create the most value for these external stakeholders?

For example, do our customers prefer to interact with a fun vendor or a serious, buttoned-up vendor?

If our company serves creative entertainment industry customers, they might prefer to interact with a vendor that makes their experience fun and leisurely. On the other hand, suppose we are selling to banks or hospitals. In that case, they are likely to expect a vendor's employees to demonstrate preparedness and discipline due to the high-risk environments these customers operate in.

Southwest Airlines is a perfect example of turning core values into behaviors. A *Warrior Spirit, Servant's Heart,* and *Fun-LUVing Attitude* summarize the airline's values. It is evident that the employees strive to make flying fun and leisurely for their core market of middle class, occasional travelers, and vacationers. It is a stark contrast to other US airlines that primarily profit from frequent professional and business travelers who are used to a more formal flying experience.

The day-to-day behaviors of all employees need to align with the internal operational expectations that satisfy external stakeholders. Core value definition starts with the articulation of these external expectations. However, we must also be able to execute these expectations.

Principle 2: Core values align with internal strengths.

With the help of human resources and the strategy & operations executive, the CEO has to take a deep introspective look at what the company is actually good at. Choosing expected behaviors that are not the company's core strengths will likely lead to disappointing outcomes.

Organizational behaviors demonstrated by employees must be consistent. External stakeholders do not do business with only one employee. They do business with the whole company. Therefore, each employee must be able to repeat the desired behaviors consistently. All employees must reproduce the same behaviors as everyone else so that external stakeholders see the company as one united front. For instance, a company would not want the resignation of a top performer to risk the entire relationship with a customer.

Taking core values from large, successful companies or being biased by social conversations in the public domain is not a great approach to define the appropriate internal behaviors.

Consider the following question:

Objectively, what are the company's operational strengths and weaknesses?

For example, a popular core value is 'do the right thing.' I have worked with multiple companies that used this as a core value. However, employees come from many geographical and professional backgrounds, and the 'right thing' is subjective.

Consider three hypothetical employees. The first has a trading background, the second has nonprofit experience, and the third has an engineering background. They will all think about the 'right thing' very differently when interacting with internal and external stakeholders. None of them are right or wrong, but their experiences vastly differ and shape what they consider the 'right thing.' Core values must align with the company's strengths and be tangible and non-interpretive.

Conversely, this is a decisive stage in the management approach development for the CEO to answer the question – *What type of people and behaviors do we want in our organization?* Although every executive wants to hire the cream of the crop, the reality is different. If one person can lift 200lbs for

$2 and another two people can lift 100lbs each for $1 each, which option do we choose? The fundamental nature of strengths and weaknesses and associated behaviors is not that simple. But we still have to make choices.

Defining the core values is the opportunity to decide the type of operational behaviors our company wants to embrace. As we discuss organization design, hiring, performance management, and compensation management, effective use of this filtering layer will prove invaluable.

Reconsider the question that I posed to my fellow senior executives in the last chapter to drive towards an aligned company-wide purpose: "Are we a high-growth, fast-paced company or a cash-flow-focused, lifestyle company?" That was not a good vs. bad or right vs. wrong choice. Instead, it intended to frame the strengths that the company's core values should incorporate. In that scenario, the company had to resolve the disconnect between our perceived strengths and the reality on the ground.

This second principle and layer of the Values Funnel Framework impacts our organizational design and the number of employees each role will need. It influences the depth of skills we can plan to hire. It impacts the expectations we set for our employees to measure their performance and how much we compensate them. It affects the quality, speed, flexibility, and cost of value creation for customers. Finally, it impacts the growth and profitability we can realistically achieve.

Principle 3: Core values are seamlessly demonstrable by senior executives.

At the bottom of the funnel, the final but equally important filter is the alignment between senior executives' behaviors and operational behaviors required to meet stakeholder needs.

> ### Consider the following question:
> *What are the day-to-day behaviors that the company's senior executives can live by?*

Ideally, we should ask this question before filling senior executive roles. Conversely, it offers an internal assessment on whether the right senior executives are in place.

A set of words and explanations is not enough to engrain the spirit of core values into the company's DNA. Core values require role models to demonstrate the true essence of every value and related theme. Senior executives are these role models. Every aspect of desired behaviors should be the natural state where senior executives operate consistently.

If core values do not reflect the natural day-to-day behaviors of senior executives, they just become words on a plaque. The broader team will not have leaders to look up to and learn what 'good' looks like. Furthermore, the misalignment between senior executives' natural instincts and documented core values will likely result in hiring and promoting employees that do not truly represent the essence of the core values. This further devalues its effectiveness.

One of the core values used by Uber's founding CEO, Travis Kalanick, was: "Meritocracy and toe-stepping – The best idea always wins. Don't sacrifice truth for social cohesion and don't hesitate to challenge the boss." Interestingly, this is a strong core value. Travis Kalanick successfully conveyed and demonstrated his idea of how Uber should behave. For years, Uber operated in markets worldwide with an 'ask for forgiveness, not permission' attitude, constantly butting heads with local governments for starting Uber services without going through the proper channels.

We may or may not agree with Mr. Kalanick. But it shows the power of a well-framed core value – demonstrability and actionability. Intending to change employee behaviors, Uber's next CEO, Dara Khosrowshahi, changed this value to a very comparable one with much more moderated behavioral elements – "We value ideas over hierarchy. We believe that the best ideas can come from anywhere, both inside and outside our company. Our job is to seek out those ideas, to shape and improve them through candid debate, and to take them from concept to action."

The change in Uber's CEO and shift in core values were also associated with turnover among other senior executives better aligned to a more evolved global brand that Uber aspired to become.

When we meet these three criteria, core values are aligned with the strategic and operational needs of the company and can be reliable guardrails.

A tricky scenario is where day-to-day behaviors that senior executives demonstrate do not adequately cover the values necessary to serve the market. This is where a company's board comes in. The board should be aware of gaps between the senior executives' abilities and systemic aspects necessary to meet internal and external stakeholder needs.

In an organization with a robust system driving towards sustainable growth, there will be significant overlap between the answers to the three layers of the Values Funnel Framework. It will result in a competitive set of operational behaviors at the bottom of the funnel that can be translated to its core values.

Core values touch every aspect of managing the organization. The CEO can measure the leadership effectiveness of senior executives and the implementation prowess of the human resources department based on the adoption and impact of the company's core values across all components of our methodology. So, how do we drive adoption?

Principle 4: Operationalize core values for practical impact.

Once the CEO has developed the core values, taking it from paper to practice is not trivial. Every employee in the company should read, understand, and live by the core values without ambiguity or interpretive differences. In addition, every item included in the core values should have a detailed articulation that communicates what to do and what not to do. But getting the core values right and in operation is challenging.

I worked closely with a growth-phase company that prided itself on the following core values: 'accountability,' 'respect,' and 'agility,' with a short sentence to support each. Unfortunately, growth stalled after a decade into the business, and the company lost 25% of revenue in a single year. Negative customer feedback had spiked due to persistent delivery quality challenges. There were no solutions on the horizon. What do you think was happening here?

First off, these three core values had no tangible alignment with external stakeholder needs. They could apply to any company in any market and did not align with the strengths of the executive team. Even more importantly, these three positively intentioned behaviors were not operationalized. The result was that the words on paper morphed into unintended behaviors on the ground.

- *Can **respect** be misinterpreted?*
- *Can one be too **respectful** when we aren't holding people **accountable**?*
- *Could one mix up **agility** with lack of discipline and lack of planning?*
- *Could too much **respect** cause executives to fail to lead employees and evolve on company fundamentals?*
- *Could **respect** lead to telling customers what they want to hear and being unable to deliver to expectations?*
- *Can **accountability** be tactical and miss the big picture?*

In this scenario, the ineffectiveness and poor operationalization of core values became one of the gaps that needed to be closed before other growth components could be effective.

Applying the first three principles during strategy development will render the appropriate themes and actionable details for powerful core values. These values don't need to be ingenious; they just have to be effective and satisfy the three principles above. But their impact will elude us if we don't bake it into every aspect of our operations. Ineffectively operationalized core values are toothless.

As we go through the remaining elements of the management approach, the core values will reappear as a constant backdrop. We must build core values into our company's offerings and how employees work with each other, customers, and other partners. We must also devise creative and standardized teaching and accountability methods to engrain our values into our company.

Our hiring and employee performance assessments will need to have the core values built in to ensure that they remain a guardrail for our decision-making around people. When new employees join us, we must conduct new-hire training across all aspects of our operations to align on how to live our core values.

All employee meetings are valuable forums to communicate impactful ideas across the organization. We must use such opportunities to influence forward-looking behaviors through core values and restrain privately consumable, non-interpretable information such as financial updates.

Similarly, larger gatherings of employees to introduce or train on new offerings and annual or bi-annual sales kick-offs are opportunities to evolve every employee's thinking on our core values continuously. It is essential to periodically retrain everyone to ensure that this all-important systemic driver doesn't mutate and create poor behaviors.

Consider the following question:

What are the tangible and impactful ways in which core values are injected into the actions and decisions made by every employee in the company?

Effectively designed core values are only a shadow of what effectively operationalized core values can be. Effectively operationalized core values will play an important part in the effectiveness of every other component, including how we design our organization and how we hire.

A.3
DESIGN ORGANIZATION TO MAP SKILLS TO GROWTH STAGE.

To grow a company sustainably, we need more than just people. We need the right people doing the right things. For example, if our company is a sports team, we first have to know our style of play and positions on the team; then, we can find the players to fill those positions. Organization design is the path to creating the most optimal configuration for our team, and hiring is the exercise of finding the players.

Let's start with an important concept that aids effective organization design and hiring.

Just because a child counts stars on a clear night does not mean they will have a reasonable estimate of the number of stars in the universe. So, why don't we tell the child to leave the estimation exercise to scientists that spent their entire careers studying the Universe? It's because we don't have the heart to tell the child about the universe's complexities, such as distances, gravity, light speed, time, rotation and revolution of objects, etc.

The point is not that we should disappoint children. But, even with adults, we often find it difficult to be objective if the truth causes discomfort.

Our inherent challenge with objectivity bleeds into professional decision-making and communication, and it can hurt an organization's access to expertise and experience. The only way to increase stakeholder value is to improve skills that directly or indirectly influence value creation.

First, corporate settings can allow decision-making based on committee and consensus rather than objective analyses and topical expertise. It feels easier to vote on difficult decisions because the vote count can be misconstrued as reliable data. It is more uncomfortable for an executive to disagree with a large group, even if objective analyses and insights indicate that an unpopular path is the right one.

If senior executives give in to this tendency, expertise, experience, and critical thinking can become overshadowed by consensus building and conformity. The latter is important, but not at the expense of the former. As a result, analytical and critical thinking employees will feel sidelined and, eventually, leave the company. Gradually, the company may only have employees that generally agree with each other but also align on a course that was not the right one in the first place. In essence, this is stumbling down *The Spiral Stairway*™.

Second, every business sector demonstrates biases based on age, gender, sector-specific experience, and a myriad of other factors. Biases are human; however, beyond a certain point, biases can cause significant gaps in the company's strengths. For example, one type of bias that young companies, especially in the technology sector, fall prey to is age. State of Start-ups, a technology sector annual surveyor, reported in their 2018 survey that 89% of respondents answered, 'yes' to the question, "In tech, do older people face age discrimination?"

When a market research firm, Statista, recently studied the median age of the largest fifteen technology companies, ten out of the fifteen had a median employee age at or below 33 years. That means over half the employees in these companies are younger than 33.

If we compare this to data from the US Bureau of Labor Statistics, Current Population Survey assessing workforce age breakdown across 283 industries, only shoe stores, clothing stores, restaurants and bars, car washes, and hobby and toy stores, which are all retail task-based jobs, had a lower median age.

A company could display other biases such as gender and sector-specific hires only. The company essentially excludes top talent with relevant expertise from hiring considerations through all these biases.

The CEO's goal is to create a system that brings together top talent and gets the best out of them, and the first imperative is to overcome biases that counter these desired outcomes. I call this state of balance between objectivity and expertise a **Comparative Advantage Ecosystem (CAE)**.

Strong leaders in senior executive roles focus on developing a CAE to drive a company further to the right of the Management Approach Maturity Model.

> **Things to Remember: Comparative Advantage Ecosystem (CAE)**
>
> **In economics, comparative advantage is an age-old idea that the most efficient and effective path expects every individual to do what that person is best at doing to create value. Conversely, placing individuals in positions where they cannot display their best qualities is suboptimal. A CAE is an environment that objectively prioritizes comparative advantage to find and deploy appropriate skills to all organizational actions and decisions.**

First, a CAE delegates decision-making authority to individuals based on objective criteria such as relevant experience and expertise, time dedicated to working on the specific problem at hand, and objective quality of work product.

A CAE does not delegate decision-making authority based on organizational seniority or job titles or reduce decision-making into popularity contests. It also ensures that each person knows the specific skills they bring to the table and focuses on those skills while internalizing others' skills and allowing them to focus on theirs.

Second, a CAE enables an organization to get beyond typical biases such as age, gender, shared educational or professional institutions, sector-specific myopia, and other similar factors. It creates an ecosystem where hiring, talent management, decision-making, and execution focus on building skills instead of spurious associations with expertise.

There is only one path to create a Comparative Advantage Ecosystem – ensure that strong leaders are in the CEO's position and senior executive roles. They become the role models that determine the behaviors that the rest of the company embodies.

Why is a CAE pertinent to a mature management approach?

The path to sustainable growth goes through an effective organizational design that fosters a Comparative Advantage Ecosystem. An increasingly maturing organizational design is necessary to acquire and retain customers as a company's market share grows. Top performers set up to do work that aligns with their strengths and expertise are the base ingredient to create the most value to meet increasingly demanding market needs.

Gallup's survey report *What Job-Hopping Employees Are Looking For*, conducted before the confounding impact of Covid-19, showed that 51% of all employees are considering a new job. The same survey asked for the motivation behind this, and 60% of respondents said that their reasons to consider a new job included "it allows me to do what I do best." Compare that to the 41% of respondents who had "it significantly increases my income" as the motivation.

Unproductive environments make employees feel the company is not utilizing their strengths. As a result, employees become bored and want to quit. Searching for a job becomes a more challenging and fulfilling project than doing the work they are paid to do.

The first step to mature our organization design systemically and continuously is to side-step common mistakes.

Principle 1: Avoid organization design pitfalls.

An effective and self-maturing organization design is crucial because it enables efficient and cost-effective scaling and increases market value creation. In addition, it ensures that every dollar that the company spends effectively finds revenue and delivers value. No one in the world will disagree with this mindset. So, why do companies often get wrapped around the axle and end up with bloated and unproductive organizations and poor staffing models? A few common pitfalls result in ineffective organization designs and staffing models.

Pitfall 1: Confusing roles and job titles.

Have you ever experienced starting a new job at a company with seemingly the same position you had at a different company, yet almost everything you do is entirely different? It is almost always the case because of the difference between roles and job titles. Most organization design challenges arise because companies rarely focus on roles.

If a role is the candy, the job title is the candy wrapper. If you choose any job title and search for it on a job board, you will see almost no relevant differentiation between the job descriptions. Do you think you will be doing similar things between those jobs? For starters, each manager will have completely different experience. In addition, the company's needs and processes are different. Often, many post jobs without a clear, in-depth description of what a person would do, particularly beyond immediate needs for the first three months.

Most organizations are too reactive. Imagine a CEO addressing an unanticipated issue with senior executives and saying, "I want it solved quickly, even if we have to hire a new person." The senior executive who owns the problem leaves that conversation and wants the issue resolved quickly to avoid another tough talk with the CEO. This executive also considers the hiring option as a directive.

The senior executive tells a supervisor about the discussion with the CEO and puts the supervisor in charge of hiring the new person with a lot less context than the CEO's original thinking. The supervisor reaches out to the recruiting team and shares his interpretation of the hiring requirements. The recruiter will ask the supervisor, "what is the job title?" The supervisor will offer one without specifying how this hire might solve the original problem. The recruiting team then searches the internet to find a job posting for the job title or will use an old job posting, and before you know it, there is a new person hired.

One of three things will happen to this new hire. One is that the original problem that the CEO faced resolved itself or was handled some other way by existing employees, maybe even before the new hire ever joined. The second is that this hire's core strengths do not fit the problem due to a misalignment between the generic job title, the hire's experience, and the company's problem. The least likely outcome is that this rushed and job title-based search resulted in a new employee that has the appropriate strengths to solve the company's short-term unique problem. However, this new hire does not have a clear long-term path, even in this unlikely scenario.

Since companies generally hire employees to meet needs beyond a few months, this tendency to use job titles to shortcut hiring leads to misalignment between a company's longer-term needs and employee strengths and experience. Such misalignment leads to a lack of productivity, employee dissatisfaction, and ultimately turnover.

Pitfall 2: Empire building.

It is human to desire advancement, more compensation, and social status. All of this can come from visible seniority in an organization and the size of the team one manages. So, we are likely to have a natural bias towards hiring more people underneath us or asking for more significant job titles. But it should never come at the expense of organizational efficiency.

In other words, the CEO and human resources must drive the company to focus on roles and not on candy-wrapper job titles. Scaling companies should have no more than one or two supervisory layers between employees who perform most of the actual work daily and senior executives who report to the CEO.

This is important for two reasons.

The **first** is cost. Quite simply, a scaling company cannot afford organizational fat if it is to achieve a sustainable growth phase. Every dollar spent on under-utilized organizational layers is better dedicated to operations that add value to external stakeholders or directly improve the company's maturity level.

The **second** is the Chinese Whispers problem. Chinese Whispers is a game where each person whispers a word into the next person's ear and asks to pass the word on. Inevitably, we misconstrue the word the more people it has to pass through. In a corporate setting where complex concepts are involved and individual incentives are relevant, creating unnecessary layers that confuse accountability and communication creates inefficiency on the simple end and lack of transparency or vicious politics on the extreme end.

Pitfall 3: Diminishing returns due to lack of prioritization.

As a company grows, more revenue starts coming in, and investors will likely offer more financing. The pressure to grow even faster often comes from success and investors demanding a return. Under these circumstances, it can be tempting to take on many initiatives to create more structure and implement new solutions to help internal operations. These might be the right things to do.

Companies often underestimate the impact of making such changes to improve their operations and end up overcommitting. A company can only work on a certain number of major initiatives at a given time, no matter how much money is available or how big the company is. The reason is that many organizational problems can only be solved in a somewhat linear or triangulating manner. Too many people running around and working in silos to solve highly dependent initiatives in parallel usually results in misaligned solutions.

Companies often overinvest in people, technology, and other assets and are forced to cut back. Laying off employees is terrible for a company's morale and a life-altering experience for employees. Alternately, the company tries to reallocate these employees into roles that may not be their best fit.

Building an efficient organization demands that the CEO prioritizes major initiatives and take a tiered approach to investing and seeing a return on the investment before investing further. Then, if done well, the company can become more efficient by simply reallocating the same resources.

Pitfall 4: Failure to reallocate employees with decreasing responsibilities.

To optimize every dollar we invest, it is essential to consider whether employee roles have become less time-consuming or unnecessary.

Imagine that your marketing team has one or more employees focused on content generation to market your offerings. It is worth considering whether this is a perpetual and consistent need. After all, how much content do we need before it becomes too much content, especially as a scaling company? Can this core skill be reallocated to another need that adds exponentially more value than marketing content after a certain period? Asking this question might even help us avoid hiring another employee in a different function.

Consider the following questions to diagnose the prevalence of organization design challenges:

Does the CEO, senior executives, and human resources use standard job titles to describe complex organizational needs?

Does the company have growing fiefdoms managed by individuals that appear self-sufficient, which indicates a tendency to build 'empires'?

Does the company have too many major initiatives managed by several owners simultaneously?

Do employees stagnate in their roles without effective reallocation?

These pitfalls are common and are symptomatic of an ill-conceived management approach. These fundamental issues will stifle efforts to scale effectively.

So, what does 'good' organization design look like?

Ultimately, we want to proactively design an organization where each role has a specific purpose, and we align that purpose with acquiring customers or creating value for them. To move to the right side of our Management Approach Maturity Model, we must embrace the following principles to optimize an organization's design and allow it to perpetually micro-evolve.

Every company starts with a minimal number of employees where each person has many responsibilities, and those responsibilities overlap heavily. This is not scalable. We have to incorporate three principles while developing an effective organizational design in the growth phase.

Principle 2: Delineate enablement & operations skill groups.

We can delineate every investment in our company, whether its people, technology, or other assets, into two groups. We invest in people, technology, or assets for time-bound projects or to perpetually create value through our operation. This delineation is our first organization design concept – **Skill Groups**. I call it skill groups because I initially arrived at this insight in the context of investment in people. But the same principle applies to everything that we invest in our company. Although we will focus on people in the context of our management approach, we will see that the identical delineation applies across all our investment choices during strategic planning.

People fall into two general groups based on their interests, aptitude, and experiences. The **first** group is most effective with time-bound efforts that have specific goals, and once that effort is complete, they move on to a different effort that solves another problem. Thus, we can consider this skill group's focus as project work.

The **second** skill group is most effective in performing an operation many times over to achieve the same results even if there are nuances between each time we perform that operation. We can think about this as operations execution. The key delineation vectors here are whether the work is time-bound or perpetual and how similar each iteration is.

In a CAE, individuals align with either of these skill groups and, as a company matures, roles should fall into one skill group or the other. Most of my experiences have been time-bound and project-based, and I am good at that. However, whenever I have been responsible for efforts in an operations execution skill group, I devise ways to make it project-like work; I am not as effective in the second skill group.

The reverse applies to anyone whose strong suit is operations execution but asked to do project work. They are likely to trivialize project work into a set of tasks, which is far less likely to achieve the intended change. In my experience, this is proven to be an invaluable practical insight in staffing teams and identifying and solving organizational risk around people and other investments.

> **Things to Remember: Skill Groups**
>
> **All investments – people, technology, or other assets – fall into one of two skill groups based on their core tendency or experience to create value through either time-bound execution of unique efforts or perpetual execution of many iterations of an operation.**

A scaling company must mature towards knowing the core skill group for every investment item and categorizing them into one of these two groups. Let's name the first skill group as **Enablement Resources** and the second skill group as **Operations Resources**. These are very different. They are equally crucial for a maturing company to drive towards sustainable growth. But mixing these two skill groups into the same employee or role is similar to mixing milk and oil. It just doesn't work. Employees or assets not categorized into either of these groups should raise questions on how to leverage them.

Let's get deeper into these two major resource categories as we will refer to these two skill groups throughout the rest of the methodology.

Skill Group A: Operations resources.

Irrespective of the type of business, many tasks need to be performed regularly in perpetuity. These might include selling efforts performed by sales representatives; marketers who create leads through manual or digital actions; service personnel who address ongoing customer needs; finance professionals who handle invoices to pay vendors and process payments from customers; the list goes on.

The commonality between these roles is that the core tasks need to be performed perpetually. Such positions form a significant portion of employees in a company. The amount of work completed by these roles can be scaled up or down by adding or eliminating resources somewhat linearly.

> **Things to Remember: Operations Resources**
>
> **Operations resources include all people (or supporting technology and other assets) that perpetually execute all day-to-day operational processes that directly lead to measurable outcomes.**

Simultaneously, a company needs to continue to improve the maturity of its operations which includes productivity of operations resources. This responsibility falls on the second group of resources – enablement resources.

Skill Group B: Enablement resources.

Improving operations resources' productivity and effectiveness, designing our offerings, optimizing operations to help employees work together, and similar such efforts are all necessary. The critical difference is that all these efforts should be timebound and clearly focus on the desired state.

These resources conduct research, develop forward-looking insights, create documentation, and socialize outcomes for others in the company to learn. Such efforts are identified and prioritized as part of strategic planning to improve productivity and maturity. Motivated self-starters and individuals who are organizational change agents should fill roles that fall under the enablement resource category.

> **Things to Remember: Enablement Resources**
>
> **Enablement resources include all people (or supporting technology and other assets) that execute on time-bound efforts that increase the maturity of operations, including the productivity of operations resources.**

Scaling companies should take a very prudent approach to adding enablement resources as their efforts are always timebound. In addition, we should vet every existing enablement resource consistently to ensure that we fully utilize them and that their strengths remain relevant.

One typical example of misallocation between operations and enablement skill groups is around sales teams.

Sales is where the rubber meets the road at most companies. The onus of revenue falls on sales representatives and supervisors, whose expertise is to execute sales transactions. Conversely, their expertise is not to define the markets that the company should sell into, develop sales and marketing collateral, or develop analytics. However, in many growing companies, sales reps and supervisors spend a large share of their time on enablement efforts such as company strategy and process design. Often, this results in poor revenue outcomes where sales reps spend too much time away from their core selling responsibilities. Meanwhile, employees in roles intended to enable sales reps are underutilized, and the revenue acquisition operations remain immature, which further hurts revenue generation.

A CAE ensures that sales representatives and supervisors focus their expertise on identifying and executing sales opportunities while leaving the market assessment, process design, and data analysis to analytical experts who are generally enablement resources.

A similar paradigm plays out in the design and development of offerings where skills to identify customer needs can be confused with those around maintaining an existing offering.

So, a scaling company must begin organization design by delineating between roles that require operations and enablement resources and aligning employees, technology, and other assets into these two divergent skill groups.

Principle 3: Increasingly specialize organization design to focus on expertise.

In addition to delineating between enablement and operations skill groups, another consideration in organization design is defining topical expertise. Even in the early stages of growth, we must define organizational roles carefully and narrowly to focus on the expertise of new employees and the exact nature of their day-to-day work.

People often describe themselves as "I work in tech" or "I am in sustainability" from an industry perspective or say that "I am a marketer" or "I am in operations" in a functional sense. If we are at a party introducing ourselves to strangers, this works. But these are very broad categories, mostly branding or aspirational, and not very practical.

To move from the left side of the addressable market to the right side, where a company's market share continues to grow, its organization design and staffing will have to shift from a generalist mindset to a specialist mindset. Specialization implies that each role in the organization design has narrower and narrower responsibilities as the company grows. In addition, the ability to execute those responsibilities will have to increase as the company acquires and serves more and more customers.

In the principle above, we formalized the two general skill groups. Now, let's formalize **Expertise**.

> **Things to Remember: Expertise**
>
> **Every employee must have specialized experiences and natural inclinations for specific topic areas that form their expertise. Expertise is the most vital attribute that an individual can bring forth single-handedly.**

When we continuously evolve our org design, it is important to articulate the necessary expertise for each role for the corresponding growth phase so that our hiring efforts can match candidates effectively to roles.

Most organizations have a sales operations function, and I have had the fortune to build this critical analytical function multiple times. Sales operations exist to deliver sales and marketing operations resources with appropriate market insights and process enablement.

One common thread across sales operations functions is the use of a CRM, and the most popular are Salesforce, Microsoft Dynamics, and HubSpot. Most sales operations teams have individuals with technical expertise in one particular CRM. But a sales operations function also requires an analytical thinker to make the process, technology, and data valuable and effective. This is very different from having technical CRM expertise.

If an organization can only afford to hire one resource, one optimal path is to hire an analytical problem-solving expert while outsourcing the CRM support needs. Alternately, formalize a CRM administration expert role while an existing analytical expert doubles as the sales operations analytical problem-solver. Trying to mix the two expertise into a single position often fails the effectiveness of both roles and the entire function.

Even in the same role, the expertise necessary shifts with the growth phase. The sales processes required for the first $1M in revenue where a minimal sales close rate is enough to meet the financial goals are not the same as when the organization captures an increasing share of its market. The sales expertise required at different phases is different.

A similar shift in sophistication applies to the design, development, and commercialization of offerings. A common error is conflating 'product management,' which is an expertise in holistic problem-solving focused on customers to create offerings, with 'project management,' where a generalist tactically oversees the activities of others who create individual parts of customer offerings. Unfortunately, companies often move generalists or hire individuals based on poorly defined past job titles into preferably customer-centric 'product management' roles resulting in a downward spiral in the quality of offerings.

It is suboptimal to have the illusion of complete coverage of expertise because the company continues to hire generalists and ask them to do things that they aren't experts at. If we acknowledge that we have an expertise gap, we can prioritize and cover those gaps when we can afford to. But, on the other hand, if we live under the illusion that we have coverage, we will never understand the root causes behind areas of ineffectiveness and address them.

I worked closely with an executive who used to say, "we will just hire some smart people, and they will need to figure it out." It didn't work. The company was caught in a generalist loop where every employee was involved in everything, and every decision was democratic or autocratic. As a result, the value created by the company slid further and further behind customer expectations and competitor strengths, while internal operations stayed immature. This company was in regression in its attempt to scale. We want to avoid this.

Even established companies can struggle if we underestimate expertise. For example, a senior executive at a large investment bank that took significant losses after investing in a defunct secondary investor framed the bank's CEO's approach as "...came in with a mindset that you can appoint anyone clever into a job, and they will be a success even if they had no experience... but that was inappropriate for risk and compliance."

It's inappropriate for any role. So, specialization via expertise is the second fundamental necessity to scale effectively.

Let's connect these two principles to formalize the term **'Skill'** for the rest of our conversation. Skill is the intersection of skill group and expertise. Skill focuses on actual work done in a specific role, not associations with other people's work.

> **Things to Remember: Skill**
>
> **Skill is the intersection point of a resource's Skill Group and Expertise combining the tendencies around time-bound enablement or perpetual operations work and topic-specific experience, knowledge, and execution ability.**

A sales rep role in a specific growth phase will need a seller with expertise to sell with constraints associated with that growth phase and falls squarely in the operations skill group. The skill necessary for this sales rep role is likely different for other growth phases.

A sales operations role in a scaling company will need to be an expert in process design, data structures, and operationalization of technology and falls squarely in the enablement skill group. The skill necessary for this role is not the same as a CRM administrator role.

Roles need to have skill requirements formalized using the skill groups and expertise vectors to micro-evolve our organization design continuously as our company scales.

Principle 4: Build an efficient structure.

Based on the two principles above, every employee should have tangible, measurable, and fulfilling work that aligns with their strengths for which they alone are responsible. In addition, a company should operate under a skill-based approach to avoid an environment with too many chiefs and coordinators. Beyond the CEO and first layer of senior executives, too many roles overseeing others' tasks alone is not scalable at growing companies. But oversight, coaching, and guidance of employees are also necessary. So, what does that look like?

Every company is different and should have a different organizational structure based on its growth phase and its offerings to the market. So, drawing an actual organizational chart isn't meaningful. But an efficient organization also has a simple structure.

For scaling companies, the CEO and the first layer of senior executives of functions such as finance, revenue generation, customer experience, offerings, strategy & operations, and human resources will be general managers. They will own and manage the development of the company's fundamentals covered in various parts of our methodology. Their efforts primarily focus on the management approach, value engine, strategy development, strategic planning, and execution oversight. The CEO is likely spread too thin if too many senior executives report to the CEO.

As a company grows, one supervisory layer for each group of similar operations employees can also be considered an operations resource. Most of that supervisor's work is a predictable set of activities to coach, support, and manage a sizable group of operations employees. This supervisory layer helps operations meet the quantifiable measures for the group.

For example, one sales supervisor who coordinates and supports the selling efforts of several sales reps on a day-to-day basis and shares accountability for the measurable outcomes of that group can be considered a valuable operations resource. In a productive organization with top talent, the ratio can be around seven or eight employees to one supervisor.

Additional operations oversight layers between direct operations supervisors and senior executives can create organizational inefficiency at scaling companies. Although such additional operations oversight layers might become necessary as a company expands the same successful offering across the addressable market, these layers are also a sustainability risk if the skill group and expertise necessary for such roles are not clearly framed.

Like operations resources, enablement resources also require work design, coaching, work allocation, and quality checks. Typically, the work performed by enablement employees is not just time-bound; it is also constantly different. Given this evolving nature of work, supervising enablement resources is more time consuming.

So, the ratio of supervisors to enablement resources is optimally four or five employees to a supervisor. If more than that, the supervisor will likely find it hard to utilize the enablement resources to their highest potential.

The specific share of operations resources and enablement resources is heavily dependent on the type of business and customers. If a company's offering centers around ongoing services, the share of operations resources as a ratio of total employees is likely high. Conversely, if the offering is a low-touch one, the company may have a much larger share of enablement resources.

In summary, an effective organization design that retains top talent to operate productively and creates increasing customer value achieves it by creating a high degree of alignment between the skill of each employee and the work expected of them and limiting unnecessary supervisory layers.

Consider the following questions when evolving an organizational structure:

How can we further delineate between enablement and operations roles?

How can we further specialize roles based on expertise to meet increasing customer needs and sophistication to address scale?

How do we further eliminate inefficiency created by unnecessary supervisory layers and poorly defined roles?

An effective organization design and mapping of skills to roles are necessary to enable the latter portions of our people agenda – hiring employees and managing employee performance and compensation.

The most significant staffing barrier that a scaling organization will face is not finding people to fill roles. Instead, it will be to define specialized skills for a greater number of positions while overcoming the generalist mindset that every small company starts with.

Consider the following question to internalize the difficulty of evolving organization design:

How do we acquire high-quality talent with the necessary skills as our organization matures while we have a base of generalists?

It won't be easy, but possible with discipline.

Our company has to embrace a Comparative Advantage Ecosystem mindset as it scales. If the CEO can engrain this mindset, the company will evolve from a generalist to a market-focused organizational design. The alignment of skills to those specialized roles will become part of ongoing micro-evolutions of operations and offerings and cadence-based strategic planning and execution macro-evolution cycles, which we will discuss in later parts of the methodology. But without a CAE mindset, the company will struggle to evolve the organizational design, and it is unlikely that true experts who can create and deliver customer value will be in the company ranks.

A.4
HIRE FOR SKILLS AND INCENTIVES TO ENABLE ORGANIZATION DESIGN.

REGARDLESS of employment rates in society, hiring someone is easy if you have sufficient resources. Unfortunately, hiring the right people for the right roles is extremely hard. But hiring is also the only path through which a new person can come in and help the company mature further.

Companies often say, "our people are the best." How could anyone know that? There is no way to assess it accurately. There are no guarantees that we will find the so-called best when we have a hiring need. Who even knows what 'the best' even means? Every person can bring something valuable to the table.

Hiring is a privilege that we must not take for granted. It is a duty to do right by all potential candidates and stakeholders. Employment is where we all spend most of our time, and our lives and families are dependent on it. I was discussing how to handle an executive-level mis-hire with a CEO when he said, "We have to treat people with respect… he has to go home and tell the family about what happened and why it happened." Such a frame of mind allows us to act objectively and responsibly. Hiring decisions have far-reaching implications on people's lives.

Conversely, hiring effectiveness is a growth necessity for a company. In addition to execution effectiveness, it dictates employee turnover, which directly affects morale. A principled hiring approach will allow us to perform this duty effectively without being overwhelmed by its weight.

In a mature management approach, we hire to staff our optimal and evolving organization design discussed in the last chapter. Therefore, we aren't just looking for interesting people; we are looking for people in the right skill groups and with appropriate expertise to fill the specialized roles framed via our organization design.

Hiring is an incentive alignment negotiation.

In my experience, you can associate many hiring mistakes with putting blinders on and thinking that hiring is just about recruiting. On the contrary, hiring is the first step in what is supposed to be a long-standing relationship. Relationships with employees continue long after they leave the company.

> **Things to Remember: Hiring**
>
> **Hiring is an incentive-based negotiation between two parties to work together perpetually after that negotiation.**

In our hiring negotiation mindset, six principles will allow us to align incentives between the candidate and company to have the best chance of a fruitful relationship. Infographic A.4 shows the key incentives on both sides and the six principles that will enable us to hire well to scale an organization sustainably.

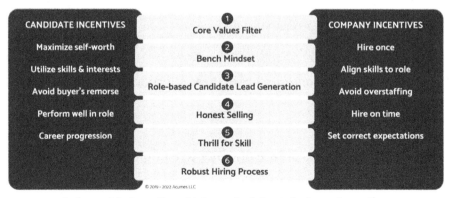

Infographic A.4 – Core hiring principles to balance incentives

Hiring goes wrong when incentives are not aligned, and information gaps exist between candidates and our company. Our goal is to avoid both.

Candidates are looking at employment opportunities to maximize their self-worth. However, each candidate independently defines self-worth, which could be monetary, the chance to do something they love, or fall into a range of other personal choices. Candidates want to join an entity to optimally utilize their skills, feel valuable in their new environment, and continue to grow. The last thing candidates are looking for is to land a job and be dissatisfied or disappoint their employer.

A company's goal is to find an optimal skill fit for our role where the incoming hire will feel that there is an excellent balance between their skills and the company's offer to the employee. There is absolutely no reason that these incentives cannot be aligned.

> **Consider the following questions to assess the hiring effectiveness of your company:**
>
> *Did you or a peer take your role and realize quite early that you were in a situation far from what they promised you or what you had imagined?*
>
> *Have you or a peer hired someone on to the team only to realize that the new employee felt oversold, or the employee skills were lacking, and now you are dealing with the fallout?*
>
> *Have you seen a layoff cycle because the company overstaffed or predictably performed poorly?*
>
> *Do key roles depict a revolving door where new employees fill that role often?*

If you answered 'yes' to one or more of these questions, the hiring approach likely needs to mature.

Principle 1: Core values create an objective alignment filter.

The foundational filter for all hiring is core values. Remember, core values are intended to be the behavioral guardrails for all employees. The CEO, human resources, and the hiring team have to ensure that no new hires feel that they have to fundamentally change themselves to fit the company and will be able to operate within the spirit of the core values. Although candidates can perform their own research and ask questions, it is hard to look beyond the walls of a company and really understand what is going on from the outside. So, it is the hiring team's responsibility to give candidates the clarity they need on core values.

Conversely, we need to operationalize core values effectively to hire highly skilled talent. Poorly defined core values or poor operationalization could lead to core values being used as an excuse by a biased hiring team to filter out strong candidates with a high degree of alignment between their skills and the role. In an immature management approach, core values can be used as propaganda to maintain the status quo of skills and groupthink, which is suboptimal to support growth.

Principle 2: Effective planning and year-round hiring enable a Bench Mindset.

When it comes to hiring, notions like "don't let 'great' get in the way of 'good'" is just a lack of nerve or planning. That mindset is often a drive to hire bodies to fill seats. If we can use all the principles we are covering here, we will hire someone with the necessary skills to perform in the role. There are no great hires; hiring someone overqualified is just a poor hire.

It takes a lot more time to make a quick hire, realize that they are a poor hire, and then spend more time moving that resource out of the organization. After all this, we are back at square one and have to go through the exercise again. Even worse, some companies allow poor hires to stay in the ranks for a significant period for spurious reasons like likability or the hiring manager's unwillingness to admit a mistake. As a result, the hire's skills are underutilized and consume precious investment.

A slightly delayed hire where we must postpone onboarding a new customer or delay a design effort by two weeks or a month is a significantly more mature decision.

The **first** scenario that could cause hiring pressure is growth itself. A revenue executive at a European start-up recently commented, "What's the biggest bottleneck in a hyper-growth tech start-up? Hiring!" This can be mitigated through effective planning.

A **second** scenario where time pressure creeps into hiring is when a company has seasonal staffing needs. But, again, for most companies, an effective corporate strategy, and a strategic plan will alleviate seasonality pressure through preparedness regardless of offering and market.

A **third** scenario is employee turnover. But turnover is predictable. Involuntary turnover, which is a choice by the senior executives and supervisors to terminate employees, implies that the intentional path not to repeat past mistakes is not to hire fast but to hire well. Conversely, if a company has significant voluntary turnover, where employees choose to leave, why would it hire too quickly without addressing the root cause of the problems causing the voluntary turnover?

All these reasons can be mitigated with effective planning and taking the time to hire until all relevant incentives are aligned. I call this a Bench Mindset, where we are in a hiring mode all year round and meeting candidates. Effective strategic planning, which we will discuss later in our methodology, will give us a longer-term view into hiring needs and limit internally propagated time constraints due to poor internal planning and execution.

Hiring with a short-term mindset is a self-perpetuating cycle that keeps the company in an immature management approach and stalling skill levels. An additional two weeks or a month spent upfront to find the right employee is infinitely better than going through the downward spiral associated with poor hires. It is a negative experience for everyone involved. So, always take the time to hire by embracing a Bench Mindset.

Principle 3: Effective role descriptions enable optimal candidate leads.

On the same night that I was drafting this chapter, I caught up with a friend and colleague who has been helping an ex-Unicorn company for several years to get to maturity and sustainable growth. Coincidently, among the many challenges he described, one was hiring the right people.

When early growth started plateauing, the CEO hired a President from a Fortune 50 company to right the ship. The new President then brought a large team of 'rock stars' from his past employer whose skills did not align with the needs of their new company. After a few months of disjointed efforts, that whole group was let go. What went wrong here? My friend described the CEO as a visionary. Unfortunately, so was the new President. The company needed a true operator as a counterbalance to the CEO.

Often, we get internal referrals about a great person someone had worked with elsewhere. Other times, companies feel that a specific expertise is missing and try to close that gap by poaching someone from a similar organization. These rarely work well.

Employee referral programs are very common, and almost every company has one. These are very popular with employees because they can influence the company's trajectory and get paid for referrals. It is also popular with senior executives and human resources because it makes hiring faster and easier and creates employee cohesion. But is cohesion all we are looking for when we hire?

No. Employee referral programs, investor introductions, and other tactics like posting the job description on job boards or using recruiting firms achieve the same outcome. It creates candidate leads, which is critical and hard to achieve if we are a growing company without a household brand name. But it is still the responsibility of senior executives, human resources, supervisors, and the hiring team to convert these leads into hires objectively. It is no different from a sales funnel.

How do we generate optimal candidate leads?

The simple answer is an optimal role description, articulating what the role would do in the most practical sense. It describes the role in a way that makes sense to an external audience. A well-defined role description attracts suitable candidates to apply or show interest and enables the internal hiring process to vet those candidates objectively.

So, hiring should start with a well-framed, detailed role description covering our organizational design principles.

Principle 4: Do not oversell or be oversold.

Buyer's remorse is real. It is a feeling of regret after making a choice, especially if one realizes that they got a poor deal. A senior executive can secretly look for a new candidate with little personal cost to the company. But for a candidate, taking a job is a life-altering decision. A candidate is likely taking the risk of passing on a more fulfilling career path elsewhere or sacrificing a promotion at their previous employer. In addition, a candidate might have made personal sacrifices like relocating.

So, a candidate has many more reasons to feel buyer's remorse than a company. If the company overstates the opportunity, it will likely result in an unhappy employee. The oversell can pertain to the environment the candidate would work in, the work the candidate would do, or the candidate's prospects at the company. Sadly, this often happens because the management approach is immature and doesn't consider hiring a full-cycle relationship.

I worked closely with a company that struggled with employee satisfaction, especially in the junior ranks staffed with many analysts. An analyst is a generic job title that could cover any entry-level job. But to a particular candidate pool, the analyst title implies that they will be using qualitative and quantitative data to solve problems. In this company's history, hiring routinely allowed several candidates who went through data-focused education programs to believe that this analyst role would use data in powerful ways. In reality, the position was more of a data processor who would perform a large amount of manual work to take reams of information from one location and make it available in another without much time or opportunity for problem-solving.

A hire who wants to use the data to solve problems would be highly disheartened if that employee had to spend their entire time doing manual grunt work. A good organization design, role description, and honest hiring approach would have saved the company years of high employee turnover, which rippled into customer dissatisfaction because the hires in the company's analyst roles would probably have never taken the position if they knew what they would really be doing.

Suppose a company has a sub-par offering that is hard to sell. In that case, it is best to attract sales reps who find that risk exciting in exchange for potentially high compensation until our offering improves. If a company has revenue or cash flow challenges, it should be honest with candidates about the criteria about their bonuses or commissions and not hide nuances in the fine print. Honesty always trumps short-term thinking in terms of hiring the right candidates.

Conversely, the hiring team must also remain objective and detail-oriented, not to be oversold by candidates who might know the right words to say or approach to demonstrate through the relatively short hiring interactions.

My recommended interview approach is to put all the cards on the table, including the company's strengths and weaknesses. It is best for both parties when candidates feel that their expectations of the role and company are essentially unchanged between the day they accept the offer and three months later. Many dissatisfied employees I have spoken with attribute their disappointment to the poor expectations set before hiring.

Principle 5: Focus on identifying the depth of skills to improve specialization.

There are many quotes out there about the importance of hiring A-players. A couple of common ones are attributed to Steve Jobs, the founder of Apple, framing the significance of hiring A-players to ensure that the company doesn't end up with a lot of poor talent through a spiral down of hiring quality. I agree with this general sentiment, but the practicality is different.

If someone tells me that all 150,000 employees at Apple are A-players, I will say that they are delusional.

First, the grading of employees is a performance assessment, not a hiring metric. Talking about A-players during hiring is silly. A person becomes an A-player only after they have performed the role for which they are hired, not simply based on their past work experience. How did the A-players at my friend's ex-unicorn fare?

Second, no one can be an A-player at everything. We must evolve past trying to find the best general employee to micro-evolve towards an increasingly specialized outfit. Instead, we want to find the best specialists to fill specific roles.

Consider the World's Strongest Man competition. Several different events with individual scores are accumulated to identify the World's Strongest Man. The winner of the whole contest isn't the best at most individual events, such as the Hercules Hold or Atlas Stone Series. Hiring with a strongest person mindset perpetuates a generalist culture where niche skills are missing over time.

Third, A-players are rare, by definition, and it is hard for scaling companies to attract perceived top performers due to lower affordability and brand than established companies. Therefore, attempting to hire A-players will inevitably lead to hiring lower-performing generalists and cause a downward spiral in both skills and performance levels.

The hiring process should reveal the core skills of candidates and how well their skill level aligns with the role we need. This principle is tough to execute without effective role descriptions and organization design, as discussed in Principle 3. A good hiring team discovers skills that even candidates don't know they have. Often candidates have skills that are unrecognized by past employers and are lying dormant for us to unearth.

Objectively searching for specialist skills with deeper expertise can create discomfort among current employees looking for advancement in a growing company. As the company's affordability and brand increase with growth, the candidate pool will likely be more experienced and skilled than the existing employees and potentially even the hiring team. If we are honest with ourselves, we have all felt threatened by a higher-skilled candidate.

Imagine a math Ph.D. holder interviewing with a bachelor's degree holder for a math teaching position where the two will work closely. The interviewer's lesser math expertise will likely negatively influence their decision, especially if they see the candidate as a competitor. So, we must purposefully choose interviewers not incentivized to keep higher skills out of the company.

The CEO must ensure the company gives hiring responsibilities to individuals who understand the broad range of skills available in the wider world and are secure in their own skin to bring on new employees with higher specialized skills than themselves. But, of course, it is easier said than done, which brings us to our hiring process.

Principle 6: Trust a robust hiring process to avoid biases.

Regardless of any CEO's best intentions, every company will have biased individuals. Sometimes we know who they are; sometimes we don't; some are better than others at disguising biases. Our hiring goal is not to eradicate prejudices because it's unlikely we will succeed. But we have to significantly reduce its influence on the hiring process to improve skill to role alignment with every new hire.

Conversely, candidates invest a lot of themselves into a job search process, and they deserve a fair shake without allowing interviewer biases to influence outcomes heavily.

I worked with a growth phase company trying hard to upgrade talent and improve the alignment of skills to roles. The CEO was onboard that a wholesale change in talent was necessary to improve the company's flagging growth trajectory. A specific change was to objectively document candidate interviews for new hires to ensure that hiring choices weren't biased and subjective. If you have a journal, you know that we tend to be more honest when we write things down.

For our first turnaround hire, I shared a simple spreadsheet with a set of criteria to objectively document interview notes individually with the three other executives I had asked to join the search. Within minutes I got a direct message: "I typically advise that we talk live about candidates. Our attorneys advise against documenting… very risky and discoverable." I know that this CEO had good intentions. But this interaction also revealed the subconscious recognition that this CEO has about what is actually happening at the company.

We want to prevent the most opinionated and influential interviewers from hiring their preferred candidates. We want to avoid a "we will know when we meet the right candidate" mentality because that is entirely subjective and perpetuates groupthink. In a growing company, we want to evolve and improve skills, without which we will stall.

Therefore, define a robust hiring process that includes at least the following considerations.

First, an effective process includes a firm set of steps that every candidate goes through regardless of the candidate lead source. Human resources must ensure that no one circumvents these steps.

Second, define a set of criteria and how those criteria will be measured that qualifies a candidate to move from one step to the next and inform all candidates about the criteria. The more objective and measurable these criteria, the more effective the process and limits subjective decisions along the way. For example, when I hire an enablement employee with problem-solving expertise, one key criterion is the person's understanding of data. For such a hiring sequence, I draft two or three discerning but straightforward questions for the recruiting firm or internal human resources to understand every candidate's expertise with data with a high degree of precision.

Third, invest in steps that allow candidates to show their skills rather than just talk about them. A very young start-up that I used to work with invested in a practical skills interview phase for all candidates regardless of role. For roles that worked closely with customers to extract value from the company's offering, the company expected candidates to learn their offering and demonstrate an ability to create customer value during the hiring process. Interviewers ensured that candidates went through a coding exercise to demonstrate skills for software development roles. Regardless of environment, I include an internally or externally focused problem-solving case for all positions I hire to allow candidates' tangible skills to rise to the top instead of their sales pitch.

Fourth, set definite interview and decision timelines uniformly used for all candidates. Intentional or not, delays can cause an excellent candidate to feel that the company is not interested or take a different offer and take themselves out of contention. Artificial urgency can allow interviewees or internal champions to influence the outcome of a hiring process even if a candidate may not have met the necessary skills criteria. Allow cadence to be a guardrail to prevent biases from influencing outcomes.

Fifth, for each role, leverage an objective hiring panel with interviewers who internalize our Comparative Advantage Ecosystem mindset and the nuances of the skill group and expertise. An interview panel that does not have the experience to discern the skills for the specific role leaves the company vulnerable to hiring for likability, other spurious criteria, or candidates who are good at selling themselves while masking skill gaps.

Lastly, document everything. There is absolutely no reason that any thought or action during a hiring process cannot be documented. However, if there are, it is time to revisit management approach components around leadership and core values.

A comprehensive but straightforward hiring process will allow the company to eliminate biases and mistakes to creep into the hiring decision.

We covered six actionable principles that will allow us to manage a skill-focused, objective, and unbiased hiring approach. We need the right people in our company to help us grow.

Consider the following questions to build an effective hiring approach:

Do we have a year-around and patient Bench Mindset for hiring based on an effective strategic plan?

Do we have a company – and role-specific articulation of the role, including necessary tangible skills, to generate candidate leads?

How do we effectively set honest expectations with candidates about the role and the company?

How effectively are core values baked into candidate assessments?

Does our hiring approach prioritize acquiring increasingly specialized skills for roles as our company grows?

What is the standard hiring process that every candidate will undergo, including assessors, timelines, and objective skill-focused assessment criteria?

We covered four key components of our management approach to build a scalable company system. We focused on the importance of leadership and core values and the necessity of an organizational design and hiring approach that creates an increasingly skilled company. Now, let's talk about how to keep our best employees and encourage the rest to upskill.

A.5
BUILD OBJECTIVE AND TRANSPARENT PERFORMANCE MANAGEMENT.

Now that we've equipped ourselves to hire the best skill fits to staff our optimal organization design, we have to figure out who our best performers are and keep them around. Start by asking yourself these questions:

Have you ever been an employee who felt that your supervisors or senior executives could not understand your true abilities and give you a fair shake? Or, maybe your skills were better than theirs?

Have you been a supervisor or a senior executive who has been part of employee assessments where you felt the conversations were not data-driven, documented, objective, or that your colleagues didn't have the experience to assess highly capable employees?

Have you worked with employees who may not even realize their true potential themselves and work in roles that are well below their abilities?

Have you ever had toxic employees on your team who lingered around because the company failed to act and remove them quickly and decisively?

Have you ever had to let an employee go when you were sure that several other employees were lower performers?

I have seen all these situations multiple times. But unfortunately, in my experience, these suboptimal situations are far more common than genuinely objective people management practices.

A revolving door of top performers in roles that match their skills, or a stagnant pool of poor performers, impedes sustainable growth. As a company scales, a comprehensive performance management approach is a fundamental requirement to ensure that the right employees are in place and motivated. A robust performance management approach will enable the CEO to counteract two human conditions – supervisory weakness and cognitive biases.

Supervisory weakness dilutes performance management.

We talked about hiring skills to fill effectively designed roles, including supervisory roles. In scaling companies, untrained and inexperienced individuals are often thrust into supervisory positions due to short-term needs or their likability. Unlike large and established companies where leadership training starts from the first day and senior executives coach supervisory responsibilities over several years, smaller companies rely heavily on undertrained supervisors.

These supervisors often manage based on subjective factors and are more vulnerable to being influenced by opinions around them. As a result, they create a breakdown between employee value and rewards and recognition because they lack the experience and confidence to stay objective.

I worked with an executive with a strong opinion about his team's contribution and considered some 'too important to lose.' I scratched my head at the reason because I saw no tangible outcomes or deliverables beyond basic expectations from these individuals. Essentially, this executive found a mutually beneficial relationship with his team by giving them organizational recognition and job security while getting their loyalty and support. However, the company was losing because this critical team needed upskilling to support its growth.

In this same company, I managed my team with significantly higher expectations on skill growth and structured, measurable outcomes. I tend not to give empty platitudes to my team members or treat people who report to other executives with less objectivity. Over time, my team's value to the organization was significantly higher than my peer's team as he continued to pursue a brand-based management approach.

Here is the wrinkle – How can our company remain fair to members of my team who are measured using an objective and quantifiable yardstick, while

A.5 BUILD OBJECTIVE AND TRANSPARENT PERFORMANCE MANAGEMENT

my peer who didn't push the individuals on his team as hard get a free pass? The correct answer is developing a comprehensive performance management approach that assesses all employees objectively and consistently.

Cognitive biases significantly impact performance measurements.

There are corporate environments that give too much feedback. There are ones that provide no feedback. Neither is optimal. The key to effectively evaluating ourselves and others is objectivity. As easy as we think it is, it is extremely hard in reality. Biases exist everywhere, including professional assessments.

Imagine working for a boss who is primarily interested in their own career and popularity instead of developing and growing the people who work for them. What if you are a highly skilled employee and your boss feels threatened by you? If you think this has never happened to you, you are being naïve.

Another professional evaluation challenge is story-building. Think of a celebrity. Chances are, we don't personally know this celebrity. But we have firm opinions about their personality, relationships, and professionalism. How is that possible? It's the art of branding or story-building triggered by spurious websites and social media portrayals.

People we work with every day also have opinions about people at work. Some of it has foundations; most of it is subjective and imaginative. A friend's favorite line is "we judge ourselves by our intentions, and we judge others based on their actions and words." Words and actions are contextual and interpretive.

And let's stop pretending – everyone lies at one point or another to meet their selfish ends.

The subjective stories become water-cooler conversations, and the stories grow arms and legs. A colleague who switched from a company with a poor management approach to one with scalable foundations described the difference as "there is a lot less talking behind people's backs here." Subjective storytelling can propel or damage an employee's career.

Workplaces and personal lives are complex. We live among other humans, and they affect how we think about ourselves. In an ideal world, we are all self-aware of our strengths and weaknesses and can rate ourselves accurately on what we do well and don't. But the positive and negative experiences that hit us every day over the years inevitably influence how we think about ourselves.

An overly confident employee can be harmful to the organization. Conversely, an employee who struggles to see their abilities positively and is not elevated to their optimal potential implies a missed opportunity for the company and a personal loss for the employee.

This fifth component of the management approach – effective performance management – is critical because an objective approach to evaluate employees' professional worth is essential to creating a productive workforce with optimal skills. Two behavioral tendencies drive the companies' need for an objective self-assessment and interpersonal assessment approach.

Dunning-Kruger Effect.

Professors David Dunning and Justin Kruger postulated and proved a cognitive bias through their 1999 study *Unskilled and Unaware of It: How Difficulties in Recognizing One's Own Incompetence Lead to Inflated Self-Assessments*. The simple idea behind this bias is that there are individuals who know very little yet believe and show very high confidence in their knowledge and abilities. The authors call this false confidence 'mount stupid.' As an individual's enlightenment increases slightly, that individual realizes how little they actually know and hits a 'valley of despair.' However, if they can continue their enlightenment journey, their confidence eventually increases slowly over a significantly more extended span of self-growth to reach a 'plateau of sustainability.'

In practical scenarios, we observe this as confidence overshadowing competence. This is a concept that we ignore in professional settings but is observable every day.

Consider the following questions to assess everyday interactions at work:

Is it easy to discern the difference between confidence and competence?

Is false confidence corrected or tolerated?

What happens when false confidence dominates over enlightened humility?

This is a cognitive bias, and individuals are often unaware of their own biases. It is also not obvious whether others' behaviors are based on confidence or competence. Such a lack of awareness about where we stand with others might make us question our competence in our professional skills and quality of work. This leads us to be mindful of a second bias.

Imposter Phenomenon.

A second key cognitive bias around skills and self-worth that impact an individual's ability to self-assess professionally is Impostor Phenomenon. This bias is essentially the converse of the 'mount stupid' phase of the Dunning-Kruger effect. This bias makes individuals underestimate their own knowledge and abilities, particularly compared to their imagination of others' knowledge or skills. The operative word is imagination, which means it is perceived and not necessarily real. Irrespective of a person's line of work or past accomplishments, most people are likely to succumb to this bias. In their 2011 publication of *The Impostor Phenomenon* in the International Journal of Behavioral Science, Jaruwan Sakulku and James Alexander show that 70% of individuals will experience this phenomenon in their life.

This phenomenon undermines confidence in ourselves and leads to underperformance or not claiming our deserved rewards. A study of high performers led to the original finding behind this phenomenon. If a company wants to keep its best talent and highest performers, how will it do so if even the highest performers face such a cognitive bias?

Given that the 'mount stupid' phase of the Dunning-Kruger effect and the Imposter Syndrome are opposites, it is likely that most human beings swing to either side of the equilibrium between these two biases. Unfortunately, this also means most employees in a workplace do not have a perfect awareness and measure of their strengths and weaknesses.

So, if an employee lacks perfect self-awareness, how will the organization have it?

Many organizations claim people are their best assets but rarely do enough to address these two cognitive biases around abilities, not to mention all the other potential biases. So, if a company wants to make a valid claim that people are their best assets, the CEO, human resources, and other senior executives have to address these natural biases that exist in everyone through an effective performance management approach.

Do you remember our second growth philosophy, Systems First? Effective performance management enables employees to do their best work in a foundationally objective personnel measurement system.

Over the past decade, many blogs and information sources have been pronouncing the death of the traditional annual review process. Many companies use tools such as Objectives & Key Results (OKRs) or 360 Degree Evaluations. However, they often give up on them after experiencing discomfort around holding employees accountable and blame these tools as too onerous.

After exploring three dozen companies, I believe the effectiveness of a performance management approach has absolutely nothing to do with the choice of tools. Instead, effectiveness comes down to our company's willingness to evolve our organizational skill level, require employees with the most skills to be identified and retained, and encourage others to grow.

Regardless of our organization's nomenclature for its performance management approach, it has to entail a few key principles. I have used the principles illustrated in Infographic A.5 a few times to rebuild the performance management approach from the ground up.

Principle 1: The goals of performance management are objectivity and transparency.

It is always best to start with understanding the company's current maturity. Almost every company invests in human resources staff and can point to spreadsheets, performance-related meetings, and annual compensation changes as proxy evidence for performance management. At the same time, executives and employees consistently admit that their performance management process is a train wreck. My work and research into scaling companies align with similar sentiments. The effectiveness of most

A.5 BUILD OBJECTIVE AND TRANSPARENT PERFORMANCE MANAGEMENT

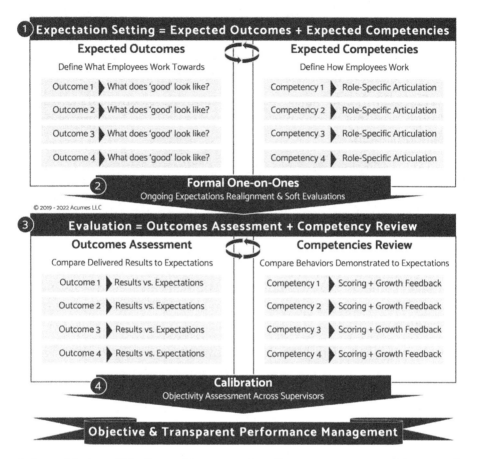

Infographic A.5 – Objective and transparent performance management framework

of these programs is poor and creates extremely political professional environments, which aren't productive or filled with high performers.

For example, I asked the Chief Strategy Officer of a growth phase company about the effectiveness of their performance management approach. He responded, "It's complicated. Yes, we have a process, but it's always an argument. It's essentially a subjective evaluation."

No single measure that we can benchmark externally will tell us the effectiveness of our performance management approach. The effectiveness can only be assessed if we agree on the goal of this component. Performance management is not intended to drive employee happiness; we need it to create clarity for employees and help them upskill to support growth.

> **Things to Remember: Performance Management Goals**
>
> **The first goal of performance management is the objective categorization of high and low performers, and the second is transparency in communication.**

The **first** crucial measure to assess the effectiveness of the performance management approach answers how objectively our organization measures individuals. The first measure is relative. People fall into a wide range of effectiveness for any given skill. If the performance assessments of individuals in the same role are clustered together, it likely shows that the organization has a poor measurement mechanism. Irrespective of the position or company's growth phase, the company must clearly distinguish between high and low performers. Even among high performers, there is a gradient.

Another measure of objectivity is skew. For example, if the overall performance for a specific skill in our company is low, but individuals are collectively assessed as highly skilled in that area of expertise, it reflects a reluctance to be objective or shows a lack of awareness about what 'good' looks like for that expertise.

Transparency is the **second** necessary goal of performance management. I used to work with an executive who handed me the reigns of an underperforming division. Before I took the role, the executive had very strong perspectives on who I should terminate on the team and relayed this to me almost daily. Yet, the company lacked any semblance of a performance management approach.

Even harder was the two-faced approach under which the executive operated. The executive would publicly and personally praise these perceived underperformers while I got private messages about how I needed to get rid of them. My efforts were focused on providing feedback to grow these employees or respectfully move them out of their roles.

But employees aren't clueless; they became paranoid about trusting my feedback and growth path or the executive's praise and "twist the knife in private" approach, as one specific supervisor who reported to me put it. Sure, this supervisor had some growth needs, but other deficiencies pinned on this supervisor were systemic challenges. The conflicting information swirl eliminated the supervisor's trust, and the supervisor influenced employees who reported to them and others. This example illustrates a transparency gap.

Consider the following questions as an internal assessment for employees to understand the level of objectivity and transparency in a company's performance management approach:

Do you agree or disagree with the statement, 'I know where I stand with the company'?

Do you believe you are a top 10% performer in the company?

Do you feel you have clarity and confidence in the process that leads to promotions and internal job changes?

Do you feel anxious about your position in the company when it involuntarily terminates another employee?

If a large percentage of employees answer the **first** question in the affirmative, it implies that the performance management process effectively provides transparency for employees.

The **second** question addresses how well the organization objectively assesses employees' strengths and weaknesses, how transparently that assessment is communicated, and the alignment of that communication with employees' self-assessment. A large share of employees answering this question affirmatively implies that our organization isn't delineating performance effectively or the employee's perspective of their strengths is misaligned with the organization's assessment. This can be a strong predictor of turnover.

A high percentage of affirmative answers to the **third** question implies confidence in the company's performance management process. You could analyze this third question further to see whether there is a significant disparity in responses between different organizational levels. For example, if individual contributors display considerable confidence while supervisors reveal lower confidence, it implies that the organization is masking the ineffectiveness of the performance management process, which will eventually surface.

The **fourth** question reveals how employees think about the performance management approach in an adverse scenario. Involuntary terminations can shake employee morale, and it is important to understand how much confidence employees have in the company's objectivity in such a scenario. For the same group of employees, the percentage of employees who feel anxious should be higher than those who disagree with the first question, where we asked whether each employee knows where they stand with the company. The key insight here is the difference. A significant difference between the two implies that the general confidence in the performance management approach is shallow and not profoundly felt when employees must make big decisions.

Once we have clarity on our level of objectivity and transparency, we can use the following principles to build an effective performance management approach.

Principle 2: Effective expectation setting starts the performance cycle with objectivity and transparency.

Professionally, I started in established and measurement-focused companies like General Electric and Accenture in their heydays, and the word 'outcomes' meant a lot. Outcomes weren't contentious because these companies were stable. However, as I gained more experience and worked in environments that missed overarching outcomes often, I decided it was time to fine-tune my definition of 'objective' performance measurement.

If we decide to yell out loud, "incoming!" and throw a ball towards a friend who instinctively catches or drops the ball, is the result of the attempted catch their doing or ours?

Rewarding a person for catching a well-thrown ball because of the right place and right time or punishing someone for dropping a poorly thrown ball is suboptimal. Instead, we want to reward individuals for outcomes they earn and avoid punishing individuals for systemic challenges.

A.5 BUILD OBJECTIVE AND TRANSPARENT PERFORMANCE MANAGEMENT

Objectivity in performance management implies that we have to go beyond measuring employee outcomes. No employee operates on an island. So, many contributing factors lead to each employee's outcomes, and no one person can control all these contributing factors.

Objective performance management primarily focuses on assessing factors that each employee can control and their contribution to outcomes affected by those factors they control. But before we measure employees, we have to give them clarity on what we expect of them. It takes significant forethought and planning to guide employees to follow a set of behaviors and activities to achieve outcomes.

> **Things to Remember: Performance Management Expectations**
>
> **An effective performance management approach starts by setting clear expectations, and it evaluates employees objectively against those expectations. It does not focus on retroactively dissecting accomplishments or failures, which are outcomes where an employee might only have a peripheral involvement.**

To achieve our transparency goal, we have to communicate effectively. Our messages have to be consistent over time – before employees set off to do their work, while they do their work, and after they finish their work. Transparent performance management implies that we measure employees only on those expectations we have communicated effectively.

Some might argue, "people want freedom in the way they work." That's just spin—anyone who believes that likely never had an actual job and was held accountable by another person. No one wants accountability for another person's unshared standards, whether it's a professional or personal relationship.

Others might say, "we have to be agile because we are a growth phase company." That's code for "I don't know how this will play out" or "details aren't my forte; you figure it out."

Setting expectations for the entire company, a large team, or one employee is challenging, requires hard work, and implies personal risk, which strong leaders must assume. However, managing people is a responsibility, where predicting the future and taking ownership of the prediction is the essence of the job.

History is irrelevant for growth phase companies. We need our fast-growth companies to evolve each cycle to sustain growth; otherwise, our company is resting on past accomplishments.

To set expectations for all our employees, we need a detailed company plan articulating our strategy and operations. We will cover the development of this plan later in our methodology. For now, let's assume that such an effective plan exists in our company. Setting expectations for each performance cycle involves two parts: **Outcomes** and **Competencies**.

Competencies help employees achieve outcomes. Therefore, our company must define and communicate outcomes and competencies with every employee that they can execute, and we can measure.

Principle 3: Outcomes are the first half of performance management expectations.

We touched on the concept of annual strategy and operations cycle to help us macro-evolve our company's maturity iteratively. Employees work within the same cycle, and that is their performance cycle. We set company-level strategic and operations goals during each cycle. Those goals need to be broken down into outcomes that each employee can influence individually or as a small group in the same role during each cycle.

One year, I was in charge of all customers at a mid-sized company. The CEO handed a few outcomes to me, and I pushed back on a few, but not enough. A simple one was to create an automated customer satisfaction measurement mechanism. But I pushed back because the automation portion was far from the company's maturity at that stage. Automating anything means we have stabilized the manual execution of it.

One of my meaningful initiatives for that cycle was to understand our customers manually through conversations to change the course of our offering and commercial approach. Once we understood the customer, we could automate getting customer input during the following cycle with effective questions to give us meaningful data. I stuck to the plan I believed

A.5 BUILD OBJECTIVE AND TRANSPARENT PERFORMANCE MANAGEMENT

in and purposely ignored the outcome, which I got dinged for in my review, and I expected that.

I could have easily created an automated survey with a few simple questions and achieved the CEO's expected outcome. But it also would mean that our company would look at spurious information and make suboptimal decisions. So, this was not a win-win outcome for me as an employee and the company.

The root cause was that the company didn't have a cohesive strategic plan dovetailed into outcomes for each employee. This outcome was also too tactical for someone in my role, where a good outcome would have been developing a growth strategy for existing customers, which I delivered. Unfortunately, such misalignment is very common, leading to employee and company disappointment.

The outcomes portion of setting expectations must feed directly from our company's strategic plan. For example, operations resources may have quantifiable outcomes such as sales pipeline conversion rate or the number of software bugs fixed. Enablement resources who handle time-bound initiatives may have outcomes such as meeting critical project milestones for their initiatives at the desired quality.

Senior executives and supervisors of operations and enablement resources are responsible for translating the company's strategic plan into bite-sized and reasonable efforts assigned to individual contributors as outcomes. Therefore, we must measure the effectiveness of supervisors on their ability to convert company-level goals into employee-level outcomes. If an employee is not clear on the quality or quantity of the desired outcome, it is a supervisory failure.

> **Things to Remember: Performance Management Outcomes**
>
> **Outcomes are the first half of performance management expectations for each employee or employees in the same role. These tangible and non-interpretable qualitative or quantitative measurements directly roll into the company's strategic plan.**

Objectives & Key Results, commonly known as OKRs, is a very popular performance and execution management approach popularized at Intel

Corporation. Google adopted it wholeheartedly. There is now an entire cottage industry around OKRs. There is no shortage of reading material or consulting services around a relatively simple idea. But I have also seen several organizations that have adopted OKRs and committed significant investment but never saw the value. Why? Companies often struggle with defining effective outcomes to set expectations.

If we poorly describe what 'good' looks like for each outcome, the desired outcomes are highly interpretive; it creates a transparency gap and invalidates the entire purpose of defining the outcome. So, outcomes must be tangible and impactful and ladder up to the company's strategic plan.

However, measuring outcomes by itself is meaningless. If our company only measures outcomes, it offers a Get-Out-Of-Jail-Free card to supervisors and senior executives whose primary responsibility is to enable their employees to achieve outcomes. This brings us to the second part of setting expectations – competencies.

Principle 4: Competencies are the second half of performance management expectations.

Think about competencies as desired behaviors that correlate with outcomes.

> **Things to Remember: Performance Management Competencies**
>
> **Competencies are tangible, controllable, and easily learnable behaviors chosen carefully to enable employees to execute their responsibilities and achieve performance management outcomes.**

A football coach shouldn't blame an individual player for not scoring goals or losing a game if factors are outside that individual's control. What if the team has very little ball possession to create scoring opportunities? What if the defensive line doesn't provide the necessary coverage?

There are observable and measurable traits that an individual can possess and work to improve regardless of anything else that happens around them. Therefore, a coach can hold that athlete accountable to only individual competencies and the outcomes correlated with those traits.

Besides translating company-level plans to outcomes for each employee, senior executives and supervisors are also on the hook to define a set of competencies and operational definitions for each competency to enable employees to achieve outcomes.

The first layer of accountability for employees is competencies, as these are traits an employee has complete control of learning and executing. Therefore, achieving outcomes set for them should be possible if employees live by the spirit of the expected competencies. Conversely, suppose employees cannot meet their outcomes after executing on the competencies at the expected level. In that case, it is a supervisory failure to develop the right competencies or a senior executive-level failure to create the environment for the employee to succeed.

Competencies are also only effective if operationalized and tailored for each role. Broad, commonly used traits are ineffective as competencies.

For example, a common behavioral trait relevant for all companies, functions, and seniority levels is 'communication.' However, telling employees that communication is a competency we will measure is not enough.

The type of communication that is important to master is different in a senior operational sales role from a centralized enablement analyst role. For example, senior sales reps need to communicate the value of offerings in the context of the price that customers will pay. We might call this competency 'negotiation.' On the other hand, an analyst will need to be good at sharing complex, data-driven concepts with a diverse audience. We might call this competency 'structured communication.'

Taking it further and comparing different sales roles, a junior sales rep responsible for talking to early-stage prospects will take notes and understand customer asks without trying to close a deal. We might call this communication competency 'active listening.'

The punchline is that we have to define specific competencies for each role, and these will closely align with the skills we define in the organization design. Next, the company has to determine the particular expectations for each position to ensure that it aligns with outcomes set for that role. Expectation setting for performance is complete once outcomes dovetail with the strategic plan and role-specific competencies that enable those outcomes. Once we do this, we can assess employee performance with confidence.

Principle 5: Use formal one-on-ones for interim alignment on expectations and soft evaluations.

Were you ever surprised by an end-of-year performance review? Were you ever backed into a corner to fire an employee and see a bewildered look on their face? No element of a performance management cycle should create a surprise.

Formal expectation setting happens at the start of a performance cycle, and formal evaluations might happen at the end. But there is a lot of time in between, and much will happen in the interim.

Even with an effective strategic plan and expectations setting with employees, we will learn new things during the execution of our strategic plan. Senior executives and supervisors will need to adapt to changes objectively and intentionally. But changing the goal post for employees without logical rationale or too often is a pervasive path to lose employee confidence in supervisors and executives and their ability to plan and manage.

No employee wants to feel like a kite in a hurricane.

Formal one-on-ones are a necessary people management tool throughout the performance cycle. This tool serves two purposes, and we will discuss the second purpose under Part E: Execution Management. Its first application offers a cadence-based, structured communication forum that smoothens the jump from formal expectation setting to a formal evaluation on two ends of the performance cycle.

The choice of the word formal is not accidental. In my experience, every organization that refrained from well-prepared, documented, and consequential one-on-ones failed to mature in its management approach. Subjectivity and lack of transparency prevailed, and these companies saw significant employee turnover, particularly among top performers.

I recommend formalizing a cadence-based, preferably monthly, supervisor-employee one-on-one process at every growing company. The

A.5 BUILD OBJECTIVE AND TRANSPARENT PERFORMANCE MANAGEMENT

process should include simple and effective documentation, preferably standardized to limit adoption challenges, that both the employee and supervisor contribute to and is accessible to the human resources team.

> **Things to Remember: Formal One-on-One**
>
> **Formal one-on-one is a powerful performance management tool that enables both supervisors and employees to continuously align and document their perspectives on actual ongoing performance compared to expectations set. It also creates a formal opportunity for supervisors to coach and support employees to bridge gaps between actual performance levels and outcomes and competencies set as expectations.**

One-on-ones will only be effective if we operate in an evolutionary mindset. If we don't empower supervisors to coach and grow employees, then one-on-ones become a gripe session where most of the conversation focuses on someone else in the company, challenges with the offerings, the sales team selling poor deals, or talking negatively about customers. On the other hand, a formal one-on-one is a tangible and objective discussion about what the two people in the room are doing.

I have experienced situations where giving feedback was impossible due to a poor performance management mindset. A few years ago, a sales operations manager on my team twice missed a deadline that we had agreed to and had communicated to the whole company. My feedback was simple: "Let's agree on a date that is reasonable, but we cannot miss it a third time." The discussion was very contentious because he didn't want to set a deadline and be accountable. He said he wanted to think about it. I let him.

The next day, I got a message from human resources that this employee complained that "John is stressing me out." I spent thirty minutes in a one-sided conversation with the human resources executive. For context, the human resources executive had not built a performance management approach after five years at the company. I listened, shared my perspective on the importance of the deadlines, and left knowing that there were challenges with the company's management approach to hold my team accountable.

A few weeks later, the sales operations manager volunteered, "I know you are right about asking me for a date. But I wanted to see what would happen if I just went around you and complained. I know how this place works, and I was right that they would just make your life difficult."

After a few months of rebuilding this function, I handed over the responsibilities and this sales operations manager to the finance executive. The finance executive fired this employee by 'eliminating his position' within a week, which surprised the employee. It completed a cycle where that employee and similar others felt the company was not objective and transparent because we couldn't set proper expectations, hold them accountable along the way, and share objective performance evaluations before making decisions.

Our performance management principles, including formal one-on-ones, are only practical if our company has effective, operationalized, and adopted core values as a prerequisite.

The CEO, senior executives, and human resources must embrace formal one-on-ones to force a necessary, all-cards-on-the-table, and documented communication between supervisors and employees at least on a monthly cadence. It allows employees and supervisors to improve alignment on the essence of outcomes and competencies throughout the performance cycle and transparently measure ongoing performance to avoid surprises at the end.

Principle 6: Evaluate only against expectations at the end of the performance cycle.

In a mature performance management approach, the employee evaluations portion at the end of the performance cycle will be easy because the difficult parts are already done. If they aren't, something likely went wrong between principles 2 and 5.

The most disheartening evaluation phase I had to manage occurred with a company that already had a performance process on paper. However, all of the principles above were missing. The company never set outcomes or competency expectations. The concept of competencies was foreign to

A.5 BUILD OBJECTIVE AND TRANSPARENT PERFORMANCE MANAGEMENT

the team. Perceived top performers were the most liked and most social individuals. Everyone operated in a generalist mindset where individual expertise was never identified and measured.

I distinctly remember that the only point of feedback that the perceived top-performing team's best performer received during the previous evaluation cycle was "[employee] should take care of self and work less." Yes, self-care is important. But this employee had four years of total work experience, and all of it at small companies with far greater growth opportunities. My company let this high performer's skill growth stall and encouraged the person to leave the company.

Performance management approaches that skip the building blocks above and give employees comfortable evaluations without providing objective and transparent feedback are not doing anyone any favors.

Employees will think they are doing well, but they aren't growing their skills or aren't aware of how strong their peers in the wider world might be. But they are also not clueless. Instead, they will live with a perpetual, subconscious awareness that they don't know where they stand. As a result, the best performers will feel underappreciated and leave.

A supervisor's primary role is to evolve the team's skills and manage their execution to achieve targets set through strategic planning. It is not to get high likability scores from their team. Instead, we should measure our supervisors' ability to set employee expectations, coach them through formal one-on-ones, and objectively evaluate them to grow in future performance cycles.

First, supervisors have to objectively evaluate each employee on specific outcomes set and provide detailed documented feedback on what worked well and what didn't. The key to an objective performance management approach is to be dogmatic and ensure that we measure employees against the spirit of the pre-determined desired outcomes. Employees should never feel that we changed their goalposts in the middle of the game.

Second, an effective performance evaluation will focus less on outcomes and more on competencies. Many aspects of success and failure are not in an individual employee's control, especially at fast-growth companies because there is a higher inherent risk than established companies.

We must evaluate employees on each competency expected of them. Competency assessments should be independent of outcomes and not rationalized to fit the outcomes. Preferably, these competency measurements are quantified, which allows an easy and reliable way to compare employees against each other. In addition, these quantifiable competencies also enable employees to internalize their own relative strengths and weaknesses.

Use competencies to guard against organizational failures affecting an employee's ability to achieve outcomes. For example, suppose we set a sales target for a sales representative for a specific offering. In that case, a delay in the launch or quality of that offering adversely affects the employee's ability to hit their target. So, it is imperative that evaluating competencies isn't a retroactive exercise based solely on outcomes.

A company that wants to hold on to high performers will focus on what each employee can achieve. Competencies are much more reflective of each employee's ability than outcomes. Outcomes often depend on multiple employees. So, it is essential to commit a significant portion of the evaluation process to objectively develop competency scores, articulate practical observations of an employee's ability to demonstrate desired behaviors, and highlight detailed, actionable recommendations to improve those behaviors.

Formal one-on-ones throughout the performance cycle create clarity on how well employees are tracking against expectations. At this stage, a supervisor following a well-laid out and adopted performance process can use the formal one-on-one documentation created through the cycle to draft the evaluation.

No one remembers all the relevant details that happened over an entire performance cycle. Therefore, it is crucial to ensure that recency bias does not influence employee evaluations. An employee can consciously change behaviors in the short-term to get an excellent review, or a negative recent experience can cause a supervisor to hold ill-will. Documented formal one-on-ones protect against such recency bias.

Combining the objective assessment of outcomes and competencies is the formal employee evaluation, which the employee will feel reflects their performance accurately if we incorporate all our principles.

Principle 7: Calibrate employees and evaluations to ensure objectivity and address supervisory bias.

Performance management in a vacuum where employees cannot be compared is practically meaningless. Some supervisors are more demanding graders. Others are much lax in their assessment of employees. So, our last performance management principle is to put all employees on a curve to compare them.

Professional environments are competitive. Attempting to hide performance levels or cluster employees into equally performing groups is equivalent to under rewarding high performers and over rewarding low performers. Eventually, we will lose high performers and encourage mediocre and low performers to maintain the status quo.

A mature performance management environment can successfully execute employee calibrations to objectively compare employees in similar roles to ensure that we are genuinely objective across supervisors. We don't want to reward employees because they work for a strong-willed supervisor or punish employees because they work for a more conciliatory supervisor.

My recommended performance management cycle culminates with a simple and effective calibration step because supervisory biases can impact employees massively. This is especially true in small companies where every cycle is different as it grows. We cannot expect supervisors to get aligned miraculously on what 'good' performance means.

Our CEO and the human resources executive can best own and manage a calibration step performed objectively if the principles above are in place. We can calibrate employees in similar roles in a critical-thinking and debate-filled exercise in a matter of hours. Senior executives must support the exercise through active participation and push to maintain objectivity and engagement. If employee evaluations remain unchanged from the beginning to the end of a calibration session, it was likely a weak discussion where all participants simply agreed with each other.

A critical-thinking calibration step allows us to align on employee evaluations, learn more about all our employees, and further align on skill gaps and challenges across groups of employees. It will enable us to close our performance cycle with our overarching goals of objectivity and transparency.

As we wrap our discussion on performance management with this final principle, we should not underestimate the level of expertise and hard work it takes to build and manage an effective performance management approach with these core principles. Finding an off-the-shelf performance or feedback management technology tool and rolling it out is confusing a technology purchase for a performance management approach.

Alternatively, copying an approach used at successful companies without internally building out the foundational principles is a lazy effort. Therefore, I recommend putting in the groundwork to create a system that allows all employees to perform optimally. Once we build a robust performance management approach, we are in an excellent position to align employee rewards with performance.

A.6
DEPLOY PERFORMANCE-BASED COMPENSATION TO INSTILL MERITOCRACY.

WE tend to expect a reward from everything we do. Spending time with friends and family has emotional rewards. Watching sports or a movie or reading a novel offers us entertainment. Meditation or prayer gives us peace and security. Charity work helps us feel more righteous or a sense of community. We are always making conscious and subconscious choices based on each choice's reward.

So, our discussion about creating a management approach and a system that brings in the right people, keeps the best, and motivates the rest is only complete once we get the rewarding approach right.

Companies and employees make reward-based decisions all the time. Recently, discussions about pay gaps due to gender and race in the public sphere have encouraged companies to look at compensation more closely. But we can't solve biases with counter biases. Instead, we must address the systemic gaps that allow biases. An immature compensation management approach is such a key systemic gap.

Imagine an effective performance management approach with clarity on who the top and poor performers are. What if the company isn't performing as expected, and we give the top performers a meager salary raise or only a small portion of their bonus? What if the bottom performers keep their jobs with only slightly lower monetary rewards?

The most likely outcome is those bottom performers are happy to hold on to their jobs, yet you will have disgruntled high performers after putting forward a strong year. High performers will probably feel slighted when they only receive a small reward for performing very well, often leading to their departure. So now we have a company that didn't do well, and high performers are heading for the exit.

A B2B technology company founder described his company's scaling experience this way, "by the time we reached 120 employees, we had to bring in a compensation consultant to address issues. Top performers did not get a good raise while we spent a lot more money on external recruiters, and then we were surprised when the best people left."

Holding on to high performers is as important for an organization as intellectual property. Top performers' skills are the asset that drives forward momentum; most other assets reflect the organization's past.

Before we discuss the principles to develop an effective compensation management approach, let's explore common pitfalls we must avoid.

Principle 1: Eliminate the common rewarding mistakes.

We have to take out the weeds before the plants can grow. We must avoid some common, costly mistakes before building effective compensation management. Compensation mistakes are easily observable to employees and can quickly harm a company's path to sustainable growth.

Some might argue that we can handle such mistakes as exceptions; not true. Every component under the management approach is about confidence in senior executives and organizational transparency and objectivity. Even a few mistakes undermine confidence in our management approach and, thus, senior executives.

Compensation is a significant grey area in most companies and creates major consternation among employees about their self-worth and career possibilities elsewhere. This opens the door for competitors to poach our employees through simple tactics like offering a small pay raise because employees feel that the devil they know is bad enough to risk another one.

So, let's talk about the common rewarding mistakes.

A.6 DEPLOY PERFORMANCE-BASED COMPENSATION TO INSTILL MERITOCRACY

Eliminate the 'squeaky wheel' fallacy.

"The squeaky wheel gets the grease" might be the #1 negative behavior reinforcement mindset of all time. Objectively, none of us would ever agree that the people who ask most should get the most compensation.

But companies often entertain power-plays directly from employees or their supervisors to secure promotions or raises. This exacerbates the situation when we lack a performance management approach. Encouraging one-off negotiations to determine compensation is suboptimal as it is not meritocratic.

Back-channel decisions often take rewards away from top performers, who tend to stay focused on delivering the expectations set for them. An organization should never want top employees to be distracted by the possibility that they might have to negotiate their way to their deserved rewards.

This mistake creeps in when we ignore our Systems First philosophy. No employee or hire is indispensable, including the CEO. If we feel that pressure, it is likely due to a lack of planning to staff effectively or past compensation mistakes coming back to haunt us. Here is an example of this mistake when I didn't think through the details and acted too quickly.

Shortly after I took over a department, an employee's supervisor informed me she wanted to raise an employee's salary because he was demanding it. So, I signed off on it to appease my new team because the current company approach allowed direct supervisors to make independent decisions. That was the first mistake.

Soon after this, someone else on the same team was gravely disappointed to find out that her base salary was 35% lower than the peer who had just negotiated a higher salary and the same supervisor came to me. The size of the discrepancy appalled me because it seemed unfair, and I allowed a sizeable correction to be made to this employee's salary as well. That was the second mistake.

Did this employee deserve a higher compensation? Maybe. But the timing and the process were all wrong. Days after allowing this change, I discovered significant salary discrepancies between employees in similar roles across the board. Furthermore, none of the compensation figures were based on performance or skill.

The right choice was to absorb the pressure and advise the supervisor to wait until the end of the performance cycle to address these challenges comprehensively. The quick actions I allowed only made the discrepancies worse. The squeaky wheel scenarios indicated a weak management approach that I set off to fix soon after.

Unsubscribe from a welfare-state rewarding mindset.

Often companies deploy 'recognition programs' where a few employees are highlighted as 'Rockstars' or 'Heroes' every month or quarter and given a small monetary gift in front of other employees. Each time, the recipients are different, and over time these programs recognize most employees.

Although the intent of such programs is employee satisfaction, top employees will likely feel duped. In such circumstances, senior executives have good intentions, and their true purpose is to motivate all employees. But such programs are often poorly developed, and their intention is miscommunicated. They do not put top players ahead of mid-tier players. So, I think about them as welfare-state recognitions. Top employees are more likely to find this frustrating and leave the company.

If a company's goal is to celebrate and motivate employees, a better alternative is a monthly team dinner, collective attendance of a sporting event, or similar perks that cannot be mistaken for performance recognitions. It is a personal insult to high performers if we frame morale-boosters as performance-related.

Avoid history-based compensation.

We get what we pay for. I never want to know what a potential hire made in their previous job or other competing offers. I trust the employee to make the best choice for their own future.

Recruiters often ask, "what is your current and desired salary?" This is a poor way to assess what an employee is worth. A company should

A.6 DEPLOY PERFORMANCE-BASED COMPENSATION TO INSTILL MERITOCRACY

have a value determination for every role, which we will cover in Principle 4. We should compensate our hires based on that value.

Assuming that the company finds a skilled employee, weighing historic compensation heavily or giving the employee what they asked leads to two possibilities. One is that an overpaid employee is filling the role because of their past high compensation. Alternatively, the company fills the position with an underpaid employee who will eventually realize their worth and leave the company.

One key responsibility of the human resources executive is to quantify employee worth. This has to go beyond just outsourcing this task or depending heavily on compensation data purchased from third parties. Our company should focus on skill-based roles and not job titles. Most references to positions outside the walls of our company are always job titles, which we called 'candy wrappers' earlier. Compensation setting must focus on the value created by specific skills, strengths, and weaknesses. Benchmarking compensation levels from job titles provide guardrails but is not the answer to what a role is worth.

In their job postings, a US-based, mid-sized technology company always includes the bullet "Competitive pay based on the work you do here and not your previous salary" in their job postings. This is the frame of mind we all need to embrace.

Do not reward employees based on tenure.

As a scaling company, we can keep government-like thinking to the side and pay for skills and performance.

Different people have different interests, and many of those interests could be outside the company walls. In addition, employees have various career goals and levels of commitment to grow professionally. So, organizations should never feel that salary increases should align with tenure. Yet, organizations resort to tenure-based rewards in the absence of a strong performance and compensation management approach. This is a shortcut to ensuring that mid – and low-tier talent stays with the organization while disappointed top-tier performers depart, seeking rewards for performance elsewhere.

So, as a first principle, we must be wary of making these common rewarding mistakes. Once we embrace a meritocratic mindset by avoiding these mistakes, we are ready to build an effective approach.

Principle 2: Compensation management must be transparent and objective.

As we build a compensation management approach, it is essential to internalize that it has the same goals as performance management – objectivity and transparency. In addition, we must cap the management approach with a reward system that mirrors our evaluations and calibrated performance management results.

First, employees should be able to correlate their performance management results to their compensation. Although performance results and compensation decisions are confidential, the organization must maintain transparency about this direct relationship to ensure that all employees are confident that they are not missing out on rewards.

Second, a compensation management approach that supports evolutionary growth disproportionately rewards high performers, encourages mid-level performers to perform at a higher level, and nudges low performers to either change radically or consider alternate employment options. Disproportionately rewarding top performers motivates mid-tier performers to improve. Overtly punishing only obvious poor performers is easy and not enough. The key is to encourage mid-tier employees to push for the top. Compensation is not just a primary rewarding instrument; it is also a quantitative mechanism to signal to under-performers about their standing.

Third, ensuring that all employees are clear on the details of their compensation packages enables transparency. Whether it's understanding how sales quotas are used in commission calculations or knowing the exact details of bonus decision criteria, employees must be able to calculate their achievable compensation themselves and should never be surprised about their final compensation.

A.6 DEPLOY PERFORMANCE-BASED COMPENSATION TO INSTILL MERITOCRACY

As simple as this sounds, the most common gap I have heard from employees during interviews across many companies is, "I don't understand how my bonus and commission number is decided!" It is even more critical in scaling companies where compensation plans radically change often to accommodate new market lessons or changes in operations. Similarly, employees need to understand their role-specific pay bands and the performance levels that will allow them to earn more.

Compensation tends to be a sensitive topic. It rarely gets discussed unless it is in a negative light, such as pay gaps. It doesn't have to be.

Netflix is a unique example that implemented a transparent compensation approach in 2017. As a result, all directors and executives know the compensation of all other employees. The company pays top employees well above market rates and provides a path for lower performers to leave. Embracing transparency solves many compensation-related pitfalls.

Fourth, develop a proactive approach and set a cadence that matches the performance management cycle. We need employees to focus on their initiatives and processes during the year. It is much easier for employees to focus on their work when we have a specific cadence for compensation discussions and changes. Lack of a formal cadence leaves employees in a mental state where they constantly think about their compensation and motivates ad hoc back-channel discussions.

A partial view links compensation to monetary schemes like salaries, incentives like bonuses and commissions, and longer-term financial rewards like stock options. However, we must think more comprehensively to scale sustainably, especially if our affordability is not high.

I broadly classify rewards into three groups. The first is rewards that offer personal satisfaction, the second is professional satisfaction, and the third is monetary satisfaction. We must use each one differently to keep high performers and motivate others through our management approach.

Principle 3: Rewards that offer personal satisfaction must be equitable for all employees.

Employees value personal satisfaction, and for every hour that we take away from personal lives, they expect compensation in some form for a fair, professional relationship. So, the first reward type is personal. It focuses on creating an equal and fair playing field for all employees.

An equal playing field is also not an overcompensating one. Companies experiment with various employee perks to attract candidates and keep employees happy. Topics that qualify for personal rewards have become even more important as more employees work from home or anywhere in the world.

However, it is not a company's place to make a value judgment between types of personal satisfaction rewards based on employees' unique needs. For example, one employee might value picking up children from school at 4 pm. Another might want to go for a run before the sun sets at 4 pm, while another might want to volunteer every week at 4 pm. And yet another might want to watch a baseball game at 4 pm.

Everyone gets happiness from different things. A company's role is not to frame which is more acceptable than another. For example, setting personal rewards can be about setting core work hours where every employee is officially in a workday between 10 am and 4 pm and the rest of the work completed at personally convenient hours of the day. Our company must avoid the tendency to judge the importance of family or health or public service or entertainment.

Another example of a personal reward is vacation days. Historically, companies offered vacation days based on roles and tenure. However, scaling companies have attempted to move to an 'unlimited vacation' policy in recent years. This incentive eliminates the need to accrue vacation day pay as a financial liability should the company decide to terminate the employee. Of course, there are good intentions behind it as well. But it is worth considering whether the vacation policy skews personal rewards.

Do certain employees take a lot more time off than others? How do we ensure that employees have an equal playing field on vacation days across roles where some roles work longer days than others, especially when personal work ethic might be different?

Consider the following questions to test the effectiveness of personal rewards:

Has the company implemented all-employee rewards designed to create more value for some employees than others?

Regardless of intention, does the company have personal rewards programs that some employees draw on significantly more than others?

Not too long ago, I offered a candidate a position. The monetary compensation was based on the candidate's skills, the role I had designed, and the peer group we already have on staff.

A couple of days later, the candidate shared that the cost of the company's healthcare policy for her entire family would be significantly higher than the healthcare perks her current employer offered. The candidate asked for 20% more in base salary to compensate for the difference in healthcare coverage because of her family's specific needs. As much as I wanted to hire the candidate, I decided I could not make that accommodation because it was unfair to her peer group. I empathized with this candidate's healthcare coverage needs. Still, I would have created an unequal playing field if I had accommodated one individual's personal needs while the peer group would not receive comparable rewards.

A company's role is not to accommodate personal rewards based on our perception of its relevance. Instead, we have to create a level playing field on personal rewards from which employees can leverage reasonably similar value.

Principle 4: Professional rewards offer a short-term incentive for high-performing employees.

If you remember the Gallup poll that we referenced in Chapter A.3, only 41% of job-seeking responders considered "it significantly increases my income" as a motivation compared to 60% of responders who believed "it allows me to do what I do best" to be a more important basis.

Non-monetary rewards motivate most high-performing employees for a reasonable period. However, we should never overlook the importance of such rewards to ensure that high-performing employees stay on the payroll. Top employees are often motivated by an opportunity to have an impact, the possibility of future income through new skills, and exposure to new challenges that help the employee grow with no association to other rewards.

There are several practical manifestations of non-monetary professional rewards. For example, we might give top performers organizational visibility through greater responsibility and accountability that align with their skills. These could include opportunities to work on important projects or invitations to critical meetings where they can observe and learn.

We could create an opportunity for a high performer to learn tangible and relevant new skills through lateral moves. If the employee has no prior experience, but the company grooms them with an apprenticeship mindset, such a move would increase their future success.

A high form of non-monetary reward can support high performers to graduate to the next stage of their careers. This could be higher education or roles at larger companies where the employee can take the next step that a scaling company cannot offer. Such a sacrifice will help attract highly skilled performers to join the company and perform strongly for a relevant period. Top consulting firms, investment banks, and law firms embrace this mindset. Experience at these firms is a mentorship steppingstone for employees to take on challenges or rewards that these professional services firms eventually cannot provide.

However, professional rewards have an expiry date for every employee. An employee's value from such a reward expires after climbing their learning curve. So, it is critical to think about professional rewards as interim and prepare for a longer-term path for the employee, and this often means a new formal role. That new role moves the employee from the tangible compensation in the current position into a new one with higher monetary compensation benefits, which we will discuss in principle 5.

However, we must sidestep two common mistakes around such role changes.

First, new roles do not imply just moving high performers into supervisory positions because they are vastly different. Companies need employees with specialized skills to excel and deliver value in their roles. For example, companies often make the mistake of elevating excellent individual contributors into supervisory roles in sales teams. A top seller adds incredible value through revenue acquisition. However, putting that same employee in a supervisory position might be a double whammy. We might end up with a poor supervisor and lose our top seller.

Second, title inflation, which implies assigning flashier job titles without corresponding changes in underlying skills and responsibilities, does not qualify as a professional reward. On the contrary, it is a lazy rewarding approach guaranteed to derail organization design, performance management, and compensation management maturity. Short-sightedness is the only rational explanation for title inflation.

I have never seen title inflation create a sustainable growth system in the three dozen companies I have worked with. Adding prefixes like 'senior' while the employee continues to perform the same role only creates an illusion of career progression, especially if we did not formally define the new role with a new set of tangible skill requirements, responsibilities, and rewards.

> *Consider the following questions to assess the effective use of professional rewards:*
>
> *Does the company leverage non-monetary professional incentives such as apprenticeship and skills acquisition to motivate top performers?*
>
> *Does the company avoid artificial professional rewards through confounding promotions and title inflation?*

Professional rewards are not the answer for all employees and roles, especially beyond a few months. Often the solution is to keep compensation simple and monetarily reward employees. So, let's talk about money.

Principle 5: Rewards that offer monetary satisfaction must be exponentially greater for high performers.

The third and most obvious type of reward is monetary. The equation for this third type of reward should be entirely quantifiable and based on the value attributed to a specific role and the performance and skills of the employee in that role.

There is no reason for monetary compensation design to be creative. It's just math. We must have a formal compensation model that every employee should know and be kept within for any role. A compensation model can accommodate both the coverage of skills and the performance demonstrated for each position.

The question, "how much should we pay for this role?" is incomplete. That question only takes into consideration the moment we extend the offer. What happens in a year? What happens when we have a few people in the same role? What happens when an employee has been in the position for a few years? Infographic A.6 illustrates my framework to design compensation for each role. There are four elements to a simple and effective monetary compensation model.

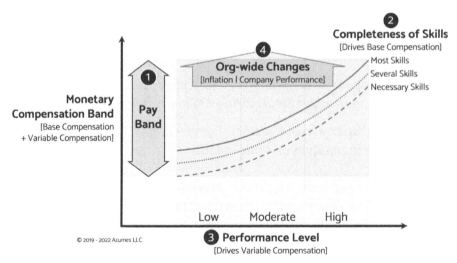

Infographic A.6 – Role-specific compensation design framework

The **first** element of a monetary compensation model is to set logical lower and upper limits for total compensation for each role. It is the pay band for the role. Besides our organizational design's skill definitions, the compensation curve offers a guardrail for the role definition. By defining the pay band, we can quantify each role. We must set intentional compensation boundaries for employees in each role to avoid the 'squeaky wheel' mistake or personal biases creeping into compensation decisions.

To start the design process, consider at least two or three performance cycles for every employee in the role. Will we have the room below the upper limit to reward a highly-skilled, top performer for multiple performance cycles? But, on the other hand, is the lower limit too low, where it might create an opportunity for inherent biases?

If you remember the mistake I contributed to in the 'squeaky wheel' story, the root cause was the lack of a pay band. The company was already paying both employees, who escalated their pay demands, above the lower limit of the pay band when I got around to creating it. The reactionary base salary change should have never happened. We should have based their compensation adjustments on an objective performance evaluation.

The **second** element of a compensation model is skills coverage. Skills coverage must dictate the fixed base salary.

When we talked about organizational design, hiring, and performance management, we covered the importance of hiring for specialized skills. The reality of hiring and performance management is that we are unlikely to find and hold on to employees with expertise in every area that we would like the role to have. Employees in the same role will have varying skill levels. A layman's proxy for this vector is the number of years of experience. However, this association is spurious, and I always look for tangible skills.

For example, if our organization has several Product Managers, it is unlikely that more than one has full coverage on all areas of the necessary expertise. There are likely many candidates who can satisfy some of the skills and very few who might meet most of them. Suppose we intentionally hire an employee with expertise in tactical management of the building of the offering, but not the customer-facing aspects. In that case, our performance evaluation for this employee should not punish them for their skill gaps.

Their fixed salary must also reflect this lower skills coverage. So, that employee can be a high performer among the lower skills coverage group.

In practice, we may augment the employee's role with some external consulting help on the customer-facing aspects. We could think about the consulting expense as a hidden compensation cost. If another employee in the same role can cover the full breadth of skills, we wouldn't need this consulting.

So, an ideal compensation model would bucket areas of expertise together and create two or three skills coverage curves to ensure we offer higher base compensation to the employees who offer higher skills coverage. The infographic visualizes how this might look.

The **third** element is performance-based, non-linear variable compensation. Higher performance levels are increasingly harder to achieve as we improve, and we should disproportionately reward improvements at higher levels.

In a competitive environment, the benefits from a top performer's same level of improvement are significantly greater than the same improvement from a mediocre or low performer.

Imagine a scenario in which our sales reps sell our company's wares in a competitive setting holding all other factors equal. In such a head-to-head setting, a mediocre sales rep improving by 20% is not likely to change the outcome as much as a top performer improving by 20%.

During a recent discussion with sales reps at a mid-sized company that struggled with employee motivation, their top sales rep rightfully took issue with their linear model. The company placed sales reps into five performance tiers, Tier 5 being the lowest performers and Tier 1 being the best performers. The company put the bottom 5% of reps into Tier 5, the next 20% into Tier 4, the middle 50% into Tier 3, the next 20% into Tier 2, and the top 5% into Tier 1. So far in the conversation, I supported the design. But the company limited the impact of all that excellent work by setting up a linear variable compensation model. They offered Tier 5 reps 80% of their expected variable compensation; Tier 4 90%; Tier 3 100%; Tier 2 110%, and Tier 1 120%.

A.6 DEPLOY PERFORMANCE-BASED COMPENSATION TO INSTILL MERITOCRACY

It takes much more work for an employee to move from Tier 2 to Tier 1 than from Tier 5 to Tier 4. In this case, an employee's reward for improving any level would be the same. Essentially, the company is motivating lower performance.

Suppose the extra compensation of moving from Tier 2 to Tier 1 was important to an employee. It is likely easier for the employee to stay at Tier 2 and take on a part-time job that pays them a guaranteed additional wage than put in exponentially more work towards the small, uncertain extra incentive.

So, always develop a non-linear monetary compensation model that rewards high performers significantly more. We want to motivate lower performers to strive to move up the compensation curve, not the other way around. Although compensation models are easiest to explain using operations roles such as sales reps, the same principle applies across all positions.

Mathematically, combining the second and third elements of the compensation model – the distinct skill-focused base compensation curves and the performance-focused non-linear variable compensation potential – must result in the guardrails we set through the first element of the model, which is our pay band.

The **fourth** element of the model is easy. Simplify compensation changes because of externalities like inflation or the opportunity to increase salaries across the role or company by shifting the entire pay band upwards. Do not address these changes at an employee level because it creates another opportunity to allow personal biases to creep in. Always accommodate externalities by shifting the pay band and delineating this fourth element from compensation adjustments centered around performance and skill levels.

You might think – isn't it easier to just negotiate employee by employee? No. Because if we spend one or two thoughtful days building and aligning on a compensation curve once for key roles, we won't have to waste hours going through stressful negotiations for each employee we hire or spend our time dealing with employee compensation issues months and years down the line.

Even for a role with one employee, which is valid for senior executive roles or cross-functional roles, the compensation cost and the expected impact are usually very high. Therefore, it is worth taking a few hours to develop the rewarding approach before spending several weeks hiring that impactful single resource.

Consider the following questions as you design monetary compensation:

Does every role have a compensation model that dictates total compensation for that role?

Does each compensation model have an upper and lower limit that sets the role's pay band?

Does each compensation model offer tiered curves to delineate varying levels of employee skills for each role?

Does each compensation curve reward top performers exponentially more than moderate and lower performers?

Are company-wide compensation adjustments made for the entire role-specific compensation model as opposed to individual employees?

I promise you, if we don't start with a compensation model and have the discipline to stick to it, we will create distrust among employees that will be hard to revert.

Principle 6: Implement a formal compensation management process.

As we design and manage compensation models, it is important to remember that every model can get distorted and needs a formal review cadence. Once we get past the first few employees, we can set an annual compensation review cadence that aligns with the performance management cycle.

Often compensation structures are tinkered with or radically changed reactively, especially when a company faces growth challenges. The inputs for these reactive modifications are usually one or two distortions that senior executives observed in the recent past. Therefore, it is best to

A.6 DEPLOY PERFORMANCE-BASED COMPENSATION TO INSTILL MERITOCRACY

review the compensation models for roles and personal benefits across all employees proactively leading up to the end of each performance cycle.

It is also important to be mindful of how we handle significant changes in our organization. For example, if our company is on a sustainable growth path, we will evolve our organizational design or processes through initiatives during the year. As these changes occur, we might be tempted to adjust compensation on the fly. Don't! It's a slippery slope that will lead us to misalignment between compensation, organizational design, and performance.

All activity throughout our performance cycle must focus on compensation administration, not design. Of course, having a design is critical. But it is crucial to adhere to its intent.

First, we must identify a Compensation Czar whose responsibilities go beyond payroll execution. One individual must be accountable to ensure that our compensation design principles are practically implemented and used. Our Compensation Czar may belong in a human resource or finance function and have other responsibilities. Regardless of functional alignment, a critical thinker must be in the role.

Second, the Compensation Czar must manage a simple and effective set of controls that ensures that every new hire fits the compensation model for the designated role. A similar set of controls must ensure that compensation adjustments align with performance evaluations. Aberrations must be escalated and addressed in short order.

Third, the Compensation Czar must work closely with senior executives and owners of major initiatives that drive changes in our organizational design and associated compensation models. As we approach each new performance cycle, this role must understand and aggregate changes necessary to our compensation approach across all three rewarding types.

In summary, rewarding starts with avoiding the common rewarding mistakes. Then, develop compensation plans that ensure that personal rewards create a level playing field. Professional rewards are an interim path for high performers. All monetary rewards must be formally designed using a compensation model that disproportionately rewards high-skilled, high performers. Lastly, limit compensation design and changes to align with the performance cycle while directing all our energy to administer our compensation principles throughout the performance cycle.

Effective compensation management is a powerful and necessary tool for senior executives to create an objective and transparent environment that encourages top employees to stay with the company and motivates the remaining employees to push the envelope on their performance to earn more.

We have now covered the six components of our management approach. We need to evolve these components continuously to maintain a mature system where we can acquire the right employees and enable them to do their best work. As we leave this first part of our methodology, remember the dart analogy that we started with. The management approach is the foundational dartboard that can absorb a perfect throw with a perfect dart. Everything else we will discuss in the remaining portions of the methodology is predicated on a mature and self-evolving management approach, without which we will likely spill our best efforts on the floor.

PART B

Value Engine Synergistically Creates Customer Value.

Under Part A: Management Approach, we explored the company's people agenda. Essentially, we answered the question – *how do we manage our people?* The maturity level of those fundamental components helps the CEO and senior executives bring together the most optimally skilled employees into well-defined roles, retain the best, ensure that the rest strive to improve while operating in a value system that aligns with our external stakeholders. We have the team.

Now, what does the team actually do?

We serve customers.

We are now transitioning from our approach to systemically managing our people to the reasons we are in business in the first place. So, the second half of our operations baseline, which comprises the intrinsically valuable parts of our business, is the **Value Engine**. It is a term that I created for the methodology.

What do we mean by serving customers? Simplistically, we are only in business to do two things. One is to create and improve an offering that generates value for our customers. The other is to devise ways to deliver that value to an increasing volume of customers profitably—nothing more, nothing less.

We must sharpen our focus and ensure that everything we do contributes to these two aspects with as little waste as possible. It is easy to get carried away with shiny objects like popular conferences and snazzy tools that promise to solve all our problems.

As a thought experiment, let's put five ultra-successful executives like Elon Musk, Bill Gates, Bernard Arnault, Mary Barra, and Warren Buffet in five separate rooms and give them five portions of a significant business problem to solve. What is the probability that they will propose five solutions that will fit together to solve the overarching problem?

My experience tells me that it is very close to zero.

We could take this further and replace them with relatively ordinary executives, who have less experience, and don't understand their biases very well.

Do you think it will be harder to agree on the best course of action? Indeed. What if the set of five were individual contributors in different roles with different incentives?

Diversity in problem-solving, choice of solutions, and risk propensity will apply to any group of employees operating independently, irrespective of their performance level or skill. But we won't have a company if every person chooses what they feel is the right course. Operating as a company is a team sport.

So, we must choreograph the efforts of all employees to act as a team, where everyone sings from the same hymn book. It is the essence of the value engine. Our value engine injects a system mindset into how we serve our customers. As a growing company, it formalizes a cohesive offering that creates value for our customers. It articulates how we work with each other to deliver that value. A mature value engine is a prerequisite to scale beyond a few employees and customers.

> **Things to Remember: Value Engine**
>
> Value engine comprises the components that create value for our customers. It includes our offerings to the market and all day-to-day operations to deliver that value.

We can only create value by having something that the customer doesn't have, doing something they can't or won't do, or knowing something they don't. The only way to achieve this is through scale. Whether our offering is an object, an action, knowledge, or a promise, we can only offer it because we are very good at it. To be better, we must do it many times. So, we must codify how we create value for our customers. This is called **Productization**, which is the first component of our value engine. Think about this part of our value engine as the answer to the question – *what do we offer our customers?*

Once we decide, design, and build our offering, we still have to deliver it to the customer on an ongoing basis. Almost every offering in the world will have portions that require constant action to create customer value. Above that, our sellers focused on acquiring new customers must take the same day-to-day steps that work for the company's chosen market. All employees who serve customer needs must be available and solve problems consistently based on expectations set. Marketers who attend conferences will establish the same expectations to prospects; engineers or designers who build the company's offerings will follow the agreed-upon method to work together.

The internalization that all such operations follow a collective way and not every employee's way is critical to developing a solid system that enables scalability and sustainable customer value creation. I call this operational system **The Company Way Processes**, the second component of our value engine. This component answers the question – *how do we deliver value to customers?*

The value engine also includes our problem-solving approach to evolve our offering. We must base our path to evolution on objective information and sound analytical principles. If problem-solving discussions are analogous to looking outside a window and using present weather conditions as evidence for or against climate change, our system to create and deliver customer value is not sound. It is only a matter of time before enough poor choices result in a catastrophic mistake.

Our wherewithal to gather objective information and use optimal problem-solving and issue resolution methods forms the third component of the value engine, **Data Usage**. This component answers the question – *how do we improve?*

These three components intertwine to form the value engine, which allows us to deliver optimal customer value, drive all employees to execute effectively and continue to improve execution over time. Additionally, these three components rest on the foundations laid via our management approach because none of this works if the right employees are not in the right roles. Infographic B.1 shows the dovetailed relationship between the management approach and value engine components to form our operations baseline.

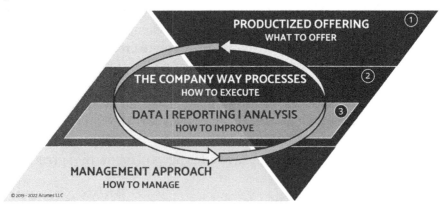

Infographic B.1 – Value engine builds on management approach to create value

Regardless of our market, our offering will likely involve ongoing actions by operations resources to deliver value, which dovetails our offering with The Company Way processes. Similarly, processes include all hiring, performance management, and compensation management activities, which dovetails with our management approach. Our data gathering effectiveness has to envelope all the other components of the operations baseline. They influence each other, and we will see the interplay throughout the rest of our methodology.

Why is a systemic value engine important?

The concepts under value engine have become layman's language. From a business perspective, this is a complication and not a benefit. We all tend to use specific words in general contexts, and over time, we lose the real intent behind important words.

When we want to search for something on the internet, we might phrase it as 'Google it,' or when we take a taxi, we might say 'take an uber,' and in these instances, we might not even use Google's search engine or Uber. Both concepts are only a little over a decade old.

How much more misused are the words I used in the three value engine components we introduced above, given that they have been part of business terminology for a long time?

So, are we getting better with these components? Data suggests otherwise.

The U.S. Bureau of Labor Statistics (BLS) publishes labor productivity quarterly and annually. BLS defines labor productivity as "a measure of economic performance that compares the amount of goods and services produced (output) with the number of hours worked to produce those goods and services (input)."

Infographic B.2 compares the annual increase in labor productivity in the United States since 1948 through various economic cycles. Each cycle in the figure starts with a downturn and includes the following recovery and economic expansion. Each economic cycle is different, which is why the length of each differs.

In an economy, labor productivity has to increase to produce more output with a given set of inputs. Therefore, the most illuminating observation in this chart is the difference in average annual labor productivity increases during various cycles.

The post-2007 economic cycle has the lowest annual average productivity increase of only 1.4%, compared to all other economic cycles except the odd double-dip recession in 1980-81. So, with all the awareness about offerings, processes, tools to automate processes, and access to exponentially more data than ever before in history, how is it possible that labor productivity growth is at an all-time low?

THE SPIRAL STAIRWAY™ – THE SYSTEM TO BUILD A HOLISTIC COMPANY

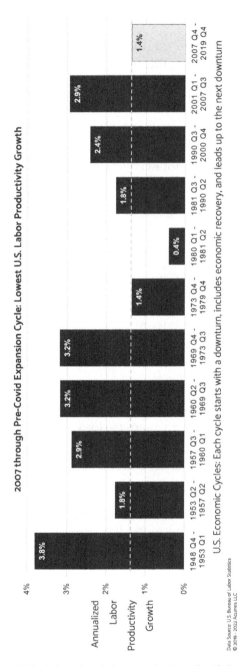

Infographic B.2 – What does low labor market productivity growth imply?

The reason is that when money is cheap, we tend to use it a lot less efficiently.

Labor productivity in a company has to increase over time to keep up with an evolving market, where competitors are likely to become more productive. In other words, a company has to create improving outcomes with a given set of inputs.

Companies have been discounting the importance of many of the foundational components that drove productivity advancements made during the late twentieth century. Over the last decade, growing companies have been relatively narrow-minded in their focus on creativity and agility while considering efficiency and discipline as the enemy of creativity.

This means hiring more people or spending more on assets to achieve slightly better outcomes rather than improving existing investments in people, technology, or other assets. As a result, it creates a lack of profitability among many companies.

We have increasingly focused more on deal-making to inflate value instead of intrinsically creating more value. Even established companies have focused mainly on finding low productivity, high-cost paths to growth. An abundance of financing implies that companies can throw more money at achieving growth in the short term via acquisitions rather than organically solving relevant problems that stand in the way of growth.

But happy hour deals don't last forever. Sooner than later, we will have to start paying the regular menu price as a collective and as individual companies.

Infographic B.3 shows my model of the productivity shift of a company's value engine. The value engine encompasses our path to revenue and our cost of achieving that revenue. The bottom left of the chart is the budding phase of our company with little revenue, cost, and almost no paying customers. As we move to the top right, we are growing and capturing more of the addressable market. The Y-Axis represents our increasing revenue which correlates with the value we create for customers. The X-Axis represents the cost of serving those customers.

Simplistically, companies can take one of two growth paths.

The first is the lower, unsustainable path where we are trying to grow at all costs. We are willing to accept that our cost of delivering value to each customer increases as we acquire more customers. We know it's not a sustainable growth path because our growth will stall eventually, and we will likely get there without a profit. So, going down this path is perplexing. But many try because it is tempting to boost extrinsic value and cash-out by handing off an unsustainable entity to someone else. The further down this unsustainable path we go, the harder it is to restore the fundamentals necessary to scale.

The preferable second path is the top one, where we are seeking increasing productivity from our ongoing cost of doing business. That is, we continue to do more with what we have. A mature value engine and its core principles will help us stay on this path. However, staying on this path is hard. There will always be a continuous downward internal and external pressure to lose discipline and take the lower suboptimal approach, which is easier in the short term but won't take us where we want to go.

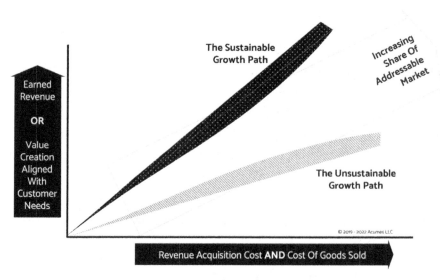

Infographic B.3 – Optimizing value engine enables sustainable growth curve

A self-assessment about our value engine and actions to improve foundational maturity is critical because it is easy to mistake a company's present maturity level. Mistaking a weakness as a strength is a path to self-destruction.

The maturity of a company's value engine has the same power. A mature foundation can help a company arrive at winning decisions and flawless execution. Conversely, a poor and misunderstood one can be analogous to trying to win a math challenge with a broken calculator.

So, what does a mature value engine look like?

Value Engine Maturity Model.

We are striving for two success factors across our value engine components.

The **first** success factor is **Repeatability**. Repeatability means each entity takes the same execution path every iteration for a given action or behavior. So, whether it's an employee, a customer, a partner, or even a tool, repeatability implies that the entity executes, in the same way, every single time or at least close to it.

The **second** success factor is **Reproducibility**. Reproducibility means that all entities collectively adopt the same behavior for every iteration for a given action or behavior. In other words, everyone does the same activity the same way.

Reproducibility is a super-set that includes repeatability.

These two success factors of repeatability and reproducibility span all components of our value engine. Building both into our value engine is our only path to sustainable scaling.

The most important takeaway from our maturity model is that all components are interdependent. They build on each other and are largely meaningless without the effectiveness of the other components.

Think about our value engine as a missile. The payload is our offering to our customers. The rocket that carries the payload is our processes. Finally, the guidance system that navigates our missile to its destination is our objective capture of data and its effective usage to micro-evolve and macro-evolve our operations baseline. Without any one of these components, our missile is inert.

Infographic B.4 shows our Value Engine Maturity Model. As a first step, I recommend that you take a moment to read through each level of the maturity model and self-assess where the company you work with sits.

As you consider these five levels, think about who might be responsible for improving the current maturity. The responsibility of driving towards high maturity levels must sit with a strong strategy & operations executive. The CEO must empower this senior executive to ensure that the company operates at a high value engine maturity level.

On the left end of the maturity model, we are operating at *Level 1: Chaos*. Here, the company primarily focuses on its own existence without internalizing that customer value creation is the only reason to exist. It also depends on individual employee brilliance to win the day across various operations. Most companies start at this end. But staying here implies that scale is prohibitive without overspending.

Many organizations make minor attempts at building maturity around the value engine components and operate at *Level 2: Ambiguous*. However, repeatability and reproducibility are not internalized as necessary success factors. So, there is a limited positive impact on scale benefits for customers or internal operations. Some misunderstand minor improvements to mean high maturity levels and remain at Level 2, which essentially stifles the organization's sustainable scalability.

I worked with a growth phase technology company where a senior executive and the supervisory layer wanted strong processes. However, their interpretation allowed each of the thirty operations employees to devise their own path to achieve the expected outcomes. This team thought that they were being "process centric." However, this is the antithesis of creating and executing The Company Way. Misunderstanding their maturity level led this team to miss targets after repeated attempts to achieve expected outcomes without repeatability or reproducibility.

We must at least evolve to *Level 3: Organized* before the customers and internal operations begin to see scale benefits. We achieve this first value stage when at least some employees have adopted effective processes designed for them and consistently repeat the same desired behaviors. However, the company is submissive to all customers and places the onus of designing the offering on them, which is not scalable beyond early

VALUE ENGINE SYNERGISTICALLY CREATES CUSTOMER VALUE

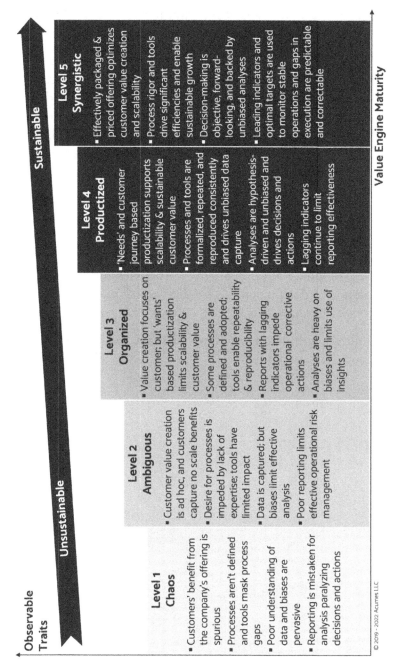

Infographic B.4 – Value Engine Maturity Model

growth. The capture and use of information is poor and largely stifles decision-making and execution effectiveness due to low return on time invested in data.

As a company moves further to the right to *Level 4: Productized*, the company has matured to develop scalable offerings by understanding the root cause of customer needs. Groups of employees in the same role execute consistently and collectively to The Company Way. Additionally, analytical roles spearhead effective decision-making and micro-evolution of the offering and processes through objective data use.

The sustainably scalable and optimally value-creating desired state is *Level 5: Synergistic*. The company's offering effectively solves the root cause of customer problems and is commercially scalable through effective pricing and packaging. The company uses objective analysis to generate insights to improve well-adopted The Company Way processes and tools continuously. The Company Way design enables predictive risk management and issue resolution using data.

Over the following three chapters, we will explore each component that drives a strong value engine.

B.1
ENABLE SUSTAINABLE VALUE CREATION VIA PRODUCTIZATION.

Every component in our methodology is important, but nothing is more important than the purpose of existence that we introduced under the leadership component. Companies can serve any combination of stakeholders, including founders, employees, investors, vendors, customers, partners, and society.

Consider the following question:

Why does our company exist?

Any data collected will be biased because it will be hard for most people to be objective about the answer.

Some companies claim an investor-first mindset. This was the traditional path for decades. Recently, there has been an employee-first wave, and many companies have jumped on this bandwagon. But, of course, there are employee-owned companies, which is a logical overlap. No choices are incorrect. But not a single company in the world is successful because it operates solely as an investor-first or an employee-first company.

Rational investors will not put a cent in our company if they don't believe our customers aren't willing to pay for our offerings. Likewise, we won't have a cent to pay our employees if our customers aren't willing to pay for our offerings.

So, who is our most important stakeholder? The customer.

Ensure our motivations align on a customer-first mindset.

Sustainably successful companies place customers first. This isn't new or revolutionary. Every methodology I explored over the years focuses on creating value for customers.

Recently, we have had many more companies funded by investors when customers aren't buying enough or paying enough. We have also increasingly given company shares to employees in exchange for lower cash compensation. But none of these changes the real end game that we will only be sustainably successful if we can generate value for customers willing to pay for what we are offering. If customers don't pay for the party, the party ends sooner or later.

Why is this important?

If we serve our customers exceptionally well, we have all the revenue and growth necessary to make our investors and employees happy and prosperous, and partners will be easy to find. But, on the other hand, if we focus on making our investors and employees extremely happy and place a lower priority on our customer needs, our party will likely end after we drink the champagne that we paid for with borrowed money.

Internal stakeholders such as founders, employees, and large investors always know a lot more about the inner workings of our company, the quality of our offerings, and motivations than our external stakeholders. These internal stakeholders are on our team. If we cannot be honest with our team, then we have serious management approach maturity challenges.

When I started working with a founder who had just replaced his co-founder as CEO, he told me, "I am going to change our company mindset from customer-first to employee-first because our employees are not happy."

As I worked to diagnose their challenges, it became apparent that the company lacked a consistent, core customer offering. Employees were unhappy when a new deal was sold because they were left to somehow provide what the sales team promised the customer. In the past, the company desired to be customer-first but hadn't matured its offering for customers. Employee unhappiness was a symptom of a lack of maturity in serving customer needs.

This is our Hippocratic Oath moment. Our growth methodology places the customer at the nucleus of all our efforts. If we serve our customers well, it will serve our internal stakeholders by default.

The CEO, the board, and senior executives must look in the mirror and ask hard questions about whether the company is truly interested in serving customers. If our priority is internal stakeholders, this is not sustainable because it's only a matter of time before current or new competitors prioritize our market space and take our customers away.

To create value for our customers, we must have something worth paying for. So, what does that look like?

'Product' is a lazy generalization of several complex value creation concepts.

If you search for a definition of the word 'product,' you will be disappointed either by its specificity like "it's a goods or service" or it's a nebulous catch-all to include anything we might create for customers.

This is an important dilemma in today's corporate environment. My first job was as a 'Product Owner' of an electronic motor that went into heating and cooling applications at General Electric. Then, over several years in consulting, I experienced many different definitions of 'product' across industries and companies. In the past few years, I have seen an even more diverse set of interpretations of this all-important word in the world of growth-phase companies. It is a nebulous word that never seems to get defined before usage.

Employees and senior executives move from one industry to another. Most employees are playing musical chairs between companies. So, how do we work together effectively and serve our customers well if all we have is a nebulous 7-letter word that no one appears to have a firm articulation of?

Can you name Google's, Meta's, Amazon's 'products'? I bet a consumer's list would be different from the list we would get from the company. So, rather than spin our wheels by restricting ourselves with this one overused word, let's focus on adding value to customers.

We will not use 'product' as a noun in our methodology because of its overuse and spurious interpretation of its meaning. Instead, we will continue to use the plain English word **Offering** as our catch-all word to describe our company's value-creating payload for our customers. So, let's keep our customer-first hat on and define two concepts – 1) flow thinking and 2) multi-directional nature of value – that underpin customer value creation principles.

Flow thinking optimizes our understanding and measurement of value.

Creating and delivering value implies that we understand how we make a difference in the recipient's life. Flow thinking allows us to internalize the life of our value receiving stakeholders effectively.

Flow thinking is the concept of visualizing everything as a process, which everything really is. We will expand its usage from just tactical processes to how we think about the market we play in and our customers' activities, in addition to our own internal operations. It is not a novel concept, but it is vastly underutilized.

> **Things to Remember: Flow Thinking**
>
> **Flow thinking implies that we view the entire world as a connected series of physical or mental actions, which includes a review, analysis, decision, communication, etc. A human or a machine may perform those actions.**

Often mistakes are made when we view a situation as a series of blocks that are not interconnected.

Let's think about the market ecosystem of the last mile delivery of consumer packages. A critical block of value is the front-door package hand-off. It sounds good, and everyone who has ever received a package at home understands what this means. But does this really clarify how much value is created? I argue not. The reason is that the front-door package hand-off is not a well-defined block by itself. The dovetailed flow of the entire last-mile delivery ecosystem determines the specific value created by the front-door package hand-off portion. How does the package recipient know when to be at the front door? How long will the deliverer wait? How many times will they return? All these ancillary actions to front-door package hand-off dictate the effectiveness of that specific value creation intent.

According to Newton's third law of motion, actions have an equal and opposite reaction. Although this isn't a physics class, the same mindset applies to how we create value. For any given situation, if we represent all the actions in our ecosystem or all the actions of our customers as a flow with no loss of information, then we are also capturing the flow of value effectively. Otherwise, we operate with spurious interpretations and expectations based on commonly misused words.

Customer value is multi-directional.

As much as we hope to deliver value to customers, we can also end up causing regret through our offering. How many times in our lives have we felt duped or felt frustrated after we bought something?

The flow of value is not single-directional. Value can flow to a customer through our offering. But value can also flow out of a customer if the customer has to make sacrifices to use our offering. Think about these value outflows as friction for the customer. The higher the friction caused by our offering, the lower the overall value gleaned by the customer. We must consider this value outflow as we design and build our offering. If we are honest with ourselves, are we creating net positive value for the customer? Or is our offering costing the customer substantial undesirable adjustments that leave their net value close to zero or negative? Our customer value creation principles must create significant net positive value, which is all the customers must pay for. Let's keep this definition in mind throughout our discussion.

> **Things to Remember: Net Customer Value**
>
> **Net Customer Value [EQUALS] Value inflow from our offering [MINUS] Value outflow due to our offering.**

Now that we have aligned on the importance of flow thinking and creating positive net customer value, how do we drive a customer-first mindset to support sustainable growth?

Principle 1: Productization is the only path to sustainable growth.

Wait! Product what? We said we are not using the word as a noun, and we aren't. **Productization** is a verb and a framework.

Customers buy from us at a fair market price because we can create value that they can't or don't want to create on their own regardless of the offering. But, as a growing company, we can only create increasing customer value to existing customers and deliver that value to an increasing number of new customers if we design our offerings with repeatability and reproducibility in mind.

> **Things to Remember: Productization**
>
> **The act of creating a repeatable and reproducible offering is called productization.**

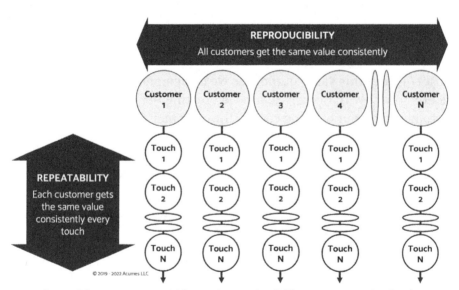

Infographic B.5 – Repeatability and reproducibility enable productization

In the context of creating value for customers, repeatability implies that we are able to deliver the same value to any given customer consistently. Thus, whether our offering is a widget, services, advice, or any other perceivable creation, the customer must predictably get the same value each time they buy or use it.

Additionally, we can only sustainably grow if we can consistently deploy our creation to many customers. This is reproducibility. Otherwise, we have no economies of scale, and we will take the unsustainable productivity path that we covered in the value engine introduction. Therefore, our fundamental goal of customer value creation is to productize because it generates the most value for customers and allows us to do so profitably.

Suppose we are offering our customers a simple widget. In that case, repeatability and reproducibility imply that we can source the core ingredients and build the widget at a large enough volume consistently that it is a lot cheaper. It is also less time-consuming for our customers than creating it themselves.

Repeatability and reproducibility don't imply making the same simple widget for every customer. For example, we could be a custom mechanic who refurbishes vintage cars. Our productization here focuses on our experience, flexibility, and ingenuity. Our repeatability comes from our ability to demonstrate this expertise for each vehicle that a customer might bring in. Our reproducibility comes from being able to show that breadth for a range of customers with similar needs. In this situation, price is likely not a relevant concern for a customer.

If we are offering our customer a service, the only reason a customer would choose us is if we can do it cheaper or at a better quality. This means we either have many people doing the same service that we can gain economies of scale, or we have gained experience by doing it many times and can deliver higher quality or bring knowledge the customer doesn't have.

Even if we own a Michelin star restaurant or a hole-in-the-wall family outlet, customers come to us due to scale. The reputation of a Michelin restaurant comes from the chef's and the team's expertise channeled into customer value. The family outlet might be valuable because of deep experience with a cultural cuisine or access to tried-and-true family recipes.

The infographic above summarizes this mindset of embracing repeatability and reproducibility to design our offerings regardless of our market. The crudest way to frame the importance of productization is that we cannot use customers as perpetual subjects for us to practice on. Beyond the first few customers, we must be good at what we're offering and continue to mature over time.

In my experience, most of the growth challenges that lead to existential crises or eventual valuation discounting come from an acceptance that the company failed at effective productization. Selling something to a few customers at a discount or a high delivery cost is acceptable at the start. But to reach sustainable growth, repeatability and reproducibility are table stakes.

Each evolution cycle must include major initiatives triggered by strategic planning to improve the productization and maturity of our offerings. Enablement resources will execute these initiatives to create and enhance our productized offerings. We will dive into this macro-evolution cycle further in the Corporate Strategy, Strategic Planning, and Execution Management parts of our methodology.

Principle 2: Why us? Align company strengths with market problem.

I am 5'10" and slim. There was never any amount of fitness training, food consumption, or mindset shift that was ever going to help me be a heavyweight boxing contender. We all have limitations. Introspection and humility will always serve us well. At the very least, it will save us an investment misallocation.

Some successful growth stories were based on right-place and right-time. There are also some stories where people buy success. But from the get-go, we agreed that our goal here is to build a path to sustainable growth that ordinary people can strive for and has a reasonable probability of success. That implies that there must be a tangible reason why we would be successful at productizing an offering.

I have seen the inner workings of plenty of motivated businesses that began with a "we want to be successful, and we will create a company!"

It is an admirable entrepreneurial spirit. But, unfortunately, this isn't usually enough.

For instance, I have worked closely with companies that tried very hard to develop technology solutions; but the know-how that got them early revenue was through resource augmentation. Without a fundamental rebuild of the entire company, including the management approach components, productizing what the resources did at each customer's desire and then baking that into a single technology doesn't come naturally to a service-minded group.

Suppose our founding and operating spirit is "we have experienced a market problem, and our experience is unique enough that we are likely to be best placed to create value for our customers!" In that case, we have a customer-focused path to sustainable growth. Obviously, anyone can say this. But only some can say this with objectivity and honesty.

Let's formally define the term **Market Problem** in our context:

> **Things to Remember: Market Problem**
>
> **Market problem is a three-legged stool that frames the situation that customers could draw value from. The three legs are 1) Non-core Activities, which encompass all customer efforts that do not have to be 100% owned and performed by the customer, 2) Voiced Pain Points, which are value-diminishing challenges that the customer is aware of, and 3) Unvoiced Imbalances, which articulate undiscovered gaps due to unfair systemic elements that the customer lives with. Thus, market problem and value are two sides of the same coin. By extension, customers are willing to pay for the market problem to be solved comprehensively.**

We will explore how to analyze our market and define the market problem in the next part of our methodology. But, for now, let's think about the market problem as the collective essence of the customer need.

At a company level, can we look at ourselves in the mirror and honestly internalize that we have something that no one else in the market has? Where does this belief come from? What are our proof points? So, it's good to ask – *why us?*

The most successful growth story I have been part of was a three-person founding team that worked in the consulting world, and they witnessed a client problem in the risk management space. They went on to build a solution for that client in a consulting project. Their company founding path codified this project that they had already successfully done once before. That's enough. They understood their customers. In my experience, this is far more unique than most companies make it sound.

Investors call this a Founder-Market Fit when they fund companies. But anytime there is a formalized term for anything, society starts overusing it. Now, every aspiring founder has a Founder-Market Fit story. So, I won't perpetuate the overuse.

The essence behind this principle is not the story itself. It is the company's understanding of its market. It can be learned and doesn't have to be natural happenstance. So, our principle here is not about coming up with a story about how one person in a company knows a lot about the market because of their experience. Instead, we will focus on understanding the market in a manner that distinguishes it from anyone else who can solve the problem.

Regardless of the company's founding path, gaining a deep understanding of the market must go beyond natural happenstance experience. The Founder-Market Fit concept only serves us to get the first few customers. The growth phase requires that we genuinely dive into the depths of how the market functions.

Incrementally, we must have the strengths to solve the market problem. Just a desire or will isn't enough. Compared to other competitors, why would we win? We will dedicate two chapters to answer our 'why us?' question under Part C: Corporate Strategy. To build and evolve our offering to solve the market problem, we must know the market better than others and hold the relevant strengths to solve the problem.

Since most high-growth companies get stereotyped as technology companies, let's use that as our example. If our technology company is trying to build an operations software, coding or technology infrastructure expertise is not the differentiating strength we need. That is table stakes because any technology sector player can code. Our market understanding and design strengths around operational effectiveness and processes must be exceptional. When building a data-centric technology solution, we need to have that internal horsepower on how data is gathered and leveraged. No amount of coding or technology infrastructure expertise will cover gaps in our understanding or strengths around data-related value creation.

Consider the following questions:

Do we have a tangible connection with the customer to empathize and understand the root cause of the market problem?

Do we have a differentiated set of core strengths to create a repeatable and reproducible solution to the root cause of the market problem?

Internalizing that we must be able to answer 'yes' to these two questions helps us confidently tackle Principle 3.

Principle 3: Focus on customer needs, not wants.

Most companies and individuals are afraid or unwilling to put in the hard work or personal risk to take a customer to a place they never imagined. But there is no reward without hard work or risk. Asking a consumer or a customer what they want and giving them exactly what they asked for is easy but not the appropriate interpretation of customer-first.

Customers are focused on their pain and not on effectively resolving their pain. Instead, customers think about getting back to core actions and decisions they consider are in their control.

I call such customer expressed symptoms and sentiments 'wants.' Addressing wants is easy. It doesn't take any problem-solving skill or ability to replicate what a customer says is painful at any cost or throw up our hands and say that it costs too much to achieve it. It can even be an excuse to say that the customer is unreasonable. Productization does not focus on addressing wants because it doesn't lead to reproducibility.

Every single problem-solving methodology highlights the importance of root cause identification and resolution tied to that root cause. 5-Whys is a root cause identification tool that drives us to ask 'why' five times to drill deeper into a symptom to address the essence of the problem. A Fishbone diagram is a tool that drives us to comprehensively assess the entire landscape and underlying contributors that result in a symptom. All such tools hint at the same message – focus on the root cause.

I call the root causes of customer wants 'needs.' A significant element of our customer value creation through productization includes our problem-solving skills, investment, and risk propensity in identifying and creating a solution that addresses the underlying need.

> **Things to Remember: Needs vs. Wants**
>
> **Customers know and share how they feel, which are their 'wants.' Our problem-solving skills must translate those wants and constraints in the market to underlying root causes, which are customer 'needs.'**

Our source of information to address problems in our market is current or potential customers. However, we must ask the right questions in the right circumstances to capture useful information to be transformed into tangible customer needs that we can solve. While gathering market intelligence, our questions and surveys must be framed to capture customer sentiments, while understanding that such answers are not the solutions. Our conversations with customers must always allow them to share their pain and feelings through open-ended questions.

Once we have objective and unbiased information about sentiments in the market, we can translate those to underlying customer needs. Then, we must productize to meet those needs, which by extension solves customer wants.

Once we embrace these three overarching principles around customer value creation, we are ready to dive into the four procedural principles to create value.

Principle 4: Customer-first implies operating within the customer journey.

Let's assume that our answers to the summary questions around 'why us?' are affirmative. We could brainstorm in a vacuum and develop great ideas that might help customers in a market we understand and try to convince customers to buy. But how would that be a customer-first mindset? It's an us-first mindset. Creating a sellable solution is only effective if it addresses a very specific and well-defined problem.

Remember, productization for customers is the act of developing a repeatable and reproducible solution to address a real-world problem.

Regardless of our market space, customers are either individuals or groups of individuals. Our offering might intend to impact their personal or professional lives. Nevertheless, every person follows a natural flow that is also a path of least resistance.

What did we do if we wanted to take a taxi at the turn of the 21st century? We walked to the corner, looked around, and when we saw a taxi with 'for hire' lights on, we raised our hands. So, what do today's rideshare platforms do?

They replicated this human flow and solved some challenges we faced as consumers. For example, these platforms placed all nearby cars on our cell phone screen. We may not have wanted to wait outside and raise our hand to get one. They replaced a hand-raising with a button push that we could accomplish without waiting outside. Even if we hailed a taxi, someone else might have jumped in front of us and snagged our cab. The platforms eliminated the possibility that someone else could commandeer our taxi. Rideshare platforms replicated our old human behaviors, systematized the steps we would take, and removed some of our hurdles.

The same principle applies if we are developing solutions for any market problem.

We are always serving a customer that operates in their own natural flow. Therefore, the act of productization is not about dreaming up a magical answer. Instead, designing our offering must internalize and optimize the natural path our customers are used to taking or create a more lucrative new path that replaces the old one. Therefore, putting a customer-first hat on implies that we are drawing a process flow for their behavioral journey, which is called a **Customer Journey**.

> **Things to Remember: Customer Journey**
>
> **The customer journey is the natural path of least resistance that any customer would take if we were not in the picture. A customer journey is a process flow with steps and hand-offs between those steps.**

The concept of customer journey is commonly accepted. However, the challenge is its practical application. Our natural flow is obvious and consistent in a familiar business-to-consumer problem-solving setting because we follow basic societal norms.

However, most companies solve niche consumer challenges or challenges other companies face. We personalize our behaviors for most consumer challenges. For example, each individual's exercise habits are more unique than hailing a taxi.

Similarly, every company is unique because of its people, history, maturity, and the market problem it is solving. Therefore, serving companies implies serving behaviors that are somewhat unique even for the same market problem.

This tendency to personalize our behaviors creates two challenges and complicates the practical application of the customer journey mindset. The **first** is that customer tendency to personalize behaviors makes solving the problem for all customers in our market space challenging. The **second** challenge is that personalizing makes commonalities between customer behaviors difficult to observe. So, how do we productize our offering to serve customers in our space if behaviors are not exactly the same?

Unless we are trying to solve a non-existent market problem, some customers will behave more similarly than other customers. In other words, there are always clusters of customers with similar enough behaviors. Let's call these clusters, **Customer Groups**. We will dive into customer groups in more detail when we define corporate strategy.

> **Things to Remember: Customer Groups**
>
> **A customer group is a cluster of current or potential customers who demonstrate very similar behaviors within the context of the market problem we are focused on.**

Clusters of customer behaviors also imply a customer journey that we can paint for each cluster. We may have to study the customer behaviors in-depth to connect the dots to paint the customer journey. We must analyze customer behaviors qualitatively to remove the noise of individualism and tease out these clusters and the common ground within each cluster. But this is precisely the problem-solving mindset that we embraced in Principle 3.

Such analysis is the answer to both our challenges to the practical application of the customer journey. Of course, we cannot serve all customers, and we cannot practically allow every customer to follow their perfect natural flow. But we can serve many customers and replicate their natural flow closely.

If we can choose the right customer group, we can tease out a customer journey that reflects the common behaviors within that customer group. I call this specific, optimal journey a **Use Case**. Therefore, an effective choice of a single use case is our primary success factor of the customer journey principle.

> **Things to Remember: Use Case**
>
> **A use case is an end-to-end process flow that reflects the common behaviors of an optimal customer group that we want to serve.**

Many companies I have interacted with struggle with the customer journey principle because of a lack of discipline to choose an optimal customer group and the skill to tease out an effective use case.

Peloton, an in-home exercise solution provider, originally built and marketed their offering for an affluent family member who doesn't have time to get to the gym and wants to exercise at home. The customer journey they focused on revolved around a person at home who was also a fitness enthusiast. It is an effective use case. The company addressed the market problem – how does one solve the needs of a motivated exerciser who lacks the time, flexibility, or interest in going to a gym? It worked.

Conversely, my exercise journey always revolved around a brick-and-mortar gym's social setting and habits. I enjoyed getting to the gym first thing in the morning on my way to work and seeing other people. I didn't mind the extra time lost because it was a social experience for me. As such, I did not fit the Peloton use case.

However, Covid-19 lockdowns changed almost everyone's exercise journey, including mine, and forced us all to try to exercise at home. It took me three stubborn months of being stuck at home to consider what a long-term home-based exercise journey might look like. I started using Peloton when my journey had converged with their original use case. I became an avid fan of Peloton classes and did 100% of my workouts at home. I was part of a large customer group that embraced Peloton because our exercise journey changed.

However, as the world reopened, how likely was my customer group to maintain our new exercise journey instead of reverting back to exercising in social settings? Peloton's productization decisions to scale imply a bet that the second customer group would continue to behave like the company's original loyal customer group. This single choice proved fateful for Peloton as data in early 2022 revealed that the second customer group's journey was shifting back to past behaviors of visiting gyms in person.

This story underlines the power of understanding customer groups and their respective journeys. A firm handle on our preferred customer groups' journey allows us to optimally create value within that use case.

Consider the following questions:

Do we have a firm understanding of the various customer groups in our market?

Do we internalize the common behaviors of customers within the customer groups?

Are we disciplined to choose one or two of these customer groups without being tempted to serve all of them?

Have we teased out the end-to-end workflow of our top customer group or two and framed that journey as our optimal use case?

These questions summarize the considerations we want to achieve through this principle.

Principle 5: Create value via comprehensive capabilities.

In our customer-first mindset, we have internalized the importance of creating a repeatable and reproducible offering in a space where we have the unique strengths to serve. We must corner a use case that can serve our optimal customers. But how do we create an offering that has net positive value?

One of the ways I kick off productization discussions is by using a planned city analogy. Some cities in the world are planned. Others aren't. Depending on the natural constraints and goals, planned cities have guidelines that dictate the city's evolution. Drone views of such cities make it obvious that there is a design and a longer-term vision behind it.

Then there are unplanned cities. An aerial view of such cities gives us little comfort that there was any method behind the madness. Such landscapes are often built for the short-term goal of creating a big mall, a skyscraper, or several large highways. The outcome is a traffic-heavy, pedestrian-unfriendly, and public transportation lacking landscape. Essentially, the freedom to build has created an unwieldy patchwork.

Designing offerings for our customers can take either a planned or unplanned city mindset. The former results in an offering that solves the root cause of customer needs and can be organically evolved to support our scale and limit customers' value outflow. The latter is a patchwork of short-term symptom-solving efforts that eventually becomes unscalable and leaves customers with higher value outflows.

From Principle 4, we strive to serve a specific customer journey, which is our use case. The shaded middle pathway in Infographic B.6 illustrates the use case for our customer group. Regardless of the market and the use case we focus on, the customer journey can always be represented as a process flow. Steps 1 through 4 in this journey connected with the hand-offs is the path that the customer flows through without us. An effective customer journey flow will frame each step and hand-off such that steps and hand-offs have tangible outcomes that the customer is generating. In aggregate, it adds up to the entire experience.

Now let's superimpose two rules of thumb to create optimal value.

THE SPIRAL STAIRWAY™ – THE SYSTEM TO BUILD A HOLISTIC COMPANY

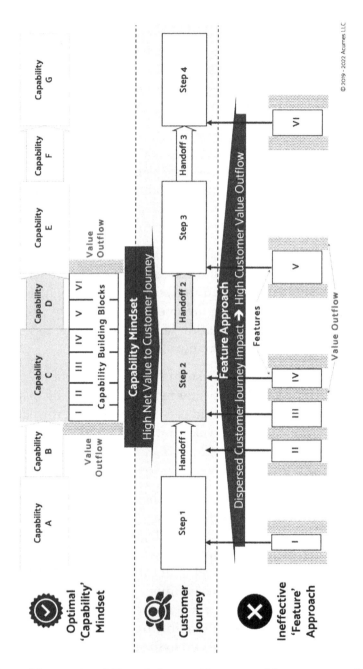

Infographic B.6 – Capability mindset enables net positive customer value

The **first** rule of thumb of optimal value creation is not to try and address the entire span of the use case, however tempting that might be. Every use case in the world is broad, whether it is a simple consumer home-based exercise flow or a more complex customer journey in a business setting. Moreover, the entire use case will require a broad set of strengths that even an established company might not have. So, stretching our limits to address all steps and hand-offs in the use case will usually distract us from effectively productizing the parts of the use case that we are strong enough to address. Of course, increasing our coverage may eventually be possible as an established and dominant player. But low net customer value with broad coverage is not the path to domination.

The **second** rule of thumb to optimize net customer value is to focus intently on a specific part of the use case that drives maximum net customer value. This means we must augment customers' journey by addressing the most impactful aspects of the market problem. Root causes of market problem congregate in specific parts of the use case. Therefore, our offering must create tangible positive net customer value by comprehensively handling the specific portion of the use case that holds the root cause of existing gaps.

So, how do we achieve this optimal value creation within a use case?

Let's formalize two terms: **Features** and **Capabilities**. A feature is a commonly used word as companies think about their offerings. However, its usage is not always effective. Capability frames a specific concept that we will use throughout the rest of our methodology to help us productize effectively.

Things to Remember: Feature

A feature is a creation in our productization effort that focuses on our internal creativity and symptom-solving. A feature is a narrow widget that solves a symptom without effectively framing the whole market problem or its root cause.

Creating a feature by itself is like putting up a residential condominium building without much thought to what will be around it. Yes, the building is fine. But how will it connect the people in the building to the rest of the world? This is our unplanned city mindset.

Disconnected features do not create much net positive customer value because each feature causes significant value outflows from customers to incorporate that narrow widget into their journey. This outflow often negates any value that the standalone feature could create. In our infographic, the shaded friction points convey the incredible customer value outflow necessary to use each feature. Therefore, this is a counterproductive productization approach.

If we build narrow widgets, they become unmanageable over time because our cost to maintain these disconnected widgets would increase. i.e., if we build features, our delivery cost per customer will likely rise beyond a small customer base. It also becomes harder to mature our offering on top of disconnected existing features. Imagine playing a game of Tetris and having a jumbled base that covers most of the playing window. Features leave us with a disorganized Tetris base that prevents us from building effectively on top.

Have you ever felt an overall body ache, while the source is a single knot in our back muscle that connects to those other achy parts? Ironing out that knot releases the pain from the rest of your body.

A capability addresses the root cause of the problem by transposing customer wants into needs. Thus, a capability is a solution that intentionally addresses the specific portion of the use case that causes the customers' broader challenges.

> **Things to Remember: Capability**
>
> **A capability is a comprehensive solution to the root causes of the market problem in our use case. It is an intentional and organized productization approach that drives scalability and positive net customer value with little waste attacking symptoms.**

Think about a capability as a modular construct that can replace an entire portion of a use case that causes most of the problems. Given this modular nature, it requires very low customer value outflow to integrate into their natural flow. i.e., a capability is a plug-and-play approach that creates positive net customer value in one part of the use case. This is because it addresses the root causes of the customer problems comprehensively and requires limited customer outflow due to fewer transitions and thus friction losses in the customer journey.

Additionally, capabilities are the only path to scalability. The market problem is often very personal to customers because they are an interpretation and a feeling that changes from one customer to another. But root causes are shared by many customers because they are objective and non-interpretive. A capability addresses a root cause that spans our optimal customers, which allows for reproducibility.

Choosing a specific capability as our value creation approach implies laying out a long-term productization plan. It allows us to organize our design and build our offering with a long-term view. The reproducibility of a capability means reducing the risk of the rising cost of delivery per customer as our scale increases. Finally, it allows us to communicate effectively with our customers regarding tangible outcomes that we are delivering.

So, our productization effort must always focus on creating one or two comprehensive capabilities that drive positive net customer value. Conversely, let's not focus on a slew of features that causes so much value outflow from customers that they create little positive net customer value. A feature can be a necessary part of a capability that delivers comprehensive customer value, but on its own, doesn't positively change the customer journey and is rarely reproducible across many customers.

For instance, a hypothetical metals manufacturer embracing the capability mindset may productize ten metal tools sold as a cohesive set targeting an urban homeowner. The same manufacturer operating with a features mindset may create ten metal widgets addressing divergent applications in an urban home.

In a real-world example, I closely worked with a software company that focused on an end-to-end spend data extraction and processing use case. At a high level, the use case spanned identifying source documents, gathering those documents, and extracting the data into a technology platform. It then transposed the data to connect with other key customer data elements, delivering the transposed data to customers, and generating insights on the end-to-end flow.

This is an enormous span to cover, even for behemoths like SAP or Oracle. But unfortunately, this company set expectations with customers that it would cover the entire end-to-end flow.

These were good intentions but impossible to accomplish for a growth-phase company.

The company deployed a narrow widget to address every part of this customer journey because the customer felt pain everywhere. One widget tried to gather documents but missed many. Another widget tried to highlight missing documents ineffectively. One widget was an extraction method that resulted in low data accuracy. Other widgets tried to interlink data with limited effectiveness. Essentially, almost all widgets left alarm bells ringing for customers and the company's resources working with customers. The reality was that customers could never remove themselves from any one of these steps in their workflow. Dealing with several transitions back and forth from the customer's natural flow to support each widget caused too much value outflow for customers. These widgets epitomize a feature mindset.

This company would have served this use case much more effectively if it had comprehensively addressed one of the steps that caused most customer pain. The biggest value creation opportunity was the document acquisition and data extraction step. This single step was the root cause of timing delays and data quality symptoms throughout the use case.

If the company had only taken ownership of the responsibility for consistent document acquisition and high-quality data extraction while leaving all the other steps to the customer to continue in their existing journey, the odds of effective productization would have been higher. This root cause solution would have been a robust capability. Customers would have been able to completely offload this step from their journey and thus embrace that value with limited value outflow to support this capability. Expansion from that core capability could have happened over time.

But this didn't happen. Customers churned off when they realized that even a low price wasn't worth the lack of comprehensive value created in any one part of their journey. They found it frustrating that they still had fires to put out throughout the entire flow. Eventually, the company stopped serving this entire use case and terminated the employees involved in the manual processing steps.

It is necessary to distinguish between features and capabilities because sustainable growth is not possible without a capability mindset. However, it is significantly easier and more tempting to create features than capabilities. It is the biggest contributor to stalling of productization maturity, which stifles overall growth. It's alluring for three reasons.

First, the most common source of feature creation comes from customer complaints or customer asks. But as we already discussed, our job is not to replicate customer wants. Our job is to solve the root causes of customer problems. Customers share their feelings, not the solutions. Companies often create features to address symptoms; however, it is not scalable. Our best-case scenario is that we have added something that makes a few customers happy in the short term.

Second, employees in the company work on projects, and it is doubtful that a single employee will ever complete an entire capability design and commercialization. So, each employee, team, or company is likely to be tempted to talk about small widgets that it can quickly create and feel accomplished about.

Third, suppose the company hasn't embraced the power of a Comparative Advantage Ecosystem that we covered under Part A: Management Approach. In that case, the productization responsibility might sit with a person or team that is more inclined on detailed execution instead of wearing a customer-first hat to identify the optimal use case and focus on a capability mindset.

Operating in a customer-first and capability-focused mindset requires a mature organization design that is staffed with skilled enablement resources who can internalize the principles we are covering and ensure that all our productization efforts focus on customer value via root cause problem-solving. This mindset can allow us to expand to another comprehensive capability over time because customers are committed to us on the first capability we comprehensively addressed. Domination always starts with comprehensive problem-solving for a specific step or a hand-off in our chosen use case through an effective capability.

If we are going to build a capability, let's understand it a bit more.

Principle 6: Building a capability is a multi-dimensional endeavor.

Remember, a capability is a comprehensive root-cause solution that fits a use case with limited value outflow for the customer. What does this look like?

If you live in an urban area, look around where you are right now. Everything around us these days is touched, moved, changed, or built. Every building, computer, book, streetlight, edible food item, sidewalk trees, etc., passed through some company.

In all these situations, the aspect that creates value involves several parts. I doubt any of us went to the manufacturing plant to pick up our laptop or phone. Even if we needed a nail to hang a picture, we don't go to a metal casting facility to get that nail. These are trivial examples. Most offerings are much more complex.

Infographic B.7 illustrates the multi-dimensional nature of a capability. Any solution that creates value comprises one or more of four dimensions – **Object**, **Action**, **Knowledge**, and **Promise**. However, we rarely consume in one of these dimensions in our complex world anymore. Instead, everything we consume is a complex permutation in these four mutually exclusive and collectively exhaustive dimensions.

The first dimension is **Object**. All goods in the world generally fall in here, including the food we consume, the energy we use, the physical phone we have, the software operating system of the phone, etc.

The second dimension is **Action**. We gain value from others performing the actions we might perform ourselves, whether due to convenience or our inability to perform it.

The third dimension is **Knowledge**. We don't know everything. We must depend on others to give us information, whether it is their licensable intellectual property or their know-how due to their experience.

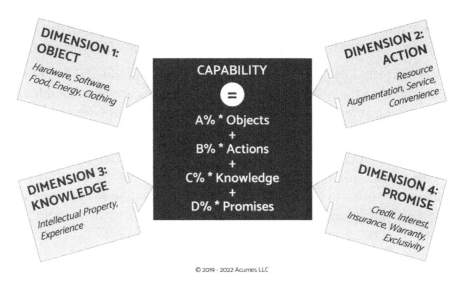

Infographic B.7 – **Capabilities are multi-dimensional**

The fourth and last dimension is **Promise**. This intangible category includes bi-directional promises. For example, an institution might give us money today in exchange for us paying interest or vice versa. Alternately, we sign insurance contracts and pay someone else to mitigate risk. Warranty is a promise of quality. Finally, even exclusive access to a thing or an action can be considered a promise.

More importantly, it is hard for us to create positive net customer value in our complex world by focusing only on one of these dimensions. Therefore, every single capability will be a solution that sits across multiple dimensions.

I hired an editor to help me put the finishing touches on this book. I am gaining value from their intellectual property as a writer and their experience helping others like me. What if my editor only offered advice? I might be able to edit myself if they tell me how. But using the advice effectively would cause me significant value outflow because editing is not my strength. My net value might be negative if I get frustrated with the process. So, my editor also performs the action of editing the book through my grammatical mistakes.

There is a tinge of warranty in our relationship because we set up our payment terms to ensure we are making progress before I pay for the work. As a single customer, I seek three of these dimensions from an editor.

Why is this principle important in our evolutionary productization mindset? Embracing the multi-dimensional aspect of a capability enables us to mature our offerings to have the highest positive net customer value possible while continuously evolving how we create that value.

For a given root cause, there can be a range of solutions that could all have the same impact from a customer perspective. In our multi-dimensional approach, we could potentially create the same value for the customer focusing heavily on any of the dimensions while augmenting with the others.

Think about a polynomial equation with four variables where we can change the constants for the variables to achieve a specific solution. The solution here is our capability and the variables are the four dimensions.

Amazon offers free shipping with a predefined guarantee on the delivery timeframe for customers paying for Prime shipping. Essentially, this seamless delivery is an Amazon capability that solves all sorts of divergent customer challenges. As a customer, do we care whether this delivery happens through the United States Postal Service (USPS), Amazon's direct fulfillment staff, or flying robots? In fact, Amazon used to deliver Prime packages through the USPS. Then, they transitioned to using their own staff. Regardless of how Amazon delivers its packages, its capability is to deliver the package for free within a given timeframe.

Amazon is shifting from operating primarily in the promises dimension of signing contracts with USPS to the action dimension of delivering themselves to whichever dimension we want to put flying robots in. The multidimensional view of our capability allows us to evolve the contributing dimensions of our capability to become more scalable and profitable.

In fact, looking at a capability in a multi-dimensional mindset is not optional because we are unlikely to create a comprehensive solution in a single-dimensional mindset.

At the software company in the last principle, my team owned and managed customers. The company referred to the software created and sold to customers as the 'product.' However, the software portion also had many of the challenges we alluded to earlier. The company ignored the vast array of action and knowledge dimension elements necessary to augment the sub-par software object to create net positive customer value. In this instance, my team struggled to deliver customer value because the company had a single-dimensional capability mindset.

So, we must think about productization as the act of creating a multi-dimensional root cause solution that can evolve and mature over time. This brings us to the last customer value creation principle – commercialization.

Principle 7: Customer value is always consumed as a commercialized package with a price.

We made a somewhat controversial decision earlier that we wouldn't use the word 'product.' So, here is the final nail in that coffin. A customer never buys our 'product.' Yes, you heard it correctly! In simple words, a customer gets what we sell.

Regardless of the market, use case, and specific root cause we are addressing, our customers always consume a commercialized version of our productized offering. The only question is whether we have commercialized well or whether our commercialization is ad hoc and reactive. Commercialization is the last step of our productization path, and it has two elements: **Packaging** and **Pricing**.

Staying with Peloton, the company introduced a corporate wellness angle to their offering in 2021 as employees working from home started returning to the office. Did Peloton introduce a new capability here? No. Everything about their capabilities remained the same except creating a new package and price to sell to companies to reach their employees, unlike previous packages sold directly to consumers. Whether this was an effective move remains to be seen.

Customers buy our packages at the price we set. So, let's explore both these elements further.

Optimal packages balance customer value via complementary capabilities.

As customers, we buy to receive value. In principles 5 and 6, we covered the importance of a capability mindset to create tangible value and avoid internally focused feature creation. We also framed the importance of creating multi-dimensional capabilities that comprehensively address root causes in our chosen use case. There is a nuance we must incorporate to apply this framework.

There is only an infinitesimally small chance of creating a precise capability that perfectly slots into a given customer's journey. Therefore, there will always be a gap between a given capability and the customer journey. That implies that there will always be a value outflow for customers to use any given capability.

Think about it this way – even the best capabilities have seasonality or customer-level variation in value.

First, we are productizing for our optimal customers. As we will discuss under Part C: Corporate Strategy, our optimal customers aren't the same. There are likely at least a couple of generally similar groups that form our optimal customer. Each customer will be different within each of those groups, even to a small extent. So, no two customers have the exact same customer journey, which means we are asking both of them to make an adjustment.

Second, no customer will ever value a given capability exactly the same at all times. Unless it's the air we breathe, we just don't use anything else 100% of the time. So, how does this time-based variation in value delivery impact the net customer value?

How do we deploy our ever-maturing capabilities to drive optimal net customer value with the real constraint of customer-level difference in mind? The answer is packaging.

Customers always buy packages. Packages allow us to normalize value delivery to each customer and across customers. Packages help us solve both the time-based and customer-level variation in value realization.

> **Things to Remember: Packaging**
>
> Packaging is the act of creating a customer-facing box with more than one complementary capability to normalize the net value created over time and across customers. Thus, it allows us to sell the same box to our optimal customers while minimizing the variance in value extracted over time and between customers.

Amazon Prime is an extraordinarily effective package that delivers at least two effective capabilities. I originally signed up for the Prime package thinking that the free shipping would be valuable. It turns out I don't buy that much stuff. But I have still been a Prime customer for a decade. Why? I attribute about half the value of the Prime package to Prime video, which is Amazon's version of streaming services and included in the Prime package. When I buy something where I get free shipping, I am willing to overlook the lack of quality shows on Prime Video. When I find a decent show to watch on Prime, I don't mind that I haven't shipped anything for free for a while. Prime is a package that accounts for my personal seasonality.

Similarly, a customer who buys a lot online and never watches Prime shows also gets a lot from the Prime package. What if a customer enjoys a lot of Prime shows but rarely shops on Amazon? The Prime package takes this customer level differences into account.

Packaging is a necessary penultimate step to commercialize our core capability because we will always have at least a small gap between our capability and the customer journey.

However, most packaging efforts are diluted into a discounting effort without focusing on customer value. Others concentrate on slapping together items that do not dovetail or complement each other as an upselling effort without creating more customer value. Putting multiple widgets into a box needs to be mature and focus on the value the box delivers across time and customers. A non-value-focused packaging effort is likely to create only a more significant discrepancy between value and price for customers causing adverse reactions in the future. Effective packaging allows us to price according to the value we are delivering.

Consider the following guiding questions to structure our approach to effective packaging:

Starting with our core capability, what is the cadence at which our customer is likely to extract the intended value from this capability? What is the risk that customers will exit the value extraction cycle prematurely? What complementary second or third capability can deliver similar net customer value to close these value gaps?

Starting with our core capability, what is the variance in value that various customers might extract at the peak use? What complementary second or third capability can offset the lower net customer value for customers experiencing it without overdelivering for customers extracting a high net customer value?

A marketing software company that I helped turnaround developed a capability to deliver high-level awareness of how effective the customers' marketing spend was. But this capability had a value creation cadence of once in six months or longer for most customers. It meant most customers were only learning something new every six months or a year. There was also a large variance in the value customers received because some customers actively managed their marketing spend much more than others. So, many stopped using this capability after a couple of cycles because they felt like they weren't learning new information often enough.

The company had a second capability that offered tactical daily actionable suggestions to customers' operations teams to act on marketing leads. The actionable suggestions from the second capability allowed customers to take frequent tactical actions and extract proportional value. But the value created by this capability may not necessarily get used by the operations teams without the overarching measurements delivered by the first capability.

Both capabilities had limitations. We packaged both capabilities together, and they augmented each other. This package normalized the value delivery frequency and the net value delivered across customers.

Embracing a packaging approach that accounts for time-based variation in value delivery and customer-level variation in value realization allows us to productize for customers and drive scale.

Leverage value-based pricing to drive sustainable growth.

Finally, to take our package to our customers, we have to put a price on it. In today's highly transparent world, where every entity has a website and third-party sources of price and value comparisons are ubiquitous, pricing is more competitive than ever before.

Perceptions about value can be created through messages on websites and social media. Any company can purchase rating services and reviews. Disinformation always existed, but each new tool introduced to help companies compete makes it even more prevalent. For example, many companies claim Artificial Intelligence but barely have automation under the hood. So, how do we price our package in our ridiculously competitive world?

Our competitive environment perpetuates an escalation of commitment to overstate the value of offerings and misdirect customers about competitive offerings. I have never found these to be effective long term, and they are ethically questionable.

Customers understand value because they usually understand their market problem after it is presented to them. Customers are willing to pay for the value created. That's where our focus must remain to drive sustainable growth. Our conversation is about dovetailed fundamentals, not one-off tactics.

My preferred framework for pricing for our package is based on reference entities. The only reference points in a market are ourselves, our competitors, and the customer. Pricing based on the first two reference points implies a lack of sustainability in the business model. Our only sustainable growth option is to grow our value for our customers, which allows us to increase our pricing for our customers, which, in turn, enables our company to maximize our revenue.

Our first option is to set pricing for our customers based on our internal operations. This is generally called **cost-based pricing**. In this mode, the company adds up the expenses incurred to deliver the offering to the customer and adds a margin on top to set the price.

The practical manifestation of cost-based pricing starts with a feature mindset to offerings. We are likely selling disparate single-dimensional features in this mode, trivializing our value to customers as a collection of widgets. We expect the customer to figure out how to draw value from our widgets. Customers will think about our widgets as commodities they can shop around for because they internalize value more than we do.

There are two primary problems with cost-based pricing. **First**, we are volunteering for an unnecessary downward pressure on price because the customer knows exactly how we create our package. If we price based on cost, we will inadvertently share our cost model with customers because we haven't enabled our sellers to discuss value.

I advise companies that customers don't need to know the sausage-making process. Effective packaging and pricing let us talk about the quality and taste of the sausage rather than nickel and dime based on what it cost us to create the sausage. Once the customer knows how our cost adds up, they will find ways to question each cost component and shrink our margins.

The **second** problem is that we will never get to increase the price beyond cadence-based increases, akin to inflation adjustment. So, we can only improve our margins in this mode if we reduce our cost. But the cost can only go down so far. Thus, we have limited the effectiveness of one of the two primary levers to grow revenue – price.

Our second option is to arrive at a pricing model based on our competitors. This is a war of attrition. **Competition-based pricing** is most common when our value creation is not unique among our competitors in a commoditized space.

Alternately, if we do not understand the customer journey and the effectiveness with which our offering addresses the journey, we might feel the need to be defensive against our competitors. It is especially true if we operate in a very messaging-focused environment instead of a value-focused one. Customers will always test us on our value proposition and our pricing by comparing us to others in the market.

Our objective awareness of our effectiveness in solving the root cause of the problem determines our confidence in addressing customer probes around comparisons with competitors. Beyond playing in a market with trivial offerings, a lack of confidence in the value created by our offering is usually the primary reason for operating in a competition-based pricing model.

Our third and preferred option is to focus on our customers and set pricing based on the value we create for them. This third option is known as **value-based pricing**. Value-based pricing is a true partnership mindset with our customers where we are taking a cut of the loot. If we create value for customers by addressing their market problem, it is only fair that we can extract a portion of the value attributed to the problem through our pricing.

> **Things to Remember: Value-Based Pricing**
>
> **Value-based pricing focuses only on monetizing the upside we create for our customers by addressing the market problem. Therefore, customers are willing to pay for value upside that directly links to the market problem, regardless of the cost to create the solution.**

To utilize value-based pricing, we must understand the incremental value that our customer group can create if we solve the market problem in the use case. The closer our package addresses the entirety of the market problem, the higher the value we are creating.

Why could Peloton price their bikes and treadmills higher than anyone else in the market in their early days? Because they primarily sought after a customer group that attributes a high value for each saved hour of time. The customer group was willing to share a portion of that increased value with Peloton regardless of what it costs Peloton to make and ship a bike and create programming.

A counterexample is my book editing services. Every quote I received for my book editing request was a competition-based price with only a 15% difference between the highest and lowest quotes. Do I believe they all offer similar value? Absolutely not! In fact, I am willing to offer an incentive model where the editor can get a share of the earnings because it is a win-win to create the most optimal outcome.

Rational customers are happy to embrace a value-based model if we take the time to understand the value we are collectively creating and our contribution to that overall value. Therefore, all the concepts we have worked through in this chapter are necessary to drive value-based pricing.

Consider the following questions to determine a fair price based on the value we deliver:

Can we quantify the ultimate value that our customers are creating in their customer journey for their own consumption or to trade with their customers?

How much of that value is attributable to the specific market problem our package effectively addresses for our customers?

How effective and differentiated is our package in addressing the root cause of the problem?

How much value outflow does our customers incur in using our package?

How effectively does our packaging normalize value delivered over time and across customers?

What is a fair share of the quantifiable net positive value that we can extract as price?

Quantifying monetary value associated with each portion of the use case isn't easy. But as a growth-phase company, we only have one or two packages to offer. So, it's worth taking the time to answer these questions. Of course, our alternative is to sell our productized offering with an unsustainable pricing model.

One of the key Impediments to value-based pricing is a lack of effective productization. If we cannot internalize the concept of repeatability and reproducibility, we will never drive the scalability of our offering. Without productization, we are likely to inflate our cost of creating value for customers. This increasing cost often distracts us from focusing on the value we might be creating for customers. Our price-setting approach quickly becomes internally focused, and we fall into a defensive mode of ensuring that we are at least meeting our cost. This leaves us with a cost-based pricing model.

I have worked with multiple companies that use the term 'value-based pricing' but actually have a cost – or competition-based pricing because they didn't follow the principles we discussed. For a growth-phase company, operating in either pricing model implies that our value is largely commoditized or our productization is ineffective. Once we enter this cycle of cost-based pricing or competition-based pricing, it is a downward spiral that is almost impossible to get out of unless we hope to be the last one standing in the marketplace, which isn't a sustainable growth mindset.

So, we must productize and become highly effective in understanding the value our packages create for customers so that we do not doubt that our value-based pricing is fair.

The vast majority of companies struggle to internalize the customer-first mindset and understand the actual value created by solving the root cause of the market problem. The starting point is understanding the customer journey and focusing on an optimal use case. Then we must productize a capability to drive positive net customer value through a specific portion of the use case. Finally, effective packaging to optimize net customer value and embracing value-based pricing are necessary commercialization principles to deploy our offering optimally.

Together, these principles articulate the offering that spearheads our value engine. The maturity of our offering and its ability to create value for customers makes our company more valuable to all other stakeholders. It ensures that our path to sell and deliver value starts on the right foot. Our corporate strategy development and strategic planning efforts will assess and improve the maturity of our productized offering. We must perpetually improve our alignment to the use case we are serving and create increasingly higher customer value.

Now let's talk about how to deliver our offerings.

B.2
SCALE OPERATIONS WITH EFFECTIVE PROCESSES.

We have the right people and the right offering. So, what do we do now?

We compared our offering to the payload of a missile headed for a customer. But we must do more. Countries spend decades developing and reimagining their long-range missile capabilities even if they have a powerful payload in its earlier stages. Our offering will only create customer value for a large portion of our addressable market and help our company grow sustainably if it employs effective operational processes and technology to support those processes along with data to enable improvements and decision-making. Together, these components complete our value engine.

We categorized our people, technology, and other assets into operations and enablement resources and supervisors for each group under organization design. Operations resources perform all the ongoing activities. This spans all functions from marketing, sales, customer management, ongoing management of our offering, finance, human resources, and any other activities that we need to deliver customer value. The specific tactics for these ongoing activities are almost exclusively dependent on our offering, the market we serve, and our current maturity level. But several fundamental principles drive maturity for processes and data across all these functions.

We will start with **Process** in this chapter. Like many other common words used in business environments, there are many opinions on what 'process' means in real life.

> **Things to Remember: Process**
>
> Process is the well-articulated set of guidelines, criteria, and conditions that we expect performers (employees, customers, partners, etc.) to execute, or technologies are designed to replicate. Processes intend to achieve repeatable (the same performer executes the same way every time) and reproducible (several performers execute the same way every time) behaviors, which in turn helps the company achieve its overall goals with optimal use of its investment in people, technology, and other assets.

Most companies talk about process rigor. Many support its criticality. However, some consider it a growth-killer, creativity-destroyer, or momentum-staller.

These anti-process sentiments are prevalent where entrepreneurial minds congregate. Such environments incorrectly presume that creativity and structure cannot coexist. The truth is that creativity without discipline sends us down an unsustainable growth trajectory. So, let's start with a fresh outlook by framing common misconceptions around the concept of process.

Principle 1: Overcome myths and awareness gaps around processes.

A strong process mindset makes everyone's life easier and creates more value for companies. No company grows slower because of process rigor; we don't value a company less because they are operationally excellent.

So, why does 'process' get a lot of flak?

The most common reason is that many employees in scaling companies have never operated in environments that scaled significantly on a sustainable track and achieved operational excellence and witnessed firsthand the benefits of such a strong foundation. So, biases surround the value of a strong process mindset. Let's go through some of the common myths.

Myth 1: Process doesn't allow agility.

Scaling companies often believe they can attribute all their success to agility. This is a misconception. Many entrepreneurs try many ideas. Many of them fail, and some succeed to find a fit between their idea and a market need. An entrepreneur must be agile in the early stages of a company to find a fit between their ideas and the market. Growing a company beyond the early stages requires a mindset change where discipline becomes just as important as agility.

Discipline in a company takes the form of processes. A clear understanding of processes enables operations to move extremely fast, not slower. Is a well-mapped and well-traveled path easier or harder to take than stumbling through an arbitrary, untraveled one? Obviously, the former.

Saying that processes slow operations down is like saying that it is faster to get in a car and start driving immediately without looking up directions or knowing the roads. Usually, it results in drivers taking wrong turns and stumbling their way to the destination, if at all.

Operations resources in companies are analogous to individual drivers in this scenario. Well-defined processes remedy the need for individual discovery of optimal paths. It allows employees performing similar tasks to follow predefined directions on the fastest route to reach the desired destination quickly and at similar times. The Company Way is essentially point-to-point directions created for operations resources through enablement initiatives that we will discuss later in our methodology.

Myth 2: Process design is resource intensive.

Wrong! Misconceptions around process development and adoption come from confusing process design and process reengineering. Process design is a preventative effort to run an efficient organization and starts well before poor operational behaviors have taken root and outcomes have started failing. Process reengineering is a cure against past sins, where an organization exists in operational chaos and outcomes have suffered.

The latter is considerably more demanding than the former because most process reengineering effort goes into change management to revert poor behaviors, which is onerous.

Imagine that your car stalled on the road. Do you think you can put your car in neutral and push the car? Most people can make some headway with effort. Now imagine that same car moving at even ten miles per hour. How about trying to slow down that car and move it in the opposite direction? It is much harder or somewhat impossible.

The physics concept that explains this phenomenon is inertia, where objects prefer to continue to follow their current path. Human beings also demonstrate inertia to keep doing things the way they have always done. As a result, managing change is challenging. We have dedicated a chapter to it under Part E: Execution Management for this reason. Most myths around the difficulty of building a process mindset come from stories where companies tried to reengineer past poor behaviors without accounting for inertia and change management and failing.

Myth 3: Process design is an option.

The choice isn't whether a company defines its processes or not – it always has processes. The only option is whether they are good or bad. Even if a company chooses not to choreograph the day-to-day activities of its critical teams, it has processes. Unfortunately, the default state is *Level 1: Chaos,* where every employee chooses their own way and leaves the organization in operational chaos.

Every human develops good or bad habits and changes them as they wish. Unfortunately, in this process chaos, the organization pays for it because it cannot explain what employees are actually doing or which activities are working well. So, the company's only choice is to improve upon the default state of operational chaos where each employee and groups of employees are operating their own way and not The Company Way.

In addition to overcoming such myths, our process mindset will be most effective if we understand and communicate its overwhelming benefits.

Principle 2: Internalize the benefits of a process mindset.

The temptation to ride a growth wave without developing consistent operational behaviors is understandable because it is easier; but not advisable. Lack of behavioral consistencies is a considerable resource tax.

Problem-solving and micro-evolutions of our operations are impossible without processes. So, let's dive deeper into the benefits of a process mindset.

No data without process.

Often data and process are considered separate concepts. Nothing could be farther from the truth, and this misconception often undermines the amount of organizational effort that goes into process design. Data is nothing more than an ongoing recording of measurements associated with behaviors demonstrated during specific steps in processes. These measurements are only meaningful if we design the process well, and the performers have adopted the design and executed it as expected. Conversely, measurements are practically useless and impossible to assess if the underlying behaviors are not well-defined or not adopted.

Let's imagine that a restaurant employee has a simple role of counting the number of people visiting the establishment. An establishment with an immature value engine will ask the employee to count. What is likely to happen when the employee counts? What if different employees are handling this role on different days?

There are several ambiguities that these employees face even in such a simple experiment where they are forced to do it their own way. An example of ambiguity is an exact definition of a visitor to the establishment. Should the employee count someone that enters the main door, takes a peek inside, and leaves without entering further? What if a visitor looks at the menu to understand the prices and then exits without making a purchase? Should the employee count neither of them or one of them or both of them? Every employee who performs this role will have a personal perspective of the correct definition of a visitor.

If you are an analyst at the head office of this establishment, how dependable are these daily tallies if you are trying to understand how visitor volume changes from one day to the next?

If you are an analyst at heart, you know what I am talking about. Making sense of information and making decisions from it is fraught with risks. We could call the information from the above scenario a 'bad' data set. But the truth is that data is just data. It is the underlying process that is bad.

One of the most important reasons to have well-defined processes is to capture coherent data, allowing us to understand the real state of affairs objectively.

Processes improve the efficiency of operations resources and supervisors.

A strong process mindset enables operations resources to focus on executing their core strengths that drive the most value. Setting up operations resources and their supervisors to stumble through and find a path to achieve expected outcomes is an organizational failure. Operations resources and supervisors would lose significant time and mindshare away from their core strengths and operate in an inefficient environment.

As a practical example, sales representatives should focus on selling activities with prospects outside the company and closing deals. However, many organizations spend too much time solving internal problems or figuring out how they should sell into the company's market. A company where sales reps spend a large share of their time not interacting with prospects is essentially throwing away a significant portion of revenue potential. In turn, the company will end up hiring several more sales reps to meet revenue goals than necessary in an operationally efficient environment. In an inefficient environment, this unnecessary spend on sales reps takes away from an investment that could eventually improve our offerings or marketing efforts to find more prospects.

To add insult to injury, in such a situation, a supervisor to those sales reps can likely only manage fewer sales reps than at a company with a strong process mindset. Even an effective sales supervisor will have to spend much more time managing each rep in a company with a weak process mindset. Every rep operates differently, and there are no economies of scale for the supervisor's activities. Now, we have a company that also needs more sales supervisors on staff due to poor sales processes, compounding the company's woes around investment allocation and future growth.

Infographic B.8 illustrates how a lack of a process mindset can cost an organization heavily with more operations resources and supervisors. The weak process mindset environment on the right side of this visual illustrates why labor productivity is lower in such conditions. This is a practical manifestation of the unsustainable growth path where the cost of delivering value accelerates faster than the value created.

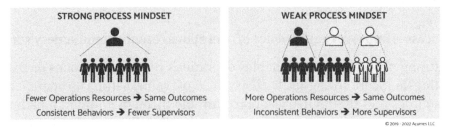

Infographic B.8 – Sustainable scale demands a strong process mindset

A strong process mindset allows operations employees to focus strictly on value-creating activities that are core to their role and align with their skills.

Operations resources must be empowered with The Company Way, which articulates solutions to repetitive problems, preventing each employee from losing time on solving the same problems independently. A process mindset doesn't just create efficiencies; it eliminates waste at all levels of the organization, allowing for increased customer acquisition and value creation initiatives.

Process design is a necessary problem-solving frame of reference.

Imagine getting lost in a huge shopping mall while looking for a specific store. What do we do? We look for a map of the mall. Why? Because it orients us and tells us where we are in the enormous complex and how to get where we need to go.

Process serves the same purpose in operational problem solving as the map of the mall does in orienting us.

If a specific operational problem arises, key players get together and discuss the problem and how to solve it. But how do these individuals communicate their understanding of the current state? Too often, senior executives, supervisors, and individual contributors talk in circles about operational problems and have little success explaining their perspectives to each other. This happens because there is no frame of reference that everyone can look at and work from to understand each other and solve problems. That frame of reference is a well-articulated process design.

We must codify process designs to ensure they can be reviewed, understood, disagreed with, iterated, and improved. Once such a codified definition that articulates The Company Way exists, problem-solving can start by using this articulation as the frame of reference – it is the single source of truth on what operations resources do.

A process mindset is the first and foundational step to maturing as an analytical organization. Once all senior executives and supervisors get beyond myths around processes and embrace its power, the company opens itself up to a world of objective information and significant efficiencies that enable the diversion of investment into initiatives that improve future growth prospects.

After side-stepping common process design pitfalls, we can deploy a streamlined set of principles to develop operational processes quickly and effectively. But before we explore the core principles of process design, let's steer clear of a few common design mistakes.

Principle 3: Avoid common process design mistakes.

One can make a few obvious mistakes when going through a process design exercise.

Avoid trivializing operational expertise and groupthink.

We wouldn't try to diagnose and cure diseases with communal voting, would we?

We would go to a doctor with years of training on specific health conditions and parts of the human body. The only difference between a health issue and a business operation is that health issues impact us personally and could have serious and immediate ramifications on our life. Business operations can feel less personal, and the impact can be slow-moving and may even only take hold after we leave that particular role. But that doesn't change the relevance of expertise in process design. Keeping our Comparative Advantage Ecosystem in mind, process design requires designated experts with solid experience.

Process design is more scientific and more studied than marketing or product development. It has proven frameworks and formulae. People dedicate their careers to this space. So, do not hand off this critical responsibility to resources without relevant experience.

The company must grant the ownership to develop a process mindset to an effective enablement resource with deep operations design skills. A scaling company only needs one primary process designer, who might also have other related analytical responsibilities. Spreading ownership will likely cost the company more through unnecessary involvement from too many individuals while rendering poorer results.

Do not succumb to a reactive top-down design.

As a company grows, senior executives naturally feel the need to understand what their employees are doing and what is working well. Of course, this implies looking at the quantitative information that the company has. But, often, as a company grows, senior executives will find that the required information is non-existent because there is no process rigor to dictate data capture.

So, what happens next?

The senior executives often ask the supervisors to collect the information needed. These supervisors, who are unlikely to be expert process designers, ask their operations resources to start regularly capturing this information; this ask is essentially process change.

The operations resources now have the additional responsibility of collecting information at an arbitrary time in the middle of their day-to-day activities. However, since this doesn't fit their usual activities, they tend to forget or ignore it or just do a poor job. Supervisors and senior executives are likely to scratch their heads to make sense of this poorly captured information.

This is a common scenario I have seen at companies where an attempt to create process and data causes more disruption and poor information. This design mistake is essentially ignoring our flow thinking. Here, our process design customers are process performers.

Process design has three stakeholder groups. Process performers, including internal operations resources, customers, and external partners, are our primary stakeholders. Processes intend to give them more clarity and predictability and ease their path to achieve outcomes, not make it more complicated. An expert process designer will base the design on what works best for performers who execute day-to-day activities, as long as it works in the company's interest.

Infographic B.9 – Effective process design focuses on performers' journey

Supervisors and senior executives, who are secondary and tertiary stakeholders, respectively, will reap the benefit of proactively laid processes and learn from consistent and unbiased data captured seamlessly through the normal flow of process performers' execution. Infographic B.9 provides a visual reminder to prioritize process performers above supervisors' and senior executives' short-term needs when designing processes to achieve optimal results.

Do not forget that processes are alive.

We often misunderstand process design as a time-bound initiative. Although a process design effort will have milestones, it is never a one-and-done effort.

A mature operations baseline implies that we are continuously learning through our data and tactically improving the day-to-day execution of every employee and groups of employees. These improvements are first reflected in the process design. Then employees adopt those improvements and execute them.

A common trap that companies fall into is the temptation to make knee-jerk changes to execution without leading with appropriate objective assessments and codification of decisions through The Company Way. Reactive and hasty changes happen when the value engine is immature. When a problem arises, senior executives, supervisors, or operations resources might present off-the-cuff ideas to remedy the situation quickly.

These unproven ideas may feel like cohesive solutions in an undisciplined and immature value engine. Suppose senior executives or supervisors ask operations resources to adopt such spontaneous ideas into their day-to-day execution while circumventing any analytical reasoning and consulting the process design expert who originally designed the process. In that case, we are essentially breaking the process. Even a handful of such spontaneous changes, however small, can completely break down a simple and efficient process design to become ineffective.

So, an effective process design will also include a governance approach owned and managed by the process design expert, where fast-paced objective analytical assessments and codification always lead to tactical improvements in design before execution changes begin. Doing nothing is often more effective than doing a lot of incorrect things.

Now, let's frame up what constitutes a good process design.

Principle 4: Leverage six design elements to optimize processes.

I spent my early years developing processes at several large enterprises, and I can guarantee that it takes years of practice to get good at it. At the same time, every employee needs to have a sense of a good process design.

Growing companies should not complicate process design with heavy methodologies because it is unnecessary. A process methodology is only necessary when a company has several process designers. A growth-phase company only needs one.

My proven approach to process design has six elements, and I've highlighted each of them in Infographic B.10. These six elements can be used to develop the foundational processes required at a company of any size. These are not complex. For each element, I will lay out a set of questions that you can use to determine your current process maturity, and you may use answers to those questions to drive improvement of that maturity level.

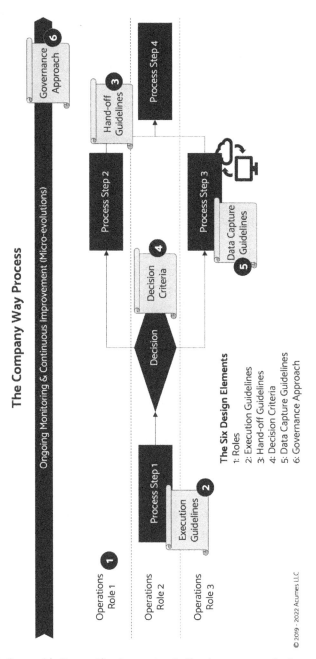

Infographic B.10 – Six elements of effective process design

Irrespective of your role in the company, look around and assess whether process definitions have at least these six elements accounted for. If not, have a conversation with the strategy & operations executive or the CEO. See what steps can be taken to get to a foundational process maturity that enables repeatability and reproducibility in operations execution and captures unbiased decision-making data.

Element 1: Cover all operations roles and their activities.

Internal operations resources, customers, and supporting external partners are the primary stakeholders of process design. Therefore, the most important outcome of a process definition is that it articulates and communicates details of day-to-day execution to these stakeholders.

First, a process design must account for every operations role. Many inefficiencies and gaps are likely left unaddressed if it doesn't cover all such day-to-day execution roles. These roles may include individual consumers or specific roles at a customer buying from us.

Second, process design must clearly articulate the entire scope of every internal operations resource. Placing a microscope on some parts of each role is not enough. Process design intends to eliminate unnecessary work as much as it means to articulate the appropriate way to execute commonly discussed topics.

> *Consider the following questions:*
>
> *Do process designs cover all operations resources across the company that have ongoing responsibilities?*
>
> *Are all execution efforts performed by those operations resources covered in the process design, including their interactions with external stakeholders?*

Asking these overarching questions across each individual role for all functions gives a strong sense of the coverage of our process designs. At *Level 1: Chaos*, these are the first two questions we need to convert to 'yes' to begin our process design effort.

Element 2: Execution guidelines dictate day-to-day actions.

Simplistically, we build a process with sequential process steps. Each step should involve a set of instructions that can convert a given input to an output, whether a human or a machine performs it. A good process step with the appropriate execution guidelines delivers the same output every time.

No human wants to feel that they are being micro-managed, and the intent of process design is not to do so. So, process design is also a prioritization exercise.

The designer must carefully choose which execution elements are most important to choreograph to achieve the outcomes without burdening process performers with too much direction. This awareness comes from the process designer's expertise in using operations technology as a process enabler and their understanding of manipulating unbiased data and performing analysis.

A process step must also have quantitative thresholds to monitor performance against. Without measurability, framing specific instructions is meaningless as there will be no way for the process performer, supervisor, or analyst to know whether execution meets expectations. We will discuss how to set such measurements in the next chapter.

Putting these two together, our second element of process design is that every process step must involve execution guidelines that are specific instructions and measurements to enable the same outcome every time the stakeholder in the role performs that step.

Consider the following questions to ensure the effective use of the second element:

What is the specific, measurable outcome expected from the execution of each step?

What is the prioritized set of key actions that each role will have to take to complete the process effectively?

What does 'good' look like for each action?

If the process designer can articulate answers to these three questions for each process step, then the company's design effort is well on its way. Alternately, take any process step in your company and ask these three questions to see whether the answers are codified, communicated, and adopted to know whether your process design is effective.

Element 3: Prevent most vulnerabilities via hand-off guidelines.

If you watch team sports of any kind, when is a team most likely to make a mistake? Mistakes often happen when the ball passes from one player to the next. It is much more uncommon for a player to drop the ball or stumble over themselves. Corporate environments are not different. The probability of mistakes is relatively low if we look at one employee's work in a vacuum, particularly with skilled, high performers.

Most operational breakdowns happen when one employee or a role hands-off responsibility to another. In all my years of process design, the culprit of most process breakdowns is hand-offs. It is a simple concept that is common everywhere in nature. Where does a plumbing leak usually occur? The joints. So, it is critical to ask a few simple but highly effective questions to ensure that each hand-off in a process is pressure tested.

Consider the following questions:

How will the preceding role logistically send the work to the succeeding role?

How will the role in the succeeding step know that work is being passed on?

Do specific actions need to be taken to confirm the hand-off?

Once the hand-off is complete, when should the succeeding role start working?

Is there a specific technology involved to record or simplify the hand-off?

These questions are not exhaustive. Instead, they intend to get us to ask the hard questions on how interactions between two roles can fail and articulate those remediations into process design.

Element 4: Decision criteria must be pre-determined.

Knowing the future is difficult. So, articulating and making future decisions is also challenging. But that's the onus of effective process design. The enablement effort to design processes includes assessing available information, predicting the decisions that operations resources or external performers might have to make, and proactively articulating that choice in the process design.

As a practical example, imagine an operations resource who handles inbound calls from prospective customers interested in buying the company's offerings. This role might have to decide to pass the call to the right sales team based on the type of customer. For example, if the company had two sales teams where one sold to large customers and the other sold to small customers, how would the call-handling employee know what constitutes a potential large or small customer? The process design should articulate exactly what large and small means for the operations employee, how to find out whether the prospective customer is large or small, what the employee should do if they cannot arrive at an answer, etc.

Putting the onus of figuring all the potential choices of answers and making the decision on the operations resource is not a good process design. Instead, to ensure reproducibility across several employees with the same role, the process design must articulate decisions that each step or hand-off entails.

Consider the following questions:

What decisions might a performer in the role have to make to move forward to the next step in the process?

Does the performer have permission to complete the task, or will a review be required?

What are the possible choices that the performer might have to choose from?

How many different ways can each choice appear in a day-to-day environment?

What should the performer do if a decision is impossible to make with the criteria articulated in the process design?

By taking a comprehensive look at every decision point in the execution flow, we can ensure that operations roles have clarity on the decisions we want them to make and specific guidelines to help the role make consistent and accurate choices.

Element 5: Be intentional about information through data capture guidelines.

We have already touched on today's ubiquity of data. This part is true. There is more valuable data available today than ever before. But it is important to think about where this reputation for data comes from. The vast majority of valuable data in the world are captured and mined by a handful of organizations, and they mostly focus on a handful of very common use cases.

Google has massive amounts of data enabled by search behaviors. Meta has vast amounts of social behavioral data. Amazon has troves of online shopping behavioral data. Netflix knows a lot about people's entertainment preferences. Major banks know a lot about people's debt worthiness. These companies dominate their space and have millions of active users.

This is nothing like what a scaling company is doing to manage its internal activities. With fifty, a hundred, or five hundred employees and similar order of magnitude for customer volume, a growing company cannot use the same data principles that big consumer-facing companies use for a few everyday market use cases.

Data capture must be very intentional and premeditated to understand internal operations or customer behaviors at a growth-phase company. Looking at spurious employee or customer information when the sample size is small will not reveal valuable information with any level of confidence. Scaling companies often struggle to make decisions using data because they do not follow an intentional path to capturing data.

So, what does this mean in terms of process design? We can tailor process design to extract just enough of the right information without burdening operations resources or external performers.

First, do not capture information for the sake of capturing information because it is a drain on process performers. It is the job of the strategy &

operations executive and process designer to predict the necessary and optimal information needs.

Second, avoid capturing complex and compounded information as we often misconstrue them during data capture. That is, don't ask whether something is good or bad. Instead, ask for the underlying information that might help determine whether something is good or bad. The company's definition of good or bad may change over time. It also prevents process performers from trying to make another decision.

Third, avoid capturing information outside the flow of steps defined based on process design elements 1 through 4. If we try to do so, we will often incorrectly capture data. Again, it is human nature to take the path of least resistance.

Fourth, make every attempt to systemically capture information because manually captured information is often spurious because human beings often make conscious or subconscious mistakes.

> *Consider the following questions:*
>
> *What are the most important analytical answers that the company might need, and which roles would that information come from?*
>
> *What is the most basic form of information we can capture to arrive at those answers?*
>
> *Are process performers asked to capture information outside their journey laid out by the other process design elements?*
>
> *Can an automated data capture mechanism be built-in?*
>
> *For the unavoidable manual information capture needs, what are the specific guidelines that the performer has to know to ensure that the captured information is accurate every time?*

When we consider all five of these questions during process design, we can capture objective information without burdening process performers. This element is critical to internalize during process design because the company only has poor information to work with without getting this right.

Element 6: Governing approach is a necessity to micro-evolve our process design.

One of the typical process design mistakes discussed earlier is forgetting that processes are alive. As a result, process design can quickly become outdated shelf decoration if there isn't an overarching governance approach.

Process governance has two parts.

The **first** is to ensure that process design always leads execution behaviors. Changing execution hastily and reactively is symptomatic of a value engine on the immature end.

The **second** is that we must tactically improve process design on an ongoing basis to protect ourselves from becoming reactive. We must monitor processes using the key measurements we set through our execution guidelines, and actions must be taken when those measurements breach critical limits. We will discuss this further in later chapters.

Consider the following questions:

What quantifiable measurements imply a performer or groups of performers aren't executing the process as desired?

What is the quantifiable measurement that would trigger a reevaluation of the process itself?

What is the decision-making path to revising the process design, including people who should be involved and who would approve the change?

Developing a simple governance approach and cadence to look at how processes are performing through reporting and improving them through analysis is our micro-evolution path to keep processes alive. A strong governance approach guards against undisciplined and ad hoc changes to execution that can rapidly take a company into process chaos.

These six elements are a simple and uncomplicated foundation to build towards most process needs of a growing company. However, it takes discipline and an expert process designer to develop The Company Way processes that are cohesive and comprehensive and adopted by all operations resources and external performers.

As you might have noticed, we went through the discussion about process design and barely mentioned technology. That is intentional because technology always follows process.

We often misunderstand the purpose and approach to leverage technology to mature our company. A mature value engine effectively leverages technology to turbo-charge processes without circumventing them.

Companies invest in technology to boost productivity, improve safety, keep records, analyze data, and make recommendations with a functional flavor or a comprehensive company-wide view. Even a small company has at least ten to fifteen relevant pieces of technology, and that number goes up as the company scales.

But then why are so many technology implementations failing, day-to-day usage frustrating employees, and not creating the efficiencies they are supposed to create? Significant amounts of investment go into technologies at companies operating in a process vacuum, trying to solve process problems, only to realize a negative return on investment.

So, let's dive into the core principles we must embrace to leverage technology to mature our value engine.

Principle 5: Internalize that process design comes before technology.

Often companies try to use technology as a silver bullet to solve their process ills because it is easy to buy something and turn it on. However, efforts to circumvent investment in basic process design by implementing off-the-shelf technology are lazy and ineffective in improving our value engine's maturity level.

Technology is never intended to be a shortcut – rather an aid. Unfortunately, a shortcut mindset leads to ineffective use of technology and eventual dissatisfaction.

In 1987, Robert Solow, a Nobel Prize-winning economist, famously wrote, "you see the computer age everywhere but in the productivity statistics."

That was true then for the early computer age, which is true now for the digital technology age.

We can replace the word 'computer age' with technology in general and the Solow Paradox, as this conundrum has come to be known, aligns with the low labor productivity increase since 2007 that we covered at the start of our value engine discussions.

For example, many companies regularly replace their CRM system, and the most common reason is "the previous CRM didn't have the right features." That's like the age-old proverb 'a bad workman always blames his tools.' However, having worked with many technology solutions over the years, it is not the technology at fault; it is the company's design, implementation, and adoption that rendered the technology ineffective.

On average, most technology platforms have become powerful enough. So, it is often not about what the technology is capable of; it is about what we are capable of doing with the technology.

Infographic B.11 shows the only path to mature to Level 3 and beyond of our Value Engine Maturity Model. We start seeing repeatability and reproducibility in our processes, which technology use enables.

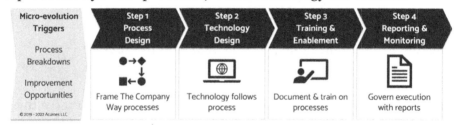

Infographic B.11 – Operations technology always follows process design

The **first** step is always to articulate the answer to operational needs, and that clarity must be evident in the process design. Always think of process design as the first step to understand the areas where technology can aid the execution of the six process design elements.

As a **second** step, the company can explore technologies that meet those needs. As a warning, it is essential not to be stubborn about initial or existing process designs and try to force technology to fit them. Processes are always malleable, and an effective process designer can triangulate between capabilities of technology choices and the process design to arrive at a design that uses the technology's best features.

Once the technology is designed, simply throwing it in front of users never works.

A strong teaching and enablement mindset is the **third** and necessary step to ensure that process designs aided by technology are adopted and used to their full potential. This is not a one-and-done exercise. Every time the process changes, a teaching and enablement mindset must follow.

A mature value engine continues to assess how well we execute processes, and technology supports processes and looks for opportunities to improve. This **fourth** step is the ongoing oversight effort of the day-to-day execution of our process governance approach. Of course, over time, changes will be necessary as we learn new information through the effective use of our data. But under any such circumstance, where a change is appropriate, it is critical to circle back to Step 1 of this cycle, which is process design.

As obvious as this cycle sounds, most environments fail to follow this discipline. Once this cycle breaks, even companies with a mature value engine can find themselves in process chaos. Breaking the value engine is quick and easy. Fixing it is near-impossible.

With this process-led mindset, let's examine how technologies can support processes in more detail.

Principle 6: Leverage operations technologies to augment process design.

If we take out buzzwords and complex categorizations, technologies fall into two groups.

The **first** group includes operations technologies that automate or simplify actions that humans perform regularly. We will focus on this because it is most relevant for the scope of our value engine to concentrate on taking our offerings to our customers through our processes.

The **second** group includes infrastructure technologies that operate behind the scenes to help a company function in the modern age. This includes computers, servers, cloud storage solutions, security solutions, etc. Although this group is extremely important, it falls outside our general conversation about the maturity of our value engine and its evolution over time.

So, let's talk about operations technologies in general and the value they can create. The value of operations technologies mirrors the six process design elements.

Manage roles and responsibilities.

Technologies allow us to separate the responsibilities of process performers in various roles from each other. Sometimes these separations are for convenience to ensure that every performer knows where their responsibilities begin and end. These separations also create necessary walls to manage information security or critical authority. These separations are required to execute day-to-day internal operations and interact with external stakeholders.

Time and time again, I have seen scenarios where employees or customers aren't able to do necessary tasks using the technology aids and have to use manual or email communication with other individuals, which breaks down their natural flow of actions. Other times, such frustrations lead to too much access to responsibilities for many individuals with few boundaries.

In such scenarios, the company is working in operational chaos because employees are likely performing tasks that do not align with their skills. In addition, external stakeholders using the company's technology might be confused and frustrated. Both of these situations are suboptimal.

There is no path for a company to leverage this technology capability unless the process design firmly lays out all the critical roles and responsibilities. Implementing a technology where roles and responsibilities do not reflect our process design is a boomerang back to process chaos.

Automate execution guidelines.

Technology solutions also help performers eliminate the need to memorize how to execute a task or information necessary to execute a task.

Most roles require a specific sequence of activities that may not follow our natural instincts. Executing those activities may require access to troves of information, including dozens of pieces of information about thousands of customers, multiple packages and underlying capabilities and enablers, their prices, etc.

Technology offers significant help for these otherwise herculean efforts. For example, technologies have workflow capabilities that can guide performers to the following predefined activity without having to remember anything at all. Technologies also have large databases where vast amounts of information can be stored and accessed at the click of a button.

What if the data is confusing and the performer cannot find the correct information? These are real everyday challenges that can look like the technology's fault.

But it is not.

The workflow paths in technologies are always flexible and configurable, and a company can choose what that path ought to be. Technology databases always come empty, and we fill them with the company's information based on historical execution. Getting these technology design elements right involves first getting execution guidelines of the process design right and driving adoption of those guidelines. Everything included in the technology for the execution comes from the process design and nowhere else.

Optimize hand-offs.

Imagine trying to complete an online application form of any kind, and when you hit the 'submit' button, you get an error code. What exactly is happening here? The technology design ensures that hand-off between you and the next person in that application process is effective. The form is likely telling you that you are not handing off enough of the correct information to the next step.

Technology can be a spectacular aid in ensuring that hand-offs are effective.

Most operations technologies can direct work to the correct next person in line. Most can do basic checks on whether the performer completed the appropriate amount and quality of work before passing to the next step.

However, this also means what 'good' looks like for each step is clearly articulated and coded into the technology ahead of time.

These are the same details articulated through the third element, hand-off guidelines, of process design. When the process design does not involve such clarity about hand-off criteria, any use of technology to aid hand-off is incapacitated. This might cause process performers to think that the technology is at fault. Far from it.

Automate or verify decisions.

As we discussed under the fourth process design element, decision criteria, every operations resource makes several decisions as they execute their day-to-day responsibilities.

The inbound call handler we introduced earlier can be aided by technology to easily discern between large prospective customers and small prospective customers based on criteria coded into a technology solution. But that also implies that the decision criteria are first clearly defined via our process design.

In this same illustrative example, imagine a situation where a supervisor decided that the criteria determining between large and small prospective customers had to change. Suppose they directly coded that change into the technology. How would that affect the call handler? How would that affect the sales team that is now likely handling a different type of prospective customers without appropriate changes in their execution guidelines or receiving training around it?

As senseless as this might sound, such knee-jerk actions are more common than you think. Technology has the power to aid decisions during execution. However, it can cause chaos unless all design elements are first passed through the process design to ensure that the overall process design and execution are cohesive.

Automate data capture and use.

When we send over that online form mentioned above, imagine that an operations resource will write down when the form was submitted so that the company can track how long it takes to process applications. A few decades ago, that was how we did it. Today we don't even think about it. That timestamp can be automatically captured in a data table the moment your form is submitted.

There are so many similar and more powerful data-related capabilities that technologies bring that require careful design and codification. For example, extending our form submission scenario further, what if the form submission had to involve support documentation and was incomplete during the first submission, and the responsibility reverts back? Should the submission timestamp get overwritten when the form is resubmitted, or should the original timestamp be maintained? The company has to make many such unique choices as part of process design for effective data capture using technology.

You can see how quickly this can get complicated. Getting it right is nearly impossible if we make these choices in a vacuum. Process design is the only path to effectively decide what, when, how, and by who information should be captured using technology.

Enable process governance.

Information gathering and charting tools are commonplace, and many are even free these days. Reporting technology solutions allow us to slice and dice information easily and deliver visual reports to senior executives, supervisors, and employees almost without effort.

But how effective are these information packets if we have not chosen the right quantifiable measurements for various execution roles? How will all the recipients of these information packets know how to act if the measurements do not highlight breakdowns in execution?

Technology solutions indeed help us. But far too often, the ease with which we can create pretty charts distract teams from focusing on whether the chart is actually useful. Instead, we must design every element to govern execution first, and then it can be built into the technology solution.

If the process-first message throughout these six technology capabilities sounded repetitive, it is on purpose. I cannot stress the importance of alignment between the six process design elements and technology capabilities and the necessity of sequencing technology after process.

Effective process design is a prerequisite to leveraging technology to support execution.

In addition to process alignment, each operations technology is only effective if it fits our broader ecosystem.

Principle 7: Ensure that operations technologies plug into our ecosystem.

Whichever operations technology we procure, it was developed by the vendor to be sold at scale. Hopefully, we are buying from vendors who have productized effectively using the principles we laid out in Chapter B.1. Best-in-class vendors provide a range of configuration options to tailor various capabilities to fit our execution needs. These configuration options can add up to millions of combinations of how each technology could be leveraged.

In our process ecosystem, these technologies must dovetail with other technologies, each serving a different purpose. Now we have multiple technologies, each with millions of configuration options. At this stage, buying a technology off-the-shelf and plugging it into our process environment must sound like a suboptimal idea.

It is.

Think about a single technology purchase to improve our process maturity as looking for one piece of a large jigsaw puzzle. This situation calls for us to remember our String of Pearls philosophy. Technology choices and design must focus on how it fits our ecosystem as much as the technology's standalone capabilities.

From an operational perspective, a technology can serve only three general purposes.

The **first** is to serve as a core technology. A few technologies solve major and broad-based problems across multiple functions. Examples include Customer Relationship Management (CRM) platforms and financial reporting systems.

The **second** is to be a niche technology in our ecosystem. The vast majority of technologies fall in this second category, where they solve very narrowly defined problems. Companies use dozens of such peripheral niche solutions. Examples may include third-party data sources, customer communication solutions, payment processing solutions, etc. To be effective, they always have to link to a core technology and potentially other niche technologies.

The **third** is a data visualization platform. Most companies also use a central database that integrates information from all core and niche technologies and is considered a single data source. Such platforms offer strong options to manipulate and visualize data. Well-run companies choose one such platform.

Beyond process-first, the most critical aspect to remember during technology selection and design is that all these technologies must link together seamlessly. Similar to our process design hand-off principle, technologies also break down most often when they link with other technologies.

Consider the following questions:

What does the company's operational technology landscape look like?

What are the overlapping capabilities between technologies that we have already chosen or are considering choosing?

How effectively will each technology solution link with other technology solutions?

Answering these three questions effectively and articulating the answers provides our company an operations technology landscape necessary to support our process design and improve our value engine maturity. If technology solutions aid effective processes in a well-designed ecosystem, we can significantly improve the repeatability and reproducibility of process execution.

Such a mature environment is a system where all operations resources work efficiently and effectively as individuals, with other employees, and with external stakeholders to deliver customer value through our productized offerings. Maturing towards using technology to execute effective processes implies that the company is arriving at *Level 3: Organized* and likely well on its way to *Level 4: Productized,* where data is effectively used.

B.3
MICRO-EVOLVE USING OBJECTIVE DATA, ANALYSIS, AND REPORTING.

THE purpose of our value engine is to create and deliver value for our customers. We started this value creation effort with our productized offering. Then we discussed our processes and enablement technology that dictates every operations resources' activity to deliver our offering to our customers. The third part of our value engine is a path of understanding how well we're doing. How do we know what we could do better on an ongoing basis?

The answer is the use of objective data.

Over the past couple of decades, big data and data science have become trendy concepts, and they have very effectively turbocharged our consumer-centric economy. However, if we dig a little deeper, the vast majority of this value from data is created by a handful of very large companies that dominate search, social, and e-commerce sectors.

Data is supremely powerful, and its application is always all around us. But mistakes are often made on purpose or due to a lack of awareness. So, it is worth dedicating a chapter for this conversation on how senior executives, supervisors, and employees might look at data objectively as a path to improve our analytical maturity.

Understanding operational information objectively is the only path to improve execution. An individual contributor must understand how the company uses its information and impacts its day-to-day efforts. The strategy & operations executive and analytical resources are accountable for identifying actionable opportunities to improve the company's productized offering and operational execution using objective information. Supervisors and senior executives are responsible for ensuring that their teams are executing effectively and can make objective decisions based on opportunities presented by analytical resources.

In a world where we throw words such as big data, analysis, data science, insights, artificial intelligence, and machine learning around very casually, we must dig a bit deeper to ensure that every employee has an objective understanding of the information they are using.

Growth-phase companies do not have the luxury of extensive historical reference points. Additionally, growth-phase companies must make uniquely new decisions far more often than large companies with troves of historical information. As a result, misunderstanding even their limited available data will have far-reaching consequences.

There are several key data principles that every employee must understand and embrace to ensure we use data objectively.

Principle 1: Data is always a byproduct of process due to Process-Data Symbiosis.

Despite being inundated with data and our efforts to use it, the data source is rarely explored. I internalized the simple idea that data is always a byproduct by solving data-related problems for almost two decades.

> **Things to Remember: Process-Data Symbiosis**
>
> **Data is the qualitative or quantitative recorded reflection of behaviors in a process, whether captured manually or automatically. I call this unbreakable relationship Process-Data Symbiosis.**

In other words, data is always a reflection of a process.

I asserted in the last chapter that there is no data without process. Now, let me explain.

B.3 MICRO-EVOLVE USING OBJECTIVE DATA, ANALYSIS, AND REPORTING

We usually see data in tabular formats. It is stored, edited, and manipulated to create charts and make decisions. But how does a data table come to exist?

If we recall our inbound call handler who directs leads to the two sales teams, one of the tasks that this employee is likely to execute is to log the information provided by the inbound caller. For example, maybe this employee asks a few questions about the caller's company, role, and the reason for their call. Each piece of information collected becomes columns in a database in our operations technology.

On one extreme, one employee could be highly talented, well-versed in our offerings, understand the company's market well, and know exactly the right way to ask follow-up questions to understand the caller. That is, the employee executes the process admirably. On the other extreme, another employee executing the same role could be undertrained and may not be a top performer and only spends a few seconds on the call before passing the caller to the next stage in the process. Here the employee is executing the process poorly.

How different will be the quality of information captured by the two employees across several calls?

Data is likely a closer reflection of reality when the first employee answered calls. For the second employee's calls, the data only reflects that employee's poor performance, while the customer information is likely to be incorrect or incomplete.

Should an analyst use all this data or only part of it? Either way, we are working with subpar data due to suboptimal process execution. This is our data conundrum.

Data is non-existent without some action, including thoughts and decisions that triggered its creation. That action is always part of a process, and that process may involve employees, both employees and external stakeholders, or only external stakeholders.

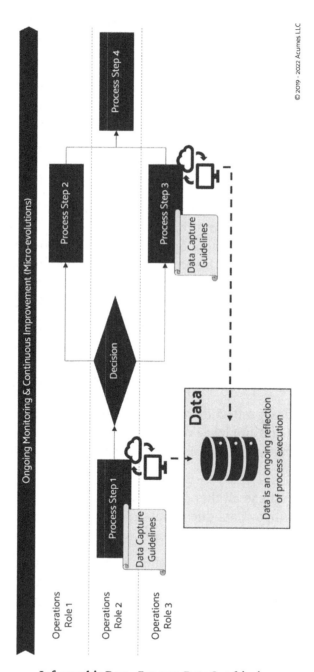

Infographic B.12 – Process-Data Symbiosis

Infographic B.12 illustrates an image of how best to think about data and its creation building up from our processes. We always collect data as a byproduct of the efforts within a process. In this illustration, two of the process steps trigger the creation of new data or change of existing data. It is a symbiotic relationship where well-designed and executed processes capture useful data and poor ones capture tarnished and misleading data.

In our example of the two call handlers, the data logged by the high-performing employee tells a story about the customers who call. The data logged by the low-performing employee tells a story about the low performance of the employee. If we just look at the data without understanding how it is being created and whether the process is being executed well, it is impossible to know which story the data is telling.

So, every exploration into understanding data begins with understanding the design and execution of the process that created it. Usage of data is rarely perfect because data itself is never perfect. It always has flaws and biases. Anyone using data to make conclusions or consuming conclusions made by others must understand the potential flaws and biases inherent in the data and how effectively it has been accounted for.

Principle 2: Data often has flaws due to process governance failures and process breakages.

There are two common types of data flaws. Both create the illusion that there is a meaningful message to be drawn from the data, but the causes of the patterns in the data are undesirable aberrations in the process itself. Therefore, every analyst should evaluate the data for various manifestations of both flaws before considering the information ready to be analyzed.

Data flaws due to process governance failures.

Imagine a growth-phase company with well-articulated and adopted process designs and process performers executing their tasks repeatably and reproducibly. Let's also assume that the data capture mechanisms gather all the correct information. In this ideal scenario, the data is likely sliced and diced by the strategy & operations executive and analytical enablement resources to uncover underlying messages to make decisions that micro-evolve any number of activities.

In a perfect scenario, where the resources perfectly understand how we expect the data to be captured and these expectations are met, all is well, and messages make sense.

However, what if the underlying messages result from disruptions in the process itself? Unfortunately, messages drawn from data are far more often a reflection of process disruptions than real trends or insights.

The sixth process design element, governance approach, which enables disciplined improvement of processes and subsequent use of technology, is the hardest to live by. I have seen large and small companies consistently fail to embrace this mindset because it requires discipline in perpetuity. Executing a governance approach is a risk management effort. It's not about all the situations it is effectively managed; it is about the situations when the governance approach didn't hold up.

In practice, failures in process governance approach may mean decisions about changes in execution are made through quick in-person conversations or via email communications without formality. If these decisions and changes do not filter into The Company Way, no one trains the employees on the changes. Governance has failed.

Moving fast is fine, but breaking discipline is not.

If we ask employees to make a change and execute without following the process design principles, the company is distorting its data. Essentially, the data before the change cannot be compared to the data after the change.

Let's use a simple day-to-day example.

Smartwatches have become very popular. In addition to many other functions, they allow users to keep track of their exercise habits. We can use most of them to track exercises manually or automatically.

Imagine that a close friend who cared about our health outcomes gave us a smartwatch as a gift and offered to be our accountability coach. We agree with the friend that we will use the smartwatch, and the friend can see how well we are tracking via the data on the smart watch's online data portal that both parties can access without even speaking to each other.

At the beginning of the first month, we agreed that we would manually trigger the functionality to track the exercise each time we began exercising. This is our process. Throughout the month, our friend is keeping tabs on the portal. We don't speak to each other because it is unnecessary. All the data is right on the portal. This is our governance.

At the end of the first month, we realized that we sometimes forgot to trigger the watch on certain exercise days manually. So, we decided to turn on the automated exercise logging function at the end of that month. Another month goes by, and we receive a congratulatory note from the friend commending us on the significant improvement in exercise habits during month two. This is akin to receiving a reward in a work environment.

The question is – did we actually deserve this reward?

The truth is that the data is most likely lying to our friend. We forgot to log some exercises during the first month, and during the second month, the watch logged all our exercises. The friend, the analyst in this example, does not know this and thinks that our habits have improved. We broke the governance pact by changing the settings on the watch without telling the friend.

Such occurrences are very common due to a lack of value engine maturity. Most organizations' data will likely contain these process governance breakdowns that could be mistaken for real insights. The only path to using this data is for an analyst to proactively do detective work and understand where governance failures might have happened. Once someone identifies these failures, an analyst could use the data within a given window between governance failures where the data is at least comparable.

Data flaws due to process breakages.

Process breakages are essentially poorly designed processes causing poor execution. When we capture data as part of poor execution, the data is poor. Process breakages pollute data with incorrect entries and offer little obvious clues as to which entries are wrong.

Let us revisit our smartwatch example to shed a practical light on this common scenario. Let's assume that our friend also planned to track the number of steps we walked each day and set a target of 10,000 steps.

In this situation, let's say that we have two watches – the smartwatch and a luxury Swiss watch that we have owned before but never came up in conversation. In our mind, we agreed to wear the smartwatch every day, but subconsciously, we intend to wear the luxury watch on the days that we have an important meeting.

How much will the friend learn by tracking our steps in an information vacuum without knowing about the luxury Swiss watch?

In this scenario, the data does not reflect the designed process, which involves wearing the smartwatch every day to track steps consistently. We could think of this as a poor process design by our friend who didn't ask all the right questions to create a process and predict the potential process breakage by the arbitrary addition of the luxury watch into the mix on meeting days.

This is a prevalent data flaw, and an analyst would have to deeply understand the process and its execution to know whether the data is sensible. Unfortunately, there are no easy fixes after the fact in such circumstances. Attempting to go back and 'fix' the entries will most likely create other distortions in the data, causing a different set of problems. Furthermore, an assumption of only using available data can backfire. What if our walking habits on days when we wear the luxury Swiss watch are significantly poorer because those are busy meeting days?

Both types of data flaws are likely hiding in most data sets. Therefore, analysts and decision-makers must be aware of these pitfalls and leverage data accordingly.

An analyst should only attempt to learn about and make recommendations with data after validating the process and execution underlying the data. Senior executives, supervisors, and employees who use data-driven decisions should have the wherewithal to pressure-test recommendations and ensure they aren't based on flawed data.

Principle 3: Data is always likely to have a capture bias or observer bias.

Unlike data flaws, which are potholes in the data itself, biases are natural human tendencies that manifest or affect the use of data. They skew the execution of processes and replicate such trends in the data or drive observers of data, such as analysts, to look at the available data in a skewed manner. Human bias around capture and use of data is akin to a poorly calibrated measuring equipment.

Cognitive biases form an entire branch of economic study, and I recommend that you explore this as a follow-on effort. In the scope of our discussion around the components that drive a mature value engine, we can broadly classify sources of biases into two themes that impact data – Biases in data capture and biases in observer mindset. Every data user in the company must understand these biases.

Biases in data capture.

We demonstrate natural biases that create a personal slant to everything we do. Then, we bring that same bias to our work. So, every performer is likely to execute the processes they are responsible for with that slant, and the resulting skew is captured in the data.

There are many types of biases that impact the effectiveness of data capture and how an observer, who could be anyone that uses data to make decisions, might use existing data.

Let us look at two examples of biases and how they might impact how operations resources capture data. Any operations resource executing a process is likely to fall prey to these.

One bias that could skew data is framing bias.

Framing bias is evident when a person uses a positioning statement that is overtly positive or negative to get a corresponding positive or negative response. Framing bias skews information received and captured in a more positive or negative direction because of the way that the person asking the question phrased the question.

Let's imagine an employee developing a new capability is asked to get customer perspectives before senior executives decide whether to continue funding the project. First, the employee would ask customers for their perspectives. For example, the employee could ask potential customers – "Would you buy our upcoming capability with three benefits that the current offering doesn't have at the same price?"

They framed this question too positively to get a positive answer, particularly if the employee failed to mention that the new offering would no longer include two existing benefits, which was a necessary adjustment to keep the price unchanged. If the same question was asked of many customers, it results in a very skewed perspective about the prospect of the new capability.

A second bias that could skew data is anchoring bias.

Anchoring bias most often applies when a person is looking for an answer to a question, and they phrase the question in a manner that nudges the responder to choose a specific answer much more likely than other potential answers.

Let's say that a customer decides to leave our company and choose a competitor and we want to understand why. An unbiased question could be, "Could you tell us the top three reasons you decided to leave us?" This question would likely lead the customer to share their own perspective. But what if the question was phrased as, "Would you say that you decided to move to our competitor because they offered you a lower price?"

Irrespective of the real reasons, the customer is more likely to provide a cancellation reason involving pricing.

These skews don't make the data wrong, technically speaking. However, the messages that analysts and decision-makers can take away from such data can be very misleading, especially if they don't understand the impact of biases and how they might have skewed the data during capture.

Biases in observer mindset.

Even if we assume that the data captured has no biases, biases can creep in as the data is being analyzed or used for decision-making. These biases occur due to personal or professional incentives and life or career experiences that have molded our general perspective about the world.

Strong analysts must take a stand on what the data might say, also known as developing hypotheses, and then assess whether the data agrees or disagrees with the hypotheses. Senior Executives have to advise the analytical team on the information they want to see before making decisions. Confirmation bias, self-serving bias, herd mentality, and narrative fallacy are all cognitive skews that can lead us astray unless all the decision-makers understand that these tendencies are always around us.

Consider the following questions to self-assess our level of objectivity when creating hypotheses:

Do I have a preconceived notion about what the decision or answer ought to be? This assesses confirmation bias.

Do I have a vested interest in proving a point and thus missing the real insight? This assesses self-serving bias.

Am I tempted to look for messages that align with the thinking of the whole group? This assesses herd mentality.

Am I tempted to create a positive storyline and search for that story in the data? This assesses narrative fallacy.

These biases are not exhaustive. They are also not anyone's fault. We all fall for it. They are natural human tendencies. However, countering them is a practiced skill and requires self-awareness. Senior executives and analysts operating in critical roles without internalizing these concepts are at risk of misleading the company. Understanding these concepts and using them in decision-making matures our value engine.

These three data principles of Process-Data Symbiosis, existence of flaws in data, and biases in data are as prevalent as the common cold but underestimating them causes existential threats to a business as bad as cancer.

Like an iceberg, the data capture principles are the significantly larger mass hidden underwater. But the groundwork is paramount. Leveraging value from the data is the smaller visible mount of the iceberg. But it has a massive impact.

A growth-phase company's ability to continue to improve its management approach and value engine depends on the effective usage of data. We always use data in one of two ways – analysis or reporting. Unfortunately, these are two very different and powerful parts that are often confused with each other and poorly leveraged. Both analysis and reporting involve graphs and numbers but serve very different purposes.

Some organizations even use catchphrases such as 'analysis paralysis,' which is propaganda against the value that could be created by objective use of data. It is not analysis that causes paralysis. It is ignorance of what constitutes quality analysis or effective reporting that creates this misconception.

Both components are the sword and shield of senior executives, supervisors, and employees on a day-to-day basis to manage and improve execution. However, analysis and reporting serve entirely different purposes. Not internalizing the difference between analysis and reporting is a massive drain on customer value, executive and supervisor effectiveness, and employee execution.

Principle 4: Analysis enables forward-looking problem-solving.

Analyses drive forward-looking improvements from our current state. It is our attacking sword. Let's start with a definition of analysis.

> **Things to Remember: Analysis**
>
> **Analysis is a time-bound objective effort to improve a given situation using data. Analyses always start with a forward-looking objective to solve a problem, find a path to improve outcomes, or quantitatively answer questions that enable decision-making.**

Once an analysis starts with the statement of the problem, the performer identifies unbiased hypotheses, assesses whether hypotheses hold true based on the available data, and recommends tangible actions to improve the current situation to achieve the objective. Such tangible and actionable recommendations are called insights.

Many corporate environments misuse the word insight, which is a considerable loss. Visually capturing charts or complex data presentations do not constitute insights.

> **Things to Remember: Insights**
>
> **An analysis must result in answers that articulate the path forward to achieve the objective that triggered the analysis, and this answer is an insight. An insight is a cohesive and actionable answer and recommendation directly drawn from the data used in the analysis. Without insights, data jugglery is not analysis.**

A good litmus test for quality analyses is to look for a sound problem statement, hypotheses to solve the problem statement comprehensively, an objective and systematic path to test those hypotheses, and finally arrive at one or more insights that chart the path forward. If any of these four elements are missing, it is likely not a quality analysis.

Imagine driving down the road, and your car starts making an odd noise. You know it's not a good sign, but you can't see any obvious signs of problems. If you are a car owner like me, you will take the car to an expert mechanic.

The mechanic is our analyst, who does a hypothesis-based assessment of what could be causing the noise based on their experience and the tests they perform. A good mechanic eliminates possibilities and provides a precise recommendation about what is wrong with the car and how to fix it. This recommendation is the insight.

Would we pay a mechanic to give us a convoluted set of tests and a list of the checks done without a clear, plausible recommendation of what we should do?

Without insights, there is no analysis.

Now let's contrast analysis with reporting.

Principle 5: Reporting predicts breakage of the expected current state.

Let's start with framing what we are trying to avoid with reporting.

I worked closely with a conversation data technology company as a turn-around leader. The company believed their biggest challenge was lead generation and that it caused the growth curve to flatten. The commercial team had a widely accepted marketing and sales dashboard built in Tableau, a data visualization platform. Whenever I tried to get some data, they referred me back to this dashboard because everyone had access to it, and they received it via email every day. It was clear that a lot of work had gone into building this dashboard, which was colorful, and it was a page full of numbers.

So, I asked a few people, "what do you usually do with this dashboard?"

Most would say, "we look at it."

I followed up with, "then what happens?" Not a single person had a good answer. They were basing their decisions on data they didn't understand or not making decisions at all.

This team's misinterpretation of what good reporting looks like is a perfect example of the danger of a lack of self-awareness about maturity that we discussed at the beginning of Part B: Value Engine. The value engine of this team was immature, and their interpretation that lead generation was the problem was incorrect, and I had to institute many of the components in this book at the company.

> **Things to Remember: Reporting**
>
> **Reporting is an ongoing effort to use objective data to maintain the status quo of a given situation and prevent adverse outcomes. Reporting continuously monitors a big or small process using previously identified and articulated metrics and compares its current measurement against a predefined threshold that signifies a breakage in the process.**

The key takeaway is that reporting does not improve the expected current state; it intends to protect against downside risk. It is truly a defensive shield, not an attacking sword.

The processes monitored by reporting can be as large as a function or as narrow as a portion of a single employee's responsibilities. Either way, to protect against downside risk, reporting must have three key elements. It involves a predefined and unchanging quantifiable metric, a threshold that qualifies what 'good' looks like for that metric, and a remediation path for threshold breaches. Without any one of these elements, reporting is not effective.

The most beautiful part about reporting is that the organization dedicates little time or effort to it once we set it up. Unfortunately, this is an aspect where most organizations fail. Spending a significant amount of time and resources to review a poor collage of data that does not have firmly defined metrics and thresholds is a major inhibitor to managing execution effectively.

Another critically important outcome of reporting is predictability.

What is the use of looking at information if it is too late to do something about it?

A practical example of a well-functioning report is a car's oil change light. The process is the car's entire systemic operation as it is designed to perform. As the owner and driver of the car, we are the senior executive or supervisor. The car's electronics are constantly 'reporting' on the volume of oil, which is the metric. It does so in the background, comparing the oil levels to a predefined threshold set by the manufacturer. A driver never has to think about it until the oil change light comes on, which is the trigger that asks for intervention. The manufacturer has designed the car to report on oil performance.

Many companies do not dedicate enough time and discipline to identify and use predictive measurements for their operations and eventually scratch their head when they break down without warning.

If you are somewhat familiar with cars, you also know that cars have an oil dipstick. Imagine a world where your car didn't have that automated oil change light. You will have to open the car's hood often, pull out the oil dipstick and see how much oil is on it. In reality, the dipsticks have a marker that shows how much oil should be visible on the stick to validate that the car has enough oil. What if this marker didn't exist?

Unfortunately, many companies operate in the dipstick scenario where even the dipstick does not even have a marker that signifies how much oil there should be.

Without a firm understanding of breakdown levels, a team that follows a path of committing significant time and effort to look at trivial and repetitive information is essentially paralyzed and will not grow sustainably.

Principle 6: Effective data ecosystem dovetails analysis and reporting.

Infographic B.13 shows my framework for a company's data ecosystem. It visually illustrates the core application difference between analysis and reporting. The center of this ecosystem must look familiar to you from our earlier discussion about Process-Data Symbiosis. It creates the necessary data we can leverage for either analysis or reporting.

The key to the data ecosystem is the diverging, non-overlapping, yet dovetailing relationship between analysis and reporting. To reiterate their purpose, analysis allows the company to assess problems and develop forward-looking solutions, irrespective of the scale or type of the problems. By contrast, reporting monitors for execution risks by comparing performance measurements against preset thresholds to trigger previously defined remediations at the breach of those thresholds.

> **Things to Remember: Analysis vs. Reporting**
>
> Analysis is our forward-looking problem-solving sword. Reporting is our risk management shield to protect against breakdowns.

Well performed analyses allow companies to identify and solve strategic and operations problems related to any part of the management approach and value engine. Insights from analyses may drive micro-evolutions

B.3 MICRO-EVOLVE USING OBJECTIVE DATA, ANALYSIS, AND REPORTING

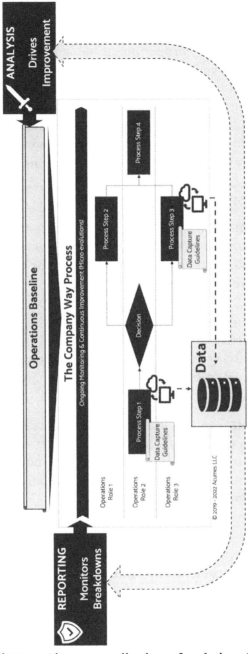

Infographic B.13 – Divergent applications of analysis and reporting

of small parts of our operations baseline or support our company-wide macro-evolutions that we will start discussing in the next chapter.

Analyses also identify the proper quantifiable predictive measurements to monitor processes and the appropriate thresholds for those predictive metrics where those processes are at risk. These are the same metrics and thresholds that we would use to set up its reporting. In other words, analysis leads to identifying predictive metrics and optimal thresholds, which are two of the three elements of effective reporting we listed earlier. Let's give these predictive metrics a name – **Leading Indicators**.

> **Things to Remember: Leading Indicators**
>
> **Leading indicators are performance measurements that offer us predictability on the likely outcome of the overall process, which allows us to take corrective actions before poor outcomes manifest at the overall process level.**

Conversely, ongoing reporting maintains a pulse on execution effectiveness using the metrics and thresholds identified through analysis and triggers predefined corrective actions when thresholds are breached. Such breakdowns triggered by reporting can reveal unanticipated problems, which leads to further analysis.

These specific purposes and intertwined relationship between analysis and reporting are critical for companies to internalize and leverage to continuously improve execution to drive sustainable growth. Failure to do so is akin to fighting with both arms tied behind the back in our fast-moving information age.

Let me share a personal experience that companies must try to avoid.

I worked closely with a highly talented data infrastructure and data tools expert who was quite a magician at linking operations technology and databases to make data available for hypothesis-based analysis and predictive reporting. However, this gentleman was not an analyst. The company mistook all the available information and charting tools to think they had achieved data-driven maturity, especially in the analysis and reporting realm.

Many senior executives and supervisors were not aware of core concepts around analysis and reporting. Senior executives would spend hours in meetings looking at charts and data presented by our data magician and going through endless discussions about what the data might mean. But the group seldom recognized impending failures in execution or made vital decisions based on forward-looking analysis. Eventually, the company lost the data magician to voluntary attrition because he felt that his hard work wasn't producing any actual results.

So, yes – paralysis can happen; but it is caused by mistaking data overload with high-quality analysis and predictive reporting and their intertwined relationship.

Principle 7: Define effective reporting metrics, targets, and limits via analysis.

Reporting allows us to monitor our company processes once we identify the appropriate leading indicators. The source of the optimal set of leading indicators is hypothesis-driven analysis as part of process design. However, it is always a critical part of a strategic planning effort to reassess and validate them. So, we will discuss my approach to revisit all leading indicators simultaneously under Part D: Strategic Planning.

To internalize what 'good' looks like for leading indicators, we must first internalize what is not a leading indicator – a **Lagging Indicator**. The names intend to be descriptive. Lagging indicators measure outcomes and are always significantly easier to identify and measure. But they offer no predictability of the outcomes. In a corporate setting, lagging indicators are often permutations of revenue and expense outcomes, which are important, but only as outcomes.

> **Things to Remember: Lagging Indicators**
>
> **Lagging indicators are non-predictive measurements of outcomes, and their measurements can be predicted by carefully chosen leading indicators.**

We will tackle the appropriate usage of lagging indicators during our strategic planning discussion. Now, let's align on a mature approach to leverage our objective data to track leading indicators via reporting.

Infographic B.14 demonstrates the simple lessons I learned as a Six Sigma Black Belt in my early career. There is nothing complex or new about it. Of course, many of you already know this. But over the last two decades, I have been surprised that many companies and teams do not internalize or apply these simple concepts to use reporting effectively.

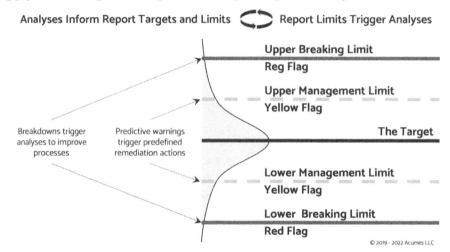

Infographic B.14 – Setting reporting targets & limits

Regardless of the situation, perfectly designed and executed processes deliver outcomes randomly around a center point – this is a law of nature. Such an even distribution around a center point is called a normal distribution. Although no processes are perfect, this is an acceptable simplifying assumption. For all practical purposes, we can assume that processes deliver outcomes somewhat randomly around a center point, even if it's not a perfectly normal distribution.

If a well-designed process is also well-executed, the outcomes stay very close to the center and do so consistently. If they are poorly executed, the outcomes spread far from the center. In Infographic B.14, this distribution of measurements of a leading indicator for a process is centered around the dark blue line in the middle. In other words, all measurements of the leading indicator fall under this distribution. Most of the measurements are close to the center; fewer are spread farther away. This simple idea that outcomes are spread around a center point helps us effectively design reporting for our processes using leading indicators.

If we are trying to hit the bullseye on a dartboard, would we shoot straight for the bullseye? Anyone who has aimed at something knows that we all have a natural skew, while gravity and other conditions take a toll on our intended actions. So, we would never go for the bullseye. Instead, we would aim for something slightly above the bullseye with an adjustment for any natural skew that we may be aware of.

Unfortunately, companies with immature value engine make a very fundamental mistake – they dedicate execution focus on not breaching the extreme breaking points and put the onus on employees to figure out how to stay within those limits. Inevitably, this results in poor outcomes.

There are three core elements to effectively tracking a leading indicator via reporting. We must identify and set them through analysis.

The most important part of a distribution of outcomes is the center point. Think about this center point as the most likely outcome if we perform the process an infinite number of times. This should be the realistic expected goal we must set for the process as measured by the leading indicator. Let's formally call this **The Target**.

> **Things to Remember: The Target**
>
> **The target is the median measurement of the leading indicator over time. Critically, this is the quantifiable outcome of the process that should be expected over time across all resources performing the same process.**

Suppose operations resources perform the process. In that case, the target must be achievable for all top – and mid-tier performers, not just the top performers, with the expectation that low performers improve. If the process involves customer actions, then this must be the expected median outcome across all customers who have adopted our processes as we strive to strengthen adoption among remaining customers. During the strategic planning process, the targets for key leading indicators must be set to this median measurement. It is the realistic anticipated output of the process or part of it.

Similarly, all operations resources must be measured against the target for operational processes they are responsible for. We must set the 100% achievement of incentive compensation against this achievable target. Top performers will likely achieve significantly higher output beyond the target and, thus, incentive compensation beyond the 100% mark.

The most important aspect of the target is that we always derive this figure from our analysis. The target is only known to us because of effective process design and measurement using objective historical data. The target is our expected outcome from the execution of the process in perpetuity, not each iteration of execution.

Why is this important? We want to avoid the temptation to use non-analytically sourced information as our target.

For example, if one of our processes is solving customer complaints, a leading indicator of customer satisfaction could be the number of hours to close complaints. However, let's also imagine that we captured customer sentiments and learned that customers are likely to be very unhappy if it takes more than 12 hours to close a complaint. What should we communicate as the desired complaint closing window with our customer service team?

Shockingly, I have seen many situations where such a customer service team would be told "we have to close all complaints in less than 12 hours." Unfortunately, most complaints will likely be closed on either side of the 12-hour mark and a significant number over 12 hours.

In this situation, we must design a process that allows us to close customer complaints at a much lower expected timeline, say 8 hours. If we created such a process where the outcomes fall on something close to a normal distribution with the vast majority of complaint closures around the 8-hour mark, we could confidently set our target as 8 hours. In this scenario, we will seldom breach the 12-hour limit.

The measurement that leads to dire consequences is not our target. Target is the expectation we set for our leading indicator, such that our process can meet all stakeholder expectations almost every single time.

In the scenario above, the 12-hour mark implies that our process to close customer complaints has failed. Let's call this the **Breaking Limit**.

> **Things to Remember: Breaking Limit**
>
> Breaking limit is the absolute edge of performance where the process or part of the process doesn't meet the minimum requirements of stakeholders, who can be internal employees performing other processes or external stakeholders.

If our performance consistently crosses this point, the company has waited too long for normal course corrections to work. So, companies should never manage ongoing operations using the breaking limit either.

Breaching this limit implies that the process has broken down, particularly if it happens several times. Infographic B.14 illustrates our breaking limits with two bold lines on both extremes. Triggering this red flag for our leading indicator is a perfect opportunity to analyze the root causes of the breaches and revisit our process design.

For an effectively designed and executed process, the breaking limit is the point that breaks the hand-off guidelines for the process or process step. So, breaking limit implies a comprehensive assessment of what went wrong.

But a process can be functional and effective while the execution lags. So, how do we manage a process beyond designing the process and setting a target? We should base day-to-day operational oversight on a more acceptable limit where corrective actions can be taken, which is the **Management Limit**.

> **Things to Remember: Management Limit**
>
> The management limit is the oversight trigger. Senior executives and supervisors proactively devise and monitor this threshold to ensure that operations resources are performing to expectations. Management limits offer a yellow flag that triggers corrective actions or coaching and training of employees to deliver to the target.

Processes will naturally deviate from the target. Performance between employees also varies. Senior executives and supervisors need an acceptable range around the target that operations resources must stay within under normal operations.

Focus on setting and using management limits is the mature path to overseeing our organization proactively. Effective use of the management limit has far-reaching implications.

First, all operational reporting activities revolve around these management limits of leading indicators, without which reports are ineffective. **Second**, ongoing individual training and coaching are triggered when performance breaches the management limits. **Third**, we can use management limits to set performance management expectations and compare the end of performance cycle outcomes.

How does a supervisor or a senior executive know that the process is working well in our customer service team or when to coach laggards? It's too late to coach someone when the breaking limits are breached because we will be doing so at the expense of an internal or external stakeholder. Processes vary around the target, so we will miss the 8-hour target often. We expect this variation. A management limit is the effective threshold, say 10 hours, that allows a supervisor to intervene and nudge the process and the operations resource back to the target.

We should base day-to-day process oversight on management limits, which drive specific, predefined remedies when breached. Often, companies don't plan ahead to articulate the particular recourse that needs to be applied when management limits are crossed; this leads to the gradual deterioration of the process to reach breaking limits. The escalation and actions associated with management limits cannot be just unstructured supervisory demands to improve performance or company expectations from external stakeholders to achieve targets. It is a supervisory failure to manage processes without a predictive definition of corrective actions.

So, we must develop and use the concept of management limits to monitor and manage processes to ensure corrective actions can be taken when performance breaches the management limit. A strong analytical team will use targets, management limits, and breaking limits for all leading indicators across processes.

Principle 8: Prioritize insightful analysis by leveraging reporting limits for monitoring.

Time commitment and cadence are necessary to optimize the company's use of analysis and reporting to drive forward towards the mature end of the value engine. Time implies how much time various resources in the organization dedicate to analysis and reporting. Cadence implies the frequency at which these resources spend time on analysis and reporting.

In today's world, where data manipulation and automation technologies are prevalent and affordable, a growth-phase company should spend the vast majority of its data usage time (say, 80%) on analysis that improves its operations baseline and solves problems and only a small share of time (say, 20%) on downside protection efforts via reporting.

There are two reasons for this.

The **first** reason is that almost every reporting aspect can be set-and-forget using automation technology if the company is mature enough to use analysis to identify the correct leading metrics and appropriate management limits. There is absolutely no reason for senior executives, supervisors, or employees to stare at reporting if they have suitable thresholds that highlight limits. Likewise, there is nothing to learn from reporting if the process is performing within these guardrails set via process design and analysis. But if the process has breached these thresholds, then it's time to take remedial action or perform analysis.

The **second** reason is that a growing company must dedicate more effort to forward-looking assessments than downside protection. Every growing company has to continue to solve its problems to improve its overall direction and execution to grow its market and stay ahead of competitors.

So, senior executives and supervisors, and where appropriate individual contributors, have to be led through review and decision-making of critical analyses developed by strong analytical enablement resources.

These reviews will require the deepest mindshare and preparation from senior executives and supervisors to understand the assessments and recommendations presented to them. These executives have to leverage their understanding of data and its possible flaws and biases to ask hard questions and ensure they make the right decisions to improve the company's management approach and value engine.

A mature company ensures that such analysis development and decision reviews are part of the company's ongoing efforts. We must set the timing of these events on a cadence to ensure that today's distractions do not inhibit such forward-thinking.

Depending on the company's growth stage and level of success with its offerings and customers, the urgency of problem-solving will differ. Thus, the specific cadence will vary from company to company. However, this frequency must never be longer than a monthly one.

These analysis-led decisions directly dictate how reporting must be developed and socialized. A skilled strategy & operations executive will ensure that operational performance reporting is seamless to senior executives and supervisors in terms of time commitment.

On the other hand, reporting aims to monitor the adherence of process execution to process design. Processes are measured using leading indicators, and escalations and remediations should kick in when processes cross the management limit.

We have to formally define ownership and cadence for report creation and dissemination and alignment with the company's decision meeting cadence, which every company must have. We will revisit this later on. It also requires a definition of escalation paths and remediation steps when management limits are crossed. The most common data usage gaps at scaling companies around reporting stem from a lack of clarity around management limits, associated corrective actions, and predefined ownership of such tasks.

Consider the following questions to self-assess whether our company has the appropriate time commitment and cadence in place to leverage value from analysis and reporting:

Does the company dedicate a significant majority of data usage time on hypothesis-led analysis (say, 80%) compared to reporting (say, 20%)?

Do senior executives, supervisors, and individual contributors commit mindshare to understand and objectively assess the effectiveness of analysis developed and socialized?

Does the strategy & operations executive maintain at least a monthly cadence to review and discuss analysis and insights?

Does the company identify leading indicators, use management limits, and use corrective actions to address aberrations in process execution?

These four assessments ensure that an organization is adequately committed to discerning value from analysis and reporting to improve its execution and operations maturity.

Principle 9: Mature use of data requires effective organization design and strong skills.

Like process design expertise, developing objective and comprehensive hypotheses, choosing the appropriate analyses, assessing the available data while being wary of Process-Data Symbiosis, data flaws, and data biases to tease out the right insights are not easily learned skills. It takes years of practice in the proper teaching environments to hone these skills.

I learned many of these concepts through formal training programs as a Six Sigma Black Belt at GE, operations training programs and operations strategy projects at Accenture, or as a strategy and operations consultant for private equity and venture capital companies. In other words, many experienced experts and situations beat this stuff into me over the years. Unfortunately, such luxury is not available to early-career employees that join growth-phase companies. Typically, smaller companies cannot afford to train their employees to a relevant extent formally. Neither should they due to a lack of economies of scale due to a relatively small employee count. So, it is up to the CEO, strategy & operations executive, other senior executives, and supervisors to lead by example on the use of these concepts.

The reality is that no classroom experience or quick-fire certification can replace learning from experienced mentors and mature work settings. As part of the organization design and hiring approach, we must ensure that our most essential hires can use data objectively in today's information age.

We live in an age where there are a lot of information capturing mechanisms, and the world's largest companies trade information. There is also a proliferation of tools that can create charts and tables for everyone with minimal effort. So, it is tempting for everyone to jump on the data bandwagon and loosely use the words 'analysis' and 'reporting' to describe any visual kaleidoscope of information.

Although data-related concepts aren't rocket science and can be mastered, it requires discipline to learn and practice to get good at it. Unfortunately, scaling companies often make the mistake of thinking anyone can be good with data and not invest in the right people to use precious information, preventing maturity growth.

First, we must fill the role of the strategy & operations executive with a resource with deep expertise in hypothesis development and forward-looking problem solving and operational risk management using objective data. This executive has to be able to do the work on their own and be able to influence the rest of the organization about operations baseline performance.

As an organization scales, this executive will require additional enablement resources with similar skills to exclusively focus on problem-solving to improve the company's operations baseline.

Second, scaling companies should never split ownership of analysis from reporting. These two components are highly intertwined, even though they serve different purposes. There is no value in splitting analysis and reporting responsibilities into separate roles because they require the same skills. Furthermore, creating separate roles can lead to turf wars about who is accountable for what instead of seamlessly and collaboratively slipping between analysis and reporting.

A well-done analysis leads to reporting, and breakdowns triggered through reporting lead to analysis.

Third, it is also critical to group these responsibilities under one strategy & operations executive. Spreading this responsibility across standalone resources under different teams creates several challenges. Separate resources under other teams may develop approaches and methodologies that create unnecessary confusion and collaboration gaps that add no value to a growth-phase company.

Fourth, this single team must ideally report to the CEO. The CEO is the only resource in a company that is empowered with a broad oversight to own and improve every aspect of a company's operations and manage downside risk across the company. Since the strategy & operations executive's responsibilities involve the same broad scope, placing this responsibility under any other senior executive with functional specialties creates conflicts of interest and a lack of independence.

> *Consider the following questions to self-assess whether we have the right people to drive analysis and reporting:*
>
> *Does the company have a single leader with deep hypothesis-based analysis and data-driven operations risk management experience?*
>
> *Does this leader own both analysis and reporting responsibilities?*
>
> *Are all analysis and reporting responsibilities across all functions combined into one team under one executive?*
>
> *Does this single owner of analysis and reporting roll up directly to the CEO for independent and comprehensive company-wide impact?*

If we can answer these four questions affirmatively, the right people are likely in place to drive analysis and reporting.

Misuse of analysis and reporting creates company-wide risks. Companies often focus on their first offering and operations that support that initial offering. But growing sustainably implies that we must continuously improve the design and delivery of offerings and the commercial execution.

A mature value engine that embraces the core principles around analysis allows an organization to chart a course to move forward on the growth curve sustainably using internally developed insights to micro-evolve its offerings, processes, and management approach.

As a company grows, the number of employees, critical initiatives, and customers increase, along with greater market and competitor attention. Unfortunately, this also means risks increase. An effective and predictive reporting approach enabled by insightful analysis will allow us to resolve execution breakages and limit downside risk preemptively.

We have now covered our value engine and management approach that forms our operations baseline. These components and principles frame our company's current maturity of people, offerings, processes, and information. Therefore, if we sell our company today, everything we have discussed so far constitutes its intrinsic value.

But to sustainably grow, we must macro-evolve. How do we do that?

PART C

Corporate Strategy Is The North Star For Macro-Evolution.

W E are at a pivotal point in our methodology.

Our management approach has a maturity that reflects our past efforts and dictates our current organization design, hiring practices, and performance and compensation management. Our value engine demonstrates the effectiveness of our past productization efforts to create value for our customers. It also reflects the maturity of our processes, technology, and data to take our productized offering to our customers. Collectively, this is our company's operations baseline.

If our past actions were perfect, we would have a mature management approach with the optimal skills and top performers. We would have a mature value engine with customers who consider us value-creating partners, and our revenue is likely growing profitably. We could also probably have achieved success so far without sacrificing fundamentals that can allow us to continue to grow.

If we have a mature operations baseline, a larger company might be interested in acquiring us, or investment bankers are trying to help us go public. But in our organic growth mindset, we will assume that we want to continue to grow and capture more of our market and create more value for customers regardless of our ownership structure.

Even in such a perfect scenario, the world around us changes so fast; we will be left behind quickly if we do not evolve to maintain and even improve that maturity level.

In reality, every growth-phase company will have significant maturity improvements to take on. We have likely not perfected our choice of customers, our offerings, or how we deliver value to customers. Corporate strategy starts our macro-evolution cycle that connects our past to our future.

Growth-phase companies commonly use the word 'pivot.' Often, it refers to ignoring and moving beyond past blunders to something else without clarity on the path forward. That is not macro-evolution. It's gambling because an arbitrary pivot is another attempt at trial-and-error.

Our effective transition from our past and present to our future starts with our corporate strategy.

Moving from our present to the future also implies making investment decisions. First, we need to decide on a path forward to use our existing investment optimally. Now imagine that we have profit that we can reinvest. Or imagine that we want to deploy new investment. Then, how do we decide what to use this new investment for?

We will discuss the specifics of how we should deploy our existing and new investment under Part D: Strategic Planning. But, as a prerequisite, we need to articulate our north star, our corporate strategy, based on deep analysis and objective decisions, without which we would be nomads walking around the desert in circles.

Corporate strategy is a necessity to drive efficient growth.

A frequent philosophical debate that I have engaged in is the importance of structure and discipline at growth-phase companies. Many CEOs and senior executives at that scale deprioritize developing a well-vetted strategy because there are so many tactical day-to-day things that are undone or are problematic, and there are never enough resources. I often hear, "I simply don't have time to do that." It is a normal human response, but it is also irrational.

A guiding corporate strategy is more critical at a growth-phase company because resources and time are more constrained, especially compared to a large established company with a significant war chest. Unfortunately, this is completely counter to how many scaling companies think about their priorities in their haste to tactically firefight problems or spend newfound investment to stimulate rapid growth without an in-depth assessment of investment effectiveness.

Imagine that you are trying to solve a company-level problem.

What if you had a time machine that allows you to return to the same moment an infinite number of times and try all possible paths to solve the problem? Think Groundhog Day.

Or...

What if you had infinite resources, both people and tools, to do what you ask them to, and between all of those resources, you get to try all possible options to solve that big problem?

If either of these were possible, we wouldn't need a corporate strategy because we could tactically try each option and eventually get to the one that works best. But that's not the real world. Companies have finite resources and time. So, a tactical, trial-and-error approach is highly inefficient to find the best growth path, especially at resource-constrained, scaling companies.

Once a company has done basic market validation to prove sufficient demand for the offering, it should develop a corporate strategy before scaling. It is the most effective use of investment, and it significantly improves the probability of sending resources down the right path to win the market.

I went in as a transformation executive at a 12-year-old managed services company where my mandate was to evolve the company's operations baseline, which had significant maturity challenges. My first week involved performing an early diagnosis of why the operations baseline wasn't supporting growth or profitability and causing customer dissatisfaction. I shared a 6-point plan with the CEO. I agreed to focus on the last five points that would drive many initiatives to mature the operations baseline. The first point in the plan was asking the CEO for a decisive corporate strategy, which was an obvious gap. The CEO agreed to own the corporate strategy definition.

Nine months later, much of the initiatives related to the five points that I owned made significant inroads. But their adoption and disciplined execution was always a challenge because the company operated in a strategic vacuum where every person could take the company in the direction they pleased. For example, choosing a specific customer group was impossible because selling followed the sales reps' instincts; use case-focused productization efforts were distracted by tactical ideas that weren't creating value. It wasn't that we hadn't discussed and looked at the strategic choices that we would have to choose from; no one was willing to commit to a decision that we could execute.

Our journey to mature our operations baseline must start with an effective corporate strategy. We can dance around this all we want, but our strategic planning that frames all our work for the next execution cycle and that plan's actual execution depends on this nebulous overused concept. So, let's make sure that the transition from where we are today in our operations baseline to our next evolutionary stage is based on a cohesive and comprehensive strategic decision.

Corporate Strategy Maturity Model.

My editor told me this quote would be cliché. But in our world of excessive information, maybe tried-and-true isn't so bad. "If you know the enemy and know yourself, you need not fear the result of a hundred battles. If you know yourself but not the enemy, for every victory gained, you will also suffer a defeat. If you know neither the enemy nor yourself, you will succumb in every battle." — Sun Tzu, The Art of War. Replace 'enemy' with 'customer,' and that describes our corporate strategy development approach.

I usually start my strategy development conversations with this quote. This frame of mind summarizes our Corporate Strategy Maturity Model in Infographic C.1.

I hope you utilize this maturity model to assess your company's current situation and then chart a course to a higher maturity state. Like our maturity models for management approach and value engine, the far left and least mature state implies a lack of corporate strategy in any sense. This leads to a reactive company without much of a forward-looking plan. This immature state is *Level 1: Reactive & Tactical*.

In this state, the company operates like a kite in a storm where the path forward is essentially gyrations from one big or small idea to the next in quick succession based on very little formal structure or analysis. In this state, a company has flatlined in terms of growth prospects or will do so in time and gives employees and external stakeholders minimal comfort that there is an actual path forward other than getting to the next day or week.

A company at *Level 1: Reactive & Tactical* is a CEO's failure.

I once led the new business division of a growth-phase company. The CEO pitched this new division to me as the company's future and how the current division that created most of its past revenue no longer demonstrated a growth opportunity. My first few weeks focused on shoring up operational challenges for this new department and improving the team's efforts in this new market. However, within ten weeks of our engagement, the CEO decided that the new market was no longer the priority. Instead, the company would start focusing on its legacy business again, implying that my priorities changed to laying off employees in the new business division.

What triggered this change? A board member asked some hard questions that the board-level executives didn't have good answers to.

The reality was that the company never found out whether the new market could have been the real future or not because a few short-term uncomfortable events led to a complete change in priorities. This exemplifies *Level 1: Reactive & Tactical*.

Moving to the right of the maturity model implies that executives have some understanding of strategic choices. But the commitment to objective

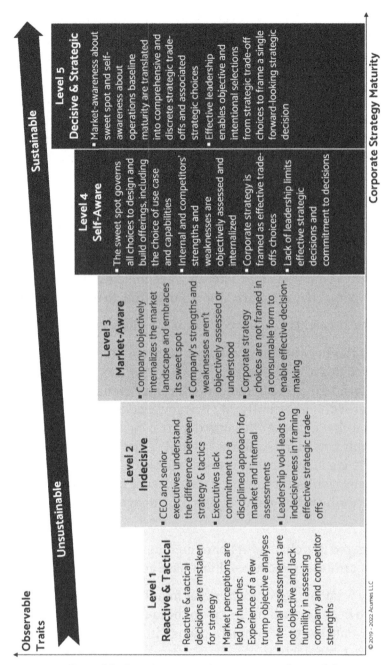

Infographic C.1 – Corporate Strategy Maturity Model

analysis and decisive choices to chart a dependable path forward is weak. In a practical sense, the outcomes at *Level 2: Indecisive* is unlikely to be better than Level 1 because the company isn't investing time and mindshare into objective information.

A good shot in the arm is often a necessary trigger to move a company from *Level 2: Indecisive* to the right of the maturity model, where valuable strategic concepts are explored and leveraged in the company's go-forward path. The reframing of the CEO's and senior executives' psyche can come from a strong strategy & operations executive, a hands-on external strategic advisor, or the board.

At *Level 3: Market-aware*, strategy development is less intuitive and reactive and more objective and analytical. Principles to embrace market awareness help a company identify its sweet spot – a blueprint of customers that greatly value its offerings and offer a large enough market to focus on.

Becoming market aware involves scientific exploration. Going after the wrong customers in a suboptimal manner is a poor return on investment and contributes to an unsustainable growth path. Although a CEO's gut feeling about these topics may aid a company to validate its market in the early stages, it will never be enough to grow sustainably. A robust internalization of critical market-focused insights backed by substantiated and objective analysis raises a company to *Level 3: Market-aware*.

Knowing who to sell our offerings to is a good start. But what should we offer and how should we deliver it?

The second piece of the strategy puzzle is knowing exactly what to offer and how to deliver that offering. To do this well, we must know our strengths and weaknesses. A qualitative and quantitative introspective exercise to define these moves a company to *Level 4: Self-aware*.

Knowing the market and internal strengths and weaknesses only takes a company to the doorstep of a good strategy because a good strategy implies translating our insights into a strategic decision. To achieve *Level 5: Decisive & Strategic*, we must develop a comprehensive set of choices and decisively choose a path forward that all stakeholders can embrace. Making hard choices comes with risk, but that's a leader's job. The company must have strong leadership to enable Level 5 maturity.

We will frame how we can create a tangible, impactful, and necessary corporate strategy for our company through the following four chapters.

C.1
INTERNALIZE THE ESSENCE OF STRATEGY.

STRATEGY became the most used business jargon of the last decade and, like others, has lost its meaning in practice. But just like the components that we discussed under Part A: Management Approach and Part B: Value Engine, it does have real meaning and purpose. However, without embracing its true essence, a company is rolling the dice on its future.

If I gave you a plain piece of white paper and a pen and asked you to draw a line, what would you do?

This is a quick exercise I have done on analytical interviews. I hope your response is to ask for more information without any doubt in your mind. Geometry 101 – even the simplest straight line has a starting point and an ending point. I ask this question to understand how a person thinks. Incredibly, a very large portion of my interview candidates draw a line right away without asking any questions and look at me with a smug look on their face that says, 'done!'

How will we know exactly where the starting point is on a piece of paper? First, you can ask for coordinates such as one inch from the bottom and two inches from the left. Then you must nail down where the endpoint is, which will require different coordinates. Do you see how the idea of drawing the simplest form of a line – a straight one – can become a material exercise?

What if your designated pen has a limited amount of very precious ink, and there is only so much of it? How does this change your perspective of the entire exercise?

Welcome to Strategy!

Our draw-the-line exercise is akin to strategy development in a fundamental sense. Strategy development is a conceptually simple but practically difficult exercise of articulating how a company can move from its present state to a desired future state.

We can think of our operations baseline as the starting point of our line. Senior executives, supervisors, and employees of growing companies often express that they know exactly where they currently are. But do they?

No company knows where they are at present without an adequate analysis of their environment and internal conditions. Therefore, it is essential to understand the precise coordinates of a company's starting point.

The same applies to where a company wants to be one, two, or three years in the future. If it's not easy to determine where a company is now, how much more difficult is it to say where it wants to be in the future?

The precious ink in our pen from the analogy is resources. We have limited investment dollars, top talent with specific desired skills, and time in the real world. Strategy development is not an exercise of wishful thinking; it is an exercise of practicality. How far can we go from the starting point with the twists and turns you must take by being mindful of our constraints?

Using this draw-the-line exercise, can you see how overused and underestimated the word strategy has become? We are dedicating an entire part of the methodology to corporate strategy because it is the lynchpin that dictates our path forward, including all investment choices, regardless of the current maturity of our operations baseline.

Principle 1: Differentiate strategy from tactics.

We often think about great chess players as great strategists. Great coaches of successful sports teams also have this quality. Unfortunately, people often associate strategy with the importance of a person's position, which is where the word's overuse comes from.

Who doesn't want to sound important?

What do chess players, renowned coaches, presidents, and CEOs have in common? They make big decisions in the context of their environment.

Others often live with or follow those decisions. Now, you might argue that we all make decisions. But the simple truth is that not all decisions are equally impactful.

A person's life might involve five, ten, or fifteen strategic decisions that offer nerve-wracking and unknown paths that can change the course of our entire life. I am not referring to events of chance such as "if I had missed that bus by ten seconds, my life would have been better because of the accident it led to" or "if I had known that the company would become such a prosperous one, I would have continued to work there." Instead, strategic decisions imply purposeful choices after considering all options and outcomes.

What is the difference between such strategic choices and decisions and tactical ones? Three key aspects differentiate strategic choices.

Differentiator 1: Outcomes are probabilistic for each choice.

The choices that a strategic decision offers lead us down a path that we have never walked before. A well-defined choice in a strategic decision will give us a clear view of what 'good' looks like for that choice, but we will not know with certainty whether it will result in the outcome we seek. We can assess our chances of achieving the outcome for each choice through the experience of others or objective assessment of information. But we will not be able to guarantee that it will lead us to the preferred outcome. This is exactly why strategic decisions are hard.

Differentiator 2: Decisions have an outsized cost.

We have to give up something to get something. A strategic decision always implies that we have to sacrifice something we consider valuable. If we cannot articulate the cost of a decision, then we are not making a strategic decision or aren't committing to a strategic decision, but just think we are.

Differentiator 3: Scale of impact.

Strategic choices are win-or-lose options. The outcomes are not passive. Instead, they often intend to create a significant positive upshot or avoid a major downside. Either way, the difference between a good and bad outcome for a strategic choice is considerable. This is precisely why it is important to frame what 'good' looks like for a strategic choice. Without a clear articulation of what 'good' looks like, we will be unable to compare each choice's upshot or downside limitation to the cost of making that choice.

Combining these three aspects that differentiate a strategic decision leads us to a simple fact: strategic decisions are not reversible. We cannot undo a strategic decision once we make our choice. We may make another strategic decision, but we cannot reverse the first one. A strategic decision always has a significant cost, and there are no refunds in the real world.

Is going to Las Vegas and putting half our net worth on one roll of a roulette table a strategic decision? The outcome implies a significant cost, and the impact of win or loss is also high. So, if we are rational, I would argue 'yes' because we have many options on what to do with half our net worth, and if we compare those options and choose this one, it is a strategic decision.

On the other hand, tactics cost us very little, and the predictable impact is also marginal. Thus, choices aren't often very relevant, and we can make many tactical decisions. Misunderstanding tactics as strategy blunts our opportunity for purposeful and impactful decisions when they matter.

Tactics and strategy are also dependent on a frame of reference. They are not absolutes. One person or entity's strategic choice can be another person's tactical choice and vice versa. A $1M investment can be a strategic choice for a small company. At the same time, a $1M purchasing approval might be a tactical decision that happens every week at a large established company because the outcome is likely guaranteed. The cost is low for their relative scale. Overlaying our three differentiating factors into the context of a given person or entity helps us focus on strategic decisions where necessary.

> **Things to Remember: Strategy vs. Tactics**
>
> **Strategy is a decision that always satisfies three conditions – probabilistic outcomes, outsized cost, and significant scale of impact. Such a choice is irreversible and contextual to the person or entity the decision pertains to. In comparison, tactics are choices with at least a relatively guaranteed desired outcome, relatively low cost, or only have a marginal impact.**

When I shared this definition with an Executive MBA classroom with experienced students, one stated – "I disagree; my start-up venture's strategy was to quickly hire the people we needed and not think too much." The student came around after a discussion. However, such mistaken associations of tactical actions as strategy are pervasive.

Our three differentiators highlight why true strategy development is uncommon yet universally associated with positions of power. But a strategic decision has nothing to do with who is making it. Conversely, people with power often make tactical decisions when strategic ones are expected.

Principle 2: Start with a self-assessment of our corporate strategy.

Before we go into how to develop an effective corporate strategy, it's good to know whether we have a history of having one. A few simple day-to-day observations will reveal whether our company has a strategic inclination or whether we are consciously or subconsciously hoping to win with rinse-and-repeat tactics.

Every company does two things: It creates offerings and delivers them. This is our value engine. Our corporate strategy guides both of these and dictates our management approach.

The commercial test.

Commercial activities include marketing the company's offerings, selling and order handling to capture revenue from those offerings, delivering the offerings, and maintaining a good relationship with customers.

> *Consider the following questions:*
>
> *Do the company's marketing collateral and channels reflect the actual value customers can receive, or is it exaggerated to the point of unrecognition?*
>
> *Are sellers clear on the breadth and depth of the value the company's offerings can create, or do they commit to value that the company cannot realistically create?*

Are customer account managers and value creation personnel comfortably able to create promised value, or do they struggle to manage customer expectations?

Misleading the market isn't a strategy. It's an unethical tactic that will backfire over time. Companies end up in the latter scenarios of these assessment questions because there is no cohesive corporate strategy or strategic plan, and execution did not follow the strategy. Not prioritizing a strategy-led approach leaves the company with little confidence in its self-worth, which is essentially the maturity of its operations baseline, leading to setting expectations the company cannot deliver.

The productization test.

We covered the core principles to enable mature productized packages and pricing that drives customer value. However, irrespective of our offering, our productization efforts must operate within the confines of an effective corporate strategy.

Consider the following questions:

Do we focus on reactively building features that customers asked for without a comprehensive capability mindset that focuses on a specific use case and the root cause of the market problem?

Do we have a slew of offerings, but none are market winners? Are new efforts to improve offerings started without effectively commercializing previous ones?

Do productization ideas created without effective market studies result in poorly executed existing priorities?

Such tendencies imply a lack of understanding about customers' real needs and a strategic decision to focus on a use case that aligns with our strengths.

Suppose we aren't performing optimally on these questions. In that case, we can expect that our early fast growth will stall or has already stalled, our organization will be drained of its best performers, and the company will likely gyrate between various tactics without success. The most rational and hard-working employees will consciously or otherwise sense the lack of direction and look for opportunities outside the organization.

So, let's codify what 'good' corporate strategy entails.

Principle 3: Corporate strategy answers the who-how-what questions for macro-evolution.

The most important strategy development concept that enables macro-evolution from our operations baseline is "we can't have our cake and eat it too!" If you are only going to remember one thing from this entire part of the methodology, remember that.

Corporate strategy is the articulation of the company's path forward that the CEO and senior executives identify and align on through objective external and internal assessments. It is the most practical evidence that allows every stakeholder to understand and align on the path to achieving the company's purpose. Moreover, such an articulation allows for optimal deployment of resources to solve the market problem and achieve sustainable growth.

> **Things to Remember: Corporate Strategy**
>
> **Corporate strategy is a single overarching decision that articulates what our company will do and will not do based on a mutually exclusive and collectively exhaustive set of strategic choices. As long as we focus on organic growth, our corporate strategy articulates a cohesive answer to these three questions: 1) Who will we serve? 2) What will we offer? 3) How will we deliver?**

We will spend the following three chapters going through how to build a strategy to answer these questions.

It is tempting to whitewash the answers to these questions with obvious responses. But it is not easy to frame a corporate strategy that answers all three of these questions cohesively. Many companies I work with confidently operate around 'Buyer Personas' or 'Ideal Customer Profiles.'

The selling team rarely actually follows these, and these situations also imply poor offerings because the team decoupled the productization efforts from these 'Buyer Personas' or 'Ideal Customer Profiles.' This is not a strategy. We must take a more comprehensive approach to ensure we have a single answer to our who-how-what questions.

Principle 4: Leverage a trade-off & choices approach to frame corporate strategy.

We need a method to translate the nebulous nature of strategy to a practical and actionable construct to articulate a single answer for our who-how-what questions. My simple framework has three parts.

First, strategy development starts with understanding and articulating how we frame our strategic choices. But it's hard to make one big nebulous decision all in one go.

We can effectively frame a strategic decision using a comprehensive set of strategic trade-offs. The concept of trade-offs allows us to break down a complex overarching decision about our company's future into mutually exclusive, collectively exhaustive decision blocks. I call these decision blocks **Strategic Trade-offs**.

> **Things to Remember: Strategic Trade-offs**
>
> A strategic trade-off is a decision switch with two, three, or four choices. Each trade-off will exhibit the three key aspects that differentiate strategic choices from tactical ones – uniquely significant impact, sizable cost to execute, and unguaranteed probabilistic outcome. Together, these trade-offs answer our who-how-what questions and add up to our overarching strategy.

Companies serve different markets and use cases and have different offerings and processes to deliver those offerings to customers. As a result, the maturity level of our operations baseline will evolve each cycle and hence never remain constant. So, we must develop a set of strategic trade-offs that comprehensively reflect our operations baseline at the current moment and our current market. A good set of strategic trade-offs is a handful of such switches covering all critical factors that answer our who-how-what questions.

A good rule of thumb is to prioritize between five and ten strategic trade-offs where each has two to four mutually exclusive choices that frame the single answer to our who-how-what question into a tangible decision board. Articulating trade-offs and related choices work because it is significantly easier to analyze and decide on a few discrete trade-offs with two or three options than compare 10 or 15 company-level nebulous paths.

Think about deciding on our next vacation. We have infinite choices to pick from. But, in reality, we seldom directly choose our next vacation. Instead, subconsciously, we define trade-offs such as type of landscape, which might include choices like beaches, mountains, cities; affordability which might have choices like low-budget or expensive; length of vacation choices like one week, two weeks, or three weeks; companionship during the vacation choices like solo, with friends, with family, etc. Our final vacation decision is simply an aggregation of our choices for each of these independent trade-offs. The same concept applies while developing corporate strategy.

The crux is that no company can do it all across trade-offs. It is not practical because every company lives within constraints like time, investment, skill, etc. Higher quality or speed usually implies a higher cost.

However, this exercise will also have to ensure that these choices leave us with a large enough market opportunity to attack and meet our company's purpose. These choices allow us to find repeatability and reproducibility within our trade-off choices.

Second, strategy is about making hard choices based on strategic trade-offs and associated choices. That's why people that decisively make strategic choices and risk their reputation and jobs to make that decision tend to make the big bucks. Identifying the set of strategic trade-offs and the associated choices is important. But it is only practically useful if the CEO, head of strategy and operations, and senior executives have the will to make decisions on each trade-off.

Strategic decisions frame what a company will do. But the converse is often ignored and leads to ineffective strategy development. Framing what a company will do also implies the company has to frame what will not be done. Far fewer executives are consciously or subconsciously comfortable deciding what we will not do. The option to change our mind is nice, but making strategic decisions comes with a risk that we make a choice that will cost us without the payoff.

A common challenge is discipline. Executives face revenue, cost, and competitor pressure every single day. Being confident in a strategic decision and staying disciplined on executing that decision is often where most companies slip. Once this discipline has slipped, we will not be able to diagnose the real reasons behind our results.

I added a **third** element as a personal twist. A corporate strategy must be readable as one cohesive sentence, using simple language, limiting any interpretive differences. In other words, based on the strategic trade-off choices, the company should be able to write one cohesive, time-bound sentence that summarizes its decision to deploy its investment most efficiently to solve the market problem. Although this sentence has no incremental information from the selections made from strategic trade-offs and associated choices, its cohesive and non-conflicting nature will validate that the trade-off choices are mutually exclusive and collectively exhaustive.

The CEO must own the act of making the strategic decision with conviction based on the insights and trade-off choices developed through the corporate strategy development exercise. The CEO's leadership enables all executives to rally around the company's north star and stay committed.

Principle 5: Strategy development is a triangulation exercise.

I was never good at it, but I spent several summers of my childhood coerced into taking oil painting classes. I now have an analogy from those months of frustration.

When I go through a strategy development exercise, I imagine it is similar to hand painting a landscape on a large oil canvas by an artist who has a clear vision of the image they are trying to produce but doesn't have a step-by-step plan for creating it.

Strategy development is a triangulation exercise. We don't start at one end of the canvas and try to perfect it before moving to the next part of the canvas. Throughout the exercise, we may revisit the same topics, such as analyzing our current offerings or how strong other players are when we learn that we need to alter our initial hypotheses. This is an important concept to keep in mind because a simple linear mindset will result in a strategy akin to a preconceived notion. Be open-minded about what you will learn through the exercise and revise your hypotheses and assessments.

In the following three chapters, our principles are not a linear path to the end. They start slightly staggered, but much of the work happens concurrently where we will have to put the paintbrush at the same spots on the canvas multiple times to add depth and colors.

Principle 6: Current operations baseline must underpin the hypotheses driving strategy development.

Like any other analytical problem-solving exercise, we have to hinge strategy development on framing hypotheses we can test about what part of the market we might serve best and how we would serve that part of the market. These hypotheses must come from the current state of our operations baseline and analyses of the execution of our previous strategy and plan.

Corporate strategy development requires a reasonable operations baseline to start from. We must have some real customers who have purchased our offering and are somewhat happy with it. Friends, family, and close acquaintances don't count as customers who have objectively purchased our offering. We must also have some semblance of an offering that works. This is critical because we need objective information to develop hypotheses.

Theranos and Elizabeth Holmes offer an extreme example to explain the importance of starting from our current baseline. Theranos was a healthcare technology company started by Elizabeth Holmes. She claimed for several years that the company had a breakthrough blood-testing offering that would allow testing for hundreds of ailments by using the company's small testing box, requiring only a small blood draw. The results would be ready in a few minutes.

It was a radical new approach because the alternative was the blood testing methods that we are all familiar with; several vials of blood taken from a person, sent to a lab, and the results are available days later. But unfortunately, Theranos lied to the world and investors, and probably themselves for several years. Their box didn't work at all. It was essentially just a front to do exactly how testing was done the traditional methods, except Theranos did it poorly because they didn't get enough blood from individuals.

I imagine the company went through at least one macro-evolution cycle. Hypothetically, what would have happened if they objectively started a strategy development exercise based on their history and the market? Basing their assessments to solve the problem on their reality anchors them to practical choices rather than a magic black box that never worked.

A strategic decision requires an effective framing of our trade-offs and choices. Developing these is a problem-solving exercise seeking insights. Problem-solving implies a vast majority of time goes into problem definition. We tend to think that we already know the solution even before understanding the problem. Trying to rush to a solution simply leads to an answer that doesn't solve our customers' problems. A key portion of problem definition is articulating hypotheses. Our approach will use our operations baseline as a grounding source for hypotheses.

Principle 7: Avoid antiquated and biased hunches by reframing strategy every cycle.

Garbage in; garbage out.

A strategic decision is only as valuable as the quality of information created and used to develop insights and frame our trade-offs and choices. Unfortunately, in today's world, information becomes outdated very quickly because the speed with which technology changes markets and the pace at which adoption happens is exponentially higher than in past decades. Change will only accelerate. So, dependence on years of passive experience in the market or what worked in recent years can become more of a liability than an asset irrespective of recent success.

This speed is a great equalizer. But it also means every company has to stay on its toes. We must renew our hypotheses about changes in our market every cycle, revise our mindset about data elements to capture and analyze, ensure we respect other market participants, reassess how they could have evolved since the past cycle, and so on.

This makes the entire strategy development exercise an open-minded, sprint research program. It involves gathering new and objective data through primary and secondary research.

Primary research refers to the process of creating the data we need through our own means. The strategy & operations executive and the analytical enablement team will have to actively capture qualitative data through structured, documented, and cataloged conversations with various types of customers, vendors, partners, and other market participants to test key hypotheses. It also includes actively capturing and analyzing quantifiable measurements of our operations baseline.

We must augment our primary research with **secondary research**. This second category refers to externally created information pulled in, cataloged, and used by the internal team. There are plenty of studies and research papers written by associations, academics, and analysts in every market that can offer additional sources of insights.

They are both equally important. But it is easier to know the quality and objectivity of primary sources because our internal resources created them. So, for instance, using a study about our market published by an association may be misguiding if a company that benefitted from the publication commissioned the study to boost their own business.

Having structured and planned discussions with customers that are unbiased, thorough, and well-documented, along with hypothesis-driven analysis of historical data, is the only path to arrive at these detailed insights. Every company should constantly be talking to their customers and capturing data objectively. However, to really understand customers' needs and mindset, we must go well beyond asking superficial questions and working with biased hypotheses about their buying approach and incentives.

Customers are normal human beings; they are often polite, guarded, and very busy. Asking customers unsophisticated questions – such as "will you continue to buy our offerings?" – will allow them to provide ambiguous answers and get back to their lives quickly. Additionally, it is easy to fall prey to biases and capture poor data during primary research with customers. It would be worthwhile to revisit Chapter B.3 to ensure that we are able to gather data that is unbiased and not flawed.

Whether our operations baseline is guided by a corporate strategy or not today, we can build a new strategy for our next macro-evolution cycle with up-to-date and unbiased data. Throughout the rest of this part of the methodology, we will explore the components that we can leverage to build that corporate strategy.

C.2
ANALYZE THE MARKET PROBLEM TO TRIGGER MACRO-EVOLUTION.

WE must take intentional steps each cycle to assess our market and operations baseline to reframe our trade-offs and choices that answer the who-how-what questions. In our ever-changing world, at least one trade-off or choice will change for a growth-focused company every cycle based on what we learned in the previous cycle. Gaining new insights to shift our north star intentionally will be hard. Our only other option is to assume that our current path will suffice. The risk is that customers evolve beyond us, and other players in the market fill the void we leave.

Many strategic blunders or lack of strategic focus arise from several factors. These might include a shallow understanding of our market, an ineffective definition of the market problem, poor or no identification of the root causes that need to be solved, and insufficient acknowledgment of strengths and weaknesses of market players to solve the root cause of the problem. Almost every strategy development exercise I've been part of had a positive shock-and-awe reaction when the company is presented with new market insights. They incorrectly assumed they already knew everything there was to know.

Strategy development starts with redefining the market problem effectively.

Let's understand the market problem using the famous Donald Rumsfeld framing about why the country's leaders made poor decisions about the 2003 United States invasion of Iraq – Known Knowns, Known Unknowns, and Unknown Unknowns. Known knowns are things we know we must know and have learned them. Known unknowns are things we know are important, but we don't know enough about them. This is learnable because we know they are blind spots. The most dangerous bucket is unknown unknowns. This is a black hole where we don't even know what we are missing. Our goal through market assessment is to reduce the size of the unknown unknowns' portion of the pie and increase the size of known knowns and known unknowns. If we think that our known knowns are most of the informational universe, we are operating in a blind-leading-the-blind scenario.

Recollect that our market problem is a three-legged stool. It combines non-core activities, voiced pain points, and unvoiced imbalances as illustrated in Infographic C.2. So, let's dive into how we develop insights around each of these to create a fresh view of our market problem as part of strategy development.

Infographic C.2 – Three legs of a market problem

Principle 1: Embrace the search for objective insights to counteract overconfidence bias.

Remember, Dunning-Krueger Effect? Every growth-challenged entity I've worked with has a loftier perspective about their abilities and understanding of their market and customers than reality. This natural bias bleeds into missing or ignoring the necessary details to evolve.

A few years ago, I led strategy development and strategic planning at a scaling technology company, which had never undergone such a comprehensive exercise. The company had grown through the sheer wit of a handful of people. But a decade in, revenue growth stalled because the company was crumbling under its own weight. The company was creating arbitrary solutions hoping one would change their fortune.

I informed the CEO that my team was beginning a comprehensive strategy development exercise, starting with a market study.

His response was, "What would you learn? I have already spoken to our customers, and I have the answers we need. So, you can stop the exercise!" The mindset permeated across the company because most people touched customers in some way. There was a lot of talk about our path forward, but no one could state it actionably.

I had a good relationship with the CEO and was willing to burn some capital and went ahead anyway. After a few weeks of engaging various market participants, my team and a few others produced tangible and actionable insights. It changed everyone's mind about what we knew. Support grew, and we framed effective trade-offs that changed our path forward. Ultimately, the board approved this new path at the end of the year.

Many scaling company executives that I speak with believe they know everything there is to know about the market they are playing in, and deeper analysis is a waste of their time. In my experience, it is not uncommon for a CEO to say, "I just told you exactly what our market is and our customers need." In contrast, a customer-facing operations resource at the same company says, "we are just making things up as we go without a clear direction."

It is easy to get caught up in everyone's view of our market or take articles published at face value and think we know enough. Very few outlets ever publish information without an underlying bias or agenda, especially when it comes to companies and markets. Most people who come on CNBC or Bloomberg and offer their views about the market are just pushing their own investment choices on the world. Despite my best efforts, my perspectives in this book will be skewed based on my experiences, and you must apply your own critical thinking to use what I am sharing.

The world around us changes fast. Our market has evolving needs. A subjective and biased strategy development team allows the world to pass by. We have one company, one market, and we do this once an annual cycle. It's best to do it well!

Principle 2: Commission a market landscape to articulate the market problem comprehensively and objectively.

To serve our customers, we have to know the problem we are trying to solve exceptionally well. What single mechanism do you use to frame new opportunities and market risks other than endless conversations based on disconnected experiences and hunches? Most growth-phase companies don't have any. How can we build effective solutions if our understanding of the problem is sub-par?

Before going further, I have repeated the word 'market' several times without stating what I mean by it. It is far from a casual concept.

> **Things to Remember: The Market**
>
> **A market is a balanced ecosystem where different players perform various activities to share and extract value in one form or another.**

Overarching balance in the ecosystem doesn't imply a fair or equitable flow of value between players. Most markets have poor business models and unequal exchanges of value between players at any given point in time. Such unequal exchanges of value imply opportunities for change. Change is good for some players, and it's not so good for others. We are just one player in our market that constantly changes.

Any mass disruption in any market is predictable based on long periods of unequal flow of value or low-value creation by players.

An everyday example of such disruption was the entry of ride-sharing applications. For decades, most major US cities operated on a medallion system that created significant value flow gaps. The city governments made out like bandits first. Then, entities that held on to medallions squeezed people who drove the taxis while passengers felt they overpaid for poor service.

The ride-sharing disruption took advantage of these value gaps and inserted new players and new types of activities. So now, ride-sharing applications have created different skews in the value created and extracted by various players who are getting transported around.

Most market shifts are more subtle and gradual, making it even more important to make sure we aren't falling asleep at the wheel. So, how do we understand our market and its problem?

We can understand and refresh our view on our market and reframe the market problem by creating a **Market Landscape**.

> **Things to Remember: Market Landscape**
>
> **A market landscape articulates our balanced ecosystem with all the relevant players, their activities, and the value flow between them. It identifies potential new opportunities and shifts that our company must address. It also informs us of risks to our current value creation model.**

A market landscape reframes our market in a cohesive view refreshed with the latest insights. It becomes our organization's single source of truth on the market and protects our company from opinions, tribal knowledge, and insight gaps.

Consider the following questions as we frame our path to internalize our market and frame the market problem objectively:

What types of companies or people are involved in our ecosystem? How will we logically group these companies and people?

What activities do each of these groups perform in the ecosystem today? How can we logically group these activities?

Which of these activity groups create value? Which of these activity groups extract value?

Where are the known impediments in the ecosystem? Where are the discrepancies in value flow in this ecosystem? Which players are undertaking activities that are not core to their existence?

How can these insights be dovetailed to frame the market problems key players face?

As we read these questions, let's hold ourselves back from thinking, "I know these answers!" Our purpose here is not to have some answers. Instead, it is to ensure that the answers are comprehensive and cohesive and reflect our market's evolving reality.

Do not be shy about details. If you feel that you do not have an audience for an effective market landscape, it reflects the organization's management approach, not your work. A quote that the CEO of a struggling company shared with each employee as we did 2-on-1 meetings with each employee was "…our challenges come from our headlines culture… we need to start reading the details!"

Principle 3: Start with the player groups who create and consume value.

We no longer live in a simple barter system where two parties come to the market to trade with each other. Every trade involves several stakeholders who have different needs and bring varying solutions to the market. It is critical to capture all the key players in the ecosystem to understand the whole picture.

In my experience, most companies tend to think about their market as a simple two-player relationship between the company and customers, with others playing a tactical vendor, outsourcer, or a selling support role. Unfortunately, this tendency is in our DNA – people preferred to think that earth was the center of the universe until the 17th century, when disproving this belief was considered controversial.

Our market landscape exercise intends to break this natural tendency to think that the market revolves around us. We should remove ourselves from the middle and see it for what it really is – a multiplayer ecosystem.

C.2 ANALYZE THE MARKET PROBLEM TO TRIGGER MACRO-EVOLUTION

Our market is an ecosystem that operates with or without us, and there are always several players.

Player groups allow us to understand the whole market in a manageable way.

It is impossible to think about, research, or analyze all the individuals and companies out there. The permutations of options will require data, computing power, and algorithms we don't have at a scaling company. But we can manage to learn about a few prioritized groups. Let's call these **Player Groups**.

> **Things to Remember: Player Groups**
>
> A player group is a similar set of entities, individuals, or companies, who we believe will behave similarly and bring a specific similar value to the market to consume a different value.

Player groups are a superset of all similar clusters in our ecosystem, including the customer groups we introduced under productization. But in our start-with-a-clean-slate mindset, we will assume we don't know our customer groups.

A player group can be customers with similar behaviors and needs. A player group can comprise companies like us with a similar operations baseline. A player group may be a set of companies that act and look differently from us but add a similar value to customer groups. Individuals or companies that our customers serve directly can form a player group using the value extracted from our ecosystem.

As a rule of thumb, avoid framing players as customers and competitors at this stage because this presumes that we sit in the middle of our ecosystem. Instead, use value-focused groupings that frame each group's purpose and comprehensively consider the most common types of players in most markets.

For instance, we want to understand our current customers' customers in the eventuality that our current customers create limited value themselves and are largely middlemen. If we have historically sold to resellers, placing the next-level value extractors on the board would be important because who we sell to and how we sell might change in the future.

Consider the following questions to map player groups without placing our company in the center:

Who are the players that gain the most value in the ecosystem? Let's call these 'primary value extractors.'

Are there players who extract a different and small fraction of the value compared to primary value extractors? If so, who are they? Let's call these 'auxiliary value extractors.'

Who are the players that extract value from the primary value extractors? Consider calling these players 'next-level value extractors.'

Which players create the most value in the market? Let's call them 'primary value creators.'

Who are the secondary value creators that complement the offerings of the primary players? Let's call them 'auxiliary value creators.'

Who are the players that the primary value extractors would fall back on If the primary and auxiliary value creators are ineffective? These are 'substitutes.'

Are there indispensable players in our ecosystem? Think of these as unavoidable portions of our market like digital and social advertising or ERP software solutions. Let's call them 'foundational value creators.'

We must put similar players of each type together in a group to account for at least 80% of each type of player.

Identifying the players in our market is not a particularly difficult task. The challenging aspect is to find the discipline and humility to ensure that we intentionally include and analyze every relevant player group. Do not succumb to the tendency to obsess over one specific type of player or group and lose sight of the complete picture.

Hubris about discounting the value that other entities can create in our market can be our downfall. If our offering is a niche data visualization solution, ignoring a group of general solutions players like Microsoft or Google with raw spreadsheet visualization tools is like putting blinders on.

So, how exactly do we group these players?

Create player groups using externally observable parameters.

The entire purpose of our market assessment is to understand how various players behave and what they hope to get out of being part of our ecosystem. So, we must group players according to their behaviors.

The path to grouping players is to develop a set of meaningful parameters with appropriate choices that effectively predict that group's behaviors. Choose a handful of meaningful parameters and two to four categories for each parameter for each type of player.

If the players in our ecosystem are individual consumers, these parameters describe a human being and their behaviors. For example, these parameters might include:

- *personal attributes such as age, gender, ethnicity.*
- *economic proxies such as employment status or type, residence neighborhood, property ownership.*
- *behavioral traits such as frequent traveler, fitness enthusiast.*
- *relationship traits such as relationship status or parenthood.*

If the players are other companies, these parameters help group companies. Such business traits might include:

- *size of the company, based on employee count or revenue.*
- *company's position in the value chain with categories like manufacturer, distributor, or retailer.*
- *company's business model like franchising model vs. direct ownership model or service provider vs. seller of physical goods; company's geographic location by country or other regional categories.*

- *environment in which companies operate, such as highly regulated vs. unregulated, etc.*

These examples illustrate how broad and situationally unique our player parameters could be. Strong analytical resources will need to inject their business acumen and analytical prowess to identify optimal parameters for each type of player without rinse-and-repeating a few canned parameters.

Let's formally call these parameters **Externally Observable Parameters**.

> **Things to Remember: Externally Observable Parameters**
>
> **Externally observable parameters allow us to group players in our market according to their behaviors, and they must satisfy three conditions: 1) Parameters must have a causal predictive relationship to the group's behaviors; 2) Every single parameter used should be unambiguous and non-interpretive, and 3) Actionable information must be available for every single parameter.**

This is one of the most time-consuming steps in our market assessment, and we must expect to iterate because getting these groupings right on the first pass is nearly impossible. Use the three conditions to pressure-test and ensure we choose high-quality parameters.

First, our chosen parameters and categories must have a causal relationship to the activities of that player type. For a scaling company, vast amounts of data are not a luxury we have. We must make do with small amounts of carefully selected data which means we have to start with solid hypotheses on effective parameters and categories that predict behaviors of different types of players.

Choosing arbitrary parameters and categories with the hope of finding millions of lines of data to analyze is wishful thinking. For instance, the religious affiliation of individuals can be a relevant parameter for the right market; but it is a stretch to presume that this parameter predicts exercise habits. Moreover, such arbitrary choices can leave us with confounding insights because we might misinterpret noise in a small data set as meaningful insights.

Second, every single parameter used should be unambiguous and non-interpretive. Different individuals should look at players and put them into the same categories for all parameters without ambiguity. For example, suppose I have 'value chain position' as a parameter and categorize a player as a 'distributor.' In that case, my colleagues should categorize that player the same way for the 'value chain position' parameter. Ambiguous parameters or underlying categories will lead to misleading takeaways.

Third, actionable information must be available for every parameter and available from an objective data provider or gathered reliably internally. Grouping players is more than an analytical exercise. We must be able to identify all players in the real world based on these parameters. If we choose a specific group as our future customers, we must be able to readily identify all players in that group to sell to without ambiguity.

As we frame our player groups, think about illustrating the outputs of this first step, as shown in Infographic C.3. This is an opportunity to generate a reasonably accurate count of the number of players that belong to each player group. This key ingredient can help us decide how much effort we should spend on a player group. We will use this data to generate our addressable market size, which directly correlates with the size of the market problem and the volume of players who experience it.

I led a market landscape assessment for an education solutions company that supported the learning experience for professional certifications using technology and service. Situationally, this client served a broad set of value extractors but considered them similar.

Our fresh look allowed us to behaviorally group these extremely different players that included professional certification organizations, industry associations, colleges and universities, training material creators, training material deliverers, and various types of learners. This act of thinking about player groups as unique was a new insight.

For instance, the company historically looked at all educators who created professional education content similarly. Through our exercise, we framed educators who created content to teach employees of companies differently from educators who created content for individuals who wanted to privately gain professional education in separate player groups. This impacted the strategic trade-offs we had to consider.

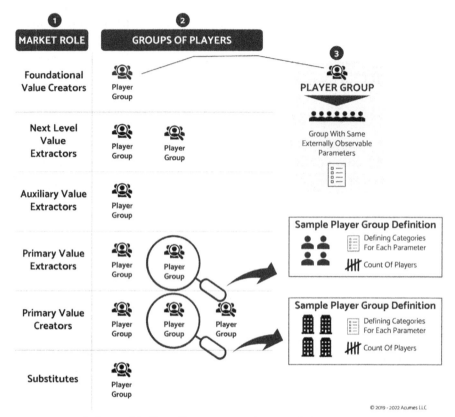

Infographic C.3 – Player groups in a market ecosystem

Principle 4: Assess player groups' behaviors to identify non-core activities.

Using common industry or functional terms unnecessarily anchors us to history. Imagine going to a large sports facility with basketball courts, volleyball courts, racquetball courts, and others. What if our skill is playing tennis and we find one wall in a volleyball court to just practice hitting a tennis ball against? Would we say that we are playing volleyball? Are we playing tennis? We aren't doing either. We are just practicing hitting a tennis ball against a wall.

People close to Uber, Lyft, and Doordash would describe them as a 'technology' company. I would describe them as transportation companies with a mobile app that is more reflective of their profitability challenges that don't have an end in sight. WeWork was also treated as somewhat of a technology company. The reality is that IWG PLC has been around for 30 years, offering hoteling concept of workspaces, and they have been a profitable company. These companies can only be seen as office real estate rental outfits. If our goal is intrinsic value and sustainable growth, then we must focus on the underlying activities in our market than gimmicks to boost our extrinsic value.

So, what are the various player groups we placed on the board in Principle 3 doing to create or extract value? How much of those activities fall under the strictures of our market? We want to understand those activities and group those activities logically.

This must sound familiar. We are applying flow thinking to build journeys for the player groups.

Understand the player groups to create logical groups of their activities.

First, we want to learn the details of activities that players go through in their hourly, daily, weekly journeys because we don't know what we don't know. Changes in activities of one player change other players' activities and relevance.

I often see companies take an easy path to use published articles received through newsfeeds. But who publishes these articles and why? Are they just marketing? Published information will rarely get into the details of how our ecosystem works. We must get our hands dirty to ask objective, critical-thinking questions and gather data to pinpoint changes in activities in our ecosystem across all player groups we placed on our market landscape.

> *Consider the following questions:*
>
> *What are each player group's behavioral characteristics and activities in the context of our ecosystem?*
>
> *With a strong understanding of the underlying activities, how can we firmly group these activities into logical groups?*

Focus on what we believe each group really does, not what they say they do. We want to build our strategy based on reality instead of marketing messages. Frame these as steps using actionable verbs where possible.

Second, as we learn and group activities, consider whether the definition of each player group changes. In this triangulation exercise, we are likely to learn that our perceptions about one or more player groups are different after we have taken the time to understand their activities. This is because we created our player groups based on behavior-predicting parameters.

If the activity groups don't align for players in the same groups, it's likely that our player groups or our information about activities is incorrect.

We should expect to learn and iterate.

This effort allows us to minimize our unknown-unknown bucket. But even the simplest ecosystems are quite expansive. We can't successfully learn about every player group and activity group. To scale sustainably, we must also focus. So, what is an appropriate border for our ecosystem?

Frame an effective scope of the ecosystem to prioritize player groups and activity groups.

Third, strategy development is about making tough decisions. Commonly accepted classifications such as industry names or functions are not effective variables to define market boundaries. It leaves too much to interpretation. We must tighten and specify the boundaries of our ecosystem such that our market landscape articulates a day-in-the-life of each player group relatively accurately. Without setting these boundaries effectively, we will try to analyze too wide a world and have no relevant insights to act on.

> *Consider the following question:*
>
> *What is our hypothesis on a logical boundary for the activity groups and player groups in our ecosystem, allowing a reasonable breadth of consideration without stretching too far?*

We must eliminate distractions that creep into strategy development discussions with a tightened market boundary.

Analyze value flow to identify non-core activities as one leg of the market problem.

As we learn about the activities of player groups, we are keeping a keen eye on our primary incentive at this stage – identification of non-core activities. They are exactly what they sound like.

> **Things to Remember: Non-core Activities**
>
> **Non-core activities are the first of three parts of our market problem. They represent a comparative advantage gap in the ecosystem. They are activities that are not a player group's core competency or preferred activity, yet ones they are forced to engage in due to lack of options or lack of internalization about comparative advantage principles. Non-core activities in the ecosystem are optimally solved through a capability that transfers the responsibility to another player group who is better at doing it or solving it comprehensively.**

Businesses that address market problems that primarily comprise non-core activities are everywhere. For example, if we think about an ecosystem as consumption of groceries for in-home use, imagine a specific player group of primary value extractors with low price consciousness and everyday grocery needs. The activity group of transferring groceries from a grocery store shelf to their doorstep can be a non-core activity. Several businesses pegged this non-core activity as the market problem, starting with Peapod over a decade ago.

But not all primary value extractors are the same in this ecosystem. I belong to a group of primary value extractors who make on-the-fly decisions based on what I see on the shelves and visual discounts. I have never gotten my groceries delivered.

So, as a **fourth** step, we must flag opportunities in the ecosystem associated with player groups to identify non-core activities, which highlight obvious value gaps, as the first leg of our market problem.

Consider the following question:

Which activities are performed by specific player groups that are not in line with comparative advantage principles?

The conceptual illustration in Infographic C.4 reflects the use of value flows to learn about our market activities, set our market boundaries, and draft early hypotheses on non-core activities in the ecosystem. Remember, strategy development is as much about what we do not do as it is about what we do. Therefore, we must develop such hypotheses and choices throughout.

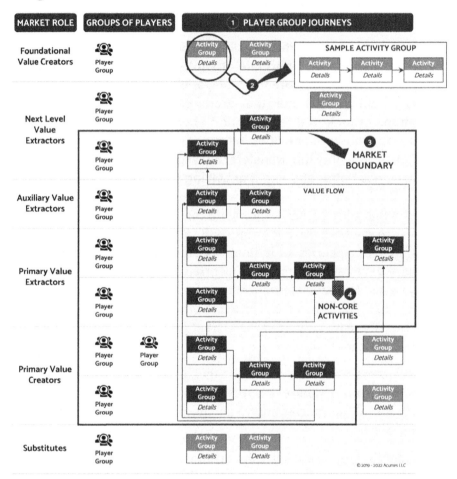

Infographic C.4 – Journeys of player groups in the market

We fleshed out various player groups' activities at the education solution company I mentioned. We further broke out educators who created content for individuals into separate player groups that focused on mandatory certifications vs. nice-to-have certifications because their activities were different. This meant that the market problem and value created would be different. This raised questions during strategy development on whether the company should serve both and how.

Additionally, the company was able to appreciate the importance of new activity groups like education content marketing and the different types of metrics that various player groups thought about in the ecosystem. These details helped assess the maturity of existing capabilities.

We also set boundaries to the ecosystem to limit distractions. Areas like 'education planning' and 'content sourcing' were set out of scope. Companies plan a diverse set of activities, and for these educators, education content was only one of them. So, we decided it wasn't critical to the ecosystem.

Content sourcing was a foundational activity offered by foundational value creators like Google or libraries, which we decided didn't impact the ecosystem enough to keep inside the boundary. It would be easy to chase opportunities far and wide without such choices, resulting in feature-building that doesn't create much net customer value.

As you can see through this example, we are already unshackling our company from historic anchors even through the early steps of this exercise.

Principle 5: Understand voiced pain points and unvoiced imbalances in the ecosystem.

We already discussed non-core activities, which capture untapped potential. When we look at activities in our ecosystem, it captures the current state of available solutions. Now, we need to assess how effectively value flows between these activity groups and across player groups to understand the effectiveness of existing solutions. This leads us to the second and third legs of the market problem – voiced pain points and unvoiced imbalances.

Is it easy to know the difference between untapped potential and gaps in existing solutions? No. Is it important to know the difference? No, because they equally contribute to our market problem definition. What is important is that we frame our analysis such that we don't miss any of the three legs of our market problem because we didn't ask enough questions.

We want to develop hypotheses and gather two types of gaps in value created by existing solutions. The act of serving our market involves both following and leading. We want to address both voiced or perceived gaps as well as unvoiced or unrecognized gaps. It matters not whether we intend to solve it all ourselves. We must explore these two aspects for all player groups because we never know where opportunities and risks sit. Infographic C.5 illustrates the type of insights we are working to gather through this exercise.

Interpreting value is an onion-pealing exercise. Our research must involve the use of structured interview guides and follow-on questions to get deeper into the activities of the player groups to understand how effectively current activities and solutions create value. Recollect the principles we introduced in productization around flow thinking and bi-directional flow of value. Our market assessment is intended to surface inflow and outflow of value for each player group.

Understand voiced pain points to follow the market in framing the problem.

As a second leg of defining the market problem, we must understand what player groups think and how they feel about value. These are the sentiments of various player groups around their activities, and they will reflect the historical experience of each player group.

Henry Ford, Steve Jobs, and others have famous quotes about the importance of staying ahead of the customers or other players in the market, which is true. But in my experience, the vast majority of companies aren't changing global behaviors from horses and carriages to automobiles or physical telephone lines to smartphones.

Loss aversion is real regardless of the scenario. Customers experience loss aversion if they feel we don't consider their obvious voiced pain points. Therefore, we must first address real or perceived sentiments if they exist.

C.2 ANALYZE THE MARKET PROBLEM TO TRIGGER MACRO-EVOLUTION

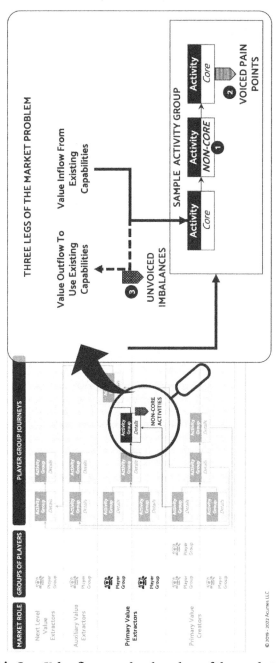

Infographic C.5 – Value flows render three legs of the market problem

> **Things to Remember: Voiced Pain Points**
>
> Voiced pain points are conscious real or perceived sentiments a player group faces. They form the second leg of the market problem. They are often symptoms of root causes, which must be addressed via new or improved solutions.

In our grocery shopping ecosystem, players like me are likely to find stock outages of certain items frustrating. Another common hurdle is mismatches between discounts displayed on shelves and actual checkout prices, which I only recognize when I get home. These symptoms help an observer frame the market problem for my price-sensitive player group's customer journey.

Consider the following questions to frame the second leg of the market problem:

What are the voiced pain points that each player group feels or experiences for various activity groups?

How effective are current solutions in addressing these voiced pain points?

Before we jump too far, we need to think about what the customer might be missing about their own world. If we only go by what the customer shares with us, we fall into the trap that Henry Ford warns us about designing faster carriages.

Understand unvoiced imbalances to lead and disrupt the market in framing the problem.

Finally, we must identify unvoiced imbalances in the ecosystem to frame the third leg of the market problem.

We are all anchored by our past. Therefore, it is easy to think that inequitable relationships are normal. However, we want to understand such inequities to possibly lead a disruption in our market.

> **Things to Remember: Unvoiced Imbalances**
>
> Unvoiced imbalances are gaps in value creation that player groups are not consciously aware of or consider the norm due to the historic ineffectiveness of the ecosystem. Imbalances often arise because an ecosystem has non-competitive dynamics due to monopolistic or oligopolistic entities dominating key activities. Solving unvoiced imbalances could lead to market disruption.

These are opportunities to disrupt the ecosystem where one or more players are offering more to the ecosystem than they are getting. Ford and Jobs would likely agree that an external party is more optimally positioned to understand the market needs than the customer due to our vantage point if we have the discipline to learn objectively.

Playing catch-up to our market by understanding non-core activities and voiced pain points is a good and necessary start. But relationships with players in our market cannot be submissive because we will miss important parts of the picture. Every player in our market has a large spectrum of activities in their life and our ecosystem likely only intersects with that spectrum for a tiny portion of their efforts. So, once we understand non-core activities and voiced pain points, we must switch roles and play a dominant one.

Customers and other players live through unvoiced imbalances that they don't speak about or recognize themselves. These are value gaps that a value creator in the ecosystem can close. The longer we focus on playing catch-up via voiced pain points and following the market, the more time we leave our market open for someone else to jump in and solve these inequities, which are often higher value-creating opportunities.

Consider the following questions:

Within the confines of each activity group, what are the unvoiced imbalances experienced by that player group due to unfair advantages held by other player groups?

What are the sources of these discrepancies?

As consumers, do we get the best quality on the shelf for the price in our grocery ecosystem? A family of beef farmers I know decided to forgo the 'organic' tag because the bureaucracy and cost were prohibitive. Additionally, marketing is not a core competency for such players. As a result, we likely miss out on access to many such high-quality options through our traditional grocery channels. Could someone break the value chain to simplify access blocked by signatories and a handful of large grocery chains? Again, it's an inequity for the consumer and the farmer, who could both benefit from better trading channels. Our goal during the problem framing stages is to identify and analyze without worrying too much about whether there is a viable solution or not.

The essence of the value creation from ridesharing platforms originated from the recognition that government-originated taxi medallions created inequities for drivers and passengers. Robinhood, primarily a stock trading platform, disrupted their market by offering consumers the ability to trade stocks without incurring fees. This was an unvoiced imbalance that everyone in the world lived with and considered a norm because all large traditional trading platforms charged hefty fees for each trade.

My market assessment effort at the education solutions company also surfaced a potential breakdown in the ecosystem. We can summarize it as "are there professional educational programs that are not creating educational value to learner groups because such programs exist solely as a tax collection mechanism for traditional accreditors?" The possibility of addressing this unvoiced imbalance presented an opportunity to disrupt the space by not accepting the current terms of trade as good enough.

Assessing the flow of value in our ecosystem helps us create a complete picture of the market problem for each player group. Additionally, it is optimal to leverage the next principle to start developing insights before exhausting all our planned primary and secondary data gathering and analysis efforts. Remember, strategy development is an iterative exercise. Using the latter half of the assessment to validate the insights we draft based on the first half would be optimal.

Principle 6: Formalize market insights to enable who-how-what trade-offs.

Every aspect of strategy development is a tedious exercise. It's not different from handling big weights at the gym. If we use it diligently, the results speak for themselves. If we do not respect the exercise, we are likely to get injured. The quality of our hypothesis development, qualitative and quantitative data gathering, and objective analyses determine the quality of insights.

In the words of a short-staffed Chief Strategy Officer of a $2B revenue company, "we have a lot of field experience on the team; but I need help to move them forward from operating on gut-feel… we are barely keeping track of our biggest competitors."

A picture is indeed worth a lot more than a thousand words because there are so many concepts we cannot explain in words without leaving room for subjectivity. Directionality is easier to show in a diagram through arrows. We can easily capture a type of value through visual cues such as a dollar sign or data, content, or raw materials icons. We can also illustrate a scale of value through size or colors. Sequencing is infinitely more apparent in a visual construct.

Once we comprehensively frame our market into a few cohesive visuals to support our in-depth research and analysis, our organization won't be held hostage to potentially biased or outdated tribal knowledge from a few people who claim market expertise because they spent years in the space or talk to customers often.

To wrap up our market assessment, we must triangulate and arrive at three sets of insights which we will need to structure the three trade-off questions that form our corporate strategy – 1) Who will we serve? 2) What will we offer? 3) How will we deliver?

First, use player groups to lead us to customer groups and a competitive set. We worked hard to keep ourselves out of the center of our ecosystem to ensure objectivity through the exercise. We learned a significant amount of information about various player groups.

We used externally observable parameters and categories to group the primary and secondary value extractors. Some of them are our optimal customer groups.

We have a deeper understanding of the primary and auxiliary value creators and substitutes. It gives us insights into where threats come from. Our probability of victory in the market depends on who else is playing in our ecosystem and their role.

Consider the following questions:

Which of the primary value extractor and secondary value extractor player groups do we hypothesize are our short-list of top customer groups?

Which of the primary value creator, auxiliary value creator, and substitute player groups do we consider competitors?

Second, a visualized market landscape, where activity groups are linked by value flows, frames journeys of player groups, including each short-listed customer group. We must validate and memorialize each shortlisted customer group's natural journey and value flow.

Consider the following question:

What is the end-to-end journey and value inflows and outflows throughout that journey for each major player group within our market boundary?

Third, hypothesize the market problem for each short-listed customer group, the likely value created for each, and our probability of being the source of that value.

We have identified the non-core activities, voiced pain points, and unvoiced imbalances of player groups. As a result, we can frame the essence of the market problem that each customer group would gain value from.

Based on our history and market feedback, we can frame the estimated probability with which a customer group might buy from us. With strong analytical skills, we can assess the value of these market problems quantitatively. Our effectiveness is also influenced by the number of value creators in the ecosystem for a given journey because we must share the market problem with them.

C.2 ANALYZE THE MARKET PROBLEM TO TRIGGER MACRO-EVOLUTION

Consider the following questions:

What is our comprehensive and cohesive framing of the market problem for each player group?

What are the estimated odds that each top customer group will buy from a value creator like us?

What is the estimated value that each customer group would gain if that group's market problem were solved comprehensively?

Developing these insights and validating them iteratively allows us to frame the market problem effectively with the most up-to-date research and analysis necessary in our evolutionary mindset. The following two chapters will draw upon these insights to answer our three critical who-how-what questions.

C.3
PIN DOWN OPTIMAL CUSTOMER TO INITIATE STRATEGIC CHOICES.

SERVING everyone is the same as serving no one. The concept of focus and serving one optimal group of beneficiaries is in every business text. We can even go back to the New Testament in the bible, and it has an often-quoted verse, "No man can serve two masters... You cannot serve God and mammon." Why? Because we will serve both poorly.

We can elevate from basic activities to tangible value creation when actions align with strong belief systems. We need similar conviction about determining our optimal customer because we are resource-constrained as a scaling company. We can only productize certain capabilities and commit to one or two sets of processes, enabling technologies, and data.

Why is focus important?

Efficiency, Efficiency, Efficiency. It allows an organization to channel its resources to go after similar customers, those easiest to sell to, and has the most to gain from its offerings. Once our scaling company has validated that some of its early customers value its offerings, we must take the time to decide the optimal audience for its offerings from among billions of consumers or millions of companies around the world.

During the early stages of existence, founders and employees are under pressure to prove the solution to themselves, early customers, and potential investors. Unfortunately, the company also doesn't have much data to rely on to decide who to sell to. So, it is rational to take a broad approach to test market viability and capture revenue, as very little reliable information is available.

C.3 PIN DOWN OPTIMAL CUSTOMER TO INITIATE STRATEGIC CHOICES

In this stage, the customers that buy from the company are early adopters who tend to be risk takers. They are most likely to try new offerings and risk living with some gaps, but this is usually a very small portion of the market.

As the company grows beyond its infancy to a relevant number of customers and revenue, it is time to fine-tune how it goes to market. A company's customers can be individual consumers or other companies. Either way, they are different enough that not everyone is equally likely to buy from the company or, even if they buy, unlikely to appreciate its offerings equally well.

Why waste time and resources going after customers who are less likely to buy? Why find and serve undesirable customers that cost too much to serve or end up being short-term customers?

There are no good reasons.

This chapter will discuss the analytical principles we can deploy to identify our optimal customer that addresses the who-to-serve trade-off in our strategy development exercise. It won't be an easy choice to make. But a necessary one.

As we go through this chapter, we must view ourselves as a protagonist for our entire player group, including our direct competitors. We want to understand who the optimal customer for the best version of our company is without being skewed by our historical mistakes or biases.

First, we will go through identifying our sweet spot customers. **Second**, we will discuss the nuances of the term customer to arm ourselves with the most insights necessary to define what we will offer and how we will deliver.

Thematically, we want to define our optimal customer in terms of externally observable parameters that we have already developed through our market assessment. A common mistake in strategy development is choosing customers through interpretive or not predictive parameters. This defeats the entire purpose because our goal is to create actionability and clarity. Therefore, we will frame our optimal customer through this chapter in objective, non-interpretive, and easily observable parameters.

A key reminder is not to use this customer choice as a branding tactic while the reality of our value engine does not have repeatability and reproducibility due to our lack of focus. Talking about focus is easier than having the discipline to stay focused.

Principle 1: Identify the sweet spot.

As soon as we validate our company's early solution to the market problem through a few good customers in the early months and years, we should focus our efforts on customers that are most likely to buy and discern the most value from our company's offerings. This is our **Sweet Spot**.

Years ago, a marketing professor compared the act of identifying the sweet spot to finding an ideal life partner. She explained it this way – "Find someone who really appreciates your good qualities and can put up with your bad qualities." I haven't heard a better analogy on this topic to this day.

Identifying the sweet spot is a highly analytical exercise of creating a mold for one or two most optimal customer groups to which we must dedicate all our investment. The sweet spot qualifies customers to whom the company proactively creates, sells, and delivers its offerings. Identification of the sweet spot is a best-case scenario analysis where we must imagine that we will operate as a mature and disciplined company. The reality of our execution weaknesses does not change what our sweet spot is.

> **Things to Remember: The Sweet Spot**
>
> **The common externally observable parameters of customers who really appreciate what we bring to the market space is called the sweet spot. It is important to note that the sweet spot is not the customer itself. Instead, it is the parameters that collectively describe our optimal customers.**

The most common misconception is that focusing on our sweet spot precludes us from having other customers. This is fake news spread by teams that lack discipline. Dedicating our company to serve our sweet spot does not mean customers outside the sweet spot won't buy of their own volition.

Imagine that our company is planning to spend $10M in our next execution cycle. We should dedicate the entire $10M to operating and evolving our value engine focused on our sweet spot. We will have enablement resources exclusively focused on designing and building our offerings for the sweet spot. Our digital marketing and branding efforts will exclusively focus on the sweet spot. We hire all new sales reps with experience and focus all their time on the sweet spot. If we apply such a focus, we will dominate our sweet spot.

However, suppose a potential customer that we didn't go after with our marketing or actively sell to comes across our company through their own efforts or references wants to buy from us. In that case, we will absolutely complete that sale if our offerings meet that customer's needs. This also implies that these peripheral customers must use our offering created for our sweet spot. We must not change our focus to make the peripheral customers happy as well. Having clarity and discipline on what constitutes our sweet spot is important for us to prioritize which customers and prospects to listen to. Not all customers are made equal.

As the domination of our sweet spot grows, such prospects we never sought out will only increase because we have an expanding value-creating offering and reputation. So, feel free to ignore the naysayers who dissuade us from identifying and committing to the sweet spot.

I use a simple three-step approach that starts with our early hypotheses from our market landscape. The three steps are:

- *Step 1: Define a short-list of customer groups*
- *Step 2: Analyze and rank customer groups*
- *Step 3: Extract the sweet spot*

THE SPIRAL STAIRWAY™ – THE SYSTEM TO BUILD A HOLISTIC COMPANY

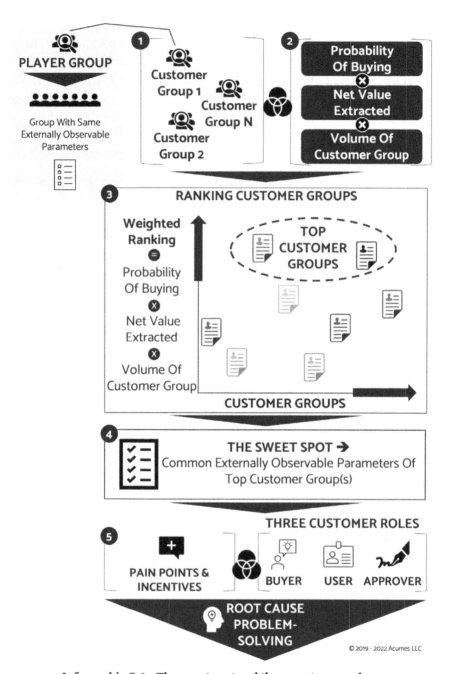

Infographic C.6 – The sweet spot and three customer roles

Infographic C.6 illustrates key elements necessary to identify our optimal customer. We move from what we know, which is our market landscape and all historical experience and data from our operations baseline, to a focused future where the company has an unambiguous definition of its optimal customer. Identifying the sweet spot is one of the most analytical portions of our strategy development exercise. Given its central nature in setting a company's strategy, it's worth the deep dive.

Step 1: Define a short-list of customer groups.

Depending on the efficacy of our market landscape insights, we should already have all the necessary ingredients to short-list customer groups. If not, this is the time to revisit Chapter C.2.

To effectively choose our sweet spot, we will need to start with a broad ecosystem mindset by including as many customer groups as possible. Rethink which value extractor groups could be relevant customer groups. We must cross-validate our market boundary with our current customers, lost customers, and prospective customers that we tried to do business with to ensure we have a comprehensive set of customer groups. This chapter will generically call all of them 'customers' for simplicity.

We will also need to know some critical information about all these customers. Customers can be described based on externally observable parameters, whether the company operates as a business-to-business (B2B) or business-to-consumer (B2C) entity. The operative phrase here is 'externally observable.' These are the same externally observable parameters we used for our player groups in our market landscape.

Over time, I added a personal clarification to my marketing professor's definition of identifying the sweet spot. The world tells us that we should not stereotype. This is true in most circumstances when we judge people on a personal basis. However, defining the sweet spot and using it effectively is 100% embracing stereotyping.

Grouping customers is a great start. But before we start analyzing these customer groups, let's do some checksums to ensure our analytical work is adding up.

A litmus test for the quality of our customer groups is to ensure that players in each group behave similarly. i.e., are we sure that customers in each group follow the same journey characterized by the activity groups and value inflows and outflows that we defined during the market assessment?

So, what does a good output from this step look like?

First, we have a handful of customer groups that cover all relevant value extractors in our ecosystem after cross-validation with our current, lost, and prospective customers.

Second, we can tabulate all these customer groups using the same three to five observable parameters, each with a maximum of four categories.

Third, we can validate that each customer group's defining categories are predictive of that group's journey.

Although mathematically, these three conditions could imply many customer groups, effective grouping and removing the long tail of customer groups with limited volume and market problem alignment based on our market landscape will allow us to create a short-list. Therefore, my recommendation would be to work towards eight or ten customer groups before moving into Step 2.

Step 2: Analyze and rank customer groups.

I won't downplay it; this second step will require strong analytical muscles and experience. In addition, the company will need to rely on solid enablement resources to stack rank the customer groups we have created.

We must base the stack ranking of these customers on three factors.

The **first** factor is the likelihood that customers in each customer group will buy from a company like ours, even if it is a competitor.

The **second** factor is how much each customer group values the offerings from a company like ours, which essentially determines how much money is really on the table to trade for the value.

The **third** factor is the volume of potential customers, whether individual consumers or companies, in each group. It would be a shame to choose a sweet spot that is so small that our return on investment will be low even if we execute flawlessly.

All three of these factors must be informed by both our market landscape and our operations baseline. The key warning here is that our strategy development should avoid being exclusively guided by our current operations baseline. Using only our operations baseline as a reference for the probability of sale or value delivered will skew us towards treating immaturity in our history as the foundational truth. Conversely, using only the market landscape as the single source of truth takes us away from our realistic limitations and might send us on a wild goose chase.

Our sweet spot customers are the ones that we can serve best in the future by striving for what is possible while grounding ourselves in our true limitations. Therefore, besides using past performance data, such as sales and marketing data and usage and satisfaction data for our offering, the strategy development team will have to collect and use qualitative and quantitative information gathered through primary and secondary research as we discussed in Chapter C.2.

Let's explore each of these factors in more detail to set quality guardrails.

The **first** factor is the probability of a customer in a customer group buying from a company like ours, but not specifically us. Therefore, we must separate the true maturity of our operations baseline from our true potential maturity.

Historical sales and revenue data are sources that could tell us which customer groups tend to buy more from us than others. However, we must start by normalizing for the difference in investment that went into selling to and building for each customer group in the past. In other words, we cannot assume that Customer Group A is more likely to buy than Customer Group B just because A has more historical sales. What if we had directed much more marketing spend to A? What if our best sales reps focused on A? Is the maturity of our processes high enough that we can rely on historical data? Using spurious or unreliable past data is more likely to lead us astray than help effective decision making. We would be better off not using poor historical data at all.

Primary research to gather qualitative and quantitative data through interviews with various players as we build our market landscape could involve objective questions to discern who each customer group might buy from and their underlying reasons. Since each customer group is a player group in our market landscape, we can preemptively ask these questions as we gather market intelligence.

Carefully conducting secondary research throughout the same exercise can help us find buying decision rationale and data for customer groups. However, secondary research is always a dance with the devil because it is hard to discern between objective, high-quality research from poor, self-serving data. Therefore, my advice is to restrict sources to trustworthy publications and always to use two or three separate sources to validate each other or use median values across multiple sources.

Exploring such analytical paths will help create an answer around probability. For a scaling company with limited data, the intention is not to arrive at a numerical probability figure with statistical significance. Creating stratification of the likelihood of buying between different customer groups is enough. The real value comes from our ability to make choices based on stratification and objective information that goes into that stratification. We only need granularity that supports objective decision-making.

Consider the following questions to internalize stratification of the probability of purchase by breaking down each customer group's likely behavior using a simple scoring construct:

What is our confidence-level that the market problem definition for the customer group is truly value creating? High = 10 points, Moderate = 5 points, Low = 3 points.

What is the likelihood that the customer group will prioritize this market problem as one that needs to be addressed if there is a solution in the ecosystem? High = 10 points, Moderate = 5 points, Low = 3 points.

How many value-creator groups, including primary, auxiliary, and substitute options, in the ecosystem could realistically solve the market problem for the customer group? High = 3 points, Moderate = 5 points, Low = 10 points.

Such simple questions are much easier to gather data for and analyze than an overarching probability of purchase. Starting with such a weighted scoring and stratification approach gives us a strong indication of which customer groups are most likely to buy from a player like us. But please don't skip all analytical work and just use gut feel to do this. It defeats the whole purpose.

The **second** factor to bake into our analysis is the value a customer group discerns from a company like ours. My recommendation is not to get carried away with placing monetary figures to value discerned as it will be based on history. For a scaling company, pricing is one of the last principles of productization to mature. Using past pricing as a measurement of value delivery will likely mislead us.

Most of the information for this second factor can come from our market landscape insights. We have already mapped our customer groups in our market landscape. We already framed the market problem for each customer group. Use what we already learned and address gaps in our data to augment our market landscape insights.

Value discerned by customers correlates with the market problem's size and scope. Customers are willing to pay for the market problem they experience if it is solved effectively. Does a customer care whether the solution is automation using technology or whether an army of humans sit behind the scenes and replicate the automation manually in an instant? Not unless the quality is different. They pay for the value created by addressing the market problem.

The value that a customer group discerns tells us how much revenue we might be able to generate from each customer. For example, it could correlate with how often they buy and how long they will stay as a customer. This second factor helps us understand the lifetime monetizable value of each customer, assuming that they buy from us.

The **third** and last factor is the universal size of each customer group. When we choose our perfect customer, we also want to make sure there are enough of such customers in the world to justify our commitment to them.

We may have already developed the size of our player groups as part of our market landscape. This is when we need it. Think about market sizing at this stage as a volume check as we choose our perfect customer. The most common reason I see scaling companies size the market is to tell the world that "we have a big market" to get more funding or keep the board at bay. I understand these motivations, but this is just a reason focused on internal stakeholders.

The more important reason to size our market effectively is to know how many customers we can really serve if we focus all our efforts.

It will give us an objective quantification of our likely return on investment. Our strategy development exercise aims not to develop a big, bloated number that can make us feel like we have a winning formula. Instead, the purpose is to create a reasonable and maybe even conservative size of the customer groups to ensure that our return on investment will be high.

The simple outcome here is a count. Forget about dollars. Factor two about value already accounts for which customer groups might generate the most revenue. If our customer groups are individual consumers because we are a B2C company, we count human beings or households or similar. If we are a B2B company, then we are counting companies, business units, employees, the sales volume of the customer's offering that our offering may augment, etc.

We must use the observable parameters and categories we defined in Step 1 of identifying the sweet spot to conduct research and calculate these counts. All the principles and pitfalls that we covered above around secondary research apply here as well. Embrace an objective bottom-up sizing to create a conservative count for the market size of each customer group.

With these three factors on the board, we know how big each customer group is, how likely each group is to buy, and how valuable each customer could be for us if they buy. By multiplying these three factors directly or through weighted scores, we can create a score for each customer group. This single or weighted score is essentially a stacked rank of our customer groups. The analytical enablement resources will have to use experience and judgment to gather the data for these three factors and complete the analysis.

C.3 PIN DOWN OPTIMAL CUSTOMER TO INITIATE STRATEGIC CHOICES

Infographic C.6 above visualizes the sequence of using these three factors to stack rank our short-listed customer groups. Our outcome is the top customer groups in our market. We are one step away from the sweet spot now.

Step 3: Extract the sweet spot.

I love it when a good analysis comes to a coasting end because of all the hard work and discipline that went into the early part of the analysis. If we do the first two steps of the sweet spot identification exercise well, Step 3 is relatively easy.

The common observable parameters that articulate our top two or three customer groups is our sweet spot if their behaviors are similar, as reflected through the journey in our market landscape. It is critical for the efficacy of our approach that both criteria are true. The shared customer journey of the customer groups we choose within our sweet spot leads us to our optimal use case as well.

The narrower our sweet spot, the more decisive and focused we are. However, we also want to choose a sweet spot that can support our company's size and growth goals.

The smaller or less mature our company is and the smaller the amount we have available to invest in growth, the more niche our sweet spot will need to be. We must make the remaining choices internalizing this self-assessment of where we are in the growth curve. Regardless, we must always keep at least the top two or three customer groups in play because we want to make a strategic decision that can go beyond the short-term. Focus on a single customer group that does not allow us to scale our operations baseline beyond that single customer group doesn't support sustainable growth. So, here are two rules to frame our sweet spot.

> **Things to Remember: Sweet Spot Rule #1**
>
> **Ensure that customers in the sweet spot have very similar customer journeys if we include more than one of our top-ranked groups. Similar customer journeys imply that these customer groups have similar market problems. A shared market problem implies we can serve them with a single scalable solution as opposed to disparate ones.**

Based on this first rule, we must look beyond the obvious ranking of customer groups to prioritize customer groups with similar journeys. If all our top customer groups have divergent customer journeys, it is critical to reassess the quality of our analysis. It is confounding that our top customers who are most likely to buy and gain the most value act very differently in our ecosystem. It is likely because we have misunderstood how value is created and consumed.

> **Things to Remember: Sweet Spot Rule #2**
>
> **Ensure that top customer groups chosen for the sweet spot have similar externally observable properties. The predictive parameters that define each customer group also heavily influence how we pursue those customers and The Company Way processes to work with each group of customers. Boxing extremely different customer groups into a sweet spot solely because they ranked high will leave us spreading our company resources thin.**

Like the first rule, the second rule focuses on the essence of the analysis as opposed to robotically picking the top-ranked customer groups without internalizing why or what purpose it would serve. The second rule ensures that we attempt to acquire and deliver to similar customers.

Illustratively, imagine that one of the key predictive parameters is age, and it turns out that our 2nd and 3rd ranked customer groups have age categories of 50-somethings and college-aged respectively, while the top-ranked group has an age category of high-school age. Therefore, it is significantly more optimal to market, sell, and deliver via our processes to high-school and college students instead of high-school students and 50-somethings. The more similar these customers are, the more repeatable and reproducible our processes can be. This is the entire purpose of developing a sweet spot – scalability.

Infographic C.7 illustrates the nuances of this final step. The table represents ten customer groups defined using five behavior predicting parameters. Each parameter has a handful of categories in which the customer groups differ. Effectively, think about each row as the unique identifier for any customer in that customer group.

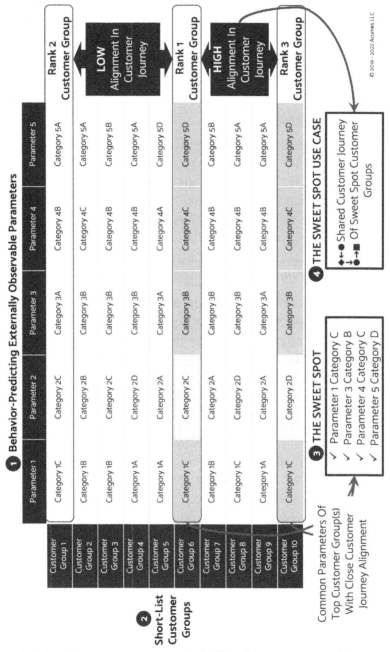

Infographic C.7 – Top customer groups with aligned journeys prescribe sweet spot

Hypothetically, we ranked Group 6 first based on our analysis in Step 2. Group 1 came in second and Group 10 came in third. Although we ranked Group 1 second, the sweet spot is optimal if we choose Group 6 and Group 10 even though they are ranked first and third. The second-ranked Group 1's customer journey is dissimilar to Group 6's. In practice, we must understand why our analysis would result in such a conclusion to ensure the efficacy of our analysis.

Given that Group 6 and Group 10 are both ranked highly enough, have very similar customer journeys, and four of the five behavior-predicting parameters match, we can feel that our analysis is correct. The sweet spot is the common parameters across Group 6 and Group 10 because they are relatively similar customers with a similar market problem that we have high confidence that we can address.

> **Things to Remember: The Sweet Spot [Refined]**
>
> **The sweet spot is the common categories of externally observable parameters of top customer group(s) with very close customer journey alignment. The shared customer journey is our optimal use case associated with the sweet spot.**

In addition to the sweet spot definition, **Addressable Market Size** is a by-product of this exercise.

We not only learned what are top customer groups are, but we also know the three ranking factors about them. We know how likely they are to buy, how much value they attribute to our offering, and how many of such customers are out there. If we multiply the quantification of the second and third factors, we have a total addressable market size for each customer group. If we frame our sweet spot around our top two customer groups and their customer journey, we should sum up this addressable market size for those two customer groups. The market size of our sweet spot is a litmus test for potential growth limitations for our company.

As a word of warning, the instinct to show growth potential and a large addressable market also leads to a temptation to include several customer groups, which breaks our sweet spot definition. This is purely extrinsic motivation and creates no intrinsic value.

As a scaling company, we must ask ourselves some hard questions, if we desire to prioritize beyond two of our similar and optimal customer groups into other customer groups with dissimilar customer journeys.

Do we have a market challenge where our customer groups do not attribute much value to what companies like us bring to the market? If so, we want to go back to our market landscape and further iterate on our research to ensure that we understand the market well. If we return to this point again, it might be time to raise the flag and ask ourselves whether we have a viable market.

Did we over-index on our past poor performance to give our entire player group a low probability of customers buying?

Remember, we are trying to perform this exercise with an objective mindset and are operating as a spokesperson for our entire player group, including our direct competitors. If customer groups tend to buy from similar players like us at a high probability, we should use that. Our macro-evolution cycle intends to improve our operations baseline and catch up and surpass others like us.

I am writing this at a coffee shop across from a candle store. Suppose our company's core capability is to produce scented candles. We can think about many applications for this capability and many paths to sell. However, a careful market assessment exercise can help group customers using observable parameters and categories. Examples may include the following.

- *Parameter 1: Size of selling institution. Categories – boutique stores, large nation-wide stores.*
- *Parameter 2: Point of sale. Categories – physical retail setting, online setting.*
- *Parameter 3: Selling institution location. Categories – neighborhood with average income 50% higher than the citywide average, neighborhood with an average income between citywide average and 50% higher than citywide average, neighborhood with an average income less than the citywide average.*

A market study can help such a candle maker choose a sweet spot that might be selling its candles to boutique stores in physical retail settings in neighborhoods with a median income at least 50% higher than the city-wide average income.

Such an articulation of the sweet spot allows this candle manufacturer to tailor its offerings. We must tailor the types of candles, the number of candles in each packet, the type and quality of packaging, the expected number of uses for each candle, and many other considerations to this sweet spot. The choice of sweet spot also drives our commercialization efforts, including packaging and pricing. In addition, the sweet spot dictates how often each end-user might buy a candle, the approach to distribute to chosen customers, and several other sales and marketing decisions.

To conclude, investing time and mindshare to identify the sweet spot is critical to deploying our value engine effectively and efficiently. It simplifies and focuses our approach to attack the market. Once the sweet spot is clear, we must then understand how customers in the sweet spot think and make decisions.

Principle 2: Understand and identify the customer roles in the sweet spot.

We framed our sweet spot, which means we can easily find our optimal customers without ambiguity. But what do we really mean by 'customer'? How does a customer think?

We need to internalize that even the perfect customer in the sweet spot has multiple personality disorders. Of course, I use those words playfully, but the meaning still stands.

Whether we serve individual consumers in a B2C space or companies in a B2B environment, a customer is a complex interplay of incentives. An individual makes decisions based on many factors. Other individuals and their decisions may influence the person we consider a customer. Likewise, a company has many roles, functions, and levels, several of which interplay to decide how value is consumed.

C.3 PIN DOWN OPTIMAL CUSTOMER TO INITIATE STRATEGIC CHOICES

Understanding what constitutes a customer in the sweet spot and how that customer makes decisions is critical before assessing how we might deliver all or part of that value to the customer.

Identify the customer roles using additional externally observable parameters.

I created a simple construct to break down every customer into three roles, irrespective of the offering or selling approach.

No matter the offering, or the type of customer, a buying decision is complex. Whether a company or a consumer, every customer has a **Buyer**, a **User**, and an **Approver** hidden somewhere within. These three roles are not necessarily separate individuals, but designing, building, and selling any offering should consider all three roles and their needs. Although this consideration is easier to grasp where customers are companies and each role is occupied by different people, the same principle applies when customers are individuals.

> **Things to Remember: The Three Customer Roles**
>
> Every customer is an individual or a company whose collective view of the market problem is a combination of individual voiced pain points, non-core activities, and unvoiced imbalances of three customer roles – Buyers, Users, and Approvers.

Each of these three roles within a customer will value the offering and commercial approach differently. A customer's overall market problem is a symbiosis between these three roles' views of the problem. Without identifying and understanding each of these roles individually, we will likely miss a necessary dimension of how the customer thinks. Each of these roles offers us a different vantage point. Buyers focus on the overall effectiveness of capabilities in addressing the root causes of the market problem. The user focuses on their own preferences and usually short-term gains. The approver focuses on the commercialization aspects of solutions.

It takes more work to dig a layer deeper and understand the incentives of each of these roles within a sweet spot customer. Still, without it, our strategic trade-offs and choices articulating the 'what' and 'how' questions will remain a shotgun approach.

Once we have framed our sweet spot, we must develop further insights to frame these three roles using additional externally observable parameters that pin-point each role. The definition of each customer role is a concatenation of chosen categories of parameters that frame the sweet spot and chosen categories of parameters that describe each role. For example, think about our definition of a customer role as a street address with an apartment number where all three roles live in the same or different apartments in the same building, where the building is the sweet spot definition.

So, we must articulate an externally identifiable definition of the buyer, user, and approver role using additional behavior-predicting parameters to complete the identification of the optimal customer.

The parameters and categories we use to identify customer roles follow the same rules we used for the sweet spot. As customer roles articulate human incentives, they are always parameters that identify humans in the context of decision-making, regardless of the market.

If the collective customer is a family, a sample parameter is 'family role' with categories such as highest income earner, dependent, and family activities manager. If the collective customer is a business, a sample parameter is 'people management role' with individual contributor, supervisor, and senior executive categories. Depending on the offering and our sweet spot, we must make these categories even more specific to articulate each role in the sweet spot.

A CEO who has a technical background might think the head of technology of a prospect is the customer. A company can easily mistake the head of the department that is buying a product as the customer because that person signs the contract. A toy manufacturer can easily think about a child as the customer because the child would be playing with that toy. However, these can be misleading assumptions because every buying decision is complex.

So, let's explore the three roles that apply to any customer in any context.

Customer role 1: Buyer.

Hands down, this is the most critical role. The buyer holds most of the cards regarding first-time and ongoing buying decisions. In addition, the buyer is usually the party responsible and accountable for addressing the specific problem for which the company has developed a solution.

We described value creation as a problem-solving exercise in our market landscape discussion. Think about the buyer role as the customer's central project manager for that problem-solving exercise.

> **Things to Remember: The Buyer Role**
>
> **The buyer role makes decisions based on the effectiveness with which our offerings meet the long-term needs and assesses the net value flow for the customer as a collective.**

Two discerning characteristics frame a buyer.

First, we are unlikely to make a sale or at least prevent a return or cancellation if the buyer is not on board. This is the takeaway if we take nothing away from this segment.

Second, the buyer is usually responsible for and closest to the problem in question and best positioned to assess the overall value of solutions. In other words, the buyer is the customer's representative who is most capable of discerning the true return on investment over time.

The buyer will be the source of information determining whether it will make an initial purchase because this role will have considered all the possibilities. The buyer is also constantly thinking about how the purchase is being used after the first purchase and will likely be the decision maker on follow-on purchases.

Interestingly, and unfortunately, the buyer role is also the one I see most ignored.

The buyer holds all the soft power and is an analytical personality. This role's objectivity and analytical facets also make the most tempting one for value creators to avoid or bypass because they ask the most demanding and rational questions. But it is a bridge to nowhere to sidestep this role and try to go after the user or the approver because it will bite back later.

In summary, we must focus on delivering our offering's comprehensive and quantifiable short-term and long-term value to the buyer.

Customer role 2: User.

The second most important role is the user. This role derives tactical value on a day-to-day basis or is directed to leverage the offering by the buyer or with the permission of the buyer. Although the buyer drives buying decisions, the user provides direct feedback to the buyer. Where there are many users, the users' needs and satisfaction become very significant, and the buyer will work to synthesize the users' needs and how much value they are discerning. Two key traits can characterize the user.

First, the user touches or is touched by our offering most often, which also means the user discerns most or all day-to-day value. Our offering's most obvious value is designed and delivered to make the user's life easier, happier, faster, or any other applicable measurement.

Second, the user could assess their own day-to-day experience and convey that feedback to the buyer. The user may also demonstrate many subconscious behavioral traits while using the offering that the buyer can observe. Thus, the user has a strong influence on the first time and ongoing buying decisions through the buyer.

Although all three roles are important, the user is also the most selfish personality.

> **Things to Remember: The User Role**
>
> The user role focuses on their own tactical day-to-day best interests and expresses their wants. The user has many other priorities or distractions and just wants the offering to meet their immediate needs despite the cost or ramifications to the collective customer or in the long-term.

It can be tempting for a value creator to bypass the buyer and try to sell to the user. However, even if a company achieves this, this is likely to be a short-term win. Over time, the buyer will learn the user's selfish incentives and block downstream purchases or trigger a return or cancellation.

The commercial approach will have minimal impact on the user. Conversely, the design and delivery of our package and the resulting net value are most interesting to the user. Those are the incentives to understand and win over the user role.

Customer role 3: Approver.

The approver is the role that holds the money bag or the pen to autograph the signature line. But this role looks to others for a buying recommendation and takes the final step of releasing the finances for the purchase. Usually, the approver is the most senior person in the buying cycle or the budget owner and is often mistakenly considered the most important.

Designers and builders of offerings, sales reps, and marketers often make the mistake of focusing heavily on the approver and taking their perspective of value as the value demanded by the customer. This is a mistake because the approver role is not a personality close enough to the user and is not the true problem-solver, which is the buyer. Chasing the approver while ignoring the buyer and the user is a path to selling an offering that will likely not get used effectively and thus hurt the length of the relationship with the customer. The approver role's incentives revolve around two aspects.

First, the approver measures success through the buyer's and user's acceptance of the offering. A good approver understands that they are a gatekeeper holding the funds, and the real value will have to be discerned by the user and buyer. Our optimal customer will have an approver who internalizes the importance of the buyer role and defers to the buyer to offer a recommendation.

Second, the approver wears the hat of the final reviewer or validator. The approver can override the analytical thinking and recommendation of the buyer if the approver feels it's flawed or incomplete. The approver can also control the timing of the decision and the price point at which they strike a deal.

> **Things to Remember: The Approver Role**
>
> **The approver role's primary incentive is commercial. The approver seeks an optimal deal with reasonable pricing and contractual terms.**

Let's walk through a practical example to internalize how the three roles transpire in real life. Consider a B2C scenario around kid's toys where my nephew and nieces are the main characters.

This story involves me, my sister, and her three kids. I am reasonably confident that their parents do not purchase most of my nephew's and two nieces' toys. Instead, every visitor appears to bring the kids a new toy that requires its own shelf in their rooms. The kids take on the user role here. They have preferences that are fairly selfish and short-term to a point where to store the toy, the best way to use a toy, or the harm it could cause aren't on their mind.

So, should a toymaker only consider the user?

No, because the children will never have toys unless someone purchases for them. If I buy a toy for them, I hold the purse and choose the timing of the purchase. So, I am the approver, but I have no idea what kids like these days or what is safe to handle. I might feign interest in what the kids say they want, but guess who I ask what I should get them? I ask my sister because she is the buyer who might have to pick up after the kids and makes me aware of her preference of what the kids should and shouldn't have.

As an approver, I am deferring to the buyer to tell me the optimal course of action so that all parties are happy. As an approver, I just have a budget in mind and how to procure the toy with the least amount of effort. Even designing kids' toys and how to sell them can be optimized if we understand the three roles of the customer and their incentives.

The same principles apply in a B2B scenario.

Let's imagine a scaling company offering a niche operations technology that supports sales and marketing operations at customers. This is a complex sales process for a complex offering that impacts many stakeholders within a customer organization.

Such a commercial operations technology requires centralized administration, user training, data management, and many other ongoing central activities, and a sales operations resource usually manages these efforts.

This position usually doesn't hold the budget. Still, it will make or break the sale because the position is considered the topical expert on process and technology to support commercial operations and is expected to synthesize differing opinions across the organization, prepare the business case after considering many vendors, and recommend the final choice. The same role is also likely to recommend canceling a contract and looking for alternatives if the value is not discerned as expected. In this scenario, this sales operations resource is the buyer.

Marketing operations resources, sales reps, and sales managers use such an operations technology daily to do their jobs. Each rep and supervisor will have personal preferences, and they will likely be selfish and depend on their unique style. As users, they will pass on their wants to the sales operations resource, who we established as the buyer. It is critical for the value creator that offers the software to ensure that it meets these users' day-to-day needs.

The budget to approve this technology frequently sits with a sales or marketing executive, who is the approver. However, in a well-run organization, the sales executive should only be interested in seeing the business case presented by the sales operations position and validating that the company is getting the best deal possible. Therefore, apart from pricing negotiations, the approver is likely to delegate all decision-making responsibilities to the sales operations resource.

Unfortunately, I often see companies trying to sell such offerings to an executive or the sales reps, who are the approver and the user, respectively, because they offer the least resistance. Inevitably, the buyer thwarts these attempts by escalating value-focused challenges, which are likely to be high in the first place because the selling company took the path of least resistance and tried to close a deal with roles not focused on the net value.

Through these two examples, I hope you can see the importance of embracing the need to understand and incorporate the incentives of buyers, users, and approvers.

We used our market landscape and our operations baseline to frame the externally observable parameters of our optimal customer and the three roles through the last two principles. Before we dive into what-to-offer and how-to-deliver for our sweet spot customer roles, let's frame our 'who' strategic trade-off choices because we will always have a hard choice to make based on what we learned.

Principle 3: Frame 'who' trade-offs & choices based on sweet spot and customer roles.

It is hard work to identify the common parameters of our top customers to form our sweet spot and the three customer roles. However, one of three outcomes will be true if we stay disciplined to arrive at these effective answers for our 'who' trade-off question.

- *Outcome 1: We went through an equally perfect strategic assessment during the last macro-evolution cycle and have arrived at precisely the same insights as the last cycle.*

- *Outcome 2: We went through an equally perfect strategic assessment in the last cycle but have uncovered a new set of insights because our market ecosystem has evolved.*

- *Outcome 3: Our strategic assessment this cycle is more mature, and we have arrived at a set of insights that are more reflective of our evolving market ecosystem.*

Options 2 or 3 likely reflect our situation, so we must make choices because our optimal customer is changing. Therefore, we will have to frame that possibility as an intentional, strategic trade-off.

For instance, a marketing technology company I worked closely with had a buyer choice dilemma that I framed as a strategic tradeoff as part of a strategy development effort. Historically, the company had considered a Chief Marketing Officer (CMO) at customers as the buyer, which meant that the offering's data capture and reporting capability was focused on a CMO. I proposed insights to frame a customer's analytics executive as the buyer going forward. This was a clutch choice because it would change how we would tailor the offering and the selling process for a cross-functional analytics executive as opposed to a CMO. The CMO was identified as the approver role through the qualitative and quantitative analysis.

Articulating these choices and enabling our team to focus effectively allows us to channel all our investment to customers that are most likely to buy from us and get the most value from us. It protects us from being distracted and serving no one effectively. Our strategy development exercise is an excellent time to draft these 'who' trade-offs and choices and make soft decisions. These soft decisions will enable us to explore what-to-offer and how-to-deliver questions more effectively.

Infographic C.8 is a simple decision framework that you can use to visualize these choices. Such a representation must have detailed analyses and supporting recommendations for the CEO and senior executives to make effective decisions.

We can frame our who-to-serve strategic trade-off choices by using the following guidelines.

We identified our top customer groups and their customer journeys through our analysis. We must choose our primary use case as our **first** strategic trade-off. A choice to prioritize a use case is a choice to deprioritize another. We must include our second and third choices as the options we are deciding against.

For the use case we choose, we will have options on which customer groups and their parameters and categories would frame our sweet spot. In other words, we could frame our sweet spot differently depending on which and how many top customer groups we choose for our prioritized use case. This choice-set changes our addressable market size and our level of focus. Framing these sweet spot options is our **second** who-to-serve strategic trade-off. Stage choices between two or three sweet spot definitions that allow a large enough market opportunity while also enabling focus.

THE SPIRAL STAIRWAY™ – THE SYSTEM TO BUILD A HOLISTIC COMPANY

	Objectively Framed Baseline State	Trade-off Choice 1		Trade-off Choice N	Proposal Rationale	Impact / Cost / Probability of Success
Optimal **Use Case**	[Current Definition / Choice]	Use Case A	vs	Use Case B	Decision Support Analyses and Insights	Analysis & Insights on Operations Baseline Impact, Investment Needs, and Probability of Success
Optimal Use Case B **Sweet Spot**	[Current Definition / Choice]	Sweet Spot 1	vs	Sweet Spot 2		
Sweet Spot 1 **Buyer Role**	[Current Definition / Choice]	Parameter A | Category A1	vs	Parameter A | Category A2		
Sweet Spot 1 **User Role**	[Current Definition / Choice]	Parameter B | Category B2	vs	Parameter B | Category B3		
Sweet Spot 1 **Approver Role**	[Current Definition / Choice]	Parameter C | Category C1	vs	Parameter C | Category C2		

Trade-off Choices for Use Case, Sweet Spot, and Three Customer Roles Articulate Who-to-Serve

© 2019 - 2022 Acumes LLC

Infographic C.8 – Who-to-Serve Trade-offs Decision Framework

Similarly, we will have to choose from two or three options for the buyer, approver, and user roles. Stage choices between the top two or three definitions for each. These are our **third**, **fourth**, and **fifth** who-to-serve trade-offs.

If we arrive at single choices for these trade-offs, it likely reflects errors, biases, and blind spots in our analytical efforts to get this far.

Consider the following questions:

What are our top two or three options for the primary use case, as defined by shared journeys of top customer groups?

What are our top two or three sweet spot options that align with the optimal use case chosen above?

What are our top two or three options for the buyer, user, and approver roles within the sweet spot chosen above, defined using externally observable parameter(s) and categories?

We must effectively articulate the impact, cost, and probability of success of making each of these choices because each choice is compelling. The quality and objectivity of every analytical step along the way are necessary to ensure we make effective decisions. Framing these strategic trade-offs and choices sets us up to dive into what-to-offer and how-to-deliver for the customer in our sweet spot and the three roles it comprises.

C.4
TRIANGULATE TOWARDS WHAT-TO-OFFER AND HOW-TO-DELIVER STRATEGIC CHOICES.

WHEN the beat of the music changes, our dance moves must change. We cannot expect to be successful if we keep our productized offering unchanged or do not evolve our processes and management approach when our optimal customer shifts and their customer journey alters.

Our strategic trade-off choices about what-to-offer and how-to-deliver can be represented as a simple game, as shown in Infographic C.9.

		COMPANY OPERATIONS BASELINE	
		STRENGTHS	WEAKNESSES
COMPETITORS	WEAKNESSES	**QUADRANT 1** Self-aware Differentiated Advantage to Serve Sweet Spot	QUADRANT 3 Not Self-aware Misidentified Market Problem
	STRENGTHS	QUADRANT 2 Commoditized Market Problem Sub-optimal Sweet Spot Choice	QUADRANT 4 Not Self-aware Sub-optimal Sweet Spot Choice

© 2019 - 2022 Acumes LLC

Infographic C.9 – Single viable strategic zone to create sustainable value

Our likelihood of successfully serving our sweet spot is highest If we play to our strengths and our competitors' weaknesses. But there are no predictable and legal paths to intentionally force our competitors to operate to their weakness. So, our strategic trade-off choices around our operations baseline must simply focus on our current or potential strengths. Of course, it's a bonus if others in the market sabotage themselves. Quadrant 1 represents this optimal zone.

Quadrant 2 implies that we are operating in a zone where our competitors bring the same strengths as we do. The most obvious reason is a difficult market dynamic where the market problem to be solved is trivial. This is essentially a war of attrition where our strengths are not differentiated and implies that we must ask hard questions about our growth and profitability prospects. Alternatively, we may have chosen our sweet spot poorly or may not understand its needs effectively, leaving us to mimic competitors.

Quadrants 3 and 4 imply strategic decisions around our operations baseline that do not align with our strengths. The most common reason for this eventuality is a lack of self-awareness where we have not objectively assessed our ability to deliver against the market needs.

This last part of strategy development focuses on framing critical choices on how to serve our sweet spot. To arrive at these trade-off choices, we must drill into the needs of our sweet spot further. If we are going to hang the future of our company on a few clutch decisions, it is important to ensure that there are studs behind those spots on the wall.

Through the principles below, we will lay out an objective path to arrive at our corporate strategy by picking up where we left off in the last chapter. So, let's reset the board for clarity as we take this final lap to frame our strategic decision. Strategy development has a single purpose – evolve our operations baseline to serve our sweet spot customers with increased effectiveness.

Infographic C.10 provides a roadmap for going from our soft decision on sweet spot customers to evolve every aspect of our operations baseline. Use it as a frame of reference as we go through each principle in this chapter. In the following two parts of our methodology, we will translate our strategic decision into a plan to achieve those decisions and execute that plan.

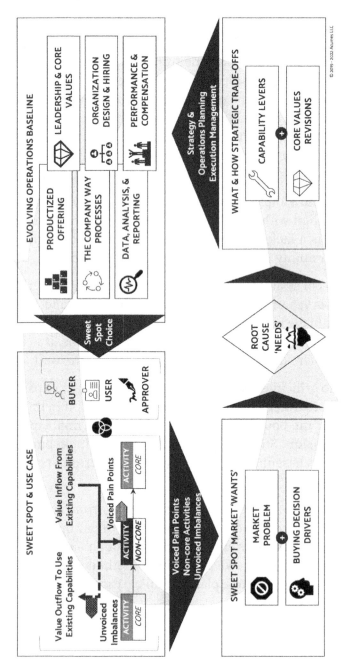

Infographic C.10 – Operations baseline and who-how-what decision cycle

Principle 1: Frame Buying Decision Drivers that help customers choose the optimal value creator.

To serve our sweet spot customer, we must understand the three legs of the market problem and create an effective solution. Before discussing how we solve our market problem, let's talk about how customers buy.

Even if we have the most optimal solution to the customers' market problem, how does a customer know that before buying? For customers to extract the value we can deliver, they must buy. Without buying, how will the customer see the value? Once a customer buys, how will a customer know how future buying experiences compare to the past?

Every relationship involves a bi-directional interpretation of behaviors.

First, customers will not have all the necessary tangible information about value creators similar to us because the use case we are focusing on is only a small part of their whole life, and we only focus on one part of our chosen use case.

Second, customers do not always think objectively and rationally about their market problem within their customer journey. Like all human beings, buyers and approvers in consumer or business buying scenarios are biased and look for short-cuts.

This information gap and lack of objectivity among customers are key enablers that encourage some market players to disseminate exaggerations and even lies to get customers to buy. If we are keeping our faith in creating intrinsic value to drive sustainable growth, how do we fend off others in the market who focus on generating external perceptions that mislead customers? How do we convince customers that we can deliver the value that we are capable of?

To ensure that our focus on fundamentals reaps its full reward, let's consider how customers buy. In addition to objectively assessing the effectiveness of the solutions through trials, customers are also influenced by what I call Buying Decision Drivers.

> **Things to Remember: Buying Decision Driver**
>
> A Buying Decision Driver is a framing of conscious and subconscious behavioral proxies used by buyers and approvers to assess, choose, and stay with a value creator in the market, especially in the absence of past experience. Buying Decision Drivers are stereotypes or decision aids that allow customers to choose optimal value creators. Buying Decision Drivers heavily depend on the sweet spot, and changing the sweet spot implies changing the Buying Decision Drivers.

We have to augment what-to-offer with an effective path to delivering it. How-to-deliver must align with who we deliver to and their needs. For example, why do the employees at a luxury clothing store dress, talk, and act completely differently from those who work at more middle-of-the-road ones? The exact same employees will likely behave differently when they move from working at a Banana Republic, an everyday brand, to a Louis Vuitton, a luxury brand. The employee's behavior and appearance are a cue for a consumer about what is offered. So, we have to uncover the behavioral proxies that we should build into our operations baseline.

We can learn about the behavioral proxies that our sweet spot customers gravitate to through the voiced pain points and activities of buyer and approver roles. Behavioral proxies are observable behaviors that customers expect to see from value creators that address problems in their customer journey.

We are all using this mindset every single day. The same mindset encourages us to dress a certain way for interviews. Investment bankers and consultants dress differently for interviews compared to software developers. Why? The interviewers' Buying Decision Drivers. The interview interactions are just a proxy for our interactions after signing the contract to work together.

> *Consider the following questions to frame the Buying Decision Drivers that allow customers to make decisions outside the effectiveness of the offering itself:*
>
> *What are the underlying processes, behaviors, and commercialization factors that the buyer and approver roles in the sweet spot use to decide whether a value creator will be a successful one to work with?*

C.4 TRIANGULATE TOWARDS WHAT-TO-OFFER AND HOW-TO-DELIVER STRATEGIC CHOICES

How do the buyer and approver interact to finalize a purchase decision?

What are the underlying processes, behaviors, and commercialization factors that the buyer and approver use to decide whether to purchase from a value creator repeatedly?

These are guiding questions; do not ask customers direct questions about the right behaviors because it is our job to figure that out. Instead, we must design situation-specific questions to understand the themes that help us answer such questions. We must also be wary of superimposing our perceptions of optimal behaviors on the customer.

Many challenges that customers feel on an ongoing basis might be unrelated to our productization efforts that deliver value by solving the market problem. However, they could be strong indicators of gaps in Buying Decision Drivers.

For instance, two of the most common value gaps that I hear from customers over the years are "I don't know what your offerings are..." or "I wish I knew you had this capability to augment what we are already buying from you..." These voiced pain points might imply a root cause of poor commercial processes where the customer feels oversold. Another potential root cause is ineffective role definitions and selling incentives among operations resources, which points to gaps in our management approach.

But immediately thinking about the solution is premature. The reality is that if such feedback came from a customer, such gaps already exist in our operations baseline. So, what is the root strategic component enabling misaligned behaviors around our value engine? Core values.

Identifying customers' buying behaviors was a common thread on many projects throughout my consulting days. As we shared insights with clients, we always diligently included action plans on how they could augment processes and offerings to accommodate these buying behaviors. However, it was evident that many of these recommendations were not being implemented effectively at many clients over time. It took me several years to recognize that the root cause of these implementation gaps came down to a lack of comprehensive shift in company-wide behaviors. The only path to achieve that shift is through core values.

Principle 2: Leverage core values as a strategic behavioral lever to deliver Buying Decision Drivers.

As promised when we first introduced core values, they have a tremendous role to play as our organization's behavioral guardrails. Core values are powerful and proactive behavioral guardrails that guide our entire operations baseline if we design and operationalize them properly.

Our strategic path to achieving Buying Decision Drivers and driving its inclusion into our value engine and management approach starts with our core values.

Remember the first layer of our Values Funnel Framework? What do our external stakeholders value? Besides solving the market problem effectively, Buying Decision Drivers is the relationship conduit between our customers and us. We don't have to fake the Buying Decision Drivers; we can live it through our core values.

When I say Amazon, what are the stereotypes that come to mind? The first few themes that come to me are 'good customer service,' 'on-time,' and 'cheap deals.' Three of their several leadership values, as Amazon calls core values, are 'customer obsession,' 'insist on the highest standards,' and 'frugality.' When I read the details behind these values and speak to employees I know at the company, I can connect the dots between their core values and my end-user gutfeel about Amazon.

For instance, 'frugality' disseminated into a company's offerings, processes, and people agenda categorically reduces the cost of operations. It focuses on developing a solution to the market problem that optimizes cost. This could directly translate to cost savings for customers. In addition, setting such a core value also enables organization design and hiring to attract employees who thrive in such a setting and dissuade employees that prefer an organization that creates a perception that poshness is paramount.

Core values must effectively set the tone for the entire company's behavioral foundation that aligns with our customers' Buying Decision Drivers. This is the super-set of behaviors that needs to guide all our actions. In our customer-first mindset, we must not choose behavior traits if they don't align with how we serve our customers.

Framing core values are not analytically complex. They are just psychologically and emotionally difficult. The development of core values requires a methodical approach to ensure their impact. I categorize core values into two groups.

The first is **Value Engine Enablers**.

> **Things to Remember: Value Engine Enablers**
>
> Value Engine Enablers are the most powerful, externally impactful core values that directly and dispassionately address the Buying Decision Drivers of customers. We can draw a direct line between the themes of such core values and our offerings' properties and The Company Way processes.

We must always start with framing this set of core values. For instance, a sample core value theme can be 'best in class,' directly influencing our productization efforts and processes.

The second is **Management Approach Enablers**.

> **Things to Remember: Management Approach Enablers**
>
> Management Approach Enablers are internally focused prerequisite behaviors that allow us to live by Value Engine Enablers.

We have to identify a set of core values that the CEO believes is critical to live by to ensure we get to bat for the Value Engine Enablers. In other words, without such underlying behaviors that largely impact our management approach, the behaviors that we want to build into our value engine are likely non-starters. For instance, a core value theme such as 'always learning' might be an underlying theme that is largely internally focused that is necessary to enable a Value Engine Enabler such as 'best in class.'

So, let's frame these two sets of core values as part of our 'how' strategic trade-off decision.

Frame Value Engine Enablers to influence productization and The Company Way processes.

Our goal through strategy development is not to wordsmith or socialize core values. Instead, we want to frame the essence of our company's behavioral themes to align with our sweet spot customers' needs.

First, we want to frame the table stakes Buying Decision Drivers for our use case as desired behaviors. These are the behaviors that we must absolutely demonstrate to have any chance of operating in our market. In a sense, none of the value creators in our use case will be successful without effectively demonstrating these behaviors. A simple example might be 'safety' in the domestic or international passenger air travel use case.

Second, we need to incorporate differentiating Buying Decision Drivers necessary to augment our solution to the market problem. If we have a market-validated solution, we have precedent. Our future solution will likely be an evolution of our past, not a radical shift. Based on our general approach to solving the market problem, what are we learning from our market analysis as differentiating behaviors that make customers choose us over our competitors? For instance, the passenger air travel use case could have a Buying Decision Driver of 'luxurious' or 'cost-effective.' Our sweet spot customers likely prefer one or the other depending on their affordability.

Third, we have to objectively identify and eliminate existing core values misaligned with our Buying Decision Drivers. Let's put on our critical thinking hat to ensure that we focus on evolution instead of being defensive about our history.

Consider the following questions to understand themes for our Value Engine Enablers:

What are the table stakes Buying Decision Drivers for our use case?

What are the differentiating Buying Decision Drivers that we need to embrace to augment our solution to the market problem?

Which existing core values are misaligned with the Buying Decision Driver insights we have gained?

Effectively synthesized themes answering the first two questions give us our super-set for our Value Engine Enablers. But we cannot be good at all behaviors because each has a cost. Therefore, we must answer the third question and eliminate ineffective existing core values.

Define two or three achievable sets of core values, while accounting for ones we would eliminate, that become choices for our Value Engine Enablers trade-off. For a growth phase company, it is optimal to identify three to five Value Engine Enablers in each option that we put forth.

The comprehensive strategy development exercise I led for a marketing technology company revealed several Buying Decision Drivers. The theme 'buttoned-up' reverberated across all value engine components as a key Buying Decision Driver, but also as a gap. The gap in this theme could be observed in the company's processes, how it launched its offerings, and even the quality of sales proposals presented to customers.

Another theme that customers asked for consistently was 'turnkey.' It implied that customers were looking for solutions that took over all non-core activities that they preferred not to do. But the company's offering required extensive implementation and ongoing attention. This was also an internally relevant theme because many aspects of execution displayed the same half-baked challenge. These two value engine-focused core values were included in a set as a strategic trade-off.

Once we frame our options for Value Engine Enablers, we must assess our remaining core values.

Assess and reframe remaining core values as Management Approach Enablers.

Framing the Management Approach Enablers is a considerably easier task because we already have clarity on their purpose. The purpose of these remaining themes is to ensure that the Value Engine Enablers are supported by how our employees think and act internally.

We must follow the same thorough process as above to assess the effectiveness of the remaining core values in supporting the Value Engine Enablers choices that we drafted above.

Consider the following questions:

What behaviors must our company embrace and live by to ensure that we can support the Value Engine Enablers?

Which of the existing core values that are not included in the Value Engine Enabler options are not effectively contributing to behaviors desired by our customers?

We must frame our optimal collection of supporting values through rigorous qualitative assessments. As an outcome, I recommend mutually complementary two or three Management Approach Enablers for a growth phase company.

Core values based on our sweet spot customers' Buying Decision Drivers frame the 'how' part of our strategic trade-offs because it articulates the essence of the behaviors we should adopt. Remember, our business exists to serve customers.

Frame the how-to-deliver trade-offs.

Our Buying Decision Drivers insights built into our core values influence how-to-deliver through our value engine and management approach in the future. Therefore, it is essential to frame the trade-off choices for both Value Engine Enablers and Management Approach Enablers before we start exploring what-to-offer our sweet spot customers. Infographic C.11 illustrates how we might represent our how-to-deliver trade-off choices.

Consider the following questions:

What are the two or three sets of Value Engine Enablers, each with three to five core values that directly achieve our sweet spot's Buying Decision Drivers, that we can realistically live by?

What are the two or three sets of Management Approach Enablers, each with two or three core values that influence our internal behaviors that support the Value Engine Enablers that we can realistically live by?

These two trade-offs are strategic as we likely couldn't include all the behaviors customers expect. Once we make these two choices on the two

C.4 TRIANGULATE TOWARDS WHAT-TO-OFFER AND HOW-TO-DELIVER STRATEGIC CHOICES

Core Values Enable Alignment of Company Behaviors with Customer Buying Decision Drivers

	Objectively Framed Baseline State	Trade-off Choice 1	Trade-off Choice N	Proposal Rationale	Impact / Cost / Probability Of Success
Value Engine Enablers	[Self-assessment Of Current Core Value Set]	Value Engine Enabler Core Value Set A1 **vs**	Value Engine Enabler Core Value Set A2	Decision Support Analyses and Insights	Analysis & Insights on Operations Baseline Impact, Investment Needs, and Probability of Success
Management Approach Enablers	[Self-assessment Of Current Core Value Set]	Management Approach Enabler Core Value Set B1 **vs**	Management Approach Enabler Core Value Set B2		

Infographic C.11 – How-to-Deliver Trade-offs Decision Framework

core values sets, we can identify the necessary initiatives to operationalize core values to impact our value engine and management approach as part of strategic planning.

Principle 3: Formalize the market problem and identify the root causes.

Before we jump to what-to-offer our sweet spot customers, we must formalize the market problem and the underlying reasons that cause the problem.

First, we need to zoom into the use case for our sweet spot customers to validate the market problem. We made a soft choice on a single journey that aligns with customers in our sweet spot. We must conduct a deeper validation of the value flow analysis that we performed through our market assessment with a deeper focus on our sweet spot to validate our understanding of each leg of the market problem.

We will have to test our final hypotheses around the voiced pain points of buyers and users. We must further explore the non-core activities and unvoiced imbalances that aren't top of our optimal customers' minds. We learn from sweet spot customers directly by speaking with them or indirectly through data gathered from our value creation interactions.

A growth-phase company must create value profitably for one problem before moving to the next. Therefore, the deep dive to frame the market problem primarily focuses on the buyer and user roles. These roles feel and experience the market problem significantly more than approvers.

We are essentially double-clicking into our use case and understanding the details of activities to a point where we can draw each customer role in swim lanes and document steps using the same six process design elements we use for our own internal processes. Visually illustrate the flow of value within this use case. How can we say that we understand our customers if we cannot articulate their day in their life and their intrinsic motivation to go through these steps?

Next, we must identify the root causes underlying the market problem.

The three legs of the market problem – non-core activities, voiced pain points, and unvoiced imbalances – are symptoms. We want to understand them and catalog them. But then we must translate them into root causes that we can solve. An effective jump from symptoms to root causes through a problem-solving mindset differentiates a mature strategy development exercise.

For our hypothetical candle maker in the last chapter, the sweet spot's voiced pain points or preferences might surround basic properties such as aesthetics or longevity. In a problem-solving mindset, the underlying factors that influence the aesthetics or longevity might involve raw material composition, manufacturing processes, storage methods, etc. We cannot devise the appropriate solution until we truly understand the root cause of the problem.

Root cause analysis is not about finding a myriad of unrelated shallow reasons, and we can't solve a wide range of disconnected root causes. Instead, our goal is to arrive at a maximum of two or three cohesive and dovetailed root causes.

> **Consider the following questions to frame the root causes of our market problem:**
>
> *Why is the user and buyer roles experiencing each voiced pain point?*
>
> *Why is the sweet spot customer engaged in each non-core activity?*
>
> *Why is the sweet spot customer experiencing each unvoiced imbalance?*
>
> *Can we drill down multiple layers into each underlying reason?*
>
> *Can we follow the common threads of underlying reasons to arrive at two or three synthesized root causes?*

Root-cause analyses will identify the essence of the reasons the buyer and user roles feel challenges or experience gaps we have identified. These are the root causes of the market problem we need to solve.

At the spend data processing company that I mentioned several chapters earlier, one of the persistent impediments that customers shared was the lack of visibility into the progress of processing the documents that the spend data was extracted from. The company had invested in increasingly complex reporting to give customers visibility about where their documents are. Over 30% of new investment into offerings went into such reporting efforts. But customers did not find value in these reports and continued to be dissatisfied.

The root cause of customers lacking visibility was that the company's software didn't effectively track progress of the documents during processing and had several blind spots. So, how can reports create clarity when the company itself was blind to processing progress? The appropriate path was to address the root cause of poor internal management of document processing without excessively focusing on the symptom of 'visibility' which resulted in reporting on blind spots.

The 'give' of addressing the root causes of the market problem implies applying analytical horsepower. The 'get' is that our solutions are significantly more effective, lasting, and scalable when applied against root causes as opposed to symptoms.

Principle 4: Utilize four capability levers to solve the root cause of the market problem.

We paused on solving the root cause of our market problem until we framed our how-to-deliver trade-off using core values because it is an important input into how we choose what-to-offer. Now, it's time for us to frame decisions about what-to-offer.

Like framing our core values sets, our goal here is not to design all the details of our productized offering. Instead, the detailed design will be part of comprehensive enablement initiatives over one or more execution cycles based on priorities we will set during strategic planning. Therefore, we must focus on the hard choices that impact our entire operations baseline during strategy development.

Mature productization efforts result in an effectively priced package that solves our sweet spot's market problem. That package has one or more capabilities that span the four dimensions we introduced under productization. A mature value engine enables data—and analysis-driven ongoing micro-evolutions to improve the exact properties of a capability or tweak a package or price. This is business as usual. But this doesn't address shifts in our market or maturity gaps in our value engine.

A mature strategy development exercise will expose gaps in our historic productization efforts or reveal a shift in the market problem via the three legs, which is a reasonable scenario in any market at least every couple of years. So, how do we strategically address our new market problem?

There are infinite combinations of ingredients to create solutions to the same root causes of our market problem, each with different effectiveness in value creation and different alignment to our strengths. A four-lever decision approach frames our optimal pathway to create the most customer value aligned with our strengths.

Let's discuss these four capability levers.

Capability lever 1: Reconfigure capability dimensions.

We laid out the four capability dimensions – action, object, knowledge, and promise – that any solution falls on in Chapter B.1. When our market problem shifts, we must comprehensively reassess the balance across these capability dimensions because subtle changes in the root cause might require a holistically different combination of capability dimensions to frame the solution.

For instance, almost all disruptive companies in the last decade simply moved solutions from an action dimension to an object dimension using software that became readily accessible on mobile devices via ubiquitous internet access and decentralized data storage. These new fundamental enablers allowed companies to address past voiced pain points, unvoiced imbalances, or non-core activities by shifting from an action dimension to an object dimension. Whether it's getting a taxi or ordering food, the essence hasn't changed. It's just a dimensional shift to software object.

Defining the dimensional balance of an existing or a new capability is not a tactical decision. It is truly a strategic decision to change the composition of our top capability or two along the four dimensions. Why?

The four dimensions around which we can build a capability require very different fundamentals.

Changes to our productized offering via dimensions significantly impact the rest of our value engine and management approach. Many processes, technology, and data components exist to support the delivery of our productized offering. Incrementally, dimensional shifts change our organization design because we require different skills. It could change our compensation models for those impacted roles.

For example, if our current approach to meet the needs of our sweet spot is heavily indexed on the action dimension, shifting to include a hardware object dimension implies significant changes to several aspects of our operations baseline. Shifting our capability to include a hardware object implies that our processes will have to be built around an e-commerce website or physical retail outlets. Such a shift might imply moving from being a marketing-led commercial model to a sales-led commercial model. It might require that we need an entirely new selling skill set focused on hardware objects.

Essentially, shifts in these four dimensions encompass the most investment-heavy, high-risk, and high-impact decisions our company can make beyond who-to-serve in the market.

Capability lever 2: Structure core building blocks to solve the market problem via capability elements.

We know that a capability is a multi-dimensional solution and our choice amongst these four dimensions is our first lever. But to set a company-wide direction for all investment, we need to dig deeper.

Each capability dimension is not as simple as just an object or an action. Saying that "we are more of a technology company than a services company" is a start, but not enough. Every solution incorporates technology to some extend!

We can only deliver each capability dimension through underlying building blocks. I call these **Capability Elements**.

For instance, an object element in our solution can be hardware or software. It could be petroleum or grains or anything at all. Depending on the market problem at hand, we might have to consider multiple hardware elements like electronic parts of varying complexity and mechanical housing to complete the hardware object dimension of the offering. Elements can include database coding, end-user-focused coding, or machine learning code for a software object. Creating value via the action dimension might imply forms of skilled labor or resource augmentation, which are very different.

Creating value via each dimension will require us to commit to one or more underlying building blocks, requiring different strengths and investments. We must choose whether we can confidently commit to a given building block that ladders up to what-to-offer. This is our second capability lever.

We must refine our view of a capability to enable further design and decision-making by incorporating capability elements.

> **Things to Remember: Capability Elements**
>
> A capability is a comprehensive solution that sits across multiple dimensions, where each dimension is an aggregation of building blocks called capability elements.

Capability elements sit within a single-dimensional silo and contribute directly to the overall value created by the capability. A combination of capability elements forms a comprehensive solution to the market problem. Each capability element requires unique strengths to design, build, market, sell, and/or deliver.

Think about the market problem as a closed door secured with two or three locks where each lock is a root cause of the problem. Each lock can be opened with a few keys, where each key is a capability. Capability elements are various potential ridges and notches for a given key. Putting the right combination together creates a good key. We must choose which ridges and notches we can create based on the tools we have.

Many considerations for capability elements are likely already on the radar in most companies. Our four-lever approach provides a structured framework to pull in internally brainstormed ideas, customer feedback, along with newly developed objective options.

Using such inputs, we must develop hypotheses on the realistic combination of capability elements across the four dimensions that can solve our market problem. As a **first** rule of thumb, if we cannot come up with at least two practical combinations of how to solve the problem, we haven't considered enough elements and combinations.

It is important to focus on using critical building blocks without creating a laundry list of tactical items. As a **second** rule of thumb, each capability element must have a major value contribution to the market problem and have a sizable internal impact on our management approach and value engine.

For instance, listing Amazon Web Services as a server option is not a consequential capability element for most software object-focused solutions unless we currently have a critical on-premises infrastructure with internally staffed resources, and this new capability element significantly shifts the net positive value created for customers.

Capability lever 3: Define effectiveness vectors for each element in alignment with core values sets.

In addition to the dimensional choice of how we build our solution and the underlying elements, we must choose the **quality, cost, flexibility**, and **speed** associated with each element.

In practice, we can take any single element in each dimension and create it with different levels of quality, speed, flexibility, or cost. To make a strategic decision that is also actionable about what-to-offer, we must expand our definition of a capability even further using these controllable aspects I have come to call **Effectiveness Vectors**.

> **Things to Remember: Effectiveness Vectors**
>
> Each capability element in any given dimension – Object, Action, Knowledge, and Promise – has four vectors of effectiveness – Speed, Quality, Flexibility, and Cost – along which we have to choose because we can only maximize on some of them at the expense of others.

No company can be good along all four effectiveness vectors for a given capability element. For example, offering an object or an action at high speed likely implies sacrificing flexibility, quality, or cost. Infographic

C.12 illustrates how we can think about our strategic choices for each capability element.

Our choices to superimpose these four effectiveness vectors onto the four capability dimensions is core to our productization efforts because offering something of high quality is a very different strength than delivering the same offering with a lot of customization. Therefore, we must decide which of these effectiveness vectors we must become good at because we are choosing not to be good at other vectors.

Effectiveness vectors is our third capability lever and is part of our what-to-offer trade-off decision.

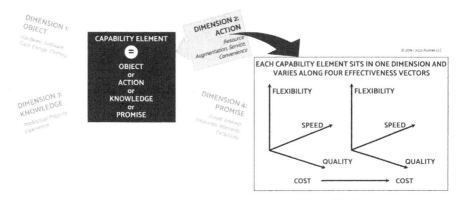

Infographic C.12 – Each capability dimension spans four effectiveness vectors

For example, highly customized and expensive Formula 1 race cars are made in machine shops that work on only two or three cars. On the other hand, a road car is mass-produced in massive factories with limited variation, quickly and at a fraction of the cost.

Our choice of effectiveness vectors also impacts our processes and our management approach. These four effectiveness vectors apply to the composition of any capability element across any offering, industry, and maturity level. Let's define them.

Flexibility is the first vector. This vector addresses the amount of variation that the company can or needs to incorporate into a part of the solution to meet the precise need of each unique customer optimally. Customers associate higher value to overall flexibility, which reduces the net value outflow for each customer. Productizing flexibility often implies a low volume and high-cost environment.

Speed is the second vector. It addresses timing precision by accommodating customer desire to receive value quickly or at precise moments. Productizing speed implies a higher cost to enable. But the higher value created offers higher pricing opportunities.

Quality is the third vector. This vector addresses the optimal investment in the appropriate quality measure such as longevity, size of impact, etc. Higher quality costs more to achieve.

Cost is the fourth and last vector. All other vectors that create value for customers cost money. So, the cost vector is the counterweight to flexibility, speed, and quality vectors. Higher flexibility, speed, or quality implies higher cost to productize.

Use of effectiveness vectors is everywhere, and we have all come across this in our day-to-day lives in established industries. For instance, I was just looking to replace all four tires on my near 10-year-old car. My search results on the online tire retailer's website are a perfect practical example of the use of effectiveness vectors for many companies selling a very commoditized and established offering. I can simplify my top three choices as:

- *Offering 1: Mileage warranty = 80,000 miles; Total installed cost = $612*
- *Offering 2: Mileage warranty = 40,000 miles; Total installed cost = $458*
- *Offering 3: Mileage warranty = 0 miles; Total installed cost = $297*

Warranty here aligns with the quality vector, and the installed cost is the cost vector. We could imagine why speed and flexibility aren't on the board for an average car tire. As you can see, we intuitively expect these trade-offs when we say, "you get what you pay for."

These four vectors are intuitive, and they are largely self-explanatory. But the application is significantly more thought-provoking. Often, growing companies with substantially less history struggle with such objectivity and try to optimize on all dimensions and effectiveness vectors, resulting in poor performances for all of them.

First, we must balance each element's value contribution to the overall capability to solve the market problem. If the root causes of the market problem indicate that a given element requires higher quality, that's the vector we must index heavily on. As a rule of thumb, we must independently frame each capability element's effectiveness vector choices.

Second, the Value Engine Enablers that we softly chose articulates thematic behaviors that our customers expect to see. Our thematic behaviors are demonstrated through our processes, management approach, and productization efforts. So, our value engine-focused core values set can also indicate which of the four effectiveness vectors we must focus on. For example, in our Amazon's core values example, 'frugality' directly points to a focus on optimizing the cost vector.

Let's consider a company that makes kitchen cabinets sold at a large retailer like Home Depot. It is entirely different in its productization efforts, which in turn changes the rest of the value engine, compared to a company that makes and installs custom kitchen cabinets directly for high-end homes. The same capability elements will vary across the four effectiveness vectors for these two companies. For the capability element of physically building a cabinet, one offers a lot more manufacturing flexibility than the other, which must come at a trade-off. The capability element to manufacture the same cabinet design in large volumes quickly focuses significantly on optimizing cost and offers limited flexibility. This is entirely different from a capability element in which a craftsman is hand-making a few cabinets in a machine shop with higher flexibility and cost.

Another capability element could be the design-thinking behind the installation of cabinets. The high-volume company's design will require significantly higher quality because it must accommodate a range of consumer tastes and installation challenges in various homes which comes at a higher cost. Conversely, the custom-cabinet maker doesn't have to invest significantly in installation design given the custom nature of its offerings. Even for the same capability elements, we can create two very different companies by altering the effectiveness vectors.

So, as a third capability lever, we must choose the optimal balance of effectiveness vectors for each capability element diligently to enable them to additively solve the market problem while accommodating our core values set as a guidepost for Buying Decision Drivers.

Capability lever 4: Superimpose operations baseline strengths to frame build vs. buy vs. borrow vs. avoid decisions.

Our fourth capability lever is our choice on whether we should and how we will acquire a capability element. Creating something ourselves is a very different ball game than using something created by another company.

Let's bring back our Comparative Advantage Ecosystem mindset. We must focus on doing the things we are good at. Irrespective of our market, it's unlikely that we will create our own email platform to communicate within our organization because someone has already built it. The same simple idea translates to any capability element on our design board.

There are three general paths to include a capability element in our solution. Either we can create it ourselves, buy it from outside, or borrow it from outside. The last alternative is not getting involved in certain capability elements. It is important to understand and decide how to realize each capability element to ensure that our strategic decision around what-to-offer is complete.

It is important to articulate how we plan to acquire each capability element because our strategic plan and execution path diverge based on the acquisition path. So, let's give our build vs. buy vs. borrow vs. avoid path a name – **Capability Element Acquisition Path.**

> **Things to Remember: Capability Element Acquisition Path**
>
> **Every company has a choice to build, buy, borrow, or avoid each capability element that is considered an option to create the overall solution. This choice is our Capability Element Acquisition Path.**

First, the clutch deciding factors on the capability element acquisition path are our ability to create the capability element and our ability to manage that capability element. We may be good at one or both or neither.

Second, the level of differentiation or commoditization of each capability element helps finalize our acquisition path. For example, if our ability to create or manage a capability element is unique in the marketplace, we should consider it a differentiation. Conversely, if several companies can throw the same amount of money at creating and managing a capability element, we should consider it commoditized.

Consider the following questions to frame our choice around the acquisition path for each capability element:

Would we categorize our ability to successfully create each capability element ourselves as a strength or a weakness?

Would we categorize our ability to successfully manage the capability element ourselves as a strength or a weakness?

Is each capability element differentiated or commoditized? In other words, is the ability to create and manage the capability element unique or common?

We can frame our optimal path for each capability element to realize it or avoid it using these questions. Infographic C.13 shows an optimal decision matrix that summarizes our acquisition pathways using these three questions.

Throughout this analysis, strength and weakness imply true potential based on the underlying fundamentals of our operations baseline, not the current performance level illustrated via metrics and market feedback. We want to improve our operations baseline continuously. Conversely, we mustn't lie to ourselves and think the improbable is possible. This is a good time to embrace our 'why us?' question from Chapter B.1.

When should we **build**? The option to create an element ourselves means we depend on our wits, skills, and experience to create it. We must do so only when we are uniquely good at it. A build option generally implies that we want to create it ourselves because it is our unique strength, and we want to maintain that strength. If the element is an object, a build option implies designing and building it ourselves because we are good at it. If the element is an action, a build option implies we train our own resources effectively on how to perform the action rather than hire resources with pre-trained experience. For a knowledge element, a build option implies

Comparing Company Strengths With Market Strengths Inform Build vs. Buy vs. Borrow vs. Avoid Options For Capability Elements

ENABLEMENT (Ability to CREATE Capability Element)		MANAGEMENT (Ability to MANAGE Capability Element)	DIFFERENTIATED (Ability to create or manage is UNIQUE)	COMMODITIZED (Ability to create or manage is COMMON)
STRENGTH		STRENGTHS	BUILD	BUY
STRENGTH		WEAKNESS	AVOID	BORROW
WEAKNESS		STRENGTHS	BUY	BUY
WEAKNESS		WEAKNESS	AVOID	BORROW

© 2019 - 2022 Acumes LLC

Infographic C.13 – Build vs. Buy vs. Borrow vs. Avoid Decision Matrix

C.4 TRIANGULATE TOWARDS WHAT-TO-OFFER AND HOW-TO-DELIVER STRATEGIC CHOICES

that we are better at creating the intellectual property ourselves than hiring external experts or licensing others' intellectual property.

There is only one out of eight paths in our capability acquisition decision matrix where we should be encouraged to build. But this is also the only scenario where we create significant value through the capability element in consideration.

When should we **buy**? Buying implies we are skipping the creation and focusing on the ongoing management of the capability element. Our optimal path to acquiring a capability element is buying if we are strong at only managing the capability element. We can buy an element from another company and include it in our overall capability. For object elements, think about buying as procuring the object creation source. In our cabinet manufacturer example, buying implies we are acquiring a cabinet production facility that we can manage going forward because creating that facility is not our forte, or it is just as easy for many others to create it. For action elements, consider hiring an entire value delivery team externally.

We would buy a capability element because it is a necessary building block of the overarching capability, but we aren't optimally placed to create it. Three out of eight scenarios in our decision matrix imply that we are buying.

When do we **borrow**? Borrowing implies that we are essentially limiting our involvement in even managing the capability element. The most common form of borrowing is outsourcing the creation and management of objects or performance of actions. Similarly, software can be white labeled for a use created and managed by someone else. We borrow when the capability element is a commodity or when our strength is not to create or manage it.

We are creating no incremental value by borrowing a capability element because another company is creating and managing it for all practical purposes. Two out of our eight pathways put us here. The only rational reason to borrow a capability element is that it complements other elements we are building and buying.

Lastly, when do we **avoid** a capability element? If we are not optimally placed to create or manage a capability element that other companies consider a differentiation, including this capability element in our overarching capability is a recipe for disaster. When there are many permutations to solve a problem, why would a capability be successful if at least one of four to six core elements is our weakness while it's someone else's strength?

Essentially, we must alter the configuration of our overarching capability to eliminate such a capability element from the design.

A consumer-facing people connector company that I have worked closely with had one core capability element of how people connect securely through technology in their overarching capability that allowed individuals to get to know each other better through virtual conversations. The company rightfully didn't consider this highly secure connectivity element a core strength that they should build themselves or buy. But the highly secure connectivity they had included in their capability was a unique strength of another company in the market that they decided to borrow from by white labelling.

This turned out to be a mistake because all the company's offerings were held hostage by this single borrowed capability element that the company could never control. The correct answer for the foreseeable future was to supplant the value created via the highly secure technology connectivity with another capability element that creates similar overall value for customers.

Just because a capability element appears effective on paper doesn't mean it is appropriate to include it in our overarching capability. So, let's summarize the rules of thumb for our acquisition paths.

We must prioritize capability elements that we are uniquely positioned to build because these are differentiated strengths that we can create and manage. These capability elements create the most value and fit our strengths.

Buy or borrow one or two capability elements that are essential to complement the capability elements that we are building. Among the few core capability elements that we consider most value-creating, limit buying or borrowing to less than one-third. Without a center of gravity that epitomizes our strengths, our capability is unlikely to be effective.

Lastly, avoid any capabilities that are differentiated capability elements that are our weakness. For example, suppose we cannot create a cohesive overarching capability when eliminating an element in the 'avoid' path. In that case, we must reassess the quality of our problem-solving efforts across the four capability levers.

A services company that I worked with was historically focused on resource augmentation and tried to create a software solution for the actions that the company was creating value through in the past. However, productizing software solutions was not a company strength. The company attempted to string together white-labelled software object elements from established vendors and even borrowed elements that the company must have avoided. The result was a collection of features that didn't dovetail because the company lacked control of any of the borrowed capability elements. Over time, the company gave up on the software capability aspirations and returned to its service roots.

Objectively framing our Capability Element Acquisition Path is necessary because it impacts our strategic plan and execution. It also impacts our processes and our management approach. The Capability Element Acquisition Path lever also ensures that we arrive at capability element combinations that can solve the market problem while staying aligned to our strengths.

Let's translate this framework into our what-to-offer trade-offs.

Principle 5: Configure four capability levers to frame what-to-offer trade-offs.

Understanding the market problem of our sweet spot and solving it might have felt easy earlier. But that instinct we all have is a "just do it!" attitude. A market-validated company cannot do this. Every problem's root cause has many possible solutions. Our four capability levers allow us to expand our thinking beyond the obvious angles and find a combination that creates optimal value and aligns closest to our strengths as shown in Infographic C.14.

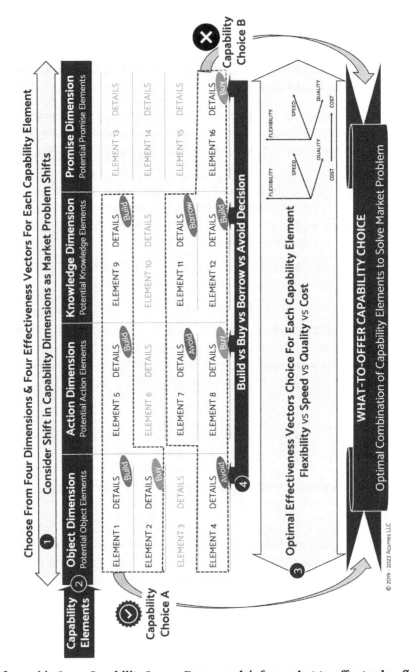

Infographic C.14 – Capability Levers Framework inform what-to-offer trade-offs

Luckily or intentionally, sustainable growth companies arrive at the right configuration of capability elements across four dimensions and four effectiveness vectors that aligns with the company's strengths and optimally solves the root cause of a well-defined market problem.

Methodically moving from framing the root cause of the market problem to proposing solution configurations is a deeply analytical exercise that requires situational awareness and hypothesis-driven analysis to connect the two sides. Jumping to a conclusion is the equivalent of hiding from all the other potential options we are not weighing.

Consider the following questions to utilize the four levers of our capability framework:

What are the combinations of capability elements, which are building blocks of a capability along one dimension, that will render a comprehensive market solution? How effectively does each capability element contribute to the overarching capability?

Which capability dimension – object / action / knowledge / promise – does each element address? Do these elements collectively offer necessary coverage across the dimensions we need to solve the problem?

What is the optimal balance across effectiveness vectors – flexibility / speed / quality / cost –for each element to create the maximum net customer value as informed by the root causes of our market problem and core values sets?

What is the optimal acquisition path – build / buy / borrow – for each capability element? Which capability elements must we avoid?

A technology-enabled services company that I worked with had customer value creation challenges because they didn't make effective choices along the four capability levers. The company created a customer self-service technology option to replace a predominantly company-performed services capability.

But the company didn't consider how the employee knowledge, which complemented the services performed in the past, would be replicated if those actions were to be replaced with a technology and customers took on the use of the technology. It turns out customers never used the technology object because it didn't include TurboTax-like user guidance that replicated the situational knowledge that the company's services employees silently included in the past.

Further, the company struggled to pinpoint its position on the effectiveness vectors. The company tried to offer high flexibility, speed, and quality and struggled along all vectors, while pricing based on a low-cost operating model. Customers perpetually question the offering's value proposition.

Decisions are hard. As part of strategy development, we want to make choices that are truly... strategic! These are the decisions that impact the whole company throughout an execution cycle, likely to require significant investment, and the choice of which implies risk.

How do we choose between all these permutations of options across the four levers? We must pick the configuration that puts us in Quadrant 1 of the game we introduced at the start of this chapter – our strengths and, preferably, our competitors' weaknesses. Infographic C.15 illustrates our what-to-offer trade-offs where our goal is to prioritize the market problem we are focused on and choose an effective path to a solution where we have clarity on the four levers we need to plan around.

This visualization gives you a structure to follow as you set up what-to-offer trade-off choices, just like our 'who' and 'how' trade-offs.

Consider the following questions while formalizing the what-to-offer trade-off choices:

What are the structured definitions of the market problems that our sweet spot customer needs solved?

Which market problem will we prioritize? What is the length of this prioritization period?

What are the optimal configurations of capability elements that form comprehensive solutions to each market problem?

Which of these solution configurations are most compelling? What is the impact / cost / and probability of success of each configuration?

Framing these productized offering-related choices brings us to the door of our final strategic decision to enable planning and execution.

C.4 TRIANGULATE TOWARDS WHAT-TO-OFFER AND HOW-TO-DELIVER STRATEGIC CHOICES

Trade-off Choices for Market Problem and Capability Configurations Frame What-to-Offer

	Objectively Framed Baseline State	Trade-off Choice 1		Trade-off Choice N	Proposal Rationale	Impact / Cost / Probability Of Success
Market Problem Choice	[Current Market Problem Focus]	Market Problem A	vs	Market Problem B	Decision Support Analyses and insights	Analysis & Insights on Operations Baseline Impact, Investment Needs, and Probability of Success
Market Problem A Solution Options	[Current Productization Baseline]	Capability Configuration A1	vs	Capability Configuration A2		
Market Problem B Solution Options	[Current Productization Baseline]	Capability Configuration B1	vs	Capability Configuration B3		

© 2019 - 2022 Acumes LLC

Infographic C.15 – What-to-Offer Trade-offs Decision Framework

Principle 6: Frame all strategic trade-offs & choices to decide corporate strategy.

Strategy development is not easy. It takes tremendous discipline and confidence to stick to the arduous, analytical, and seemingly repetitive yet necessary triangulating approach. If we choose to go down this path, at least one person will tell us that this is a waste of time because they feel the answers are obvious. Remain confident because our exercise is not about some of the insights that align with the existing hypotheses. Some gut instincts will align because otherwise, we wouldn't have a functional business. Strategy development is more about all the things that our gut instincts will miss and misalign with the reality of our market, which will hurt us downstream.

"What gets us into trouble is not what we don't know. It's what we know for sure that just ain't so." – Mark Twain.

In addition to having many relevant insights, following such a comprehensive and cohesive framework allows us to know that our unknown unknowns are minimal.

To recap, we went out of our way to consider our entire ecosystem. We took an analytical approach to frame our sweet spot customer and understand our customer's various personalities – the buyer, user, and approver.

We went deeper into framing our market problem in the context of our sweet spot customer and their Buying Decision Drivers. Rather than addressing these symptoms, we covered the importance of analytically understanding the root causes to develop solutions for.

We then considered opportunities to reassess and formalize two sets of core values to evolve our organization's behavioral guardrails. The first set directly influences our value engine and thus addresses Buying Decision Drivers. The second enables our management approach and the necessary internal behaviors to support the Value Engine Enablers. These two core values sets are our how-to-deliver trade-off choices.

We used four capability levers to frame our what-to-offer strategic choices which ensure that our market problem is addressed by an effective combination of capability elements. These elements must cover the relevant capability dimensions while focusing on the right effectiveness levers of flexibility, speed, quality, and cost to solve the problem. We also validated the overall value each capability element would create by considering our acquisition path, which helped us frame the optimal configuration of these elements as a comprehensive solution.

There is no side-stepping the reality that this is a challenging analytical exercise to frame the jigsaw puzzle that is our company's north star. Yet, if we have the discipline to pursue this path, we have the power to articulate our company's future in a single strategic decision.

The strategic trade-offs framework allows a single source of our corporate strategy that can be accessible to every employee in our company because it has no sensitive information. It helps us align all teams and employees under a single cohesive decision.

Often companies take a silo mentality where the 'who' questions are tactically answered independently by marketing and sales teams, core values are created by human resources with no dovetailing with any other 'how' aspects of our company, and 'what' decisions are handled independently by teams that manage the offerings. Unfortunately, this leaves companies without a single corporate strategy. We cannot mature without a single dovetailed strategy.

Let's wrap up our strategy development effort by packaging the soft decisions and insights to frame a single strategic decision. Infographic C.16 memorializes our corporate strategy for the upcoming strategic planning and execution cycle. Although I often dissuade the use of templates as they minimize important ideas to filling a box, leverage this structure as a minimum quality guardrail. Let's break this down into five components.

First, consolidate the 'who,' 'how,' and 'what' trade-offs, choices, insights, and soft decisions into a single view. The essence of this final step is to make a single dovetailed decision. Our String of Pearls philosophy implies that every piece on the board impacts other pieces. If they don't, it is essential to question whether the trade-offs and choices are impactful at all.

Second, firmly articulate the baseline state and propose the optimal evolved state for each trade-off unambiguously. Include at least a second

THE SPIRAL STAIRWAY™ – THE SYSTEM TO BUILD A HOLISTIC COMPANY

		Objectively Framed Baseline State	Trade-off Choice 1	vs	Trade-off Choice N	Proposal Rationale	Impact / Cost / Probability Of Success
Who-to-Serve	Optimal Use Case	[Current Definition / Choice]	Use Case A		Use Case B	Decision Support Analyses and Insights	Analysis & Insights on Operations Baseline Impact, Investment Needs, and Probability of Success
	Optimal Use Case B Sweet Spot	[Current Definition / Choice]	Sweet Spot 1		Sweet Spot 2		
	Sweet Spot 1 Buyer Role	[Current Definition / Choice]	Parameter A | Category A1		Parameter A | Category A2		
	Sweet Spot 1 User Role	[Current Definition / Choice]	Parameter B | Category B2		Parameter B | Category B3		
	Sweet Spot 1 Approver Role	[Current Definition / Choice]	Parameter C | Category C1		Parameter C | Category C2		
How-to-Deliver	Value Engine Enablers	[Self-assessment Of Current Core Value Set]	Core Value Set A1		Core Value Set A2		
	Management Approach Enablers	[Self-assessment Of Current Core Value Set]	Core Value Set B1		Core Value Set B2		
	Market Problem Choice	[Current Market Problem Focus]	Market Problem A		Market Problem B		
What-to-Offer	Market Problem A Solution	[Current Productization Baseline]	Capability Option A1		Capability Option A2		
	Market Problem B Solution	[Current Productization Baseline]	Capability Option B1		Capability Option B3		

Who-to-Serve, How-to-Deliver, and What-to-Offer Choices Frame a Single Corporate Strategy Decision

ILLUSTRATIVE FRAMING OF A SINGLE COMPREHENSIVE & COHESIVE STRATEGY STATEMENT

WHO-TO-SERVE	HOW-TO-DELIVER	WHAT-TO-OFFER
Focus on USE CASE B customer journey… with customers in SWEET SPOT 1 and… Buyers are PARAMETER A | CATEGORY A1… Users are PARAMETER B | CATEGORY B3… Approvers are PARAMETER C | CATEGORY C2	Deliver Buying Decision Drivers via CORE VALUE SET A1 …while… Internally enabling Management Approach via CORE VALUE SET B2	Prioritize MARKET PROBLEM A… and solve via CAPABILITY CONFIGURATION A1 …and… Shift to MARKET PROBLEM B in X period And solve via CAPABILITY CONFIGURATION B3

Infographic C.16 – Comprehensive and cohesive corporate strategy trade-off decision

choice and possibly a third choice for each trade-off. If we cannot frame competing choices that are compelling, we should ask whether we have explored our options effectively enough.

Third, include the analytical rationale behind each proposed evolved state and the analytical reasoning to move past choices. Senior executives must understand that deciding to choose a proposed choice is also a decision against the choices we are moving past.

Fourth, articulate the three differentiating factors of a strategic decision for each trade-off – the impact, cost, and probability of success for each choice. Our current reality influences the cost of achieving our desired evolved state. It is naïve to imagine that achieving a strategic choice would be easy or guaranteed just because we make a decision.

Fifth, the strategy & operations executive must lay up the ball for the CEO to take the final shot of formalizing the strategic decision based on the proposed evolved state. It is tempting to make a couple of the easy trade-offs and leave the rest unattended. However, that's why executives make the big bucks – to make tough choices.

Not making a choice or making cut-the-baby-in-half choices are not options. If we cannot forgo a compelling choice on 'who' we will serve and then hope that our 'how' and 'what' trade-off choices will be effective, we are in for a rude awakening when we execute.

Every single strategic trade-off must have a decisive choice. Collectively, these choices must solve the root cause of our prioritized market problem and address the Buying Decision Drivers for our sweet spot customers. This is our corporate strategy!

Over the last four chapters, we have objectively and insightfully addressed the three incredibly powerful questions of who-to-serve, how-to-deliver, and what-to-offer to evolve our operations baseline.

Many growth-phase companies choose to guess the answers to these questions. In my experience and analysis, the growth trajectories of those companies do not align with their purpose. Beyond getting lucky, the only way to know our path forward is through rigorous analysis.

The power of our approach is that we can influence our entire company, the board, our customers, and other external stakeholders. We have done our due diligence on the market, our customers, ourselves, and our competitors objectively.

In the next part of our methodology, we will have to plan how to invest during the next execution cycle. We will build that plan confidently based on the corporate strategy we decisively laid out and memorialized for everyone's consumption. The CEO doesn't have to fear whether plans are resting on quicksand. Functional executives have clear direction and evidence on why the path forward was chosen.

PART D

Strategic Planning Charts The Path To Corporate Strategy.

SCALING a company beyond early-stage growth without a strong strategic plan is analogous to running blindfolded. We will likely lose a lot of time and resources stumbling and course-correcting with no guarantee that we are going in the right direction. Planning can be the difference between sustainable growth as opposed to a stalling growth trajectory.

Macro-evolution requires a mature strategic plan to lead execution.

Every company with more than a few hundred thousand dollars in revenue has some form of a plan for the next year and beyond. Strategic planning has similarities with our discussion about process design. Our only options are developing and operating according to an effective strategic plan or operating in chaos without a plan. A so-called plan in someone's head that changes all the time is not a plan at all.

Our operations baseline can self-evolve tactically through objective data analysis on an ongoing basis. But to grow sustainably, we must evolve our entire operations baseline comprehensively. We kicked off our macro-evolution cycle with corporate strategy. Strategic planning is the second of the three parts of our macro-evolution cycle.

A strategy & operations executive told me, "I don't think strategic planning is necessary... we just need to focus on growth." A few days later, a VP of Strategy who reports to this executive said, "I am sure [the executive] would disagree... but I don't think we have a plan at all. I wish we had one." Even though almost every company dedicates time and effort to planning, a deep internalization of what constitutes an effective strategic plan and belief in its true power is hard to find.

First, a company's strategy at a growth phase must be refined on a cadence to stay ahead of evolving competitive landscape and customer needs. Staying stagnant strategically is a path to losing market leadership. Translating such a strategy into day-to-day execution requires an effective strategic plan.

Second, operations maturity must evolve to keep up with strategic shifts and growth. In-house skills necessary to execute key initiatives must mature over time, and operations responsibilities must evolve to accommodate market shifts and our scale. However, making these decisions ad hoc without structure is chaos. Strategic planning provides a structured path to align these operations maturity changes with corporate strategy.

Third, growth-phase companies often use linear scaling approaches and rinse-and-repeat tactics that imply investment without maturity. This tactical scaling approach can result in the misallocation of investment to underperforming enablement and operations roles and assets. Strategic planning provides a structured path to avoid such investment pitfalls.

Fourth, most growth-phase companies aspire to increase valuation and exit via a buyout by new private investors or an Initial Public Offering. The intrinsic value of our company rests with our operations baseline. Increasing our valuation for a rational investor implies maturing our operations baseline. Our strategy & operations cycle is the only pathway to evolve our management approach and value engine holistically, and this path goes right through an effective strategic plan.

Incrementally, effective planning is also a day-to-day necessity.

Effective strategic planning is the only path to manage execution.

When I was younger, I was an impatient driver, and when I saw traffic, I had the illusion that somehow weaving between lanes allowed me to pick the one that would get me to my destination fastest. This illusion was based on zero information to support my choice of which lane I would switch to and when. Looking back, it feels silly. We all do this. All these lane changes are not getting anyone anywhere any faster. Instead, such lane changes are causing chaos or probably resulted in the accident that slowed traffic in the first place.

A scaling company has similar challenges as a driver on the highway. Many people around us, such as investors, the press, and social media, make us feel that we must somehow move at a certain pace that makes these observers approve of us. We take indications equivalent to the road's maximum speed limit to decide how fast we should be going. Scaling companies love to make statements like, "we grew 100% last year!" But not every company can or should.

We are looking for extrinsic validation by internalizing such hollow measurements about our company and ourselves. The reality of our world is always more complex.

Setting tangible and realistic expectations allows us not to panic and weave around when the reality of our market and our execution to create value hits us. Effective strategic planning is the single most effective magic wand that frames a realistic path to our destination.

A weak strategic plan that sounds exciting but is not reality-based becomes a tool for budgetary approval for the next cycle but does not have the core components to help us execute effectively. By the end of the first month of our execution cycle, such a plan will likely get derailed and send our frenzied executives searching for new ways to achieve unrealistic outcomes that we set ourselves.

This will make all employees feel that our company has no coherent path to our destination, and just like our customers, will voice or, even worse, conceal their sentiments. Regardless of their role, every employee can feel the motion sickness of a gyrating company even though they don't know why it is happening.

Without an effective strategic plan, the executive team's management will likely reflect a lane-changer in traffic. Unfortunately, as exciting as lane changes might feel for the driver, it only makes things worse for everyone else along for the ride.

Strategic Planning Maturity Model.

Strategic planning is like tax season for most executives and analytical players. We will use the term execution cycle to frame the time window that the planning exercise should shape.

Commitment to developing a solid plan enables us to solely focus on executing flawlessly during the execution cycle. Conversely, a lack of commitment to planning leads to a lack of confidence in the plan. This results in poor forward momentum and a continuous waste of organizational resources throughout the execution cycle. We will end up perpetually reworking the outcomes that could have been well-developed during planning.

The most critical success factor for planning is the intent behind planning. If we use planning as a means to an end that we believe we already know, it's a waste of everyone's time. On the other hand, strategic planning is a powerful part of our evolutionary growth methodology if we embrace that the treasure is truly in the path.

Infographic D.1 explains our five-level Strategic Planning Maturity Model. This reference point can help us self-assess our company's planning maturity. As we go through the following four chapters that explain how to build an effective strategic plan, use this infographic as an outline.

When we first introduced our methodology, we talked about its dovetailed nature. The maturity of the first three parts determines our strategic planning success.

How mature is our management approach? If we have an immature management approach, we will struggle to run an effective planning exercise. We cannot think as a collective unit while also challenging each other. That balance only exists in environments with a mature management approach.

STRATEGIC PLANNING CHARTS THE PATH TO CORPORATE STRATEGY

Infographic D.1 – Strategic Planning Maturity Model

How mature is our value engine? How can we learn from our past if we do not have a customer-focused offering and our processes are in chaos with poor data capture and usage? If we can't operate objectively and analytically on a day-to-day basis, we will likely struggle to do this during planning as well.

How mature is our corporate strategy? If all else fails and we are in dire straits with our operations baseline maturity, we could develop a strategy to reinvent our company. But have we developed an effective corporate strategy based on the maturity levels we covered in Part C?

As we get closer to Part E – Execution Management, everything about our operations baseline, past maturity growth efforts, and strategy and planning actions that create our macro-evolution wave will become necessary. Without it, our execution efforts will reflect a team on the field chasing a ball without a game-winning plan.

There are no shortcuts unless we somehow get lucky with a magical offering that was a runaway hit, and we can get away with riding that wave. But that only applies to a very small percentage of companies. The rest have to earn the market victories.

With these realities in mind, let's consider the effectiveness level we could plan to achieve. Obviously, we want to work on the right-hand side of our Strategic Planning Maturity Model at Level 5.

On the immature end, *Level 1: Ad Hoc* represents a company with no real plan. Inbound advertisements or ideas picked up from conferences are mistaken for maturity growth projects, most of which get scrapped after the initial investment or have no return on the investment. Executive motivation and discussions focus internally on showing short-term revenue or growth, deprioritizing identifying an effective path to achieve it. Customers are considered a means to an end.

Moving to the right, *Level 2: Linear Scaling* represents more structure. But planning focuses on financial outcomes and budget allocation. The planning process doesn't focus on strategy or the evolution of fundamentals. Instead, the company will likely allocate a budget to repeat the past and measure outcomes. This maturity level epitomizes a rapid scaling mindset and doesn't prioritize sustainable growth or profitability.

At *Level 3: Strategy Led*, we are starting to get serious about strategic planning instead of financial forecasting and budgeting. The most relevant upgrade here is that we are focused on hinging our path forward on a cohesive corporate strategy, which assumes that we have a mature strategy. Here, we internalize the importance of macro-evolution of our operations baseline, and we develop projects to achieve our strategy using a structured planning approach.

Being strategy-led is one thing. But how we run our business is a different matter. *Level 4: Operations Focused* implies that we prioritize the controllable aspects of our operations as opposed to just hoping that our outcomes come true because we are investing. At this level, we will focus on the impact of our strategy-led evolution on our operations using leading indicators. We will set optimal leading indicator targets and limits to manage execution. We will also start prioritizing efficient investment considerations.

Our planning efforts can achieve the highest maturity by adding an investment effectiveness layer on top at *Level 5: Investment Optimized*. We will ensure that our investments in our time-bound efforts and operations baseline are optimal at this maturity level. We will optimize the overarching return on investment in the medium – and long-term by carefully evaluating every aspect of our investment. Company-level outcomes are effectively framed using lagging indicators and defined as byproducts of customer value creation-focused execution measured via leading indicators.

Over the following four chapters, we will discuss the components that allow us to build a *Level 5: Investment Optimized* strategic plan.

D.1
BUILD A STRATEGY-LED, OPERATIONS-FOCUSED PLAN TO ENABLE EXECUTION.

STRATEGIC planning can feel like Groundhog Day. So, here is how it often starts.

Revenue-focused CEOs and CFOs kick off strategic planning season by engaging senior executives with a rallying cry... "We had some challenges this year. But those were anomalies because... you know... we are still a great company... we are the best... Next year will be the best we ever had... our investors are behind us... customers love us." The exercise starts here without any rigor on any of the components discussed under Part C: Corporate Strategy.

Then comes the ask... "we want you to define your plans to meet our revenue goal of $75 million ... that's what we already agreed with the board... we want your plans to be strategic and align with everyone else's plans... got it?"

Does this sound familiar? Every planning scenario that starts with this ends with a collection of disjointed projects that do not achieve its goal or corporate strategy, which is likely to be missing.

Why does this happen?

Most scaling companies do not engage in an effective strategic planning exercise because they do not have a corporate strategy. The successful ones were one-hit-chart-toppers with their first offering and brand, and the rest are barely keeping their head above water. Moreover, most do not have a growth plan beyond linear scaling by throwing more money at symptoms of problems.

Strategic planning intends to frame a realistic path to achieve our corporate strategy. In our sustainable growth mindset, we are not running a one-hit-wonder company. We do not believe that the game's opening five minutes settles the outcome. Instead, we believe in an analytical and evolutionary approach to maturity growth via effective strategy and execution cycle after cycle. A methodical approach to strategic planning is crucial for this growth path.

Principle 1: Strategic planning must hinge on a mature corporate strategy.

The most pivotal principle of strategic planning is that it must always start with a strong corporate strategy. The macro-evolution portion of *The Spiral Stairway*™ must start with corporate strategy and flow through planning to define a game plan to execute against. Even with some core strategic decisions articulated, it takes significant discipline to go through an effective planning exercise due to the rigor and patience it demands.

A mature operations baseline can tactically go through a micro-evolution through the effective use of data and ongoing analysis. We can improve each process in the same direction that we have been going. We can enhance each capability based on objective data we gather from customers. However, all these improvements are tactical and generally stay within the scope of a specific process or capability or the details of a specific role. These tactical improvements are micro-evolutions and do not address company-wide direction.

> **Things to Remember: Strategy-Led Planning**
>
> **Our who-to-serve, what-to-offer, how-to-deliver trade-off decision triggers the macro-evolution of our operations baseline. Corporate strategy is the north star that starts our macro-evolution change wave where strategic planning always follows a mature corporate strategy.**

I am a huge soccer fan. Unfortunately, having a talented attacking team with a clear game plan to score goals is a rarity. There is an observable difference between teams with strong goal-scoring abilities and those that don't. The teams that don't have a genuine belief in their goal-scoring plan and skills tend to run forward until about 20-odd yards from the goal post and hit the ball hard, seemingly with eyes closed. When this happens in successive attempts, it's clear that they lack a game plan or skills to get through the defense using their dribbling or passing skills to get closer to the goal post and find a realistic scoring opportunity.

Starting with a poor strategic decision or ignoring an effective strategic decision will nullify planning effectiveness and leave the company to take long, blind shots at macro-evolution, hoping for results. Instead, corporate strategy-led planning focuses on sustainable and evolutionary growth based on fundamentals.

Decoupling strategy from planning is one of the most common failure paths among companies.

However, companies often make the mistake of kicking off strategic planning from a cold start. In a strategic vacuum, plans are built on spurious foundations. Senior executive intuition and reactive choices to competitor movements without analytically framing the best course of action will lead our company astray. Such inputs alone are not cohesive or comprehensive and often leave companies questioning their path throughout the execution cycle.

A 'whale strategy' is an example of a suboptimal hinge-point that I have seen at multiple B2B companies. Its recurrence is predictable, primarily when a company operates in a strategic vacuum.

First, it is a poor sweet spot definition to say that we are just going to go after customers who would be very big in terms of revenue, hence the 'whale.' How could anyone know which specific customers will bring in significant revenue unless we have psychic abilities? So, this is essentially an ocean fishing expedition hoping to catch a whale in a small boat. But that isn't scalable.

Second, such a planning hinge-point usually has no relationship to our company. It is an outcome-based tactic chosen due to a lack of confidence in the operations baseline. The thought process in these circumstances is "it would be much easier to find one or two big customers who will meet all revenue goals even if we do whatever they want." Usually, it doesn't work at all. Even in situations with short-term benefits, the companies become enslaved to one or two large customer's bidding and struggle to serve any other customers effectively.

We dedicated significant effort and discipline to arrive at the strategic tradeoffs and a single overarching decision around those tradeoffs because we want it to be our company's north star. We must find the discipline to follow this north star.

Principle 2: Strategic planning is not financial forecasting or budgeting.

The Chief Strategy Officer of a publicly traded company recently shared his view on their planning efforts as, "The finance team manages the exercise. They call it a strategic plan, but that's just ignorance... All they have is a financial plan." On the same day, the operating partner of a large private equity firm shared the same view about what he wanted to change in their portfolio companies – to focus on a real strategic plan.

Sadly, financial forecasting and budgeting are mistaken for strategic planning across most companies. Why would we call it 'strategic' planning if we don't design it to be strategic?! Strategic planning must focus on the market, not internal dynamics, and strategy and operations, not financial goals.

How does a financial outcomes mindset derail strategic planning?

The word 'growth' is hard to avoid. It's hard for a CEO or CFO to not think about the top-line and bottom-line outcomes of the income statement. But worrying too much about the outcome leads us to play poorly.

When a CEO and CFO set specific revenue or expense goals, they practically torpedo objectivity in the planning exercise. Whatever any company's website says, every executive and senior position is constantly trying to prove their effectiveness to keep their jobs.

If a CEO and CFO ask for a $75 million revenue goal in the next cycle, that's exactly what they will get during planning. Through every single stage in the exercise, every executive will likely come back with projects that magically lead to a total revenue of $75 million.

First, anchoring is a bias that skews even the most objective individuals. What is the probability that the asks from the CEO and CFO didn't influence executives to say, "we can get there!"? Very low.

Whether it's building an arbitrary feature or a brand-new website development or hiring an entirely new lead generation team, each executive will state that the total output of their projects will help the company get to $75 million. It won't be $70 million or $80 million. It won't be a discussion about whether $75 million is realistic. Instead, the exercise anchors everyone to the idea of $75 million as if their job depends on it.

Second, herd mentality is another very powerful bias. If executives collaborate, how likely are they to have objectively different recommendations? Why would anyone put deep thought into the calculations of a math problem if all the focus is on getting to an answer that everyone already knows? When we framed $75 million as the revenue goal, we took away the incentive to focus on the 'how.' In such financial outcome-focused planning, the evolutionary efforts are likely nebulous and do not dovetail with the company's strategy or operations baseline.

The most important output is the alignment between strategy and execution – i.e., the path to achieving the strategy and how to measure that path. Without such strong alignment, a financial forecast is just an aspirational guess or extrapolating past performance.

Without operations focus, an aspirational or history-based plan will always lead to one of two outcomes. We will either miss revenue or expense goals because we didn't develop a tangible path to achieve results. Alternatively, we will under-achieve the company's real potential because we couldn't identify and execute against the market problem we could have solved, processes we could have improved, or other fundamental improvements within our grasp.

> **Things to Remember: Financial Forecasts**
>
> **Financial forecasts are company-level lagging outcomes derived from well-developed strategy-led and operations-focused planning deliverables. Unfortunately, the reverse is impossible if financial forecasts are set with spurious extrinsic motivation.**

Company-level revenue outcomes only matter to shareholders. Customers do not care whether our revenue went up or down. If employees are not shareholders or compensated based on financial outcomes, neither do they. Vendors or partners only care about our financial outcomes to a point where they are comfortable with the payment terms they give us or a long-term partnership they might invest in. In fact, external parties do not know the financial performance of most growth phase companies anyway because results aren't publicly shared.

Financial outcomes are the responsibility of the CEO and the CFO. These outcomes provide a guardrail for investment thresholds. Beyond these thresholds, it is suboptimal to let extrinsic outcomes influence the strategic plan. Suppose the reality of the maturity changes in the operations baseline to achieve an effective strategy does not lead to these desired financial outcomes. In that case, it is on the CEO and CFO to realign its purpose-level expectations with investors and owners.

A budgeting mindset is equally ineffective.

One of the major organizational design pitfalls that we discussed under the management approach was empire-building. I observed this tendency early in my career, and I told myself that I would always be an objective team builder. However, some years later, I fell into the same trap of feeling a desire to add more people to my team or add areas outside my purview. It's a human tendency to fortify our environment and today's working world encourages us to be promoted every year and build large teams.

This human tendency kicks into high gear during strategic planning. During this period, we make investment decisions for the upcoming execution cycle. It is tempting to make a land grab for investment to hire support staff because employees feel overworked, or a popular new technology is available on the market. Such ideas are only worth investing in if they are objectively correct, align with our strategy, and how we plan to mature our operations baseline and scale it. Otherwise, these are just random ideas that are spurious reasons to divide the budget.

When we described 'whale strategy' earlier, what could be the subconscious thought process of such a team? It is not driving a maturity shift in the operations baseline. So, what is it achieving? It is a wrapper to approve a budget to make investments and hope for the best. It allows the team to invest more without a real strategy or a plan to mature.

Alternatively, we must avoid allocating investment to unvetted channels. A friend who advises venture capital-backed companies on marketing topics told me about turning down clients because she wanted to work with the companies that understand their investment decision. One specific example was "these two founders want to immediately spend $30K to $50K every month on advertising because they got $2 million in [early stage] funding. I just feel uncomfortable agreeing to this. I don't think they realize this will be a waste."

Strategic planning can waste organizational resources if the primary output is a budget allocation for another year of business-as-usual execution or spending hoping for outcomes. Moreover, it often implies deploying investment towards unsustainable linear growth tactics and functional empire-building where functional executives are focused on building their teams in a silo.

Principle 3: Operations focus effectively translates investment into outcomes.

Strategic planning must focus on how we will achieve our strategy, not on aspirational outcomes that we may have trouble replicating.

The world constantly measures and talks about extrinsic outcomes. It's preferred not because it is better. It is because it is easier. If we are watching a football game, anyone can look at the scoreboard on the screen and tell who is ahead or likely to win.

But what if we didn't have a scoreboard on the screen? Can most people look at the state of play and say who is winning? Some can. It takes a keen observer looking at how the players are walking, talking, their energy level, urgency, confidence, and the tactics deployed to know who is likely ahead and who has the momentum.

The same principle applies to thinking about a business. Of course, anyone can look at past revenue or profitability trends and say whether a company did well or not. But what good is it to know something after it has already happened?

> **Things to Remember: Operations-Focused Planning**
>
> **Operations-focused planning is about predicting future outcomes by optimizing and measuring behaviors.**

We can truly predict our outcomes if we know the quality and quantity of actions we take and the decisions we make. In a pre-Covid world where employees were in the office, imagine taking a lap around the office at 4:45 PM. What we see on that lap can tell us more about the revenue trajectory than any aspirational goals we set.

A turnaround executive described his last failed turnaround experience as "there were six of us in the office after 4:00 PM on Fridays consistently with the remaining 1500 people having packed up and gone… meanwhile, we were still bleeding revenue every quarter." So, again, it's not about the big talking points but the many small actions and decisions that add up to outcomes.

So, our strategic plan must focus on how we operate. Although connecting intrinsic behaviors to extrinsic outcomes is complicated, and it takes discipline and analytical muscles to do it, this is necessary.

We can think about our whole company as one giant process flow. A process is a black box that converts inputs to outputs. Any output depends on two aspects: the process and the inputs. From a strategic planning perspective, our company-level goal is the output. Based on the principles we already discussed, we will frame extrinsic outcomes such as revenue and profitability with the relevance it deserves – as an outcome that ladders up from how we run our business.

The input is our total investment. But just agreeing to invest is not enough. It is a royalty mindset without a strong basis in reality to just focus on the outputs and inputs. So, what does this investment go into?

The process that converts the investment inputs to outcomes is our ever-maturing operations baseline. The hardest part of strategic planning is articulating the improvement and performance of this black box. What is the macro-evolution we want to drive in our operations baseline, and how will it perform during execution as we evolve it? This is where the real magic happens. The key differentiating factor of sustainably growing companies that create intrinsic value is not the inputs and outputs; it's the evolving black box that performs the conversion.

Infographic D.2 illustrates this input-process-output model of our company.

Thematically, our planning approach will primarily focus on four aspects.

First, we will focus on the maturity improvement of our operations baseline to align with our corporate strategy, which our time-bound enablement initiatives will drive. I think about our collective enablement efforts as a cocoon enveloping our current operations baseline and transforming it into a more mature one.

Second, driving this macro-evolution via enablement initiatives requires investment, and we will call it the **Enablement Investment**.

Third, we will also focus on the maturing metrics and targets of our productized offering, our processes, our data gathering and usage, and our management approach, which collectively reflects the performance of our evolving operations baseline. This is the tangible operational performance of our company.

Fourth, the operations baseline requires investment, which we will optimize – not necessarily always increase – through our planning approach, and we will call this **Operations Investment**.

Together, these four aspects result in the extrinsic outcomes we seek, which are our company goals.

D.1 BUILD A STRATEGY-LED, OPERATIONS-FOCUSED PLAN TO ENABLE EXECUTION

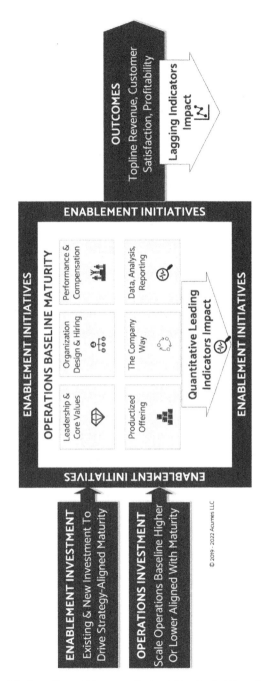

Infographic D.2 – Input-Process-Output Strategic Planning Model

This won't be easy because we will likely feel pulled towards revenue and expense discussions, how many employees we can hire, or boast about the big customer we could win. We need strong leaders on the executive team who can withstand these tendencies and focus on our operations baseline, which is the only path to value creation.

Principle 4: Disciplined, analytical, thought leadership is necessary to build an effective planning team.

A company's investment in the planning exercise is people and skills. Putting the right people – those with an objective and analytical mindset – on the task is the only path to a successful exercise.

Every company is different, and employees add even more differences. Thus, sticking to our don't rinse-and-repeat mindset, proposing a one-size-fits-all planning team structure wouldn't be optimal. Instead, planning requires a few critical roles and specific responsibilities.

Role 1: Strategic planning lead.

Strategic planning requires a quarterback, who we will call the planning lead. The CEO must delegate this responsibility because it requires serious attention to operational details and analysis. However, this role must have the complete backing of the CEO. In addition, the role must demonstrate two essential skills.

First, the planning lead must have strong business acumen around strategy and all business functions, an analytical mind, and a good handle on potential pitfalls associated with poor strategy development, planning, and execution. The role also should have experience running planning efforts, without which the company is risking its time, resources, and the company's trajectory on someone learning on the job. The planning lead is accountable for defining the planning approach tailored to the company's needs, choosing the right individuals required throughout the various stages, and moderating all problem-solving, reviews, and decision-making to ensure the plan is comprehensive and cohesive.

Second, this role must demonstrate leadership. Ineffective leaders often underestimate the emotional Implications and complexity of strategic planning. Planning can lead to poor results that range from tactical ideas cobbled together, on the ineffective end, to a land grab for the budget by various teams, on the harmful end. Strategic planning will not make everyone happy because it should be a disciplined, trade-off exercise. The path to make choices cannot be a split-the-pie-evenly or a command-and-control CEO-mandated approach.

The planning lead should be an independent thought leader who can stand firm and balance all the information available to arrive at the most optimal outcomes using dependable frameworks, while seeking depth of rationale and details on all critical building blocks of the plan.

Role 2: Executive sponsor.

In a growth phase company, this is the CEO and the CFO. The CEO is accountable to the board for the company's execution plan built on an effective strategy. The CFO is accountable for the company's financial forecast and management against that forecast. Both aspects are outcomes of strategic planning. The executive sponsor is the dispassionate referee in this exercise.

The executive sponsor must stay fully engaged by consuming and understanding all relevant analyses and findings and actively police all participants for objectivity. The role must also bring holistic perspectives around market dynamics and investor interests to the table. Lastly, the sponsor must be a strong advocate about the importance of staying focused on the corporate strategy and building a plan that focuses on fundamentals.

If the executive sponsor is not fully engaged, decisive about making decisions based on objective findings, and advocating adherence to the planning approach, the exercise is at risk of not driving the necessary organizational changes to grow further.

Role 3: Analyst.

An analyst does not imply someone who simply slices and dices data. This role must have a firm handle on our productized offering, processes, and data usage and is responsible for objective analysis and insight generation throughout planning. This role remains joined at the hip with the planning lead and executes on direction from the planning lead.

Role 4: Objective functional representatives with a company-first mindset.

This is the most challenging role to fill appropriately for a growing company. Everyone is busy, and many hires are functional operators, not cross-functional thinkers. Strategic planning requires a team that can put the company-first hat on. Every player involved must find a way to solve for all the colors of a Rubik's cube, not just the color each person likes. It is a company-first exercise, with a laser-sharp focus on strategy and operations. So, the specific individuals tapped to get involved are situational.

This role is also the all-important conduit between the strategic plan and the rest of the company. These individuals will help develop initiatives to improve the maturity of our operations baseline. They will support the identification of metrics that demonstrate the maturity and execution of our operations. They also must think critically about investment trade-offs to arrive at a plan that aligns all stakeholder needs. Finally, beyond planning, this role must evangelize our single company plan when it's time to execute.

None of the responsibilities above are functionally focused. Strategic planning cannot be along functional silos. The individuals stepping into this role should operate at a high objectivity level.

Companies often swing to the extremes of over-inclusion or under-representation. On the one hand, including key players from every team responsible for any topic impacted by strategic planning might seem appropriate. Alternatively, the executive sponsors might try a command-and-control approach by only including a minimal group based on seniority or organizational position. Neither extreme will work.

During one of the recent planning exercises I led, the company brought together every department lead into the exercise. This is a very common occurrence. However, the Chief Technology Officer was the only one who asked hard questions, challenged groupthink, and brought a prove-it-to-me attitude. Many others were disengaged until it was their turn to talk about their own functions when they mainly spoke about their spending plans with limited details on how those plans would really drive maturity. As a result, the quality of the plan suffered.

We must apply our CAE mindset to create a work-based staffing model for the planning team. We need a small, hands-on SWAT team staffed with individuals who can influence up, down, and across an organization and bring a critical thinking and analytical mindset to the exercise. Unless senior executives are very hands-on with designing and performing analyses, and ideating and detailing enablement initiatives, they are better off serving as executive sponsors. Planning is a complex exercise, and it requires the core team to be comfortable with creating and consuming details.

In summary, staffing for planning is more about quality than quantity. Therefore, a small, objective, and influential group of thought leaders are the most optimal candidates for the four key roles on the planning team.

Principle 5: Leverage a three-phased comprehensive and cohesive strategic planning approach.

Strategic planning follows the same triangulation theme as corporate strategy.

Astronomers could relatively easily state the expected path of the earth around the sun if there were only two objects. But the moment we add in the moon or any number of other planets, it's no longer a simple formula to determine its path due to all the interdependencies of gravity and position.

As we go through the key components of strategic planning, we will discuss related concepts together. But it is important to understand that every single principle is like an object in the universe. Their mass and position affect all the other ones. It is an iterative triangulation effort. Nothing we discuss will be a drafted-once-and-done effort. We will have to revise and reconfigure every aspect to get to a plan that gets us closest to our corporate strategy and desired overarching outcomes, while being realistic about where we are today and the world around us.

Strategic planning does not have to be a heavy time or resource-intensive effort for a growing company if we start with an effective and decisive corporate strategy. The company likely only has one core capability with one or two auxiliary capabilities and one brand. The same commercial operations resources generally sell and deliver everything the company offers, making resource planning relatively straightforward.

Tailor approach to our past planning maturity.

Like many concepts under our methodology, the planning approach is not a one-size-fits-all answer. Instead, the most critical consideration is our starting point.

> *Consider the following questions to assess current planning maturity:*
>
> *Have we performed a structured strategic planning exercise in the recent past?*
>
> *If so, was the strategy development, maturity growth initiatives, and execution cycle effective?*
>
> *How mature is our value engine, particularly processes and data?*

These self-assessment questions provide a litmus test on prerequisite steps we must take prior to heading into a planning exercise, optimally well in advance of the cycle.

First, past annual budgeting exercises don't count as planning experience.

Second, if past efforts were unsuccessful, we are likely starting with challenges around our management approach, including behavioral alignment issues and a lack of a CAE.

Third, being positioned on the Value Engine Maturity Model's immature end implies significantly more pre-work requirements, including manual data gathering and insight generation to assess the market and internal operations.

Executive sponsors must internalize the current maturity level of the management approach and value engine and the importance of being open-minded and objective about hearing and sharing difficult messages about current maturity, performance, and need for improvement. We also need a skilled strategic planning team, including a strong planning lead and demonstration of executive sponsor commitment.

Infographic D.3 illustrates the core components of a mature strategic planning exercise. Regardless of our current planning maturity, we will have to go through all the components laid out here. Based on our existing maturity, chewing off what we can swallow is better. If we try to jump from the Strategic Planning Maturity Model's left side to the very right side, our team will be ill-equipped to handle the exercise and necessary follow-throughs.

The three strategy-led and operations-focused phases.

Three phases of strategy-led and operations-focused efforts form our strategic planning approach.

The first phase is **Enablement Planning**. Here, we decide how we evolve from the current maturity level of our operations baseline to a higher maturity level that aligns with our strategic trade-off choices, which also enables higher performance.

Why is this 'change' mindset important? Just because we made a strategic decision one evening at the end of the strategy development effort doesn't mean our operations align with that direction and performance when we arrive at work the following day. Our operations baseline is exactly where it was. It will take Herculean efforts that we have to plan and execute to reach our evolved state where our strategic choices are part of our day-to-day operations.

> *Consider the following questions to prepare for enablement planning:*
>
> *What meaningful efforts will increase the maturity of our operations baseline to align with corporate strategy?*
>
> *How will we prioritize these efforts?*

The second phase is **Operations Planning**. Here, we will outline exactly how our operations baseline will perform from the start through the end of our execution cycle. This is not trivial because our operations baseline is a living and ever-improving entity. As we improve our alignment with

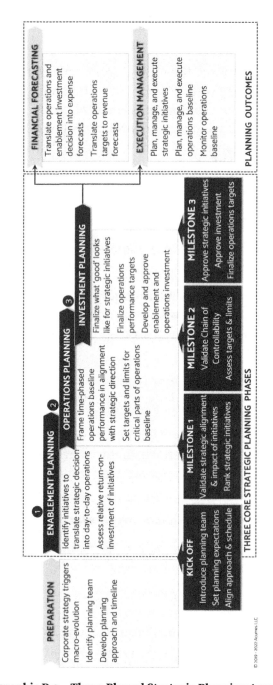

Infographic D.3 – Three-Phased Strategic Planning Approach

our corporate strategy, the performance of various operations baseline components improves.

Consider the following questions to prepare for operations planning:

How will we characterize the current performance of our operations baseline?

How will our operations baseline perform over time as we evolve it through enablement initiatives?

The third phase is **Investment Planning**, which demands that we take our enablement and operations plans and ready them for execution. This requires investment decisions. Saying something is a lot harder than doing it. In the next part of our methodology, we will have engaged every enablement and operations resource in our company to execute flawlessly. But we need to build a bridge from saying what we will achieve through our execution cycle to how we will do it.

Consider the following questions to prepare for investment planning:

What are our investment considerations and decisions for both enablement initiatives and ongoing operations?

What are the expected aggregate operations targets and likely outcomes based on our investment decisions?

We are effectively building a bridge from our corporate strategy to how we execute through these three phases. They lay out the marching orders for the enablement resources to work on major initiatives. The operations targets adjusted over time set guardrails for all operations resources.

Leverage milestones as accountability guardrails.

Given the planning team's experience, the gap between the company's strategy and current trajectory, and investment availability or constraints, the amount of work required for planning will differ. Regardless, it is important to make incremental progress, collectively align on progress, challenge conventional and subjective thinking, and improve each element objectively.

The choice of the collaborative approach for planning is dependent on the planning team composition, geographical and time zone spread, and similar logistical aspects. Historically, planning meetings were elaborate multi-day collocated affairs. Milestone reviews can involve elaborate, broadly attended conferences with fun kick-offs and icebreakers.

On the other end, the core planning team can get together in a room for a few tedious and intense hours to review key deliverables and dismiss the meeting to iterate deliverables offline. As we increasingly work remotely and globally, we learn to collaborate with others in more constrained circumstances.

The more important part is to ensure that every planning team member is well prepared to lead insightful and objective discussions. Most of the effort must go into structuring critical questions to answer and tailoring frameworks that help us arrive at optimal decisions. Smooth proceedings of planning review milestone meetings are essential to ensure that the proceedings don't encourage a herd mentality.

Optimally, at least three milestones are thematically included in our approach to ensure that our three phases effectively push us towards a strong plan.

First, begin with a formal planning kick-off to set expectations. Use this opportunity to state our corporate strategy to guide our planning exercise. The CEO and planning lead must lay out the planning approach and specific roles and responsibilities.

Second, use the first progress checkpoint to pressure-test initiatives that align the operations baseline to strategy. Utilize this session for early prioritization of our enablement initiatives for the next cycle. The discussions and feedback will lead to rework and improvement of initiatives.

Third, we should have a relatively strong handle on how our maturity growth initiatives impact our operations baseline by the second progress checkpoint. We will have set aligned, predictive targets on our operational performance for the next cycle.

Fourth, a final approval checkpoint ensures that the planning team collectively approves the accountable success factors for initiatives and operations performance targets. The final strategic plan also aligns the planning team on the investment that would go into necessary maturity growth and operations scale.

Combining our three-phased approach with an iterative, milestone-based review-and-improve mindset is a minimum requirement to stay true to the essence of our treasure-is-in-the-path planning approach.

Derive financial forecasts from strategic planning outputs.

We can derive the financial forecast from key outcomes from the planning phases. Operations targets directly translate to revenue outcomes. The investment decisions translate to our expenses and cash-flow decisions. The financial forecast helps the CFO manage the company's financial health.

As discussed earlier, anchoring planning with financial outcomes is the most common strategic planning mistake. Attempting to start with aspirational growth goals and force-fit strategy and operations into such goals is equivalent to putting the cart before the horse.

Planning efforts should develop a comprehensive strategy-led and operations-focused plan. The planning team should take responsibility for developing all deliverables outside the financial forecast, which the CFO and finance team will build based on the strategic plan. Developing a strong foundationally dovetailed plan simplifies the creation of and quality of derived outcomes such as financial forecasts and board-level presentations for alignment and approval.

Now, let's dive into *Phase 1: Enablement Planning*.

D.2
TRANSLATE STRATEGY INTO OPERATIONS WITH ENABLEMENT PLANNING.

THE purpose of enablement planning is to define how to evolve our operations baseline at a macro-level to engrain our winning corporate strategy.

This means we must mature our management approach, productized offering, processes, and data acquisition and usage where collectively these components deliver our strategic trade-off choices. As we know, these four parts of our operations baseline are symbiotic, and they influence each other heavily.

> **Things to Remember: Enablement Planning**
>
> **Enablement planning is the first stage of strategic planning, where we define an optimal path to engrain our corporate strategy decision into our operations baseline. Incorporating the who-to-serve, what-to-offer, and how-to-deliver strategic trade-offs into our operations baseline evolves it intentionally and proactively at a macro-level to meet increasing customer value needs and serve more customers.**

It is important not to mistake enablement planning for the identification of quick wins.

In a recent strategic planning readout, the details of a sales function's enablement plan to drive incremental revenue amounted to: "Define Ideal Customer Profile; Source knowledge; Ensure sales and marketing wins; Use contextualized demos." This nebulous proposal poses some questions.

Are these items technically incorrect? *Unclear.*

But are these specific to any company? *No.*

Is this detailed enough? *No.*

Did this align with the company's strategy? *No.*

Details, depth of problem-solving, and alignment with strategy are necessary parts of planning. There are three steps to enablement planning.

First, we must clearly frame our current operations baseline maturity and how far our leap to the evolved state, which reflects our strategy, needs to be. To build a bridge, we have to know the state of the ground on both sides of the river and the span of the river. This first step is a gap assessment. Setting off on a path to our evolved state without an effective gap assessment is akin to planning to build a bridge without internalizing the lay of the land.

The **second** principle covers the development of **Strategic Initiatives**, which we also refer to as enablement initiatives. Once we know where we are, where we need to be, and the distance we need to cross, we need to lay out the specific packages of work that can get us there. If we framed a comprehensive and cohesive corporate strategy, this would not be a small leap we could accomplish in one simple initiative. Instead, to reach our evolved state, we will need to define and dovetail several initiatives covering various components of our operations baseline across different parts of our company.

> **Things to Remember: Strategic Initiatives**
>
> **Strategic initiatives are comprehensive projects that mature our operations baseline. They inject our corporate strategy into our company's future operations execution. They dictate how we make both enablement and operations investments and the realistic, measurable outcomes our organization can achieve over time.**

Third, we don't get to do everything we want because we live in a world of constraints. We decided our strategy with a visionary yet approximate timeline such as one, two, or three years. We did not analyze exactly how long it would take to achieve the strategy and did not consider what it would cost us to get there. This falls into strategic planning. So as the last step, we must prioritize the most impactful efforts that we can realistically achieve with our available or appropriate amount of investment for the next execution cycle. This third principle of enablement planning prioritizes strategic initiatives, which begins to shape one of our key inputs in our process-model view of our company – enablement investment.

Principle 1: Assess Operations Baseline Gaps to achieve strategic decision.

The current maturity of our operations baseline reflects the effectiveness of our past strategy, planning, and execution cycles. And we can't change our past.

We have also fixed our endpoint through our who-how-what trade-off choices. We must figure out how to make the leap from today's operations baseline to our evolved operations baseline. To leap to that evolved state, we have to know the details of our starting point very clearly. The framework for this comparison has five elements. Infographic D.4 illustrates them.

The **first** element is our strategic trade-offs with our decisions articulated. Let's place these decisions on the left side of our framework. Anchoring our framework with the trade-off's decision ensures that our enablement planning efforts align with our new corporate strategy. Even when we have effectively framed a corporate strategy, planning and executing that strategy is far from a foregone conclusion.

The **second** element of the framework is the introduction of functions. Throughout our methodology, we stayed away from the concept of functions purposely. The vast majority of success factors in a company are cross-functional and apply to everyone equally. We intend that our company-first mentality will break down silos and ensure that the same principles and rigor apply across the board.

D.2 TRANSLATE STRATEGY INTO OPERATIONS WITH ENABLEMENT PLANNING

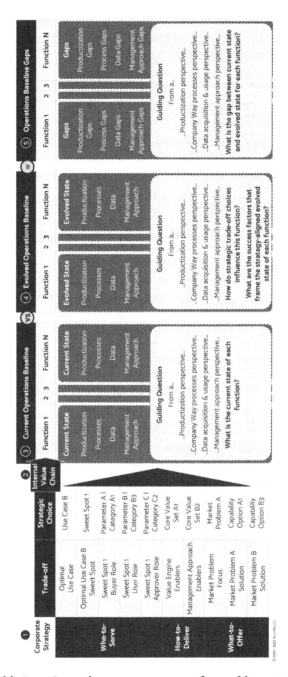

Infographic D.4 – Operations gap assessment for enablement planning

But during execution, individuals do the work. Strategic planning is the bridge between our company-wide strategy and every employee and asset, which sits under a function.

We must bring back our flow thinking and focus on how we create value for customers on a step-by-step basis and use groupings from that value flow as functions. This focus on our value creation flow articulated by our processes is essential because planning for the future based on our existing reporting structures reflects our past hiring patterns. It's best to assume that it's not perfect – it never is. In our 'work-based' organization design, we want to continuously shift our company to align with the flow of work that creates value.

> **Things to Remember: Functions**
>
> **Functions are logical groupings of roles, which mirror the roles in The Company Way processes and are filled by operations resources. Effective functions use internal value creation flow as the basis for grouping roles.**

For instance, lead generation is a crucial function regardless of the market. The roles and processes ensure that the company is attracting prospective customers effectively. How often do you see a formal function synonymous with 'lead generation'? Rarely, based on over three dozen companies that I have worked inside and several other companies I have collaborated with. Often this critical function is piecemealed into sales and marketing teams. Everyone seems to understand 'marketing' and 'sales.' But these teams are never the same between any two companies; so, why do we always use these two buckets? Convenience! This is suboptimal. If lead generation is a critical value-creating function, we want to call it out as such, regardless of which senior executive owns that team.

With this flow mindset, list out five to seven most relevant functions as the second element of the framework. This list is optimal if it correlates with our processes instead of groups of humans and their reporting structure today. The reverse will backfire. We want to identify our gaps based on how we create value, not how we hire people.

The **third** element is assessing the current state of affairs for each function across every component of the operations baseline, once we have the first two elements set up as pillars. Again, recollect the intertwined view of our operations baseline – aspects of our productized offering, processes, data usage, and management approach must all dovetail.

Consider the following question to frame the current state:

What is the current state of each function from a 1) productized offering, 2) processes, 3) data acquisition and usage, and 4) management approach perspective?

For a lead generation function, understanding our current state implies having an insightful grasp of existing processes and data collection effectiveness. This can include the effectiveness of advertising that creates inbound interest and proactive outreaches to start selling efforts and related data gathering and reporting. Our current state assessment may also include the effectiveness of our productized offering's pricing and packaging and how we present it to prospects along with organization design, staffing for roles, and incentive compensation around lead generation roles.

Our insightful takeaways to this question for each function are the starting point of our macro-evolutionary change efforts. It is worth determining whether a strategy effectively guides our current operations baseline as an ancillary consideration. An alternative is that we are not guided by a strategic decision today. The difference is that starting from an immature and chaotic operations baseline will require a significantly higher change management effort than starting from a mature strategy-led environment where effective micro-evolutions are prevalent, and the company is familiar with effective macro-evolutions triggered by market shifts.

The **fourth** element is to draft what 'good' looks like for our evolved state of the operations baseline for each function when we fully operationalize our strategic decisions.

Consider the following questions to frame our evolved state:

How do our strategic trade-off decisions influence each function from a productized offering, processes, data acquisition and usage, and management approach perspective?

What are three or four of the most relevant success factors for each function in the evolved state?

To compare the current and evolved states, we need to articulate success factors that are important in the evolved future state, while knowing its current state. Conversely, highlighting challenges in the current state will help us ensure we have framed the appropriate optimal behavior in the future state, even if it is table stakes.

Staying with our lead generation example, we want to frame the three or four success factors of our evolved state processes and data capture. Similarly, we want to frame optimal lead generation skills required and related incentive compensation. Conversely, we must highlight potentially obsolete skills on staff in the current state. The same goes for the commercialization aspects of our offering.

However, information for the sake of it isn't useful. It is too early to jump to specific productization or process details in the evolved state.

At this stage, our goal is to simply set guardrails on success factors that allow us to develop the specific projects that will enable our strategy. We can leverage our analytical details from our strategy development exercise to draw a rough picture of our evolved state for each function. For example, we already know which capability elements we will need to build, buy, or borrow. We know the essence of the behaviors expected via our processes and the skills we have to demonstrate based on our deep exploration into Buying Decision Drivers. Superimposing these onto functional components gives us the information we need. We will continue to build depth of detail and revise both the current state and evolved state definitions throughout our planning.

The **fifth** and final element is to comprehensively frame our **Operations Baseline Gaps** based on the current and evolved state. We must articulate the delta between the answers to the guiding questions for element three and element four for each function along the four operations baseline components. Think about this as our shopping list that we have to address in the next principle, where we will identify the initiatives that can help us cover as many of these gaps as possible. Infographic D.4 offers a high-level visual structure to build this gap assessment.

Consider the following question to frame our Operations Baseline Gaps:

What are the gaps between the current and evolved states for each function from a productized offering, processes, data acquisition & usage, and management approach perspective?

Although we must perform this gap assessment for each function, consider this an initial information-gathering step. Silos destroy cohesive and comprehensive problem solving and execution. Our path to addressing these gaps will need to be cross-functional.

A common suboptimal path to enablement planning is to ask each senior executive's team, not function, what projects they will do. This is akin to operating without a corporate strategy. The answers will be disconnected blocks of ideas that fit in a silo and are formed based on instinct without directly connecting to our corporate strategy.

This brings us to the development of company-wide, cross-functional strategic initiatives.

Principle 2: Draft cross-functional strategic initiatives.

How do we enable our corporate strategy and move from the current state of our operations baseline for each function to the evolved future state? We develop and execute strategic initiatives to close the gaps we identified.

> **Things to Remember: Strategic Initiatives [Refined]**
>
> **Strategic initiatives are the comprehensive and cohesive, mutually exclusive, and collectively exhaustive packages of time-bound enablement efforts that evolve our operations baseline to reflect our corporate strategy.**

A mature operations baseline implies that work flows through and between functions seamlessly without interruption. By extension, maturing any component of our operations baseline, whether it's our management approach, productization, processes, or data usage, doesn't sit in a single function because of our flow approach. This means it's ineffective to focus on evolving any function, like lead generation, from the current state to the future evolved state independently. For instance, changes to lead generation processes will have to dovetail heavily with changes to selling to a prospect, which in turn will have to dovetail with how we manage a customer that we have successfully sold to.

Cross-functional problem-solving is significantly more effective.

First, attempting to box in projects in a function inevitably means operating in a block mentality where we are missing continuity and dependency between related efforts across functions.

Second, planning and executing closely related evolutionary efforts across functions create significant economies of scale by limiting duplication and conflicts in work and better accountability by keeping related efforts under a single owner.

Third, no company can drive progress on many initiatives without fatigue. A reasonable number, say between eight and twelve cross-functional and comprehensive initiatives, is optimal. The scope of these initiatives will be broader as a company grows.

So, we shouldn't mature each function independently when there are hand-offs and dependencies across functions. Strategic initiatives allow us to achieve meaningful shifts from the present state to our evolved future state across multiple functions and closely related strategic tradeoffs. A strategic initiative may address one or more components of our operations baseline based on the Operations Baseline Gaps we need to close.

Set three quality guardrails for effective strategic initiatives.

In their simplest form, strategic initiatives achieve our desired state. But that's too much of a simplification. A founding CEO once asked me how often I see successful projects. My tongue-in-cheek response was – "80% of projects fail…" There is some truth to this, but context is extremely important. I have personally been part of several large failed initiatives, some costing over $100M. The COO of a different company quipped, "I don't think I have been part of a major change effort ever if I were to be really objective..." So, we need to align on what a 'good' strategic initiative is.

First, the most effective strategic initiatives are uniquely tailored to achieve our company's strategy by evolving our operations baseline. Half a strategy is no strategy at all. We want to ensure that all our strategic trade-off choices are translated into our operations baseline via strategic initiatives.

This single attribute alone justifies why a cross-functional strategy & operations executive or advisor must own planning. Breaking silo thinking is hard. Ensuring that every component we need to address across all our trade-offs and functions is not trivial. One person must be accountable to ensure that the strategic initiatives collectively achieve our evolved state for all functions in alignment with our strategic trade-offs.

This also means these initiatives will never be the same from company to company because operations baseline starting points and end points are different across companies. In our String of Pearls philosophy, no rinsing and repeating.

During strategic planning efforts at a company where I was an external planning advisor, we struggled to arrive at effective strategic initiatives, which cost the company later on. The company had just hired several new executives. It was one of the situations in my life when that 'whale strategy' came up. This case manifested as a rinse-and-repeat initiative that originated from the new sales executive hired from the sales group that exclusively sold to large customers at an established company. Thinking that the same tactics would work in an unrelated market and at a growth-phase company was a poor assumption. As a planning advisor, I also failed to stop the excitement behind this rinse-and-repeat idea which was disconnected from the company's strategy. Months later, the founder told me that the 'whale strategy' failed during the execution cycle.

As a **second** quality guardrail, strategic initiatives must always be defined to address tangible Operations Baseline Gaps. We must define a comprehensive set of strategic initiatives to ensure that they collectively take us to our evolved operations baseline, which implies focusing on closing our Operations Baseline Gaps.

At the company I mentioned above, the marketing executive pushed for a single bucket of spending by framing an initiative that replicated a popular marketing approach called account-based marketing I have seen across companies. This would have accounted for a 200% increase in marketing spend. But we considered: What is the Operations Baseline Gap that this new marketing approach specifically addresses? Why is this specific initiative important in achieving the company's strategy? Asking more in-depth questions changed the image of this proposal during enablement planning.

The **third** quality guardrail is a comprehensiveness check. Visually place the strategic initiatives on a grid with our trade-offs and functions to ensure that every Operations Baseline Gap is covered, and we are not missing any relevant components. Ensure that lack of strategic initiatives across trade-offs, functions, and operations baseline components is a proactive choice to maintain the current state.

Consider the following questions as a litmus test for the quality of drafted initiatives:

Does the roster of proposed strategic initiatives effectively cover all the strategic trade-off decisions across all functions?

Does the roster of proposed strategic initiatives collectively cover all Operations Baseline Gaps to its intent?

Does a lack of strategic initiatives at intersections of strategic trade-offs, functions, and operations baseline components imply a purposeful choice not to evolve?

Infographic D.5 illustrates how we can define and map cross-functional strategic initiatives comprehensively. Our goal through this enablement planning phase is to place all the relevant efforts on the board so that we can prioritize the set of initiatives we will focus on during the next execution cycle.

D.2 TRANSLATE STRATEGY INTO OPERATIONS WITH ENABLEMENT PLANNING

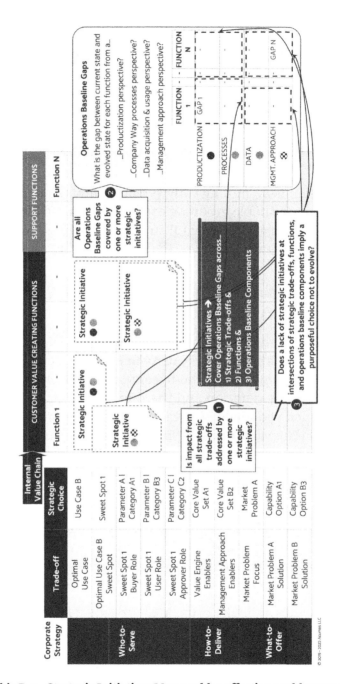

Infographic D.5 – Strategic Initiatives Map enables effective enablement planning

Draft strategic initiatives using four rules of thumb.

Developing strategic initiatives from our gap assessment is a qualitatively analytical exercise. We started with two sets of inputs. One set of inputs is each function's current state and the corresponding evolved state that accommodates our strategic trade-off decisions. The second set of inputs are components that require evolution for each function, whether it is the management approach, productization, processes, or data. Together, this formed our Operations Baseline Gaps.

If we stay disciplined, drafting early versions of our strategic initiatives can be a relatively simple grouping exercise. We group our Operations Baseline Gaps to create meaningful strategic initiatives. Given our goal of breaking down functional silos, the planning lead must manage this exercise.

Then, leverage the following rules to transform our Operations Baseline Gaps into the first draft of our strategic initiatives.

First, group gaps with most interdependencies together. Problem-solving is optimal if the same people solve interconnected problems. For instance, to improve our alignment with who-to-serve, we will likely have to address gaps in both lead generation and the sales functions. These are also highly dovetailed with delivering value to those customers because we set expectations for value delivery through lead generation and sales. So, why solve customer acquisition and retention gaps around who-to-serve trade-offs separately? These answers depend on each other, and they are optimally solved together. This example represents one of the most common incongruencies in companies. Customers are attracted by a lead generation function that sets early expectations that the sales efforts do not align with. Furthermore, the sales efforts set certain expectations to encourage customers to buy; but what if the value delivery function cannot deliver accordingly?

Second, group gaps in similar components together. For instance, process changes are easier to complete together than half of one process and half of management approach component changes, all else being equal. Addressing each specific component requires unique skills and experience, and we can optimize our resourcing and interaction requirements by bucketing similar work together.

Third, start with a mental estimate of the level of effort and create groups with roughly similar completion efforts. We don't want to devise strategic initiatives requiring significantly different workloads. Prioritizing and managing these initiatives can become messy if our initiatives are not of reasonably similar size and complexity. Resourcing can be a challenge.

The **fourth** rule is that our strategic initiatives do not overlap. Overlapping strategic initiatives imply duplication of efforts and conflicting points of view that become hard to resolve downstream. Consider this attribute a soft rule at this stage because it is important to be comprehensive first. We will further flesh out strategic initiatives through various planning and execution phases. We will have the opportunities to improve the definitions of our initiatives.

These four rules of thumb give us a fair start for framing our strategic initiatives. Use the three guardrails in Infographic D.5 along with these rules of thumb. This is our opening bid on moving from our current state to our evolved state. Once our planning team has our evolutionary path laid out, prioritizing is important.

Principle 3: Stack rank strategic initiatives to prioritize.

Our goal of the first strategic planning milestone is to arrive at a prioritized set of strategic initiatives. We want to apply pressure on the quality of the strategic initiatives and focus on the more impactful and cost-effective ones. Think about this principle as preparatory activities, key outcomes, and the follow-through actions around the first planning milestone to arrive at our initial prioritized set of strategic initiatives.

To compare and prioritize strategic initiatives, we need to have some meat on the bones for each. Over the years, I have learned that it is hard to get even key members of our planning team to understand the implications of our strategic choices and frame our path forward effectively without a purposeful design. Although the strategy & operations executive can take the lead on these efforts, senior executives and supervisors will have to engage and dive into the details to frame and choose effective strategic initiatives.

If we have a skilled and supportive team on board, we can use a thoughtful and methodical approach to arrive at objective prioritization decisions. Prioritizing our strategic initiatives is a return-on-investment decision.

Once we validate the completeness and coverage of our strategic initiatives, this prioritization exercise offers a formal assessment of the efficacy of our initiatives. Putting on a return-on-investment hat allows us to pressure test and fine-tune our strategic initiatives before we prioritize them.

Stack ranking is a powerful tool. Being forced to slot initiatives one above the other focuses our minds on finding clarity and performing necessary analysis. In addition, it will inject much-needed debate and discussion in a planning exercise.

Return of a strategic initiative is its impact on operations.

The return portion of a strategic initiative is the tangible outcomes that align with our strategic decision. To stack rank our proposed strategic initiatives, we must know their impact. Attempt to stack rank our proposed initiatives from *high* to *low* based on their impact on the operations baseline. In the prioritization framework in Infographic D.6, this is the vertical axis.

Consider the following question:

What is the strategically aligned operations baseline impact of each strategic initiative?

We must always be able to quantify the impact of strategic initiatives on our operations baseline via leading indicators, even if it's zero. Some strategic initiatives are necessary to lay a foundation for other initiatives. We must internalize their purpose as well. This is a tedious, analytical exercise that we will save for *Phase 2 – Operations Planning*.

Additionally, we will never be able to compare the impact on various parts of our operations baseline quantitatively because each metric is different. This is precisely why folks often do return on investment calculations in dollars. But this is a folly. Attempts to use revenue impact or cost impact are often quantification-for-the-sake-of-quantification. There is always a many-to-one relationship between fundamental drivers such as strategic initiatives and operations performance and lagging indicators such as revenue and expense. Moreover, the drivers of these lagging indicators are so interdependent that narrowing the likely impact source will be practically confounded.

Our best path to assessing the impact of strategic initiatives is weighted scoring using our understanding of the qualitative impact on our operations baseline. We will have to identify each proposed initiative's qualitative and tangible success factors. We also want to draw a robust scope for each initiative. As we consider the impact of an initiative, we want to ensure that its scope is comprehensive enough to have the necessary impact. We also want to understand the dependencies between the initiatives because it determines the importance of each of them.

A strong planning team can devise a ranking method that fits each planning cycle's needs. Consider these three-ranking variables to develop a weighted impact score.

First, the impact of an initiative correlates with the number of strategic trade-offs the initiative addresses across functions. For example, count the number of grid spots in Infographic D.5 each strategic initiative covers. The higher the number of grid spots covered, the higher the impact score.

Second, count how many other proposed strategic initiatives depend on this single initiative. The higher this number, the higher the foundational impact score will be.

Third, in addition to the breadth of coverage, we want to consider the comprehensiveness of that coverage. How many operations baseline components does each initiative address? Addressing the maturity improvements along productization, process, data, and management approach is far more impactful than just addressing data usage evolution, thus a higher score.

> ***Consider the following questions to create a sample of variables to stack rank impact of initiatives:***
>
> *On a scale of 1 to 5, 5 being the highest, how broad is the coverage of each initiative across strategic trade-offs and functions?*

On a scale of 1 to 5, 5 being the highest, how foundational is the impact created by each initiative?

On a scale of 1 to 5, 5 being the highest, what is the depth of impact of each strategic initiative across operations baseline components?

We can multiply or average such individual impact scores to develop weighted scores for impact at the initiative level. This is our numerator for a return-on-investment comparison.

The relative cost of impact enables weighted investment comparison.

The cost of completing an initiative is the denominator to assess return-on-investment. However, we do not need to finalize enablement investment choices during enablement planning. Assessing the exact cost of each initiative is an arduous task, and we only want to do so during investment planning for prioritized initiatives. Our goal in this phase is to prioritize the most critical initiatives and eliminate poorly defined ones. To do so, we need a relative weighting of investment across initiatives.

To assess the investment needs of each initiative, we want to have a reasonable early understanding of the path to completing the effort. Although we considered the scope of an initiative as we thought about its impact, we want to take a second look at the scope with the cost of implementation in mind to assess whether we scoped too wide. Then, apply downward pressure to arrive at an optimal scope while balancing impact. Like impact scoring, our goal is to stack rank initiatives in terms of investment.

Consider these three variables to develop a weighted cost score.

First, approximate the initiative execution cost by estimating the number of enablement resources and supporting infrastructure required for each initiative. The higher the execution cost, the higher the initiative's cost score.

Second, changes to our organization are a cost as it distracts operations resources from their primary focus of creating value for customers. Therefore, a higher estimated disruption implies a higher initiative cost score.

Third, every initiative takes time for impact; a longer estimated time to impact implies a higher opportunity cost score due to this initiative.

Consider the following questions to create a sample of variables to stack rank relative cost of initiatives:

On a scale of 1 to 5, 5 being the highest, how high is the execution cost for this initiative compared to others?

On a scale of 1 to 5, 5 being the highest, how large is the organizational disruption from this initiative?

On a scale of 1 to 5, 5 being the highest, how long will it take for the strategic initiative to impact the organization?

Like our impact scores, we can multiply or average these individual cost scores to arrive at a relative weighted investment score for each initiative for comparison purposes.

Prioritize strategic initiatives as a soft choice.

Together, these scores allow us to create a stack ranking of our strategic initiatives on the grid in Infographic D.6. We want to work on initiatives with the highest impact and require the lowest investment. Conversely, we will likely deprioritize initiatives with the lowest impact and high investment needs.

Consider grouping the initiatives in each of the four quadrants of *high* and *low* impact and investment levels as a preliminary prioritization for the remainder of our planning efforts. As we will see through the following two chapters, we must have a firm grip on the strategic initiatives that we will prioritize and their impact on operations to manage our company predictably.

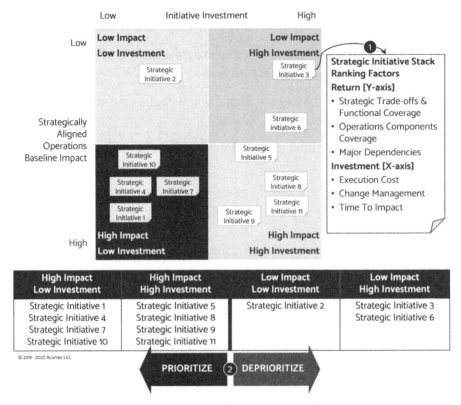

Infographic D.6 – **Strategic Initiative Prioritization Framework**

Our takeaway from this prioritization effort is soft choices of initiatives that form our enablement plan. **First**, we must identify a prioritized set of strategic initiatives that we know we can afford to invest in and will help us move our operations baseline to an evolved state that aligns with our corporate strategy. **Second**, as shown in Infographic D.6, imagine drawing a line between the initiatives we will build the rest of the strategic plan around, and the ones we do not believe are plausible or affordable.

Similar to making strategic trade-off choices, stack-ranking and prioritizing allow focus and actionability and are significantly more important than the perfection of the exact rank. Through our prioritization effort, once we place initiatives into the four quadrants, it doesn't matter whether an initiative was third or fourth if they are both in quadrant 1 and are at the top of our priority list. Translating our corporate strategy to tangible evolution of behaviors on the ground is difficult and emotionally taxing. Formal, structured, and tangible strategic initiatives help us achieve this transformation.

Turning around the performance trajectory of a data services company that I worked closely with involved moving the company from a service-focused offering to an object-based offering leveraging technology.

One of the significant changes that had to happen was how the company sold its offering. The company's home-grown sales executive continued to sell services even after the CEO and the board had agreed to a shift to a technology-focused solution. They had made this choice since growth had stalled and there was low customer satisfaction for services. However, there were no strategic initiatives to transform the operations baseline components around the sales function beyond asking nicely. Over several quarters, the sales function continued to sell an increasing number of services projects that it had never done before, while other employees focused on enabling the strategic shift. Eventually, the sales executive trumped the CEO, the board, and the company strategy.

An objective strategic initiative prioritization exercise can be the difference between effective strategy on paper and effective strategy implemented. This prioritization effort of our strategic initiatives to frame our macro-evolution pathway wraps up the enablement planning phase and kicks off planning of operation's performance through our execution cycle.

D.3
PREDICT UNIT-LEVEL PERFORMANCE VIA OPERATIONS PLANNING.

THROUGH strategic planning, we need to formalize our company's overall expected evolving performance throughout our next execution cycle. The interim step towards arriving at such an overall prediction is operations planning. So, let's talk about what's unique about operations planning before getting into how we go about it.

Remember, the performance of our company is the additive output of operations baseline components across all functions. Executing every portion of our operations baseline creates tangible value directly for our customers or indirectly to support activities that create value for customers.

The overall outcomes produced by our operations baseline is a simple multiplication of two things – the outcomes generated by each employee or asset in our operations baseline and the volume of those employees or assets. The concept of framing outcomes generated by each employee or asset is called **Unit Economics**. It reflects the true maturity and execution effectiveness of our operations baseline.

> **Things to Remember: Unit Economics**
>
> **Unit economics is the concept of measuring the maturity and execution effectiveness of every relevant part of our operations baseline at the lowest controllable unit, which could be an employee, a portion of an employee's time, a machine, or any other asset.**

Operations planning frames the true intrinsic performance potential of our operations baseline. We will arrive at the expected performance of each operations resource or the outputs of each machine or other assets we use in our processes. We want to know what we can achieve at the unit level without conflating the specific number of employees or other assets contributing to a given process.

> **Things to Remember: Operations Planning**
>
> **Operations planning focuses on maturity and execution effectiveness, not scale. It creates a unit-level performance blueprint for our operations baseline, giving us the flexibility to moderately change our scale up or down through investment decisions.**

This will answer questions like – What is the expected performance of an average resource in each role in a specific part of our operations baseline? How many widgets can a given machine used in a process produce? What is the expected value created for an average customer by a specific capability in our offering?

For example, our operations plan will remain the same if we have 20 sales reps or 25 sales reps because all baseline components will remain the same regardless of the exact staffing counts.

This is practically important because we are more interested in the fundamentals in an operations-focused approach. Throughout our execution cycle, we will have variability in scale due to employee churn or volatility in the volume of other assets. Therefore, it is essential to know what we can expect from our operations baseline on a per-unit basis at any given point in time to delineate between maturity and execution problems and scale limitations.

Using this backdrop, let's cover the core operations planning principles that we must build through the second phase of strategic planning.

Principle 1: Embrace controllability and predictability via Chain of Controllability.

The maturity of our operations baseline and its effective execution reflects our company's performance. This is all we can control. Our operations baseline directly influences our aggregate revenue and expense, which are compounded and lagging outcomes. This internalization is the most significant difference between our planning method and most used financial forecasting approaches, which are not actionable or predictive.

In physics, a fulcrum is part of a force transference system that allows us to apply only a reasonable amount of force to an accessible position and transfer significantly higher impact to a distant or less accessible point. We use this concept every day in our lives.

In this same force transference mental model, we can design our company's work via our operations baseline so that it has the desired impact on the outcomes that we can't directly control. We apply force in certain places and measure the outcomes elsewhere. I call this model the **Chain of Controllability**.

> **Things to Remember: Chain of Controllability**
>
> **The Chain of Controllability is the structured path to translate meaningful enablement efforts into impact on outcomes measured via lagging indicators. This structured path goes through our maturing operations baseline measured via leading indicators.**

Infographic D.7 – Chain of Controllability enables predictive and actionable plan

The Chain of Controllability focuses our attention on what we can influence and thereby design a system that will predict our future outcomes based on what we can influence. Nothing about this concept is particularly new from what we have already discussed. It's a matter of application. We must focus operations planning efforts on internalizing the importance and power of the relationship between four parts that form our Chain of Controllability. These four parts are:

1. Strategic initiatives that improve the maturity of operations baseline
2. The adoption and execution of our ever-maturing operations baseline
3. The performance measurement of our operations baseline via leading indicators
4. The overarching outcomes measured via lagging indicators

Infographic D.7 shows the relationship between these four parts. Before we take any actions, let's internalize how the Chain of Controllability works. Let's examine the four links in our chain.

The **first** link is the injection of operations baseline maturity from strategic initiatives.

Our company's future performance will reflect the impact that the strategic initiatives, which we defined and prioritized via enablement planning, can inject into our offerings, processes, data, and management approach. Our prioritized strategic initiatives impact the actual work we do to create value. Therefore, strategic initiatives are our first controllable. They do not directly impact outcomes; they only impact our operations baseline.

> **Consider the following question to internalize the first link in the Chain of Controllability:**
>
> *What will be the direct maturity impact of strategic initiatives on our operations baseline?*

The **second** link in the chain is to predict the relationship between the actual maturity of our operations baseline and the adoption and execution against that maturity. On paper, a strong sports team doesn't always mean that results on a given day or during a given season align with the team's true potential.

We will dedicate the entirety of the next part of our methodology to execution management for this reason. Through strategic planning, we must understand and slate the difference between the true potential of our operations baseline and the realistic likely execution expectation. If we do not know the difference between the two, we might blame execution for systemic problems, or we might blame systemic problems for poor execution.

Consider the following question to internalize the second link in the Chain of Controllability:

How effectively will the ever-maturing operations baseline maturity be adopted for operations execution?

The **third** link is our ability to measure and delineate between maturity and execution of our operations baseline using leading indicators during the execution cycle. As we introduced under our value engine discussions, leading indicators measure our operations baseline at the specific spot where work gets done. They measure our execution via our productized offerings, processes, and the enabling management approach.

Through operations planning, we will have to define or validate the set of leading indicators that can quantify the effectiveness of both maturity and execution effectiveness of our operations baseline.

Consider the following question to internalize the third link in the Chain of Controllability:

What effective measurements can convey the maturity level of various parts of the operations baseline and simultaneously delineate execution strengths and weaknesses from the true potential of the operations baseline?

The **fourth** link in our Chain of Controllability is the translation of leading indicators to externally relevant lagging indicators. The relationship between leading indicators and overarching company outcomes is the same as the relationship between root causes and symptoms.

Lagging indicators are always a compound measurement of an eventual outcome. We always accomplish such outcomes by completing small contributing parts that are the components of our operations baseline. Therefore, we can never impact a lagging indicator directly.

D.3 PREDICT UNIT-LEVEL PERFORMANCE VIA OPERATIONS PLANNING

Think about a lagging indicator as the measurement of the success of the heavy arms of a crane, accomplishing the outcome of moving a large amount of dirt. If we wanted the crane to move even more dirt than it is capable of, can we just wish that it does? Do we focus only on adjusting the heavy arms? No! It might require us to redesign the crane entirely to handle more weight. The design might have to change the levers in the cockpit for the operator's use.

Consider the following question to internalize the fourth link in the Chain of Controllability:

How do we translate leading indicators that measure the work we do daily to results that articulate the overarching success or failure of the company?

Our approach focuses on creating an operations plan based on leading indicators that directly correlate with lagging indicators that are often permutations of revenue and expense. The benefits are two-fold.

The **first** is **controllability**. We exert all our efforts on influencing the aspects we have control over, which are the components of the operations baseline. We have no direct control over revenue or expense because they are always multiple degrees separated from tangible actions.

The **second** is **predictability**. Focusing on measurements of our operations baseline implies that we can predict our lagging indicators well before the actual events. The whole purpose of planning is that we want to know what will happen in the future. Literally! If we can only say with confidence that we will miss our revenue or expense goals after we slide behind on actual revenue or expense performance, what was the point of planning in the first place? Leading indicators that measure our operations baseline gives us predictive powers to alter our course.

My amateur beach volleyball team wanted to win games despite our poor skills. We had a single measurement to determine our likelihood of success – how well we handle serves. Since volleys never last long in amateur games, our plan was simple – send a very high percentage of serves over the net while serving and send the ball back over immediately when receiving. Our serve handling measurement was the single most effective indicator and predictor of our overall scores and wins in our early playing days.

Similarly, our goal through operations planning is to effectively create or refine this Chain of Controllability across all operations baseline components and functions.

In my experience, the lack of internalization of this principle is one of the common failure points in planning that send companies down the financial forecasting-is-strategic planning path. Geniuses and savants can often go from A to D without going through B and C. Unfortunately, most people don't have such gifts, and we need to work through problems. It is tempting to jump to predictions, but we might be confusing confidence with competence.

Developing a Chain of Controllability will not be easy. The planning lead will have to take ownership of this cross-functional effort. Additionally, the mental gymnastics necessary to build a predictive and controllable chain from strategic initiatives to outcomes is high. These principles will test the objectivity and analytical skills of the planning team.

Principle 2: Map operations to leading indicators and lagging indicators.

Our path to maturing our operations baseline to meet our new corporate strategy and achieving higher revenue and profitability aligned with our purpose started with enablement initiatives. Enablement initiatives will drive improvement in parts of our operations baseline which improves our leading metrics and enhances our lagging indicators. This is our proactive, predictable, and methodical path to sustainable growth. Prior to operations planning, we prioritized key enablement initiatives. Now, we must translate the impact of strategic initiatives into our operations plan.

Define leading indicators that measure maturity and execution across functions.

We must apply the principles we discussed under Part B: Value Engine to measure our operations baseline processes and steps using

D.3 PREDICT UNIT-LEVEL PERFORMANCE VIA OPERATIONS PLANNING

leading indicators throughout the execution cycle. Recollect Process-Data Symbiosis. Remember that The Company Way processes dovetail with the management approach, our productized offerings, and how we deliver those offerings to customers. It is the only path to gather and use data effectively.

We might choose a single leading indicator to articulate the performance of an entire process, or we might use more than one leading indicator to convey a crucial step's performance. We make these decisions as we design and mature components of our operations baseline. Strategic planning offers us a proactive opportunity to validate the efficacy of these definitions.

Infographic D.8 illustrates a small part of our operations baseline. Our only path to creating more value for our customers is directly through the tangible operations baseline components across functions.

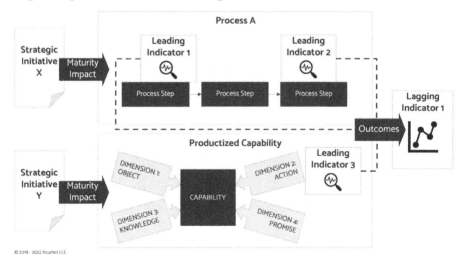

Infographic D.8 – The power of leading indicators

The performance of every process involves complexities, and the design of our leading indicators must accommodate the incentives of the roles performing each process or process step. Let's stay with our lead generation function in our operations baseline. One of the common ways for companies to generate leads is to perform outreach to prospective customers. A simple leading indicator could be the number of outreaches performed. If we conduct more outreaches, it will positively impact our overall company outcomes, such as the number of customers and revenue.

But could outreaches be executed poorly? Absolutely. Some employees may not be motivated enough to understand the prospect well enough before performing the outreach, even if our process execution guidelines set specific expectations. So, we may have to consider a secondary leading indicator around the execution effectiveness of outreaches in this process.

Similarly, we can measure a productized capability with one or more leading indicators. For instance, if we can measure whether a customer uses our offering as part of their journey, it is a powerful predictor of whether they will continue to buy in the future. I've illustrated this measurement in Infographic D.8 as Leading Indicator 3.

Remember, a leading indicator is a simple measurement or a simple ratio that directly measures either or both the maturity and execution of a part of our operations baseline.

Leading indicators are easy. They are not complex measurements with several factors in the numerator and denominator. Instead, they measure what one employee or a group of employees in the same role might do. They measure how effectively a specific part of our productized offering creates value. It's best to keep it that simple. The more confounding a measurement is, the more uncontrollable it is.

Think about the choice of leading indicators as an effort to contain a liquid that will flow in the path of least resistance. Our operations baseline's maturity and execution effectiveness are like such a flowing liquid. So, how many walls do we have to build to contain the liquid? That's how we think about choosing and defining our leading indicators. We want to select the optimal set of leading indicators that can collectively help us understand the maturity of our entire operations baseline and the internal or external human behaviors that determine its execution effectiveness.

Infographic D.9 illustrates the concepts to define leading indicators as a framework that you can use as part of your operations planning efforts. Consider all components of our operations baseline – productized offerings, processes, data, and management approach – across all functions. The choice of leading indicators must consider all our functions.

The choice of leading indicators can stay within a function, span multiple functions, or just hand-off between two functions.

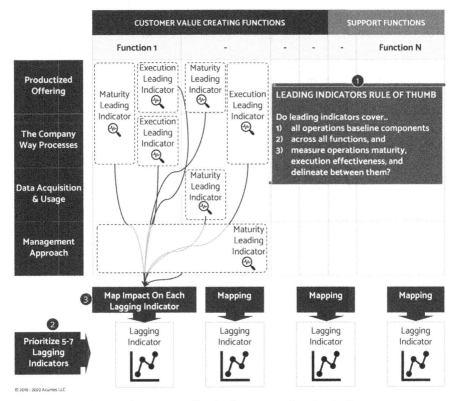

Infographic D.9 – Leading indicators vs. lagging indicators

The planning team must be able to identify the circumstances in which we need multiple indicators to frame our operations baseline's maturity and execution effectiveness. The choice depends on current maturity and execution effectiveness. It also depends on whether we have slated a strategic initiative that is expected to shift maturity that requires its adoption in the next cycle, which implies we must measure execution effectiveness.

Are you worried about too many leading indicators? Don't be – because effective target setting and reporting that we will discuss in Principle 4 ensures these require no work unless we cross certain thresholds. If we have leading indicators that breach thresholds, we really should have been monitoring them anyway.

Consider the following questions as rules of thumb while assessing and refining leading indicators:

What simple measurements can directly set expectations and monitor our work to create value through every management approach and value engine component?

Do these chosen measurements cover all functions comprehensively?

Do they measure both maturity and execution effectiveness, especially in areas where our corporate strategy will shift our operations maturity via strategic initiatives?

Defining these leading indicators is a starting point. We will iterate them as we map them to lagging indicators, set targets, and create our execution plans because a critical thinking planning team will refine the quality of the strategic plan throughout.

Map leading indicators to compound lagging indicators for external use and storytelling.

The primary practical application of lagging indicators in a company is storytelling. Revenue and expenses are just compound measurements, often determined using accounting rules common to all companies. Measurements such as 'churn,' which states the total revenue that we lost because we lost customers, are so complex that it is hard to internalize what it really means. Such measures never tell us why the measurement is what it is. Instead, we must undergo a situational root cause analysis to understand why such measurements went up or down.

Additionally, accounting for revenue and expenses is unique to each company because the underlying operations are never the same between companies or over time. The result is that benchmarking lagging indicators across companies or over time doesn't really tell us anything actionable.

Lagging indicators have a use, and we must choose five to seven for the whole company. They are perfectly normal to use for external reporting for an audience that just wants to know how our company is performing without being involved in the details or helping us get to results. But this same interest in lagging indicators from external stakeholders creates a tendency for executives and supervisors to operate and manage the business using lagging indicators exclusively. This is problematic.

Lagging indicators are very tempting. They require very little work to define because the world just wants to know the outcomes. If our management approach is immature, lagging indicators are tempting because they can be used as a stick to manage supervisors and employees without giving them a specific path to achieve those lagging indicators. In our lead generation example above, it is very easy for a supervisor to demand more high-quality leads from employees who work hard to find them. Demanding results is not hard. The hard part is to design a way that makes it possible.

Unless we are in an established business ticking along at a small growth rate with meager profitability and not evolving our operations, planning using lagging indicators implies a lack of a real plan to manage the company.

The relationship between a lagging indicator and leading indicators is often complex. This relationship is multi-variable calculus. Every lagging indicator has a one-to-many relationship with several leading indicators. A lagging indicator may not improve until multiple leading indicators collectively improve. The impact of each leading indicator on a lagging indicator may also not be linear.

At one of the companies that I helped turn around, a major internal challenge was the rift between the marketing and sales teams. The sales reps incorrectly didn't attribute much value to the leads handed to them by marketing lead generation resources and worked on only the leads they self-generated. In this circumstance, a common lagging indicator called 'sales pipeline,' which reflects likely revenue based on high-quality prospects in the sales process, will remain unchanged regardless of the number and quality of marketing leads created. Here, we ran separate strategic initiatives to improve the hand-off process between sales and marketing teams and used leading indicators to measure this hand-off and improvements in marketing lead generation activities, both of which influence a lagging indicator like the sales pipeline in a mature process.

We can simplify these complexities by focusing most of our efforts on leading indicators. So, we need to understand an approximate relationship between our leading indicators, which we can directly control, and the resulting lagging indicators. In a growth-phase company with no public reporting responsibilities, fretting about exact future measurements of lagging indicators is not a good use of resources.

Infographic D.8 Illustrates this relationship between the work we do in the form of processes and offerings, measuring them using leading indicators and relating them to outcomes measured via lagging indicators. Use the tabular framework in Infographic D.9 to map the many-to-one relationship between leading and lagging indicators comprehensively.

Consider the following questions to map leading indicators to lagging indicators effectively:

What are the top five to seven lagging indicators our external stakeholders are interested in?

Which of our drafted leading indicators directly impact these five to seven lagging indicators?

What is the approximate level of impact (direct correlation, partial correlation, etc.) between the leading and lagging indicators?

What are the dependencies between leading indicators for improvements to be observable within the lagging indicator?

In our fundamentals-focused planning approach, we focus on leading indicators and draw a reasonably effective estimation of impact from our leading indicators on extrinsically relevant outcomes such as customer satisfaction, number of customers, new revenue, revenue retention, cost of goods sold, etc. This mapping helps the CFO and CEO translate the reality of our operations baseline to externally reportable outcomes.

Once we have mapped our leading and lagging indicators, we also have to understand the timing of the impact of our strategic initiatives through our Chain of Controllability.

Principle 3: Define strategic initiative impact timeline on leading and lagging indicators.

So far, we discussed what the level of impact of strategic initiatives through our Chain of Controllability looks like. But 'when' such an impact will manifest is equally important. So, let's incorporate how strategic initiatives, operations baseline, leading indicators, and lagging indicators relate over time.

> *Consider the following questions to build an operations plan that accurately reflects changes in maturity as we move through the next execution cycle:*
>
> *When will strategic initiatives trigger operations maturity improvements?*
>
> *When will operations resources adopt improvements and realistically reflect maturity improvements in execution?*
>
> *What is the time-sequenced impact of maturity improvements on overarching outcomes?*

Whichever sports we consider, every team starts the season with enthusiasm and excitement. But are they playing at their best at the start of the season? No. If we normalize for psychological breakdowns, injuries, and similar setbacks, we expect every team to learn more and play better as a season progresses. The same maturity growth trend applies to our business. Our maturity growth comes from our effectively executed and adopted strategic initiatives.

To predict the performance of our operations baseline, we must internalize when our strategic initiatives drive improvements into our operations baseline. Effective maturity growth via our strategic initiatives implies that our leading indicators will improve through our execution cycle as we effectively implement more initiatives. Lagging indicators will reflect improvement in our leading indicators in due course. We want to know when these improvements kick in.

Enablement Roadmap determines timeline of maturity impact.

At the start of each execution cycle, we will start exactly where we finished the previous cycle. The performance of each component of our operations baseline reflects the effectiveness of the strategic initiatives we have effectively implemented until that point in our company's history.

With no maturity shifts in the components of our operations baseline, we must assume that the next cycle's starting performance is the same as the ending performance of the current cycle. Under this scenario, the best we can do is short-term tactical scaling of more of the same. For example, we can hire more sales reps to sell exactly the same way and same offering. We could offer the same capability without increasing the value created. But we would be sacrificing sustainability because more sales reps become unwieldy to manage with scale without maturity growth. In addition, the same offering has less net value for customers over time because value creation feels inflation, just like currency. Hence our maturity growth path.

The time to impact our strategic initiatives determines improvement in our operations' performance, and thus our growth and profitability increase through our execution cycle. Therefore, as we create our operations plan, we must incorporate the time-phased release of impact from strategic initiatives on our operations baseline.

We must create a tentative timeline for our prioritized strategic initiatives. We will call this timeline our **Enablement Roadmap**. For now, let's think about the roadmap as a simple construct where we add a start date and an end date for each initiative. Over the next several chapters, we will further detail our initiatives and bolster our Enablement Roadmap.

We cannot work on all our prioritized initiatives simultaneously. Nothing will get done. We must stage-gate our strategic initiatives based on dependencies between them – we might have to complete some before others – and practicality around enablement investments because the same resources might have to work on one initiative after another is complete.

In Infographic D.10, element 1 illustrates how we can think about the phased approach to strategic initiatives that builds on our preliminary enablement initiative prioritization.

D.3 PREDICT UNIT-LEVEL PERFORMANCE VIA OPERATIONS PLANNING

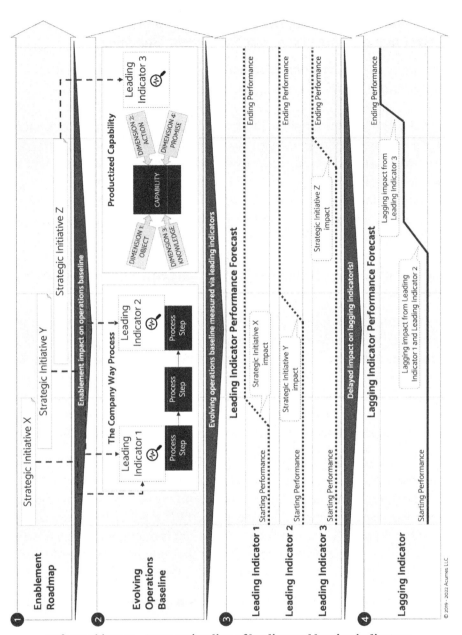

Infographic D.10 – Impact timeline of leading and lagging indicators

Consider the following question to draft our strategic initiative execution timeline to start our Enablement Roadmap:

What is our high-level timeline to start, execute, complete, and transition each strategic initiative among the prioritized strategic initiatives?

The left side of the infographic illustrates the starting point of our execution cycle. Let's simplify our company to just one capability and one process, measured via three leading indicators. Our performance will reflect these three leading indicators at the start of our cycle. Regardless of how much we wish our lagging indicators to perform at a higher level, it will always be a trailing aggregation of the tangible performance of contributing leading indicators.

Leading indicators closely track improvements injected by strategic initiatives.

As strategic initiatives improve our value engine and management approach, the measurements of our leading indicators will ramp up as operations resources adopt these improvements. The impact timeline of leading indicators solely depends on the adoption effectiveness if we successfully complete strategic initiatives to drive maturity improvements. It is important to note that our operations performance ramp reflects both maturity improvement and execution alignment to the new maturity level.

We can evaluate this ramping in operational performance by the performance upticks from the start and along the way as we complete each related strategic initiative. Each of these improvements is a crucial time stamp for our operations-focused plan. This is one of the key payoffs around embracing leading indicators. We will immediately know whether the enablement investments we commit to are working without waiting for company-level outcomes to show improvements.

Consider the following questions to frame impact timeline on leading indicators:

When will each leading indicator show maturity improvements triggered by effective completion of strategic initiatives?

What is the reasonable adoption timeline where execution effectiveness will ramp up to increased maturity created by strategic initiatives?

In our lead generation example, a hypothetical enablement initiative that aligns with the how-to-deliver strategic trade-off could be to change our approach to create leads from outbound outreaches to inbound advertising-driven leads. Now, we can track a leading indicator like '% of sweet spot leads from advertising as a ratio of the total.' Then, as the related enablement initiative approaches completion, we can immediately see the uptick in this leading indicator without having to wait for company-level outcomes such as new sales revenue.

Lagging indicators will display a significant delay in improvement efforts.

No one in the world will disagree with the importance of leading indicators. But these are just words, not actions based on true beliefs if we let lagging indicators run us ragged. I can't stress this enough. But, unfortunately, in my experience, lagging indicators have a nicotine-like addictive effect on many executives.

It is critical to internalize that our lagging indicators will always see a significantly delayed uptick from our strategy development, strategic initiatives, and operations improvements demonstrable via leading indicators. As compound metrics, we also never really know why they are going up and down by just looking at them.

The chart at the bottom of Infographic D.10 illustrates this delay and compounding nature of lagging indicators. In our operations-focused planning, there is no new information that we will learn from lagging indicators that we cannot learn from leading indicators. However, we must understand and incorporate the impact timelines of lagging indicators.

Why? Because when external stakeholders ask questions about overall performance, we will feel the pressure to give them some good news. If we lack clarity on when our controllable aspects – strategic initiatives and operations baseline execution – will impact our lagging indicators, we will likely feel the need to act irrationally and take knee-jerk actions.

This happens when a company doesn't have a firm handle on its Chain of Controllability and the true nature of lagging indicators. If irrational reactions set in, it essentially drives executives and key resources to deviate from our well-laid-out plans. If that happens, we are operating without a plan. For example, I used to work closely with a revenue executive who loved saying, "the long-term is important, but we just need results now!" My response was typically, "How do you suggest we do that?" Unfortunately, the reality is that this executive limited the effectiveness of sustainable growth opportunities at that company.

Consider the following question to frame a credible understanding of the relationship between leading and lagging indicators:

When will the compounded impact of improving leading indicators be observable in our five to seven lagging indicators?

To summarize, we must have iteratively triangulated towards a high-level timeline for our strategic initiatives at this stage in our planning efforts. We must also understand at what points in time our planned strategic initiatives will impact our operations baseline and improve our leading indicators and when we expect to see improvements in lagging indicators as leading indicators improve.

Use the framework in Infographic D.10 to define a realistic timeline for strategic initiatives while internalizing the impact on operations baseline, its measurement via leading indicators, and lagging indicators.

Principle 4: Setting leading indicator targets will anchor operations baseline performance.

We discussed how we would leverage our enablement initiatives to mature our operations baseline at the start of our Chain of Controllability, which is core to our operations-focused planning approach. We know the linkage between our strategic initiatives and our lagging outcomes; we also know the timing of impact throughout our chain. Now, all we have to do is set targets across this chain while intertwining the impact timeline. Setting analysis-backed targets enables us to set organizational expectations on how our operations baseline will perform throughout the execution cycle. This is our operations plan.

Another common pitfall I have seen through planning efforts at various companies is for teams to volunteer for unachievable targets. Senior executives or supervisors often feel that future performance can be significantly better than past performance because they are involved. It's a form of optimism bias. It's a human tendency to think that "this time, it will be different!" In a poor planning approach, this optimism is based on spurious rationales such as a new senior executive or subjective learning from past mistakes. But these aren't tangible evolutionary shifts.

Even individuals will struggle to shift personal behaviors without a tangible enabler. For example, how many alcoholics say that they quit every so often? Going to rehab is a tangible enabler. Similarly, our improved future targets will require directly related enablers.

Let's build on principles from Chapter B.3 and lay down the guardrails for effective target setting to round out our operations plan. Infographic D.11 summarizes the minimum viable outcome that we must create for operations planning. The four guardrails below highlight the key parts to implementing this framework to formalize an operations plan.

Guardrail 1: A comprehensive set of leading indicators ensure company-wide coverage.

Operations plans speak to every employee and executive alike. Operations resources live and breathe the components of our operations baseline, and their performance is set and measured using our leading indicators.

So, the spine of our operations plan is the comprehensive set of leading indicators that we developed and validated in the principles above. At this stage in the planning effort, we must ensure that we use the indicators we developed. The left side of our framework above illustrates this guardrail. This guardrail ensures that our operations plan comprehensively covers our entire operations baseline.

Measurement gaps often act like the slope in the bathroom floor that attracts all the water flow. Failure points via maturity gaps and execution ineffectiveness often shift towards these blind spots.

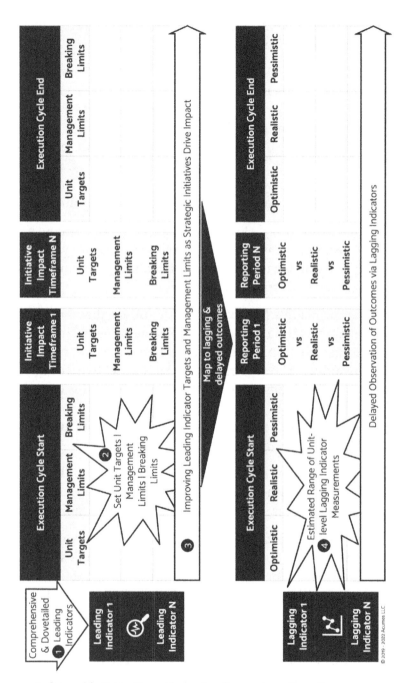

Infographic D.11 – Operations plan forecasts unit performance

Guardrail 2: Leading indicators will require targets, management limits, and breaking limits.

We must know how we expect our organization to perform on that measurement for each leading indicator. We must leverage analytical rigor to set operational performance expectations. The targets must reflect the reasonable unit economics performance expectations based on maturity at any given point in time. The measurements that we can hit for our metrics should not be defined in a vacuum or be based on desired outcomes.

Remember our discussion about creating effective reporting. Reporting is a powerful risk management tool if we set optimal targets and limits. This is the most opportune and purposeful moment in our entire strategy & operations cycle to analytically identify targets that can help us repeatably and reproducibly achieve necessary performance levels for each component of the operations baseline across all functions.

We must also set effective management limits for each leading indicator that trigger corrective actions and supervisory intervention for each leading indicator.

Imagine trying to monitor a comprehensive set of leading indicators without effective thresholds! It will be akin to trying to find a person who we don't know visual details of by looking at feeds from several security cameras showing hundreds of people. Strong reporting with management limits is like knowing this person's face and having facial recognition software. Without it, we will likely pick out an arbitrarily interesting and incorrect person, not the actual person. Therefore, setting management limits for leading indicators is a necessity.

The breaking limits for our leading indicators, which identify situations where our operations baseline is at risk of an unpredictable breakdown, are also critical to reassess and reset throughout our operations planning effort. As our operations baseline matures, the worst-case performance expected also gets more stringent.

Guardrail 3: Targets, management limits, and breaking limits will evolve with operations baseline maturity over time.

The targets, management limits, and breaking limits evolve as our operations baseline matures through our execution cycle. The impact of our strategic initiatives must lift our performance expectations for leading indicators. Precision is pertinent here. We want to be realistic about our impact timeline.

If we are too optimistic, we have set ourselves up for failure. If we sandbag, we are poorly allocating investment to protect ourselves from the risk of failure at everyone else's expense. The planning lead must devise effective analyses to quantify the impact of each strategic initiative on portions of the operations baseline that we highlighted under Principle 2.

One effective approach to arrive at reasonable figures is to estimate optimistic, realistic, and pessimistic scenarios for each leading indicator. Triangulating from three such figures often renders a reasonably precise target and management limit.

Our starting performance as we ring in the next execution cycle must equal our performance when we finish the current cycle unless we finish a strategic initiative at the turn of the cycle. No wishful thinking must convince us to set elevated operations baseline performance targets. Then, establish the expected performance targets and limits that align with completion timelines of enablement initiatives. The third guardrail is this time-based adjustment of operations performance targets and limits triggered by strategic initiatives.

Additionally, we must proactively look for dependencies in our operations baseline and enablement initiatives, thus between leading indicators. In our lead generation example, what if we trained our lead generation resources to deliver incremental leads, but our enablement efforts to generate interest in the market via advertising spend or branding efforts are not complete? Target setting must be dovetailed across leading indicators to ensure realistic expectations and account for dependencies, especially time lags.

Adhering to these three guardrails will help us translate all the inputs that we developed thus far into a single plan that articulates what our organization will do operationally.

Easy, right? On paper, yes. But lagging indicators will always tempt us to abandon discipline and skip the use of leading indicators. So, we must adopt a fourth guardrail to ensure that we can predict our operations' lagging performance at a unit level.

Guardrail 4: Frame unit-level outcomes using lagging indicators.

Our goal through operations planning is to set an operations blueprint for our organization. But we will be surrounded by extrinsic conversations about revenue, expenses, and growth rates. In my experience, the best way to stay focused on aspects that we can control is to be able to effectively answer all questions about how the aspects we can control will influence aspects we cannot directly control but are outcomes others care about.

Like setting performance expectations for leading indicators, our goal is not to predict aggregate outcomes. Instead, by this second milestone of strategic planning, we want to predict lagging outcomes while staying with our unit economics mindset.

We have already mapped our leading indicators to our lagging indicators. We already have an estimated time to impact from our improving leading indicators. We must create a simple mathematical model that estimates the outcomes via our prioritized five to seven lagging indicators. Our goal is not to be exact. As a growth-phase company, all we need is to estimate optimistic, realistic, and pessimistic scenarios for each chosen lagging indicator for key moments in time through our execution cycle. These key points in time can be the turn of fiscal quarters or months.

For example, for a lagging financial metric like 'new sweet spot revenue from the existing offering,' we can predict 'new sweet spot revenue from existing offering per sales representative' as part of our operations plan. The work we have already done informs us of the strategic initiatives that would support the maturity growth around the specific offering and how we sell that offering. The 'total new sweet spot revenue from existing offering' is simply an operations investment decision on the number of sales reps, lead generation resources, various thresholds of advertising expenses, etc.

Such investment decisions will be part of the final planning phase and directly build on the maturity level articulated by our operations plan.

I have included this fourth guardrail in Infographic D.11 to complete the minimum set of answers that we can work towards to draft our operations plan. This operations plan enables us to conduct a second planning milestone review with the planning team to align and improve our Chain of Controllability.

The concepts we discussed aren't complex. But getting these concepts right under the pressures of time, priorities, and personalities can be extremely difficult. The CEO's leadership and the maturity level of the company's management approach will determine effective operations planning through these analytically demanding stages.

D.4
OPTIMIZE SCALE AND OUTCOMES THROUGH INVESTMENT PLANNING.

GROWING sustainably by focusing on fundamentals implies committing to the groundwork discussed through corporate strategy and planning thus far. Our alternative is to skip those foundations and sign-up to invest in the existing maturity of the operations baseline. We likely did the same in the past cycles if our current tendency is to invest poorly. Investing in an immature operations baseline is akin to using all our cash to barely cover the interest on a credit card balance while continuing to rack up more debt.

> **Things to Remember: Investment Planning**
>
> **Investment planning is the third and final phase of an iterative strategic planning exercise where we translate soft decisions from enablement planning and operations planning to finalize both enablement and operations investment and formalize forecasts for company-level lagging indicators.**

First, we need to approve what good looks like for our prioritized and tiered strategic initiatives and solidify our investment choices into these initiatives. Strategic initiatives are difficult to execute and derive maturity from because we expect they will change our company, and change isn't easy. So, before we formalize and approve our initiatives and begin execution, we must agree on what good looks like for each strategic initiative.

Second, we need to formalize our operations investment choices for each controllable resource or asset contributing to our processes to achieve the unit-level leading indicators we laid out in our operations plan. Operations investment choice is a scaling multiplier decision triggered by maturity level improvements in our operations baseline. Therefore, we must decide when and how much we will scale a specific portion of our operations baseline and what maturity improvement will trigger each scaling investment.

Third, to firm up our unit economics-focused operations plan, we must finalize our leading indicators and targets based on our strategic initiatives' impact and enablement investment choices. Superimposing our operations investment decision on top of this finalized unit-level operations plan gives us the scaled measurements of our operations baseline performance.

The above outcomes provide the CFO with all the tangible inputs necessary to create a detailed financial plan that forecasts revenue, expenses, and cash flow. These core outcomes also give our fundamentals-focused company a cohesive and comprehensive plan to execute effectively in the next execution cycle.

> ***Consider the following questions to anticipate the principles that form investment planning:***
>
> *What does 'good' look like for every strategic initiative that will translate our strategy into our operations?*
>
> *What will be our enablement investment to support our strategic initiatives?*
>
> *What will be our operations investment to deliver customer value through our operations baseline?*
>
> *Based on our finalized operations plan and operations investment, what will be our company-level outcomes?*

Principle 1: Investment decisions balance affordability and impact.

To make money, we must spend money. Every dollar we spend on our operations and enablement efforts is our investment. But what is the right amount to spend? In our sustainable growth mindset, we don't believe that careless investing will help us grow sustainably.

There are two simple guardrails to an overall investment decision. One is affordability, and the other is the tangible impact of the investment.

Affordability is the upper threshold for investment.

Affordability implies our ability to invest without risking the financial health of our company. This means we want to remain in a relatively stress-free cash position as a company where we can afford to pay our bills, keep our employees, and serve our customers effectively even if we face headwinds. It implies only taking on interest-bearing debt that we can afford without being consumed by the risk of default. Affordability is the CFO's realm.

Our company may or may not have profits. If we are running at a loss, we need external funding from an investor or a bank to keep investing as much as we have been. Do we have profits? If we have profits, what is the correct share of those profits to reinvest during the next execution cycle? As our affordability police, the CFO will work with the CEO and the board to identify relevant investment thresholds for our next execution cycle.

Impact, the second guardrail, is the realm of the CEO and the planning lead. What can each dollar we spend get us in intrinsic maturity growth and extrinsic outcomes?

Just like resources, we categorize all our expenses in our company into two categories – operations and enablement. We must formalize our investment decision on both these categories for the execution cycle through strategic planning, which must depend on their impact.

Impact has to consider the maturity improvement we can realistically drive in our operations baseline through enablement initiatives and the operations baseline scale that the maturity level can support. There are realistic limitations to such impact.

Our planning impact assessment must be realistic on how fast we can execute enablement initiatives due to dependencies and availability of decision-makers and other company-level constraints. Additionally, we can only scale our operations investment to a maximum level. At this point, we are destroying the unit economics of our operations plan, which is equivalent to maturity decline. The ceiling created by these impact thresholds could be below our affordability, so we must stay prudent and not overspend.

We must also decide our total enablement and operations investments in a manner where we are optimally balancing these two categories between each other. We want to invest in enablement efforts to stay ahead of our scale to ensure that our operations investments go into a mature operations baseline. Conversely, we do not want to overinvest in enablement where our maturity level is significantly higher than our operations' scale, leading to lower overall outcomes than our operations baseline can produce. We must strike this secondary balance between operations and enablement investment.

The planning lead can work with the CFO and the finance team to ensure that the strategic plan stays within the guardrails of total investment and cash flow constraints without mudding the primary focus on investment impact.

Principle 2: Finalize strategic initiative impact via steady state definition.

The first step of the investment planning phase is to nail down what 'good' looks like for our prioritized strategic initiatives.

How would we consider that decision if we were to sign up for a running race? First, we would like to know whether it's a marathon or a 5K. Next, we'd like to know which city and time of the year the race is because elevation changes and temperature impact the race. The list goes on; we want to know the factors that determine success before training for or participating in the race.

The same goes for strategic initiatives. We must frame what 'good' looks like for all our strategic initiatives during investment planning before finalizing our plan to ensure we are crystal clear on the expected impact and investment requirements.

The impact of strategic initiatives is far from guaranteed.

Strategic initiatives, which are enablement projects that evolve maturity and move our company closer to achieving its corporate strategy, don't just start and end. Unfortunately, an unsophisticated 'get it done' tactical mindset is a common path to failure.

After running so many implementation projects over the years, I have had the realization that most initiatives fail if we objectively measure outcomes and don't try to spin the outcome as a success. Failures transpire in two forms.

The **first** type of failure is that initiatives fizzle away and do not achieve the objective and measurable outcome that was its original intended essence. This often happens due to a lack of clarity on their intended improvements.

Many strategic initiatives start by intending to achieve nebulous outcomes that the people involved don't even agree on or understand and eventually don't go anywhere.

The **second** type of failure is regression. Even among the successful initiatives that achieve the desired improvements by completing the execution phase, many fail to maintain those improvements over time. Strategic initiatives can achieve the desired improvement for a short period due to intense attention and investment, but the performance can slip back after the initial excitement.

Gravity is a practical reality. What goes up will come down unless the necessary energy is expended to fight gravity and keep the object at the higher state. Executing strategic initiatives to improve organizational maturity and productivity has a similar constraint. Imagine training for that running race, and we got ourselves to a pace that made us proud. What if we stop running for the next six months? Likely, our running speed dropped back to what it was before we trained for our race.

The root cause of both these failure modes is a lack of clarity about what 'good' looks like for strategic initiatives and an internalization that maintenance of that 'good' state isn't trivial. I call this articulation the **Steady State**.

The steady state definition articulates strategic initiative success factors.

Infographic D.12 illustrates the maturity trends for well-run and poorly run initiatives. Poorly run initiatives tend to look for quick improvements without dedicating the design and build effort to truly mature fundamentals, which is impossible to maintain over time. The dotted line represents the trajectory of such doomed efforts.

For example, a common strategic initiative that companies take on is the implementation of software solutions such as CRMs and ERPs to automate or streamline operations as the number of employees increases. It's the right choice. But what if we dilute the initiative to buy a software solution off the shelf and quickly turn it on without effective design to ensure it aligns with our processes or has strong governance? We could get employees to use it very quickly, and they might even appreciate it for a few weeks. But without proper design, governance, and training, the software will quickly become the wild west. It will regress our maturity level because the software's effectiveness will drop as more bad information and poor usage pile up. So, where do we end up? We lost our investment in an initiative that devolved after initial success. This is a very common storyline when a company does not internalize the concept of steady state.

> **Things to Remember: Steady State**
>
> **Strategic initiatives do not end when the execution plan is complete. Instead, they go through a heavy lifting execution phase to complete a certain set of tasks and deliverables to improve current performance and achieve the desired maturity level. Then, the evolved state has to be embraced and maintained. This evolved state that requires perpetual maintenance is called the steady state.**

An initiative moves into a steady state when we achieve the desired, measurable maturity and productivity improvements and transition the responsibilities from enablement execution resources to long-term operations execution resources accountable for executing at the higher maturity level. I illustrate this trajectory with the bold line in Infographic D.12. This is our desired execution path for each strategic initiative, which drives three benefits.

D.4 OPTIMIZE SCALE AND OUTCOMES THROUGH INVESTMENT PLANNING

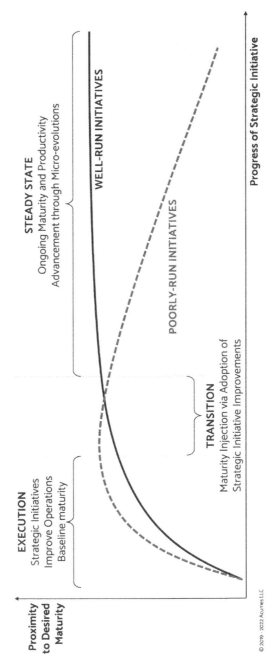

Infographic D.12 – Importance of strategic initiative steady state

First, the end justifies the means. A clearly articulated desired state allows strategic planning to predict each initiative's realistic investment needs and maturity upside. In addition, an accurate depiction of the steady state is necessary to firm up the targets and limits we drafted as part of *Phase 2: Operations Planning*.

Second, we tend to rationalize and put a convenient spin on situations when conditions turn sour. For example, execution can take longer than expected, or high quality may be harder to achieve than anticipated. Unless a steady state is well articulated ahead of time, there is a strong likelihood that we will settle for 'good enough' results far from the original intent as deadlines slide and unanticipated obstacles turn up. Starting with a strong articulation of the steady state helps the company and individuals involved hold themselves and each other accountable to achieve the essence of each strategic initiative.

Third, the idea of maintenance of maturity is not obvious and guaranteed. In real-life projects, I repeatedly use the specific term – steady state – to highlight the importance of perpetual maintenance. Formalizing enablement initiatives must always involve a clear internalization of what the steady state is. It drives clarity on the level of performance we have to maintain as we go through planning, design, and building through the 'execution' phase and push for organizational adoption during the 'transition' phase, which comes after execution.

> ***Consider the following question to take enablement plans to an executable state:***
>
> *For each prioritized strategic initiative, what is the impact on the operations baseline we want to hold ourselves accountable for through qualitative maturity improvements and leading quantitative indicators?*

So, what does a 'good' steady state definition look like?

Formalize and approve strategic initiative impact on operations baseline.

In previous planning phases, we developed high-level impact and timeline details during enablement initiatives prioritization and Enablement Roadmap development. But we need to get deeper. Documentation, reviews, and memorialization are often underrated. Strategic planning is not just an opportunity to think and talk about what we will do. It is a time to write down what we will do so that our analyses and insights are more formal, and we can hold ourselves and the organization accountable for the promises we make.

Consider the following questions to detail processes & data capture and usage impact for each prioritized initiative:

What are the expected qualitative improvements in processes and data?

Which operations roles must embrace improvements?

How will adoption and improvements be measured and monitored?

Which leading indicators will quantify process improvements and by how much?

Consider the following questions to detail productized offerings and related pricing and packaging impact for each prioritized initiative:

What value-creating capability improvements will be delivered?

How will these improvements be evidenced via pricing and packaging?

Which leading indicators will quantify productization maturity improvements and by how much?

Consider the following questions to detail management approach impact for each prioritized initiative:

What are the expected organizational design, hiring, and performance and compensation management improvements?

What are the new skills required to execute the improved processes, capture or use higher quality data, or deliver value through evolved offerings?

These answers will ensure accountability on impact throughout the next execution cycle. Framing impact with downstream accountability in mind ensures that we are basing our strategic plan on firm grounding instead of hopeful desires.

These answers also flow directly into finalizing our strategic initiatives' impact on our leading indicators. Framing these answers makes a business case for whether we are ready to allocate investment for each of these prioritized strategic initiatives. Without knowing what we will achieve and when, how can we frame what it would cost to achieve it? Why would we approve an initiative without such a case?

In addition to addressing our investment decision during planning, such a clear framing of the steady state allows us to start execution management of enablement initiatives with confidence and clarity.

Imagine a group of executives going through a planning effort and framing a major nebulous initiative without many specifics... Then the initiatives are presented to the board and even the whole company as critical for our maturity shift... Then, we hire an enablement resource to manage that initiative... would you want to be that enablement resource? They are set up to fail. This pattern is all too common. We want to avoid it.

Doing our diligence at this stage ensures that we are effectively planning our enablement initiatives and readying them for execution.

Infographic D.13 visualizes the central role of strategic initiative steady state definition. Effective framing of steady state informs of their impact and ensures that we are ready for effective execution post-planning. Without effectively framing the steady state for each initiative, we cannot objectively finalize our enablement and operations investment.

Principle 3: Formalize enablement investment for strategic initiatives.

Enablement initiatives are not trivial to execute and transition. They require investment in the short term that does not become a perpetual cost burden. Enablement investment planning must be managed surgically because of this short-term nature. We want to execute our initiatives without investing beyond the time horizon we optimally need them.

Initiative planning always feels easy to strap together by just putting some names and dates down. But often, these end up being throw-away, lazy efforts that give planning a bad brand. The truth is that we could predict most aspects of how an initiative would play out if we reserved some thoughtful time to ask deeper questions and identify answers.

D.4 OPTIMIZE SCALE AND OUTCOMES THROUGH INVESTMENT PLANNING

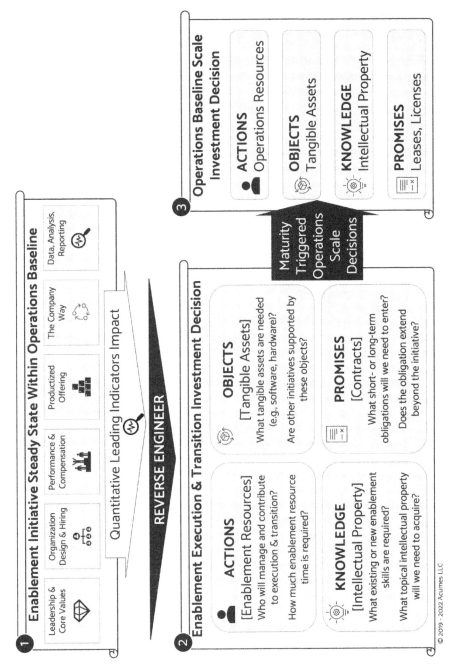

Infographic D.13 – Strategic initiatives' steady state trigger investment decisions

> **Things to Remember: Enablement Investment**
>
> **Enablement investment is the time-bound allocation of finances to execute and adopt prioritized strategic initiatives until hand-off to steady state operations.**

The following three guardrails will help formalize enablement investment.

Guardrail 1: Frame enablement investment needs for each initiative using four capability dimensions.

Each enablement initiative implies an investment. We started with the end in mind by defining the steady state for each initiative. Now, let's reverse engineer from a final vision of where we want to be and identify a cost to achieve that steady state.

We channel the enablement investment into the cost of running these time-bound initiatives. The cost must cover complete staffing of enablement resources and all technology, infrastructure, and knowledge support to run those initiatives. In most markets, most enablement investment goes into people resources.

Remember the four dimensions of capabilities we used for productization and what-to-offer trade-offs in chapters B.1 and C.4, respectively? Our four-dimensional capability framework also effectively structures our investment needs to complete enablement initiatives because solving an external market problem is no different from solving an internal one through a strategic initiative.

First, think about all the actions we will have to take to accomplish each initiative. This line of thinking helps us firm up our investment in enablement resources – number of resources, the share of time we will need from different resources, the role each will play, etc. If we do not know this ahead of time, how will we know whether an initiative we have prioritized can get executed?

> *Consider the following questions for each strategic initiative:*
>
> *Who will manage and contribute to execution & transition?*
>
> *How much enablement resource time is required?*

Second, we must consider all the object dimension requirements necessary to execute each initiative. For example, we might need existing or new software, hardware, or other tangible assets, especially if such a thing is either impossible to find or is cost-prohibitive. It is also important to consider whether such an investment is beneficial across other initiatives so that we can share the investment burden across initiatives.

Consider the following questions for each strategic initiative:

What existing or new tangible objects or assets will we need (e.g., software, hardware)?

Do these objects support other initiatives to ease the overall investment burden?

Third, to evolve our maturity level, we might need knowledge or skills that we do not have in-house. An obvious example is specific skills that are required to improve maturity. For instance, we might want to invest in external advisory support for our internal enablement resources who do not have experience in a niche topic.

Consider the following questions for each strategic initiative:

What niche enablement skills are required?

What topical intellectual property will we need to acquire?

Fourth, we live in a world of obligations through contracts and informal expectations. For an enablement investment, this is the least prevalent dimension; but it is important to consider if a unique situation calls for a considerable cost of enablement. To maintain a higher maturity level, we might have to agree to contingencies with external parties.

For example, we might have to enter into an informal agreement with our large customers. They may be willing to test our new capability as we design and build it in exchange for offering it to them for free for a considerable period of time. This delivery beyond testing will have a cost without revenue, and that cost is part of enabling the initiative that matures that capability. It is essential to consider such hidden costs as we finalize the expected cost of each strategic initiative.

Consider the following questions for each strategic initiative:

What short-term or long-term obligations will we need to enter to execute this initiative?

Does the obligation extend beyond the needs of the enablement initiative without fitting into our operations baseline?

Using these four comprehensive capability dimensions helps us formalize the total investment needs for each initiative. As part of the investment planning phase reviews and approval with the planning team, we must document, discuss, iterate, and align on an execution plan, including investment requirements, for each enablement initiative. We can further refine these plans during execution management if we approve the initiative.

Consider the following question as an overarching guardrail for each strategic initiative during investment planning:

What are the investment elements – considering object, action, knowledge, and promise dimensions – necessary to plan, execute, and transition to a steady state for each initiative?

We must consider the investment needs across all dimensions because one dimension without another may prove a waste altogether. For instance, assigning enablement resources to manage an initiative without investing in knowledge gaps in the form of niche consulting advice might render our enablement resources' work ineffective. Once we have defined initiative-specific investment, it's time to make our overarching enablement investment decision.

Guardrail 2: Leverage three tiers of enablement investment to guide prioritization.

Every company has investment constraints, particularly growth phase ones. Even if we have the luxury of spending significantly more than we earn because of new investments, loans, or even profits, we must practice constraints. Having cash in the bank doesn't mean we have to spend it, especially if we know that the return on investment is limited beyond a certain point. Diminishing returns is a real phenomenon.

In the late 2000s, there was a slew of reporting about highly paid athletes living in financial distress. Over 75% of professional American football players were in financial distress by the 5th year of retirement. Over 60% of professional basketball players in the US were in the same situation. If we simplify all their reasons, it all comes down to poor investment choices that arise from the sudden influx of spending power.

Companies aren't different. Every company that contacts us to sell something when news about a funding round or public listing comes out is no different from obscure relatives suddenly contacting someone that came into new money.

The truth is this – regardless of the size of the company and the amount of money we can afford to spend, we can only juggle a certain number of major initiatives that have a relevant impact. Maturity growth in any of our operations baseline components must become embedded into our DNA before investing in additional related initiatives. Otherwise, maturity improvements are a few tough days away from regression.

It's hard to decide whether each initiative is worth investing in or not in a vacuum. So, we build further from the Strategic Initiative Prioritization Framework in Chapter D.2 and our initiative-specific execution investment needs framed above. The second guardrail is for the CFO and the CEO to set investment tiers for the planning lead. I recommend three logical tiers.

The purpose of this tiered approach is to decouple initiative-specific biases from influencing our decisions. Infographic D.14 illustrates the conceptual tiers overlayed on our Strategic Initiative Prioritization Framework.

The first tier of enablement investment is the current investment. Unlike Operations efforts, enablement efforts are time-bound. Therefore, our company will always have existing enablement investment within the overall company-wide expenditure. Given its time-bound nature, current investment can and must be recycled. Since we will always have the current enablement investment, it is **Tier 1: Current Investment**.

Existing enablement efforts will need to transition to a steady state by the time we are ready to begin our next execution cycle. So, it is important to ask whether the current enablement initiatives progressing through the

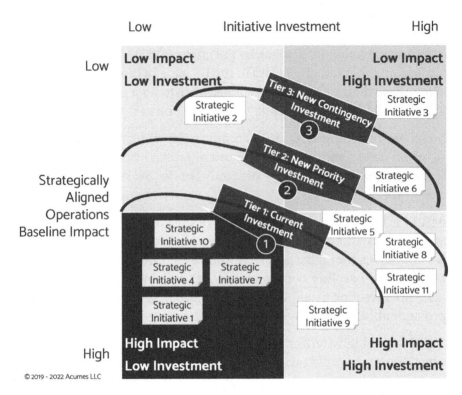

Infographic D.14 – Tiered investment prioritization of strategic initiatives

present execution cycle align with our new corporate strategy. If they do not, should they continue?

We must avoid two Tier 1 investment pitfalls.

First, companies often fall prey to the equivalent nature of growing plaque around Tier 1 investment by considering it allocated without any effective return in the upcoming cycles. In other words, environments with an immature management approach and poor execution management do not effectively redeploy existing enablement investment. This stagnation results in a stale Tier 1 investment. When companies raise external funds, it is tempting not to address the efficacy of the existing investment.

Second, as our company grows, we must consider whether we have to further mature this existing enablement investment. We may have to hire new skills externally instead of existing ones as our enablement initiatives become more complex. We may have to upgrade existing technologies or tangible assets to handle the increasing sophistication of the initiatives we have to manage. If existing enablement resources cannot support increasing sophistication, they are likely to be ineffective in executing increasingly complex initiatives.

Consider the following questions to reassess Tier 1: Current Investment:

What is the total Tier 1: Current Investment?

Which of the four dimensions and initiatives are these investments allocated to?

Should the company at least maintain existing Tier 1 investment, or should it be reduced?

Can we effectively redeploy 100% of our Tier 1 investment? (We must be able to. Understand and address reasons we cannot)

The second tier of enablement investment is **Tier 2: Priority New Investment**. This is incremental to our current investment if it is necessary to execute must-do enablement initiatives to mature our operations baseline. Obviously, this isn't a luxury that every company has. Incremental investment ideally comes from our profits. However, this new investment can also come from external funds raised that we don't deploy in the existing cycle.

The enactment of Tier 2 enablement investment must be contingent on effective use of Tier 1 investment. Throwing good money after bad makes matters worse because we end up with a large, poorly managed organization that is more challenging to fix than a smaller, poorly managed organization.

We must source the guardrail for potential incremental investment from the CFO and CEO based on the company's financial health.

Consider the following question to guide Tier 2: New Priority Investment decision:

What is the total incremental enablement investment that the company wants to unlock without conditions?

The translation is that Tier 2 investment is approved to drive incremental maturity growth.

The third tier of enablement investment is **Tier 3: New Contingency Investment**. Again, there are many reasons to split new investment into a readily approved bucket and a contingent bucket that gets unlocked when positive execution performance reveals itself in the future.

Investing in too many efforts simultaneously usually results in limited progress on any of them. All strategic initiatives have dependencies, and we must internalize the optimal sequencing of initiatives. One of the conditions for unlocking Tier 3 investment can be hitting key milestones of other dependent initiatives.

> *Consider the following questions to prioritize stack-ranked strategic initiatives into three tiers:*
>
> *If we need to invest further, what is a realistic Tier 3: Contingency Investment we can allocate to strategic initiatives?*
>
> *What are the execution performance triggers on Tier 1 and Tier 2 strategic initiatives to unlock Tier 3 investment?*

As the **first** rule of thumb, we must leverage our Tier 1: Current Investment to perform the 'high impact' and 'low investment' efforts, our top priority. If we continuously mature our Tier 1 investment effectively, these initiatives are already approved through prioritization.

The **second** rule of thumb is to skew our prioritization to include 'high impact' and 'high investment' instead of 'low impact' and 'low investment' efforts. The slant of our tiers in the prioritization infographic is emblematic of this proactive choice. As an evolving company, higher maturity growth of fundamentals and alignment with strategy is worth the investment.

As a **third** rule, always eliminate approximately 10% to 20% of the least favorable strategic initiatives identified. There are always poor ideas floating around; it's unavoidable. The few initiatives we ranked at the bottom are unlikely to be effective even if we prioritize them.

Guardrail 3: Leverage Initiative Investment Map to optimize total enablement investment.

Guardrail 1 and guardrail 2 allow us to define a relatively precise investment requirement for each initiative and the total investment that our company can afford through the three tiers. But we have to take one final step to ensure that our final enablement investment decision aligns with all the work we've done through the three phases. Why?

Multiple companies I have worked closely with have fallen prey to the athlete-financial management challenge. Year after year, increasing Tier 1 investment flies under the radar without effective redeployment through maturity growth in skills and effective execution management. Through annual budgeting, companies add Tier 2 new enablement investment on top of a poorly leveraged Tier 1. As a result, the impact of Tier 2 is often just as low because it is impossible to hold Tier 2 investment accountable if we can't hold Tier 1 accountable. The result is increasing enablement investment and decreasing tangible results to show for it.

I recommend using the **Initiative Investment Map** framework in Infographic D.15 to ensure that we have a single dovetailed and verifiable outcome from our enablement planning efforts. The details included in the framework are illustrative to provide context on how you might leverage it.

The **first** element of this framework is our prioritized strategic initiatives, which require no additional context.

The **second** element is mapping our strategic initiatives to our strategic trade-offs and operations components. As we are wrapping up strategic planning, we must ensure that we haven't lost our way through weeks of discussions, debates, and iterations. It is important to ask ourselves – "Do the steady state definitions of the prioritized strategic initiatives align and cover the strategic trade-offs and operations baseline component gaps we used to define them?"

If we have lost our way and our strategic initiatives do not serve the purpose that we defined them for, we have to take a step back and revisit our earlier principles. Sadly, agenda-driven planning efforts often result in breaking this link.

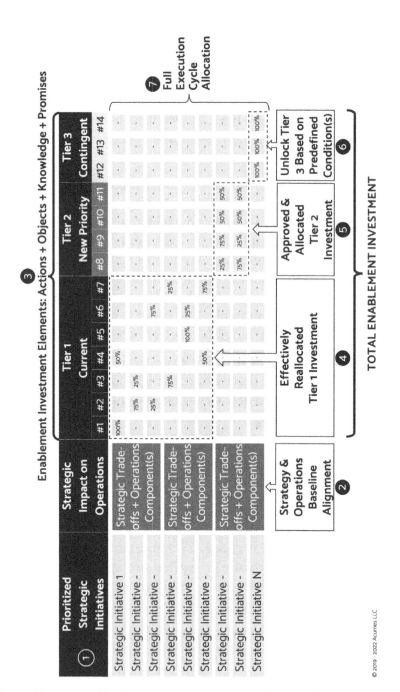

Infographic D.15 – Initiative Investment Map prescribes enablement investment

D.4 OPTIMIZE SCALE AND OUTCOMES THROUGH INVESTMENT PLANNING

The **third** element is the comprehensive framing of all our critical enablement investment elements across all four dimensions for all strategic initiatives. The Initiative Investment Map ensures that our final enablement investment decision is optimal. To do so, we must put all existing and proposed enablement investment elements for all strategic initiatives on the board. In the illustration, these are slated simply as '#-.' This would be the name of an enablement resource or a specific enablement asset in real life.

A planning exercise of a larger company with higher employee counts can group very similar employees into one enablement element. I recommend that the planning lead make such adjustments to ensure that relevant investment elements are reflected adequately without making the use of the framework too unwieldy.

The **fourth** element is mapping the utilization of each Tier 1 – Current Investment elements to specific strategic initiatives. We must associate the share of each enablement element that we would require to each strategic initiative.

Planning is also an opportunity to assess the need to mature current enablement investment. For example, do we have an enablement resource that we invested in for a past initiative but do not have the skills to contribute to any future initiative? Leaving the mapping for this niche enablement resource as 0% across all initiatives helps us objectively assess how to leverage this resource rather than allocating the resource to an initiative that could fail both the resource and the initiative.

Yes, this is an emotionally taxing and sensitive exercise. But, unfortunately, planning for an entire company always is.

Similarly, we must perform the same exercise with proposed new enablement elements via Tier 2 and Tier 3 investments. Mapping in Tier 2 and Tier 3 enablement elements forms the framework's **fifth** and **sixth** elements. We must perform the same diligent exercise of mapping utilization with the best of our knowledge based on all the planning analyses we have conducted.

Consider the following questions to stage fourth through sixth elements of the Initiative Investment Map framework:

How effectively can we mature our operations baseline via strategic initiatives with only Tier 1 investment if we stagger the initiatives to recycle our investment optimally?

How effectively can we mature our operations baseline by adding Tier 2 investment?

Which initiatives can we place under Tier 3? Conversely, which initiatives will we deprioritize?

The **seventh** critical element of this framework is comprehensiveness to cover the entire execution cycle. It is crucial that we assess the allocation of every enablement investment element throughout the execution cycle and not at the highest points of utilization. For example, if we have an enablement resource or plan to hire one to concentrate exclusively on a single strategic initiative that lasts three months but have no other initiatives allocated, the utilization over a year-long execution cycle would be 25%. This is a good indicator that we should be redeploying this investment to complete other strategic initiatives rather than adding more.

Although it is unreasonable that we will fully utilize every investment element throughout the execution cycle, our goal is to approve only enablement elements slated for close to 100% utilization.

Cash-rich, growth-phase companies can be tempted to invest without removing unneeded resources or underleveraged assets. We can avoid overstaffing and padding middle layers with supervisors or acquiring equipment and technology with a low return on investment through this systematic approach. The Initiative Investment Map provides a rational and structured approach to ensure the company remains lean and efficient.

Once all seven elements are incorporated and vetted, the Initiative Investment Map directly forecasts our total enablement investment for our next execution cycle. This directly feeds the expense side of the financial forecast after overlaying the market price for these enablement investment elements. The CFO and finance team can develop expense forecasts by adding in the market price of the enablement investment elements like the fully loaded cost for compensation, technology licensing cost, equipment purchase cost, etc.

Formalizing the impact of strategic initiatives and enablement investment leads us to finalize operations investment decisions.

Principle 4: Formalize operations investments as efficient scaling decisions.

We are now ready to finalize our operations investment, the second half of our entire investment decision. Operations investment accounts for every dollar that goes into our operations baseline.

Imagine pointing a flashlight at an object and looking at the shadow behind. Our enablement plan and operations plan framed the intrinsic performance of our operations baseline, which is analogous to the actual object itself. The operations investment decision is the angle at which we shine the light. The shadow is the total performance of the operations baseline. The shape of the shadow doesn't change; only the size changes.

The CFO and the finance function already manage our operations investment on an ongoing basis. As part of strategic planning, we shouldn't worry about whether the exact start date of an employee is at the beginning of one month or the next and whether that implies an occupancy cost in the building that we all work in. We are not trying to define our exact monthly expenses. These cash flow management aspects are part of the financial plan that the CFO and team will build based on our strategic plan.

Every CFO needs to operate with a revenue and expense forecast. If the planning lead and the CEO fails to develop an effective operations plan and operations investment decision to feed the financial plan, the CFO is in a bind. They react and step in heavily into the strategic planning exercise, which dilutes it into financial planning.

There are many similarities between our considerations to make enablement investment and operations investment. All investment, regardless of reason, is always channeled into one or more of our four capability dimensions. Operations and enablement require efficiency considerations where we want to reassess our past investment choices. They both require effective allocation to purpose – we should allocate enablement investments to enablement initiatives and operations investments to specific parts of our operations baseline.

The biggest difference between operations and enablement investment is that each specific operations investment decision is perpetual. In contrast, enablement investment is timebound until the enablement initiative transitions to steady state.

> **Things to Remember: Operations Investment**
>
> **Operations investment is the financial allocation decision to perpetually scale up or scale down specific components of our operations baseline across all functions while keeping the scale within the current maturity level of operations. Operations investment decision is an approximation and accommodates for real-life variances in translating investment decisions into expense forecasts.**

The following five guardrails will help us develop our comprehensive operations investment decision. The **Operations Investment Map** in Infographic D.16 is a simple but detailed and comprehensive framework to ensure that our operations investment decisions objectively incorporate these five critical guardrails.

Guardrail 1: Operations investments must always directly link to operations baseline components and functions.

Sometimes the simplest things are the hardest. It is important to start operations investment discussions by internalizing 'why' we are investing. Operations investment decisions often go wrong because we focus on 'what' we are investing in before knowing 'why.'

Why are we making operations investments?

Operations investment must directly channel into the operations baseline components – productized offering, processes, data usage, and management approach – within the core functions that we defined in enablement planning using our flow thinking.

We have all bought something that we saw on TV or the internet because it seemed exciting at the time, but we never ended up using it because

D.4 OPTIMIZE SCALE AND OUTCOMES THROUGH INVESTMENT PLANNING

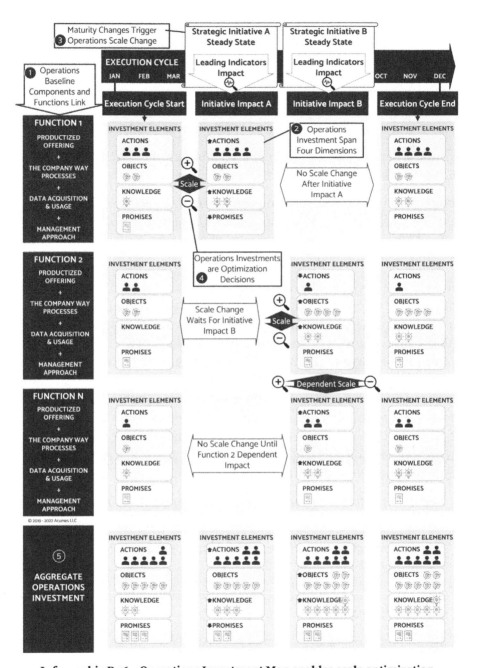

Infographic D.16 – Operations Investment Map enables scale optimization

we never thought about the application. We have the right to do this with personal funds. But it's not acceptable with communal funds, which is what operations investment is.

Starting with decisions about the number of employees or assets focuses on the 'what,' not the 'why.' The context of the investment channels is vital to ensure that our natural biases on what we invest in do not lead us astray.

In our framework above, we positioned this guardrail on the left side as an anchor to ensure that every operation's decision relates to a specific reason.

Before putting investment options on the map, we want to understand the function within which an investment would sit in using our flow thinking and not historic organizational charts. Then we must consider operations baseline components for each function.

We want to ensure that the details of our productization efforts associated with each function confirm the investment's need. We need to ensure that we effectively mature the function's processes in our operations baseline and the investment element clearly aligns with those mature processes. We want to ensure that any data management-related investments are tangible ongoing needs instead of solving a short-term tactical challenge. Short-term needs must be part of an enablement initiative in the first place. From a management approach perspective, we might invest in a manager-employee one-on-one software solution that enhances performance management and coaching or a solution that creates clarity on incentive compensation for each function on an ongoing basis.

Consider the following questions to relate operations investment to our operations baseline functions and components:

Using a flow thinking around creating market value, what function will the investment item sit in?

Within each function, how will this investment directly create customer value through our productized offering?

Which processes will this investment be part of within each function?

What are the data capture and reporting aspects that this investment will contribute to in perpetuity within each function?

How will this investment perpetually support or enhance our management approach components within each function?

To prevent creating a bloated organization, we need a robust answer to all these questions to ensure we do not mistake a confusing short-term need for a perpetual need. Moreover, it ensures that our operations investment truly dovetails into the actual business we are running instead of spending on random ideas we believe might work.

I led the annual strategic planning exercise at a marketing solutions company where some executives believed that the key challenge was a lack of leads to drive the commercial engine. This was only a symptom. Yet, the sales executive proposed hiring a sales development representative (SDR) manager and several SDRs. The idea was that this team would create sufficient leads for the sales reps.

It is a plausible idea because an entire cottage industry churns out SDRs. But beyond that, the proposal lacked an answer to – *why would this work at our company?* Nothing about the what-focused investment proposal tied back to existing operations. After several grueling but non-productive discussions about the importance of framing a strategic initiative that creates a connection between the investment and existing operations, it was approved.

After several months of hiring and staffing, this SDR team proved ineffective at creating leads, and eventually, the company disbanded the entire team and terminated almost all those employees. The reason for this failed investment and heartache for many was that it focused on what the investment was and not why it was the right investment. In addition, it didn't tie to the company's existing functions or processes. Nor was there an enablement initiative to evolve processes to accommodate the new operations investment.

In our operations investment decision, we want to avoid such a pitfall. So, always start with framing our maturing operations baseline components across functions as the first guardrail. The source of our investment reason is our operations baseline, not shiny ideas pulled from thin air.

Guardrail 2: Operations investment span all four capability dimensions.

The first guardrail holds us accountable to ensure that our reason for operations investment is evident in our maturing operations baseline, not external ideas. The second guardrail is to ensure that 'what' we invest in is comprehensive and cohesive. All elements we could direct operations investment into fall in our four capability dimensions, just like enablement investment.

What operations elements will we invest in?

Operations investment falls into four capability dimensions – actions performed via resources, objects that we buy or borrow, knowledge that we acquire, or promises we make with external parties. Effective operations investment implies that every investment choice is impactful because our choices are synergistic and address all necessary dimensions. Therefore, we need to catalog the critical operations investment elements across functions like our enablement investment elements.

> *Consider the following question to frame Guardrail 2:*
>
> *What are the specific investment elements – action, object, knowledge, and promise – necessary for each function to execute across each operations baseline component, including productized offering, processes, data acquisition and usage, and management approach?*

We must consider all four capability dimensions to ensure our investment catalog is complete. Multiple capability dimensions of the four are often necessary, and without the necessary dimensions, the others will prove ineffective. It is important to consider the dependency between investment elements objectively. A decision to scale in one dimension, such as resources, might imply that we also have to scale in other dimensions to support that first one.

Operations resources for a specific process such as sales, customer support, or services that are part of our offerings imply operations investment elements along the action dimension. For example, hiring more operations resources in one role implies they perform more actions. But performing more actions in one role might impact another role, such as the supervisory layer for this role or objects such as tools or knowledge such as information that we might have to invest in complementarily.

So, as a second guardrail, we must catalog the operations investment elements relevant to each function and its operations baseline components. The source of these elements is the effective documentation of our operations baseline components across functions and strategic initiative steady state definitions where we might have future improvements slated for the upcoming cycle. Once we have our 'why' and 'what' constructs in place, we can consider the timing of 'when' we need to make operations investments.

Guardrail 3: Operations investments must be triggered by maturity changes.

The timing around investment is the most significant conceptual difference between operations and enablement investment.

When will we trigger operations investment?

The two key timing aspects of operations investment are: 1) operations investments are perpetual, not time-bound, and 2) operations investment changes must always align with shifts in maturity in the operations baseline triggered by strategic initiatives.

The **first** aspect aligns with our message throughout our methodology. We must base our operations investment decisions on the understanding that the investment is perpetual. If there is a doubt about this, we are likely confusing a poorly defined, time-bound enablement effort as ongoing operations. The root causes of this confusion are often a disconnected organization and planning process. Enablement initiatives may not be defined and refined collaboratively with functional executives leaving them in the dark. Functional executives may work in a silo mindset without leveraging enablement resources outside their purview. Avoid such siloed thinking at all costs.

The **second** aspect around timing is operations investment triggers.

Imagine playing a video game, where leveling up implies extra tokens to acquire more potent tools or weapons to deal with a higher level of play. From an investment planning perspective, the more tokens are the unlocking of operations investment to acquire higher scale across all four dimensions we covered under Guardrail 2. The higher level in the game is the maturity growth of our operations baseline via our initiatives.

Scaling without maturity is a house of cards that will crumble. The planning team must agree on the specific maturity improvements that need to be demonstrated by leading indicators in our operations plan to trigger the operations investment changes. If you think back to the timing principle of our Chain of Controllability under operations planning, these are the exact same points in time that our leading indicators tick up in performance because strategic initiatives are driving maturity improvements.

Say, we want to increase the number of sales reps from 5 to 15 to align with a new capability launch. We change the game by scaling the number of sales reps by 3x. But when will that new capability be ready? Hiring and training 15 sales reps too far ahead of that value creation capability improvement is a waste of investment.

Even if nothing else changed, the maturity of how we sell would need to shift if our sales team is growing three times. So, this hiring investment trigger must align with the completion of enablement efforts on how we sell. Unfortunately, I have seen too many companies that assume that this scale shift will produce more revenue only to realize that the company fell backward into a management approach and process nightmare with little incremental lagging outcomes to show for it.

These decision triggers are illustrated via the vertical columns in our Operations Investment Map framework. Strategic initiatives are completed as we move from left to right, and various parts of our operations baseline are evolving.

Our execution cycle starts exactly where our current execution cycle ends. So, always reserve the first column of our framework for our starting point: our current operations investment in our operations baseline.

The remaining columns are our operations investment triggers that must align with our enablement initiative impact timeline. These directly flow from our operations plans, where we set leading indicator targets and limits and the timeline of impact. Our operations investment triggers align with our operations baseline performance upticks that we can measure via our leading indicators.

Guardrail 3 allows us to align the impact of strategic initiatives on operations baseline with the timing of related operations investment choices.

Consider the following question to frame Guardrail 3:

What are the time triggers where our operations investment elements will require dialing up or down in alignment with our strategic initiative impact on our operations baseline?

We do not need to be robotic to remain disciplined. Hiring more sales reps in the example above takes time. Our intent is not to wait until the maturity of operations baseline is elevated even to start our hiring efforts. In fact, we must optimally trigger such an operations investment in tripling the number of sales reps with the completion of a strategic initiative that matures the pertinent management approach and value engine components and executes the time-consuming act of hiring the new sales reps.

Guardrail 4: Operations investment is a maturity-based optimization decision.

Finally, we are in a position to put some numbers down. Our discipline to take a methodical approach will pay off because our investment proposals in this guardrail will not be guesses.

How will we invest?

Operations investment decision is an investment optimization decision. It is not an add, add, add decision. Throwing good investment after poor operations is terrible management.

So, we must rationalize operations investment to ensure that we invest in high return on investment portions of our operations baseline. A prudent mindset implies that we rationalize existing investments while making new ones in conjunction with maturity changes in our operations.

This involves reconsidering existing expenses on the operations baseline that doesn't need to exist as we mature. Companies often think about cost-cutting as a separate effort compared to investment decisions. That is an immature mindset.

We developed a unit economics-focused operations plan in Phase 2 precisely for this reason. We want to scale up on mature and high-productivity parts of our operations baseline, and we want to limit investment in low ROI parts of our operations baseline.

Maturity improvement of our operations baseline is not only an opportunity to add more fuel to the fire, but it might also be an opportunity to remove too much wood that is stifling the fire from burning well.

A common reason for scale rationalization is dimensional changes due to evolution. Investing more or maturity improvements in one dimension might allow us to scale down on elements in another dimension. For example, suppose we choose to scale on the object dimension via automation software. In that case, it might be an opportunity to scale down investment in the action dimension by reducing people operations resources.

In a recent planning effort that I led, a director who managed a customer onboarding team was very excited about the need for project managers on his team due to historic execution challenges. However, the team already had several technical resources doing this work with low effectiveness. The rationalization of "they are already working too much" is lazy. We needed to repurpose the poorly utilized investment in technical onboarding resources in conjunction with approving hiring new project managers.

Strategic planning must encourage such complex but necessary discussions.

So, through this stage in our operations investment efforts, we must propose an optimal scale of investment in each operations investment element we identified via Guardrail 1 and Guardrail 2. Obviously, these operations investment proposals must also align with our timing guardrails.

> **Consider the following question to frame Guardrail 4:**
>
> *What are the 1) optimal and realistic, 2) maximum, and 3) minimum scale for each operations investment element within a function, considering all four dimensions of outlays – action, object, knowledge, and promise – and in alignment with the optimal investment timing trigger?*

Operating at the optimal and realistic scale ensures that our operations can deliver the leading indicator performance targets we set via operations planning. This answer can be zero for poor existing investment elements, allowing us to cut waste. Framing the maximum scale for each element tells us how far we can dial up each investment element without compromising the maturity of our operations baseline. Setting this upper threshold protects us from compromising the unit economics of targets and limits in our operations plans. Lastly, the minimum threshold tells us how far we can dial down on each investment element without wrecking the unit-level performance targets and limits that we set in our operations plans considering dependencies on other parts of our operations.

In our solid object and its shadow analogy for operations baseline maturity and scaling, we want to shine the light, which is our investment, firmly within a range where the shadow isn't too big and blurry or too small and unrecognizable.

Leveraging this framework keeps us accountable for looking at operations investment as an optimal scale decision instead of a perpetually incremental investment decision. Often growing companies make investments without rationalizing impact. Strategic planning offers a critical juncture to reevaluate past operations investments.

At a company I worked with, the customer executive purchased a high-end package of a third-party solution for a few hundred thousand dollars. This gave all customer-facing resources the license to find nice-to-have customer information by going to the third party's website. However, there were no processes on its usage, and no one really used it for two years. A million dollars sounds like nothing these days, but tiny drops of water fill an ocean. We identified and cut this investment through strategic planning.

Strategic planning and our Operations Investment Map offer that moment at least once in our macro-evolutionary cycle to ensure that our operations investments align with our maturing operations baseline.

We can build out our Operations Investment Map in a tabular format to state optimal, maximum, and minimum scale for each operations investment element with the functions and operations components as one vector and impact timing triggers as the other vector. Then, these scale figures can be directly translated to operations expense figures by the CFO and the finance team, just like we did with enablement investment.

Applying this diligence to translate our strategy into enablement and operations plans and related investment decisions is necessary for the finance team.

Guardrail 5: Aggregate operations investments offer a financial planning feedback loop.

Our operations investment decision faces similar constraints as our enablement investment decision. Our company has an overall affordability threshold, which the CFO owns and manages. Our proposal via Operations Investment Map allows us to go through an iterative refinement cycle with the finance team to approve a final operations investment decision based on our strategy and operations.

The proposed operations investments that we mapped to our operations baseline will need to be reviewed and approved by the CFO and the finance team, who will own and manage the financial plan. Cash flow constraints are real for a growth-phase company. Several iterative cycles will likely be necessary to arrive at a finalized operations investment plan that allows the CFO to stay within the affordability thresholds and buffers.

Our answers to the scale questions in Guardrail 4, where we identified a scale range from maximum to optimal to minimum, allow us to tweak the scale of our operations baseline in a manner that stays true to the operations baseline maturity and operations plan. This also supports the finance team's overall investment constraints.

These five guardrails allow us to develop a rational and optimized operations investment decision that aligns with our strategy, evolving operations baseline, enablement initiatives, and the expense forecast side of the CFO's financial plan.

Principle 5: Evolved and optimally scaled operations baseline translates to effective performance targets.

Our enablement investment and the corresponding initiative steady state outcomes are the driving belts for our macro-evolution. The operations investment decision frames the optimal scale for our operations baseline. Combining these decisions articulates the company-wide performance that our optimally scaled operations baseline can produce across all functions and components.

Superimposing our operations investment decision on top of our finalized unit economics-focused operations plan gives us the scaled measurements of our operations baseline performance. These are the overarching performance predictions that we must use to measure our functions and operations baseline components throughout the execution cycle via reporting.

We must build a leading indicator performance prediction at both the unit and aggregate levels. This becomes our final approved **Aggregate Operations Plan**.

To operate with our Systems First philosophy, we have to know the difference between the system failing the people as opposed to people not leveraging an effective system. The corrective actions must be different for these two situations. Components of our management approach around performance and compensation management will not work if we cannot pinpoint where our people excel or underperform. We will be unable to assess and improve our value engine if we cannot understand where our system is failing us while the people are doing their best.

> **Things to Remember: Aggregate Operations Plan**
>
> Aggregate Operations Plan predicts our performance for the next execution cycle. Therefore, it must include approved versions of 1) comprehensive and cohesive set of leading indicators, 2) unit-level targets and limits for every leading indicator, 3) aggregate targets and limits for every leading indicator to incorporate our operations investment decision, and 4) evolution of unit and aggregate targets and limits over time as our maturity improves and operations investment shifts over time.

It's a fair question to ask why we meticulously parse these individual measurements. This should seem like a trivial point to say that if we have a lead generation resource who could get us 10 leads and invest in 10 such resources, we should have 100 leads. This is 2nd-grade math. True. But in the emotional throngs of day-to-day execution, this simple math gets confusing.

Where is the breakdown if we only get 50 leads a month instead of 100? The root cause of the low output of 50 leads can be poor execution of some lead generation resources through a systemic problem that limits their ability to generate leads.

Effective unit-level targets and aggregate targets for all critical leading indicators help predict the root cause of breakdowns without daily mouse hunts during our execution cycle. On the other hand, perpetual issue resolution will jangle nerves and bend reality, and employees, supervisors, and executives could start behaving irrationally.

A mature operations baseline and planning exercise ensures that performance expectations are comprehensive and cohesive before the execution cycle starts. In addition, it protects us from playing whack-a-mole once execution starts.

As you can see, a high level of maturity in all components of our operations baseline is necessary even to identify the right leading indicators and targets and execute towards it in the next cycle. Choosing poor leading indicators and targets that do not reflect the flow of a mature operations baseline will backfire during execution.

Our finalized Aggregate Operations Plan wraps our strategy-led and operations-focused planning effort. These are the outputs that we expect our operations baseline to produce. These are the targets that we will keep ourselves accountable to during execution.

We sign our names under these dotted lines...

These are also the operations performance targets, in conjunction with our mapping of leading indicators to lagging indicators from operations planning, that the CFO can use to predict our topline and extrinsic outcomes.

Principle 6: Aggregate Operations Plan and investment decisions forecast financial and extrinsic outcomes.

We need to forecast extrinsic outcomes for two reasons – financial management of our company by the CFO and simplistically sharing external messages of our company-wide performance. Most externally reported outcomes are revenue related. We want to predict how much money will come into our company each day, week, month, and year, because we should fund much of our investment with our revenue.

Creating a financial plan is strictly in the CFO and finance team's court. Forecasting financial outcomes can be seamless if we effectively develop the components of our strategic plan. We can model the revenue forecast directly from our Aggregate Operations Plan powered by our unit-level operations plan and operations investment decisions. Also, we can derive our expense forecast directly from our enablement and operations investment decisions.

If this view seems overly simplistic, it is the silver lining associated with a focus on the fundamentals. Poorly executed strategic planning efforts often spend significant time and effort on revenue and expense calculations because the finance team has no tangible inputs. Then, when the company misses those forecasts on the high or low end, there is little clarity on the root cause. A forecasting exercise focused on the company's fundamentals remedies this issue and allows us to create a plan built on controllable aspects.

It is important to note that revenue and related permutations are not strategic or operational metrics. In fact, it is not even easy to calculate revenue if we consider accounting rules. It is also notoriously hard to decipher.

I took on the responsibilities of a customer executive at a company I helped turn around where it was extremely hard for me to have a pulse on the company's performance when I took over. Operational measurements were non-existent. Meanwhile, revenue from customers was spread across the entire customer relationship length. When the largest customer informed us that they would not renew for the following year, the revenue metrics showed no change for several upcoming months until the new year started. Not a single report in the company nose-dived even when the largest customer canceled. We cannot manage execution with financial metrics. I had to build an operational measurement system from scratch at this company.

Financial metrics can also create incentive challenges. Imagine a big customer signing a three-year contract, then canceling six months later because the customer wasn't getting what they expected. What if the sales rep blames the offerings and the employees responsible for creating customer value? What if the customer value creation-focused employees blame the sales rep for over-promising? Who is accountable for this revenue? There is no good answer because thinking in revenue is a mess strategically and operationally. Most companies' executives, supervisors, and operations resources live with this ongoing strife created by financial measurements. The few runaway successful companies do not feel this measurement strife because of the innate nature that they are doing well, and operations problems fly under the radar. If they face challenges, living and breathing financial outcomes will backfire for them too.

In addition to revenue metrics, we likely want to forecast other lagging outcomes such as customer counts, revenue per customer, or customer satisfaction. Using our operations planning approach, all such lagging metrics have one or more leading indicators that give us predictability and controllability.

Outside the CFO's cash management and external reporting needs, we can live and breathe our Aggregate Operations Plan, our strategic initiative steady state definitions, enablement investment decision, and operations investment decision throughout the execution cycle. Our revenue and other extrinsic outcomes will likely be stellar if we execute effectively using these four planning outcomes. If we do not, they will likely suffer. It's that simple!

As we wrap up strategic planning, it is worth remembering that we have yet to play the real game.

PART E

Execution Management Dictates Outcomes From Operations.

OUR pre-season preparation is now complete. It's time to play.

Any sports team's execution through a season is like an annual execution cycle for a company. Top racing outfits invest in preparing every minute until the lights go off and the first race starts. Such teams have the right drivers, pit crew, top-of-the-line car, and race tactics to execute flawlessly during the season.

When I was a Six Sigma Black Belt at General Electric, we classified projects into Six Sigma projects and Nike projects. We followed a Define-Analyze-Measure-Improve-Control Six Sigma framework for important efforts. The methodical approach was worth all the mistakes we avoided. But we classified one-off tactical tasks differently. Those were "Just Do It!" projects, as framed in the Nike motto. Evolutionary efforts to grow sustainably beyond the market validation phase fall in the former bucket.

We have established a management approach through our past execution cycles, including components that dictate our people agenda. We also have our value engine, which is why we are in business. It articulates our customer offering and how-to-deliver that offering. Together, this forms our operations baseline.

EXECUTION MANAGEMENT DICTATES OUTCOMES FROM OPERATIONS

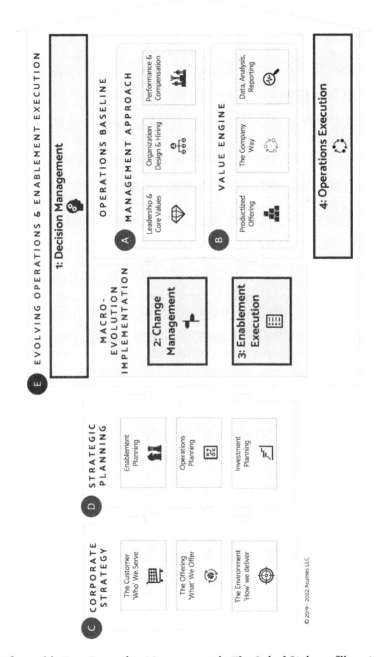

Infographic E.1 – Execution Management in The Spiral Stairway™ context

But we can't stop with what we have. We have to evolve the maturity of our operations baseline every execution cycle. We reframed our corporate strategy and created a strategic plan to guide our path forward. Our strategic planning efforts culminated with initiatives to take our operations baseline to the next maturity level and our Aggregate Operations Plan to execute that maturing operations baseline.

What now? It's time to shift focus. Infographic E.1 pivots *The Spiral Stairway*™ to put Execution Management in the crosshairs. It illustrates why we need more than a 'just do it!' mindset to drive evolutionary success.

In this final part, we complete our macro-evolutionary cycle by executing our enablement initiatives to improve our operations baseline and effectively executing our ever-maturing operations baseline to create customer value.

But a racing season brings its own challenges.

What makes execution complex is that our growing company is constantly changing. If we aren't evolving, we are sliding backward. Our execution cycle is our opportunity to climb another level of organizational maturity that allows us to further evolve our offerings, processes, and management approach, capturing more customers and creating more value for them.

In our racing season analogy, it is much easier to use the exact same engine and chassis design as last season because it requires less work and implies fewer risks. A newly designed engine might have reliability problems; a new aerodynamic design might create unanticipated balance issues. But we have to push our design parameters forward. We can comfortably drive around the track with last year's car, but our competitors are likely to be a lot faster. So, evolutionary change is not optional.

There is one major difference between a racing season and our company's execution cycle. A racing season runs only nine months. All sports teams have an off-season to recalibrate before the following season. However, our company execution cycle runs all year, and we don't get to stop our value engine at any point. We start each execution cycle with the management approach and value engine that we finished the previous cycle with. So, we have to upgrade our operations baseline seamlessly as the execution cycle progresses.

This reality that we don't get to stop to evolve is the core reason for companies to abandon an evolutionary mindset. If we succumb, the only changes come from reactions to events that hurt the company. Unfortunately, those reactions are often shortsighted and decoupled from an effective corporate strategy.

Does this mean that we never get to mature rationally and proactively? No! It just takes forethought and discipline. Think about our execution management as refueling an airplane in mid-air. It is possible with the right approach, skills, and tools.

Effective execution management has two goals.

The **first** is the meticulous execution of our ever-maturing operations baseline starting on Day 1 of our execution cycle to achieve the targets we have set during strategic planning.

The **second** goal is effective execution of our strategic enablement initiatives and injection of resulting maturity improvement into our operations baseline. As the execution cycle progresses, we set more challenging targets because we are counting on maturity improvements to feed in from our enablement initiatives.

We will also cover fundamental components that allow us to manage execution effectively through these final four chapters. We will discuss the importance of effective decision-making at all levels to support execution. Enablement initiatives drive change, and change is difficult. We need a framework to manage change.

So, let's start by framing what 'good' execution management looks like.

Execution Management Maturity Model.

Assuming that our prerequisites are in place, we have the opportunity to execute to achieve our two goals of maturity growth and increasing operations target achievement. Infographic E.2 shows our Execution Management Maturity Model. Self-assess where your company is on this spectrum.

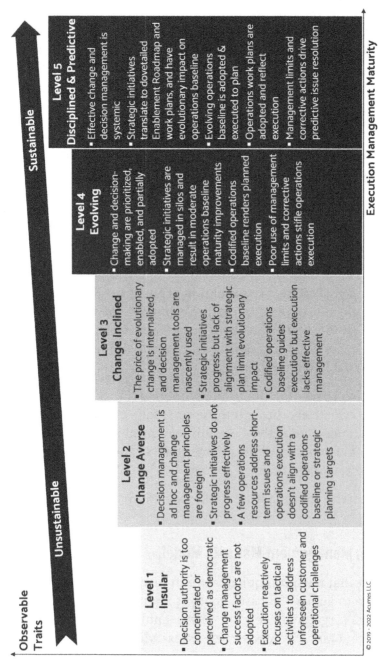

Infographic E.2 – Execution Management Maturity Model

The left side of our maturity model, *Level 1: Insular*, epitomizes an organization in trouble and operating like a small family business. Here, all decisions and discussions flow through a few people. Execution is survival focused. Many customers are unhappy with the offering. Operations resources struggle to stay above water with customer relationships or sell new deals through sheer will. Enablement resources are powerless to drive maturity improvements.

As we move to *Level 2: Change Averse*, the company has some breathing room to mature. But systemic components around decision-making and change management necessary to support maturity growth are non-existent. Enablement resources will have little impact regardless of effort. Instead, operations likely focus on salvaging existing customers through issue resolution.

Level 3: Change Inclined organizations understand that change and decision enablement are challenging but necessary. Sporadic use of decision and change management frameworks allows some progress in enablement initiatives. However, maturity gaps in execution management result in many incomplete enablement efforts or cause a lack of impact due to deviation from the original intent. Ad hoc audits will show moderate adherence to the operations baseline, but operations execution lacks planning and proactive management due to limited work tracking.

At *Level 4: Evolving* maturity level, over 50% of senior executives and employees have adopted structured change and decision-making tools. This supports enablement initiatives to achieve an acceptable completion rate and inject maturity improvements into the operations baseline. Operations baseline execution is planned. But operations management and issue identification and resolution have room to mature.

The payoff from improvement to *Level 5: Disciplined & Predictive* is immense. Accepting core principles behind decision and change management ripens the organization to strive for change and embrace maturity shifts delivered by enablement initiatives. Our enablement initiatives investment pays off without drag caused by poor adoption and execution management practices. The operations baseline evolved through our enablement initiatives are managed effectively using structured plans and predictive monitoring. Issue identification and resolution follow mature process designs.

Execution management implies that we are bringing all our employees onto the field. A few key resources played an outsized role to kick-off our macro-evolution through corporate strategy and strategic planning. That changes here.

Under Part A: Management Approach, we covered the importance of two resource types – enablement and operations resources. Throughout execution management, we will see the criticality of delineating between these two groups, whether they are people or assets. Employees who own and execute enablement initiatives must think and work entirely differently from those who manage and execute our operations. Without this differentiation, our enablement initiatives will likely fail to mature our operations baseline, and our operations baseline will suffer from a lack of execution discipline.

The idea of improving our operations baseline via our enablement initiatives is simple. But, achieving it is not easy. It requires discipline and change management expertise from our strategy & operations executive and all enablement resources. Operations resources, supervisors, and senior executives will have to be disciplined and execute to the spirit of our operations baseline. These employees will also need to embrace a change mindset and support the enablement resources in injecting maturity shifts into the operations baseline. The CEO and senior executives will need to enable a system that supports effective decision-making and embraces evolutionary changes.

With these responsibilities in mind, let's dive into the first component of Part E: Execution Management.

E.1
OPTIMIZE EXECUTION USING DECISION-MAKING FRAMEWORKS.

IF we take a step back and think, everything we do professionally is either an action or a decision. There is nothing else. Actions lead to decisions, and decisions lead to actions. Actions intertwined with decisions help us reach outcomes. Without decisions, actions won't help us arrive at desired outcomes.

Every execution cycle implies thousands of important decisions. Some decisions lead to new actions, and others do not. So, how do we make decisions collectively? Does our company have an effective decision management approach? Or are we relying on a few loud souls to make all our decisions?

A robust decision-making approach builds trust and objectivity while saving eons of lost time and circular discussions. It drives productivity and positive outcomes. The success of our enablement and operations actions depends on the effectiveness of our decision-making. So, we will start our execution discussion with decision management.

We live in an era of tools. There is no shortage of communication methods, and many tools help us access and share information quickly. They give us reminders to act. But we are also bombarded by notifications. We stare at gadgets and perform digital activities for many hours of the day. 'Smombies' is a word coined to describe our obsession with tools. It is short for 'smartphone zombies.'

Are these tools making our actions more decision-ready? Some are, and some are not. It depends on how we use them.

Management experts will tell us to shut off emails and focus. Successful business leaders boast about never attending meetings. We wouldn't disagree with these sentiments. But among mere mortals like us, many employees boast obscure measures like, "I have 200 unread emails!", "I respond to messages within the hour!" or "My meeting calendar is full for the rest of the week!"

Obviously, there is a disconnect between conventional wisdom and what happens in real life.

Slack, a popular messaging platform, frames its mission as "Make work life simpler, more pleasant and more productive." Sure, Slack is easy and fun to use. We can share an incredible volume of information. But what happens to the words, pictures, and files that we share? Is there any evidence of tangible collective productivity improvements? Are we piling more information onto each other? Most senior executives and supervisors I have spoken to find such channels distracting. Why the disconnect?

Actions do not constitute outcomes. Regardless of how many meetings we attend or emails we write, it is meaningless if those actions don't result in relevant outcomes. The path to outcomes involves decisions.

Work environments face significant inefficiencies starting with never-ending strings of meetings. Lack of decision-making and ownership structures usually makes matters worse, leading to more meetings. When do we get to do actual work, such as thinking, reading, and writing? Endless discussions without progress stifle strategic and operational maturity.

We want to drive efficient decision-making. Strong decision-making attains outcomes with fewer actions. It eliminates red tape and perpetual revisiting of the same topics that cause discussion fatigue and a sense of hopelessness. A well-implemented decision-making toolkit that allows the company to self-manage seamlessly can be a game-changer. It simplifies day-to-day decision-making and rules of engagement.

Both enablement resources which execute time-bound initiatives and operations resources that execute on our operations baseline need systemic support via effective decision management tools. Internal inefficiencies in both groups are often a symptom of a lack of rules of engagement.

We will cover four tools, which collectively create a holistic decision-making structure to drive better outcomes. The four tools are 1) delegation of authority, 2) formal one-on-ones, 3) decision meeting cadence, and 4) collaboration technique. We must build these tools into our company's system.

Principle 1: Embrace delegation of authority as a decision tool.

In line with our Comparative Advantage Ecosystem mindset, outcomes are easiest to achieve if experts make decisions.

Delegation of Authority describes pushing permissions to make decisions based on predefined criteria. An organization that doesn't empower experts will not scale well. The intent is not to exclude individuals but to formalize the lowest threshold of expertise necessary to decide on topics and, thus, improve efficiency.

> **Things to Remember: Delegation of Authority**
>
> **Delegation of authority creates zones where different experts have unilateral permission to make decisions based on topical expertise and accountability.**

CEOs won't be successful if all decisions go through them. Likewise, senior executives won't be successful if all decisions go through their peers or the CEO.

Using the CEO as an example, some topics could stay out of the CEO's zone to empower a fast-moving organization. These are choices unique to each company and framed based on the skills built into our mature organization design. Let's consider a few examples.

We can delegate hiring decisions around skill-based roles. A Comparative Advantage Ecosystem will focus on skills interviews and depth of experience. Supervisors and senior executives can handle this. The performance management approach must tackle personnel decisions without escalation to the CEO. An objective human resources executive who has developed a strong performance management approach can oversee this.

While a CEO is a great asset to manage relationships with the top few customers, getting involved with customer relationships below that top tier isn't optimal. Of course, all revenue is important; but the CEO's active involvement with customers beyond the top few reflects a lack of confidence in sales and account management executives and revenue-generating operations roles.

A CEO owns the corporate strategy but needs to delegate the development of corporate strategy and planning to the strategy & operations executive. Delegating the development stages enables the CEO to be the owner of the strategy instead of trying to contribute analytical components and insights while being stretched thin.

A company will always have several major initiatives. Once initiatives are defined and scoped as part of strategic & operations planning and operationalization, we must delegate the ownership of execution oversight to appropriate senior executives and supervisors.

These examples illustrate that going through such a proactive exercise of assigning accountability creates more leverage for senior executives to focus on decision-making on topics in their zone of expertise.

Incrementally, decisions occur at all organizational levels. Therefore, it is essential to streamline the path for operations and enablement resources to convert their actions to outcomes.

Each enablement initiative has an owner and a few internal stakeholders we identified through strategic planning. We delegated this group of employees the authority to plan and execute the initiative while being held accountable for its completion.

Operations resources, supervisors, and senior executives involved in process execution will need to leverage authority granted to them via process design. For example, if a sales rep wants to send a heavily discounted proposal to a customer, it may require approval from a supervisor. Conversely, by empowering the sales rep to reasonably discount the sale price without approval, we incentivize smaller discounts and faster operations.

Consider the following questions to enable effective and faster decisions via delegation of authority:

What are senior executives' and supervisors' expertise and accountability zones where they are empowered to make unilateral decisions?

How effectively are enablement and operations resources empowered to make day-to-day decisions on their enablement initiatives and processes, respectively?

Delegation of authority is necessary to drive decision-making. But all employees need coaching and issue resolution support to leverage the authority effectively. Formal one-on-ones address this.

Principle 2: Formal one-on-ones double-up as a decision forum.

We introduced formal one-on-ones in Chapter A.5 as a tool to drive ongoing performance management expectations and ongoing evaluations. Decision management is the second application of formal one-on-ones.

Employees interact with superiors often when they are in the same workspace. Some interactions involve employees asking clarification questions or for tactical help. Others involve coaching on skills and offering advice on role-specific challenges. But these are likely ad hoc, and they are not enough to drive decisions and outcomes. Instead, employees and supervisors must leverage structured, cadence-based formal interactions called one-on-ones to enable decision-making.

Informal one-on-ones are popular because they require no work. Unfortunately, they often turn into glorified venting sessions. It is a missed opportunity that could be an intentional decision forum.

Cadence-based, formal, documented one-on-ones serve as bottleneck relievers and opportunities for escalations. It allows employees to plan and prepare to highlight significant challenges they cannot solve or require help with. Employees must prepare and present options and demand decisions from supervisors.

We must design formal one-on-ones to readily identify outstanding future decisions, which will otherwise get ignored until it's too late. One-on-ones force employees to use the forum as a deadline to present options for decisions. These are not discussions that happen naturally in most companies; structured one-on-ones enable it.

Structured one-on-ones also give employees predictability and control over their time. Supervisors shouldn't use ad hoc interactions to change priorities for employees. In alignment with our performance management approach, changing employees' goal posts too often leads to an unproductive environment where employees are always reactive.

Consider the following question:

Has the organization built a systemic decision forum of at least one documented and forward-looking monthly vertical check-in between every employee and supervisor to support issue resolution and decisions?

Additionally, we must avoid two common mistakes.

First, ensure that one-on-one check-ins don't devolve into backward-looking status discussions. Beware of execution environments that lack work tracking because they dilute one-on-ones into reactive and ineffective work management forums. Instead, we should cover such details through the normal course of executing strategic initiatives or operational processes.

Second, a common misconception or excuse to circumvent this formal forum is the mindset that "it is unnecessary to wait for such formal one-on-ones to discuss major challenges or make key decisions." On the contrary, the lack of structured, forward-looking decision-making that formal one-on-ones enable creates an illusion that reactive problem-solving is the only option. In these cases, one-on-ones likely already degraded into informal conversations.

One-on-ones complement other decision tools and reduce reactive and unprepared decision discussions. They encourage enablement and operations resources to proactively seek advice or approval on decisions to drive outcomes efficiently.

But decisions made during one-on-ones need to be communicated or may require further escalation. Decision meeting cadence offers an organizational decision forum to address that.

Principle 3: Decision meeting cadence enables organizational efficiency.

Have you been part of organizations where senior executives and supervisors spend a significant amount of time preparing for one big meeting after another? For example, senior executives are often unavailable for forward-looking decisions for several days before a board meeting. Then, there are internal executive meetings and all-employee meetings. They require preparation too.

Such meetings are essential. But we also need these critical decision-makers to help run the business. So, I recommend an efficient three-stage decision and communication ladder that enables the whole company to dedicate the majority of time to evolutionary improvements and operations baseline execution.

Every company needs a core group of decision enablers. Let's conveniently name this group **Administration Group**. This group often mirrors the stakeholders involved in strategic planning. The group includes senior executives and the most important topical experts. Too small a group implies that we aren't delegating enough. Too large a group implies that we have passengers who aren't contributing enough to be on board.

First, the administration group must be hands-on and partake in a periodic, preferably monthly, structured session to assess the company's state and make decisions. The optimal owner is the cross-functional strategy & operations executive. The well-prepared session allows the administration group to assess the progress of strategic enablement initiatives and analyze operations execution and breakdowns. Not unlike formal one-on-ones, this forum enables proactive decision-making and communication at a company level.

We don't want these monthly administration group meetings to become tactical. We can individually consume financial and enablement initiative status reports. We also don't want these discussions to become live problem-solving sessions. A good decision forum requires prior problem-solving and insight generation so that we can prepare decision options ahead of live discussions. The disciplined strategy & operations executive must moderate preparation, execution, and follow-through.

Second, every company has a board of directors. Independence and expertise characterize its effectiveness. Packing the board with observers or friendlies doesn't enable growth or objectivity. An effective board offers the CEO and senior executives thought partnership to make difficult decisions and provides a constructive accountability forum. Before formalizing decisions, we can present the top few organizational decisions to the board for input and feedback. Interacting with the board using a mindset of "share the best version of the good news and hide everything else" creates no value.

Third, all-employee meetings are an excellent opportunity to communicate major decisions and gather employee pulse. We want to instill awareness about the organizational progress and challenges transparently without spin. Let's not forget; employees worked on all the details. They know the truth!

This 3-rung decision and communication ladder covers the same topics tailored for its audience. However, these forums usually are scheduled based on the availability of certain executives or board members. Major meetings require the latest information. Whether it's revenue and expense data, the status of major initiatives, or analyses to support decisions, presenting outdated information is not an option. This perpetual challenge limits the effectiveness of problem-solving and related decision-making, which is the real purpose.

The simple root cause is a lack of scheduling and execution discipline. Setting a purposeful and firm cadence that creates an information ladder allows us to focus on execution and less on talking about execution. Infographic E.3 illustrates my recommended decision meeting cadence in the context of the other decision tools in this chapter.

E.1 OPTIMIZE EXECUTION USING DECISION-MAKING FRAMEWORKS

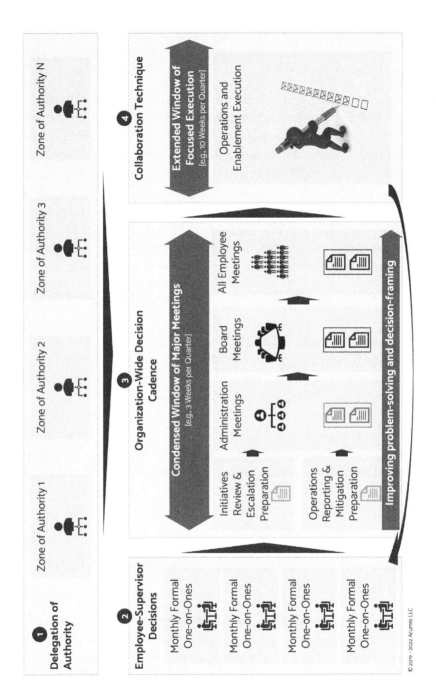

Infographic E.3 – Four decision management tools enable execution

Such a coordinated and intentional approach reduces time elapsed between major meetings and allows us to problem-solve and develop decision considerations incrementally.

Operations reporting and related analyses and strategic initiative status reviews and escalations should work up from formal one-on-ones where we make the first level of decisions. Next, the administration group meetings enable decisions that require higher authority and visibility. After that, board meetings offer a higher decision layer. Then finally, we can share key details with all employees. We can schedule this sequence during a three-week period each quarter. Then, for the remaining two months of a quarter, formal one-on-ones can be managed such that they lead directly to monthly administration group meetings without incremental meeting preparation cycles.

> **Consider the following question to assess current decision meeting effectiveness:**
>
> *Do we have a streamlined and effective decision-making and problem-solving ladder starting from administration group-level problem-solving discussions to a board-level meeting culminating in employee-level communication without causing a tax on the company?*

Such a cadence quarantines all major meetings into a small window of time. As a result, it avoids reporting, analysis, and other content rework. This also allows all resources to use the remaining time to focus on execution that drives forward momentum. It also focuses on problem-solving and decision-making and improves productivity at all levels.

Principle 4: Collaboration technique differentiates productive organizations.

The first three tools enable structured, formal decisions. More minor ongoing daily decisions need to progress to reach this decision-making level. We need to set guardrails around how employees interact to make decisions. I call this conceptual tool **Collaboration Technique**.

Conventionally, presenteeism implies that an employee could be at work without performing productively due to sickness, exhaustion, personal reasons, or lack of motivation. This is obviously not optimal.

What if the ailment that employees face is just a lack of appropriate organizational governance where they are present, attend meetings, and respond to emails without tangible work products? We can stretch presenteeism to cover situations where we use facetime and speed as proxies for work quality. This version of presenteeism can affect all employees. It leads to an ecosystem heavy on activities but low on outcomes.

Everyday employee collaboration must lead to effective decisions to move initiatives and operations forward. Sustainably successful companies embrace two collaboration techniques: 1) the ecosystem expects actions and decisions to be memorialized, and 2) the ecosystem embraces a SWAT team mentality. As we increasingly work with employees who don't physically sit next to us, these techniques become even more important.

Memorialization is the first collaboration technique.

I borrowed the usage of this word from a strategy director who described their core challenge in one phrase – "lack of memorialization." Many of the company's discussions and decisions lacked any documentation trail. This is a critical gap at companies that are attempting to grow fast. Unfortunately, the word 'documentation' often evokes the same emotion as 'taxes.' Such environments often dedicate minimal effort to framing foundational decisions and choices. This tendency often leads to revisiting the same decisions and discussions with little forward momentum, costing us exponentially more time and resources.

Organizations that don't set firm expectations on preparation for interactions and substantiation of solutions throw away vast amounts of organizational efficiency. We also risk the same unpreparedness to creep into interactions with the outside world, including customers, vendors, partners, and the board.

So, we must set company-wide expectations around documentation quality and behaviors that precede and succeed all collaboration events. Group discussions are always seeking decisions based on inputs prepared. We might solve a problem, agree on a plan, or address potential risks. If we cannot document the discussion to drive decisions, let's ask whether the collaboration was necessary.

Collaboration should drive towards desired outcomes and start with the necessary inputs. Collaboration events should include evidenced articulation of the event. Some prefer a prose documentation format; others prefer slides. Either works as long as we standardize. The important part is the quality and comprehensiveness of the ideas, how they relate to each other, and how well articulated they are.

Consider the following questions to set memorialization expectations for all employees:

What information should each collaboration event owner include as inputs?

How do we frame decisions?

How do we memorialize the collaboration event to avoid losing value from the interaction?

Who should memorialize decisions and discussions?

How must decisions and follow-through actions be managed?

How long must key decisions hold before we revisit them?

Bureaucracy is not our goal. We want to drive deeper thinking and analysis to limit poor ideas from consuming resources. We want to avoid decision paralysis due to a lack of structure and preparation. In addition to memorialization, we can optimize participation levels in collaboration events.

A SWAT team mentality is the second collaboration technique.

It's never optimal to have too many cooks in the kitchen. Employees at all levels need to discuss critical problems and make decisions effectively without big gatherings. This implies operating in small groups without drawing too many resources. In a Comparative Advantage Ecosystem, roles are skill-based.

The first decision-management tool delegates authority. Now, only necessary experts must collaborate to make decisions without a committee of observers. If done effectively, it should result in a drastic reduction in meetings.

However, this requires prior creation and consumption of memorialized artifacts. Small groups must not operate in a vacuum. SWAT teams must communicate decisions and discussions broadly in a format that others can consume. Otherwise, small groups making fast decisions is analogous to going rogue. We need to allow the rest of the company to stay aligned without verbal debriefs. If we resort to communicating progress verbally, we create another meeting, which invalidates the entire purpose of a SWAT team mentality.

There are many other collaboration techniques that we could explore. But these two are necessary maturity drivers to enable effective execution.

Our four fundamental decision management tools are necessary to move beyond early-stage execution, where founders and the CEO make all decisions. We must enable employees to seamlessly make and contribute to decisions to execute increasingly complex enablement initiatives and sophisticated operations successfully.

However, decision-making tools assume that all employees have the same incentives. But no two people have the same worldview. Such diversity in thought makes decision-making and alignment difficult, especially around enablement initiatives that drive evolutionary change. So, let's discuss change management.

E.2
EMPOWER MACRO-EVOLUTION WITH EFFECTIVE CHANGE MANAGEMENT.

In this final part of our methodology, we enable and manage all employees to execute daily against our strategic plan. Change management is the backbone of effective enablement execution to stay on our evolutionary path.

In our evolutionary growth mindset, we are not merely executing on an ongoing basis. As our company grows, the alignment of incentives between each employee and the company's purpose as a collective will diverge as we hire a broader spectrum of people. Additionally, our value engine will need to become more sophisticated to serve more customers and create more value. Supporting such diverse incentives and needs requires maturity improvements in our offerings and operations.

Each cycle, we will fundamentally improve our operations baseline through enablement efforts. Our operations resources embrace those improvements to execute at higher productivity, quality, transparency, or other relevant qualifiers individually and collectively each cycle. This is *The Spiral Stairway*™ to the next maturity level.

The catch is human beings don't just embrace improvements created by others. We tend to be stubborn and stuck in our ways. Some human beings are not motivated to self-evolve because the comfort of the current state gives them personal rewards. Others prefer to evolve in the direction of their own choice. Some might even like to evolve things so much that nothing gets a chance to take root before the next idea comes up. In short, our evolutionary agenda is habitually hard for stakeholders in our company.

To evolve, we must change. Our evolutionary mindset will always be hard because change is hard. To embrace change and move together collectively, we have to set expectations and build necessary structures that enable change intentionally. That's **Change Management**.

Forward-looking evolution is significantly easier than fixing past sins.

My entire career has been a kaleidoscope of change programs, and it's amazing how often change efforts fail despite honest intentions from all parties involved. The primary reason is that most change programs are reactive and start too late for the change to be effective.

I have performed several challenging surgeries for growth companies in recent years, and a turnaround is nearly unachievable and exponentially harder than getting things right early on. By the time a company is in a turnaround mindset, the fundamentals have been left unattended for far too long. The biggest reason for the disintegration of fundamentals is failing to embrace an evolutionary change mindset early on.

Companies in these situations find it easier to fix obvious symptoms while deep wounds continue to fester, and the company continues to regress. Gluing together a badly broken vase is a theoretical possibility; in my experience, it is just too many shards to put back together. I have tried enough times to advise that we take on an evolutionary growth mindset from the get-go. Let's focus our change management efforts on the happy path of maturity improvements that drive forward momentum instead of waiting until mistakes add up to where we have to dig ourselves out. It is nearly impossible.

So, let's cover the core principles to enable a system that embraces change.

Principle 1: Leverage Pressure Valve Framework to set expectations.

After racking my brain for years to figure out how change programs can be effective, I arrived at a framework with fundamental change ingredients that we can apply in any scenario. The framework builds on two ideas of change. The first is that hardship is necessary to enable change, and embracing hardship helps us set the right expectations around change. The second is that change's effectiveness always correlates with the weakest portions of the effort.

Hardship is the core enabler of change.

Of the three forms of rocks on earth, igneous and sedimentary rocks are the original forms. The third type is metamorphic rocks. The dictionary definition of metamorphism is "alteration of the composition or structure of a rock by heat, pressure, or other natural agency." These evolved rocks are formed by the transformation of igneous and sedimentary rocks with the natural application of extreme pressure and temperature.

The evolution of living organisms follows the same theme. Demanding environments allow an organism to become better at adapting to that environment.

I love my gym classes. Every instructor that I have taken classes from would say, "pain is gain," "if you aren't uncomfortable, you might not be using a large enough weight," "don't stop now; change is happening just when you want to stop!", etc.

This all seems obvious. But then, why do most companies assume that change efforts will just work, and everyone will be holding hands and singing throughout when we attempt to change behaviors?

My answer is lack of experience or leadership.

Take any major policy issue that our country has kicked around for decades with many charismatic politicians stepping up. But unfortunately, most politicians fail to make changes stick because they pander and do not communicate that change requires compromise.

The good thing is that a company is not a democracy, per our Comparative Advantage Ecosystem mindset. Topical experts and hierarchical roles enable decision-making and accountability. Effective communication of expectations is necessary for a corporate setting to ensure that behaviors align despite divergent incentives.

It took me a decade and a half of deep corporate explorations to internalize and start evangelizing the mindset necessary to drive change. Until then, I was ashamed to admit that change was difficult because I felt it reflected on my ability to drive change. In order to make progress with our evolutionary mindset, we must embrace the reality that hardship is the core enabler of change. A counter-argument is just naiveté.

Change impact correlates with the weakest portions of enablement efforts.

Another epiphany around change management was the repeated observation that the impact of change always correlated with the least effective part of the change program, and the highest effective part had a limited impact on the quality of the change.

So, do I mean that if we worked really hard and perfected our responsibility on a change effort, it may not correlate with the quality of change? Exactly, if there is a single other weaker portion on the change program, the impact of the change correlates with that weaker portion.

A long time before I started working with growth-phase companies, I was leading the operations design portion of an enormous transformation effort at an established wholesale distribution company where my firm had several teams on the ground. First, my team spent months redesigning the company's processes and roles. Then, we worked with technical resources and their executives for a few more months to build that design into a new Enterprise Resource Planning software. The entire design and build were reviewed and approved many times across many stakeholders. To this day, I stand by the quality of that work.

There was one last step left – let the client employees use what we built, and our firm's software security team came into play. Despite weeks of rational discussions, the security team manager decided that the best way to let clients start using the new software was to give all of them pretty much full access. Unfortunately, this team didn't internalize the concept of roles, as we covered under the process design chapter. The rollout resulted in complete chaos where client employees and supervisors were confused about whether they could use all the new tools they saw on screen. Some started using them prematurely, which resulted in business actions conflicting with the client's financial controls.

The senior executives of the design and build teams coached and managed supervisors like me quite well. The design and build were optimal. However, one very narrow set of actions where one small team didn't take the work others had done seriously, didn't take repeated warnings, and weren't managed properly resulted in the client questioning the entire program. This is a typical example of how change programs go sideways; the least effective portions dictate impact.

Putting together the hardship is the core enabler of a change mindset, and the change impact correlates with the weakest portions of enablement efforts epiphany; I arrived at a view that helps me work through change management efforts.

The Pressure Valve Framework.

The Pressure Valve Framework is a practical concept that I developed to prepare CEOs and other executives on the seriousness and complexity of successfully achieving change.

It may be the engineer in me, but my mental visual about change management is a water management apparatus illustrated in Infographic E.4. This simple view encapsulates the three core elements of a change management effort.

Water is the ubiquitous source of our lives, and it is as common as human emotions and incentives. It flows to wherever gravity allows it, or other external pressures direct it. We have all felt a water leak and spillages to know that there is little controlling its flow unless it's well contained. Human behavior is not very different. It needs to be channeled for collective benefit. We have already covered the tools under Part A: Management Approach and Part B: Value Engine to do so at an organizational level.

At an initiative level, we can imagine the outcome we are seeking through our enablement initiative as an increase in the water level in the tall vertical portion of our apparatus. This change in water level is the **first** element – the change impact. We clearly articulated the steady state we want to

E.2 EMPOWER MACRO-EVOLUTION WITH EFFECTIVE CHANGE MANAGEMENT

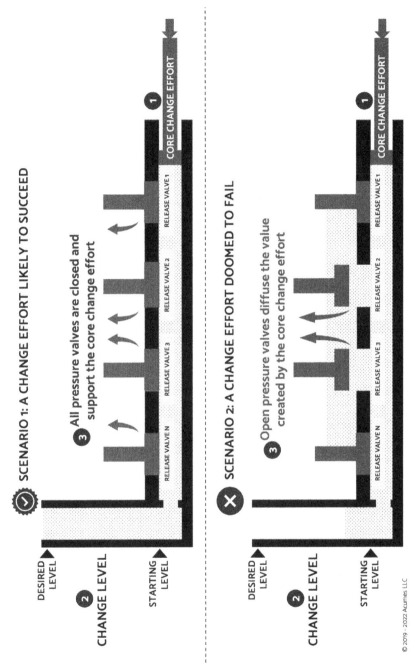

Infographic E.4 – Pressure Valve Framework empowers change management

achieve in our operations baseline for each enablement initiative that drives organizational change. This steady state is the high water-level mark.

The **second** element is the change effort, creating a detailed execution plan for the enablement initiative and its flawless execution. The piston on the right side of our visual symbolizes this effort. The water level in our apparatus or the resulting steady state of our initiative doesn't happen because we wished it would, or someone just announced it is the new normal. There is always work that needs to go in to enable that steady state.

We will dive into how to manage an effective enablement initiative in the next chapter. But, for now, let's say that a poorly run enablement initiative will imply that the overall change will not take effect, and we are unlikely to reach the steady state. Think about this as a piston that doesn't apply enough pressure to push the water higher in our apparatus. Regardless of any other factors, poor management and execution are common potential failure points.

The **third** element of change management is pressure valves. Pressure valves are risks in achieving the steady state of our strategic initiatives.

Over the years, I have noticed that the word risk was often watered down and not very actionable. So, I started using pressure valves as a more actionable way of thinking about ways that an initiative can fail. For example, in our water level apparatus, pressure valves are escape routes that release all the pressure our enablement initiative creates to move the water level.

A pressure valve has the power to negate all of our change efforts. The summary list of items that could constitute pressure valves is also the table of contents of this book. Essentially, a pressure release valve can arise from any component or principle we discuss.

Through the next few principles, we will internalize the importance of pressure valves and how to address them to ensure that our enablement initiatives have the highest likelihood of success.

Principle 2: Alignment on steady state vision of strategic initiatives is the first pressure valve.

I am drafting this chapter at the tail end of the book at a somewhat early phase of my overall manuscript. Why? Because if I can firm up the ending of this narrative, which includes execution of operations plans that align with our corporate strategy, I have set myself strong guardrails on how I want to explain various topics that help us communicate effectively to reach this grand finale. Running an enablement initiative that is driving operations changes follows the same logic.

The first pressure valve of any enablement initiative change effort is the clear articulation of steady state and strong alignment on that definition. We prepare the steady state definition for each initiative as we finalize our strategic plan. This is worth reiterating because lack of clarity and alignment around the steady state is the most common failure point of a change program.

Categorizing a change effort as a success or failure requires an objective definition of the steady state. The vast majority of projects lack a clear articulation of what 'good' looks like when it is done, and this often muddies the reality of whether the desired change took effect. It might result in a 'mission accomplished' claim without any tangible impact to go with it.

Articulating the steady state was a good start. But before we set off on driving change, it is important to align on the steady state with key stakeholders. Lack of such alignment often derails change efforts.

We can decide the specific tactics to reach alignment situationally. It depends on the level of change the initiative is driving, the sensitivity around the operations baseline components we are changing, the current maturity of the management approach, and most importantly, the incentives of other stakeholders. First, we must write and illustrate our steady state definition. Then, we can conduct meetings to discuss it with all key stakeholders one-on-one or in a group. We may even ask everyone to sign off on their alignment formally.

The reality is that I have royally failed at getting through a change program after all stakeholders boisterously supported the change multiple times after all such alignment tactics. People don't always share what they think publicly and act privately in their best interests. Conversely, I have successfully driven change with a well-aligned stakeholder group with nothing more than an email to share the steady state view.

This alignment stage will offer an early indication of our probability of success if we understand stakeholder incentives.

Consider the following questions to assess alignment on change:

Do we believe that the key stakeholders are truly engaged?

Do we believe that the key stakeholders have aligned incentives and believe that the end goal is to increase our company's maturity and do not have conflicting motivations?

Do we believe that the key stakeholders are the true experts to support the initiative, keeping our Comparative Advantage Ecosystem mindset? i.e., Do they actually understand what is going on?

Are we convinced that none of the stakeholders are passively aligned but actively misaligned?

Are we convinced that no stakeholders would sabotage the change efforts in due course?

I recommend being a realist and considering these questions before jumping to the next success factor. A 'no' answer to any of these questions implies that we are carrying an open pressure valve – a misaligned stakeholder group – into our enablement effort. Document the answers and articulate the nuances around the alignment gaps. Ensure that this pressure valve is visible to the administration group and is highlighted via the decision meeting cadence. It's not fair to put the weight of improbable outcomes on the initiative owner's shoulders alone.

Principle 3: The price of change is the second pressure valve.

In alignment with our Comparative Advantage Ecosystem mindset, companies aren't democracies. Even in a democracy, we choose leaders who write policies that sometimes benefit us and other times only others. A weak management approach triggers a common change management failure point creating an illusion that every employee or most employees have to agree with the steady state for a change to be the right or necessary course of action.

Enablement initiatives that drive change always imply an alteration in the behaviors of some or all employees. Change requires discomfort. That is the pressure in our Pressure Valve Framework.

Newton's first law of thermodynamics, also known as the Law of Conservation of Energy, states that energy can neither be created nor destroyed; energy can only be transferred or changed from one form to another. In plain English, this means we can't have something for nothing.

It is truly shocking how many executives, supervisors, or employees feel or speak as though we can break natural laws and achieve change without sacrificing much. As simple as this pressure valve is, it is worth placing it on our checklist on its own, given the frequency of this misconception. There is always a price to pay for change to take hold, and that price always includes discomfort.

I led an enablement initiative to mature the sales prospecting operations where sales reps worked based on individual preferences and were selling into the same prospects creating diminishing returns. Although every executive was onboard with this necessary natural maturity shift, the sales executive and sales supervisors felt that creating formal prospecting lists would remove the freedom and creativity that the reps valued. But this was a pain that had to be embraced. The change effort did not take root for months until a new executive and supervisors willing to coach the sales team to embrace the change were on board.

If anyone tells us that change can come without a cost, they have either never managed change or are placing unfair expectations on the change initiative owner. So, let's always embrace the simple principle that we will have to make sacrifices to achieve higher organizational maturity. That price is often not spending more money. Regardless of how much we spend on fitness coaches and gyms, higher fitness levels imply going through physical discomfort ourselves.

Consider the following questions to highlight the price of change:

What is the price demanded by the change from various stakeholders?

Have we communicated this price using our decision meeting cadence?

It can be tempting to shield the stakeholders and impacted audience from this reality. That's just delaying the inevitable. Set the appropriate expectations and socialize broadly upfront to avoid surprises. The human desire for arbitrage is the second pressure valve we must manage.

Principle 4: Unilateral support for the strategic initiative owner is the third pressure valve.

However large or small, every enablement initiative needs an owner. We slated this owner as we approved the initiative during strategic planning. This owner is responsible for detailing the enablement initiative's steady state and aligning the organization about the price to pay. The owner will only be successful with the unilateral public and private support of the CEO, senior executives, and supervisors.

Why is this an important principle at this stage?

People often don't attack other individuals in professional settings because it's impolite. Instead, we consciously or subconsciously attack what they do, undermining their credibility and work effectiveness. The price of change often creates enough consternation that people resist or fight back. Inertia is natural. It's physics! People do the same thing.

It is also a human tendency to offload risk onto others. For example, the adage about finding someone slower than us when chased by a bear reflects our human tendency to let someone else take the heat when uncomfortable situations arise.

This is an important principle because as an enablement initiative picks up speed and moves closer to steady state, the price to be paid starts coming due. In the early stages of an enablement initiative, the onus falls on the change owner and the core resources to do the groundwork necessary. It is only in the later stages that the impacted stakeholders start to feel the pressure to change. This is the stage when the impacted audience begins looking for pressure valves. The CEO, senior executives, supervisors, and influential employees become paths to relieve the pressure with the change.

An easy manner for the other stakeholders to attempt at harmony is by trying to empathize with the impacted audience and questioning the initiative or the owner. That's the release that the impacted audience needs to stall change.

The time to challenge an enablement initiative is not during the execution and change management phase. An enablement initiative is in the execution management stage for one reason only – the initiative was framed as a path to achieve the company strategy and was prioritized over other strategic initiatives.

> *Consider the following questions as illustrative sentiments from the CEO or senior executives that will undermine the initiative and initiative owner:*
>
> *Is this enablement initiative still important, or should we prioritize a different strategic initiative?*
>
> *Could the initiative owner do something to remove all discomfort the impacted audience will face?*

Change requires all relevant stakeholders to pull in the same direction in intent and actions. However, change also creates a different type of organizational pressure valve – a tendency to rationalize.

Principle 5: Accountability structure to protect against rationalization is the fourth pressure valve.

Regardless of the best intentions and efforts of the CEO, the senior executives, and the initiative owner, the successful completion of an enablement initiative with major ramifications can prove unnerving at clutch moments. Unfortunately, many people tend to cave in at those difficult moments. A less impactful and less mature steady state might feel acceptable because it reduces the pressure for change felt by our impacted stakeholders.

As humans, we naturally tend to rationalize, also known as choice-supportive bias. Rationalization is a cognitive bias where we create unsubstantiated reasons for why a specific choice or outcome makes sense. In the context of driving enablement initiatives, the initiative owner and the organization are likely to feel tempted to avoid the discomfort around change and use the avoidance as a rationale to support a suboptimal steady state. The common anecdote "don't let good get in the way of great!" makes me chuckle because it's a common rationalization to avoid feeling the necessary pressure associated with change.

How do we counter this? The simple answer is to create accountability structures. We all tend to deliver more and with higher quality when we are held accountable and limit our natural tendency to rationalize subpar outcomes. The same applies to our strategic initiatives. Let's discuss three lines of defense for this.

The **first line of defense** is performance management. Every strategic initiative's steady state must be an expected performance outcome for the initiative owner. This creates a direct incentive for the owner to drive initiatives to the intent of the steady state articulated in the strategic plan. The enablement owner's supervisor can leverage formal one-on-ones to coach and support decision-making to ensure progress and closure of pressure valves.

The **second line of defense** is our decision meeting cadence, where we must review strategic initiatives. It offers an internal accountability forum where we can assess our progress towards the steady state. The forum also offers an opportunity to escalate pressure valves and drive decisions to close those pressure valves.

The **third line of defense** is the company's board of directors. Almost every company has this built-in accountability partner. An operationally minded and engaged board offers a cadence-based opportunity to collectively assess the progress and challenges around our strategic initiatives, which are critical evolutionary changes that the board must oversee.

All three of these lines of defense are necessary and must not be circumvented. However, a symbolic use of these three lines of defense will not be enough. The key success factor for these accountability partnerships to serve their purpose is objectivity and transparency. As we move from

E.2 EMPOWER MACRO-EVOLUTION WITH EFFECTIVE CHANGE MANAGEMENT

the first line of defense to the third, the audience in the accountability forum is further removed from the details of the enablement initiative.

How many of us have been asked how things are going during a challenging phase in our life, and we responded, "I am doing great!" Human beings tend to try to fix a broken situation before admitting difficulties. If we read the newspaper regularly, most corporate issues metastasize and blow up before the involved parties own up to the existence of a problem.

I have overseen all the post strategic planning initiatives for the entire company during a few execution cycles. This involved creating and managing the three lines of defense. In my experience, there is a strong correlation between the maturity impact delivered by initiatives and the level of objectivity and transparency with which we manage them with the three lines of defense. For initiatives that are laggards and fizzle out over time, it is tough to engage the enablement owners to share the progress of initiatives and leverage the whole company and external advisors to maximize the probability of success. So, embrace the accountability structures because they exist to help.

__Consider the following questions to assess the effective use of accountability structures:__

How effectively are enablement initiatives built into performance management expectations of owners and stakeholders?

How effectively are decision management tools leveraged to manage change initiatives?

How effective is board oversight? How objective and transparent are the CEO and executives in engaging the board on initiatives enabling macro-evolution?

Once we embrace these five principles, we have systemically supported the enablement initiative owner to drive change forward. However, change efforts can also fail when initiative-specific pressure valves are not closed.

Principle 6: Identify and manage initiative-specific pressure valves.

Without a doubt, someone will challenge the enablement owner. Tactics deployed by stakeholders impacted by the change might have questionable professionalism. This is par for the course. The #1 quality of an enablement initiative owner is conviction. Such a change owner is a strong leader and is willing to take a stand to accomplish the change during the challenging later stages when the pressure on the impacted stakeholders to adopt is the highest, and they look for pressure release valves.

Companies often attempt overhauls and dedicate very little time and mindshare to ensuring those changes stick. The funny thing about change management is that it is less about what we do; it's more about what we don't do. Everything we don't do is a pressure valve, and it destroys all the good work we put into it.

The enablement initiative owner is not a project manager who is checking off boxes. The owner must genuinely commit to driving the change because the pressure created by the change will always look for a release path. The change owner must dedicate a significant effort to identifying and closing these pressure valves. Outside of the four organizational pressure valves discussed above, an enablement initiative's success depends on closing topic-specific release points.

The enablement initiative owner must identify, monitor, and escalate any potential failure point. In a CAE, responsible experts can help the enablement owner close each valve tightly to support the change. The ability to receive support from other skilled resources is critical. This is precisely why we are discussing execution management at this late stage in our methodology. The fundamentals necessary to support maturity shift don't materialize overnight. We will need a mature management approach and value engine to drive effective change.

Consider the following question to identify the pressure valves that can derail each change effort:

What are the realistic impediments, given the current maturity of our management approach and value engine, that moderately or strongly limit the effectiveness of the desired change?

The closure of these pressure valves becomes part of our enablement initiative scope. Therefore, we must plan and manage their closure during the execution of the enablement initiative. The initiative owner may take responsibility for some of them. Other stakeholders may own and tighten the remaining pressure valves.

We must go into the critical enablement execution phase with a firm scope of how likely our initiative will fail.

If you believe that one of the above pressure release valves will remain open regardless of our execution efforts, STOP! You might think that you can push through against all odds if you are like me. But believe me, if one pressure valve is open, we are highly likely to fail. It's irrational to commit significant resources into an initiative that we know will fail unless our three lines of defense accountability structure commits to helping close all initiative-specific release valves.

These principles that build on our Pressure Valve Framework allow us to address the organizational and enablement-specific pressure valves that can stand in the way of our evolutionary enablement initiatives.

A recent conversation with the CEO of a 100-year-old insurance company sums up this chapter. The CEO took over about five years ago and successfully revitalized the company's stagnant trajectory in the very established industry. This is a rare scenario because usually, most such stories end in disappointment. We can pick up the Financial Times or Wall Street Journal and see at least two or three stories each week of failed transformation efforts ending in the departure of the CEO. When I asked this CEO why he succeeded, he quickly replied, "we have a clear vision, and we are determined not to let anything get in the way!"

We always have a choice between embracing the necessary pressure to evolve and being comfortable by maintaining the current maturity level. That choice flows from the fundamental components of our management approach, value engine, corporate strategy, and strategic planning. If we want to be a cash-flow-focused, low-growth company, our strategy primarily involves trade-off decisions that are easy to achieve. Then our enablement initiatives in our strategic plan are likely demanding very little maturity growth, and thus very little pressure is necessary to drive the initiatives forward. This is why many refer to cash flow businesses as lifestyle companies. There is nothing wrong with this purpose; it is a trade-off choice. So, the various components of our symbiotic growth methodology anchor how we want to and can afford to execute.

E.3
CONNECT STRATEGY TO OPERATIONS VIA ENABLEMENT EXECUTION.

WHEN I present various parts of the methodology, I kick off the Execution Management section of the conversation with a picture from the TV show *The Office*. One of the characters makes a very tasty-looking pot of chili and grins from ear to ear, indicating how pleased he is with his creation. The next visual is him carrying this pot of chili into the office and falling over and spilling the chili all over himself and the floor. We are doing the same thing if we stumble during execution after all the hard work during strategy development and planning.

We exhaustively discussed the importance of ensuring that our strategic enablement initiatives dovetail with our strategy. But why would we spend a dime on an enablement effort if it doesn't have an evolutionary impact on our operations?

I spent a significant period in my career trying to piece together how to dovetail strategy and operations. Sure, there is a lot of information out there about both strategy and operational improvement. But the answer has always seemed spurious about the connectivity between the two. Real-world applications where they are tied together were much harder to find until I finally arrived at the following key insight.

> **Things to Remember: Strategy and Operations Connectivity**
>
> **Strategic initiatives are the enablement efforts that link strategy to operations. Strategy is on paper; our operations is in the real world. Something needs to stitch them together. Strategic initiatives enable that linkage. The strategic initiatives that we carefully identified and prioritized through our strategic planning exercise are the magic key that aligns with our strategy and evolves our operations to mature further in alignment with our strategy.**

This is how the rubber meets the road for our String of Pearls philosophy. Don't chase after shiny objects unless they perfectly align with our core strategy. It will be a waste of our precious resources. And don't allow strategic initiatives to get decoupled from tangible operational evolution because they would be meaningless.

Obvious, right? Not exactly. One of the biggest reasons that sent me down the path to attend a business school and explore several companies to figure out how to tie strategy to operations was this seemingly obvious, but hard-to-find linkage. Early in my career, I spent years on large transformation projects that cost clients tens of millions. Despite the incredible amount of organizational investment and change management efforts, these projects had questionable operational maturity impact. I was part of a major change program when the client asked us to stop the work and hired another consulting firm. My firm was invited to take on work when our competitors faced a similar fate.

So, the success of enablement efforts is not always apparent, especially when we are trying to achieve operational impact in scaling environments where we have so much more day-to-day issues and distractions and so little investment and experience to draw on.

Every strategic enablement initiative has a single purpose – mature one or more components of the management approach and value engine to close specific gaps and evolve to the steady state that we identified during strategic planning. We have failed if we do not achieve the desired steady state definition.

Enablement resources are dedicated to planning and implementing strategic initiatives intended to improve organizational maturity and operational productivity. Strategic initiatives can range from short sprints that involve limited enablement resources to major efforts that consume the company's attention for months. However, before we go down the execution path, we must clearly articulate the desired steady state for every strategic initiative at the tail-end of strategic planning.

Nevertheless, executing on slated efforts and successfully maturing our operations is a tall order. So, why is it so hard to perform seemingly straightforward tasks based on a plan to achieve relatively achievable improvements in organizational maturity and productivity?

Principle 1: Internalize common manifestations of enablement execution failures.

Whatever the scope of an initiative is, the probability that it will miss the mark is very high if we do not effectively develop the steady state and execution plans. Even if these plans are well developed, implementing initiatives can be troublesome. Therefore, before we address the principles to maximize our probability of success, it is good to internalize the general themes that trigger failure.

Change of priorities.

Change of priority is the most used code for "we are admitting defeat without saying so!" Initiatives often start strong with kick-off meetings and forward momentum for the first month or so. After that, however, senior executives often change their minds about commitment to the initiative or what it should achieve based on limited new information. This mindset usually happens due to two reasons.

First, the initiative may not have a comprehensive rationale behind it in the first place. This implies that the strategic planning effort that drove the initiatives was poor or the commitment to our corporate strategy is weak.

Second, outcomes will always lag effort. Improvements do not appear overnight. Senior executives must internalize this time lag and have the discipline to stay the course on strategic initiatives and see them through to the end regardless of the consternation that our organization will feel because we are instituting change.

Change of personnel.

Senior executives may change. Enablement resources implementing initiatives may resign. Such personnel change is par for the course at any company. However, companies tend to mothball existing plans or change directions because new individuals are on the playing field. However, personnel changes are not a good enough reason for going off course. Companies must stick to their system, including their corporate strategy and associated strategic plan. Our plan to implement an initiative should only change if we reframe our corporate strategy comprehensively and then our associated strategic plan.

Another symptom of this problem is passing the responsibility of the same initiative to different owners over time with limited real progress in the desired outcomes. This is another method of kicking the can down the road. These are symptomatic of the company not leveraging our decision management tools effectively.

Check-the-box outcomes.

Another indicator of an initiative failure is a declaration of victory without demonstrating measurable improvement in our operations baseline or disclosing strong deliverables that are proxies for productivity or maturity impact. These symptoms likely imply that these initiatives have fizzled into a check-the-box exercise during execution. This indicates that several components of our management approach and decision management tools have failed to drive accountability.

Embracing execution progress and outcomes objectives is uncommon because it is easier to avoid difficult conversations in the short term. But as a collective, all stakeholders involved with the company will suffer. Therefore, we need to keep these symptoms in mind as we go down the path of enablement implementation.

Principle 2: Be agile without using Agile as a crutch for poor execution.

Not unlike our human tendency to take easy money and potentially lose focus on the ultimate value we can create using the easy money, a great execution methodology called Agile can be used well or used as an excuse for poor behaviors. Agile is a project management framework primarily created for the software development space, and its usage has expanded. Many have embraced it as an improvement over a more traditional approach to managing projects called Waterfall.

Waterfall generally focuses on long-term planning and execution. Waterfall was commonly used in larger companies with established project managers and large budget projects with many resources. Over time, many jobs and certifications grew around Waterfall, where project managers became a staple in most execution environments. However, Waterfall usage went too far to a point where projects started failing because poor practitioners didn't adapt to new information and changes in the project's environment.

When Waterfall started showing blemishes, the proponents of Agile saw the opportunity to propose the importance of being adaptable and nimble through the execution of projects. This is great.

However, the proponents of Agile focused so much on short-term practices such as stand-ups and sprints for work that they could complete in the short term that they lost sight of the big picture. Agile intends to enable reasonable adjustments to the path forward. It does not intend that we don't have a vision or clarity on the path forward, or that we change the vision or path on a whim.

An optimal approach to execution management is in the middle. Waterfall's strengths lie in its focus on laying out the big picture and connecting the execution details to that big picture. Agile incorporates good practices to inject new learnings and adapt the details to reach the desired outcome without being too strict about the path forward.

Our enablement execution management takes the best parts of both Waterfall and Agile and avoids the downsides of both. We must work with a crystal clear vision of the steady state and a well-laid out plan to achieve that steady state while managing the execution to incorporate objective new information into the plan and the steady state.

The world has all but shunned the Waterfall mindset during our recent growth-at-any-cost era. But history tends to repeat itself for a good reason. The use of Agile can become an excuse for poor execution management behaviors because of its flexibility.

Agile does not stand for making stuff up as we go along and not admitting that we don't have a plan. The essence of the approach does not recommend a 'change our mind at the drop of a hat' philosophy of running the business.

I used to work with an executive who insisted on using the word 'agile' as an excuse to operate in a world of perpetual firefighting. Work was limited to tactical emails or conversations based on Post It notes, and every strategic endeavor became watered-down into gyrating tactical actions. Such a short-term, task-based mindset is not enough to strategically evolve a company.

For enablement initiatives to have an impact, they must be driven by an overarching steady state view, a strong work plan, and an adaptive approach to iterate the steady state view and the work plan when relevant and objective information is found through proactive means. So, let's dive into the building blocks of balanced enablement execution management.

Principle 3: A comprehensive Enablement Roadmap organizes initiatives centrally.

The first step of enablement execution beyond systemic empowerment via effective decision and change management is to manage the Enablement Roadmap drafted during strategic planning. It addresses resource constraints, dependencies, and communication of enablement efforts at a company level.

You must be thinking – roadmap as a tool is cliché. We have all been frequently disappointed by the broken promises made by roadmaps. But we can't blame a simple tool with a simple purpose for the flaws of the workers who created those roadmaps.

> **Things to Remember: Enablement Roadmap**
>
> An Enablement Roadmap is a living timeline that comprehensively frames strategic initiatives in a visual format with time on the X-axis.

A Gantt chart is a roadmap. There is nothing complex about it. Unfortunately, that also makes it dangerous because anyone can create one in a few minutes, and it is hard to know whether it is an effective one.

Roadmaps that seem good and do not deliver or don't seem cohesive have the same underlying root causes. First, they may lack an effective overarching corporate strategy. Second, they may not have cohesive enablement initiatives that dovetail with the corporate strategy. Third, the execution team may lack the skills and experience to deliver against the strategic plan that includes our strategic initiatives. We have already learned the principles to sidestep the first two root causes. We are addressing the third root cause in this chapter.

Inherently, a roadmap must never have any new information. Every single piece of detail on a roadmap comes from our strategic plan. Use this as a rule of thumb – if our roadmap has information that does not perfectly jive with our strategic plan, our roadmap will fail. We drafted our Enablement Roadmap during enablement planning and formalized all necessary inputs during investment planning.

First, an Enablement Roadmap articulates dependencies very well. An effective roadmap offers a single tool to validate that our top-of-the-house strategic initiatives meet the bottom-of-the-house actions, and nothing is amiss. A detailed roadmap offers connectivity between our prioritized strategic initiatives and detailed executable plans, which we will discuss soon. It allows all employees to understand and act, while also enabling us to monitor progress.

Second, a strong Enablement Roadmap is also a compelling communication and alignment tool internally and externally, assuming that we are good at delivering against it. One of the most critical aspects of preparing for change through an enablement initiative and managing that change is to share the whole story before we start.

Have you played Billiards at a bar? Of course, any competitive opponent would ask us, "what's your play?" before we take a shot.

All stakeholders want to know our company's plan to macro-evolve. Every employee wants to know how their actions each hour of their day add up to the big picture. We must be able to articulate that connection. Customers want to know the future of their partnership with us because it is a determining factor in their choice of an offering. Corporate partners would want to understand how effective our relationship would be in the future.

Our strategy and strategic plan are for internal use. We cannot share our plans externally because the details of our strategy and plans are intellectual property. Therefore, we need a consistent and straightforward way to communicate with everyone about our path forward. An effective Enablement Roadmap shares the details of our path forward to all stakeholders.

Third, the Enablement Roadmap is also one of the alignment tools we can leverage for change management. We have already discussed how every human being in a company has its own incentives, and some of those incentives can be impediments to effective execution. Employees who do not have full access to or do not have the appetite to consume our strategic plan cannot plead ignorance if we can communicate using an effective Enablement Roadmap.

What does a 'good' roadmap look like?

Given the throwaway rate of roadmaps, it is worth getting into the specifics of what constitutes an effective one, and each of us can look for signs of their effectiveness. Let's consider four rules for a good roadmap.

The **first rule** of a roadmap is that a growth-phase company has one cohesive roadmap that covers all functions. Roadmaps often originate in functional siloes, the most common being a 'product roadmap.' But a functional roadmap only paints part of the picture and is thus incomplete. A function is only part of a company. If our roadmap is a comprehensive validation and communication tool, how can it be effective with only part of the picture?

To take an offering to market, we have to evolve commercial maturity via management approach components such as org design improvements, hiring management, and compensation design. In addition, some enablement initiatives may also mature value engine components around the commercial team, which will have to dovetail with the offering that these resources are selling and delivering.

The **second rule** of an Enablement Roadmap is that it includes all strategic initiatives and only strategic initiatives. A roadmap must be comprehensive for each strategic planning and execution cycle.

Suppose we feel that a strategic initiative prioritized during strategic planning is not worth its space on a roadmap. In that case, our planning exercise likely included pork-barrel politics where someone slipped in one or more enablement initiatives that do not align with our strategy. To reiterate, all strategic initiatives identified as part of planning must be on our roadmap.

Additionally, adding unplanned new efforts is a common way to fail enablement execution. If we feel compelled to include an effort that is not a strategic initiative that didn't seem relevant during planning, we must ask ourselves why it is relevant during execution. Did we just make a mistake during planning?

If so, it is necessary to go back and include the initiative in the strategic plan and rework the resourcing, timelines, and related investment decisions. If we do not, we are essentially breaking our entire plan. How do we know this new arbitrary addition doesn't distract from everything else we had planned to work on? How do we know this new initiative is more important than another one we had prioritized? "The CEO or the board said so!" is a lazy answer. We might need to revisit the entire strategic plan if it is a relevant strategic initiative.

This is not to say that we cannot simplify or articulate our strategic initiatives in layman's terms on a roadmap. But if an employee asks a question about an initiative on a roadmap, it must drive straight back up to our planning efforts without ambiguity.

The **third rule** of a roadmap is that the book-ending parameters of a strategic initiative must align with the details we laid out during strategic planning. For example, if we framed a strategic initiative to be executed and adopted in three months, we must reflect that time window on the roadmap. That must be the same timespan used to build detailed enablement initiative execution plans. Misalignments will imply that the impact of our strategic initiatives will not align with the underlying conditions that our Aggregate Operations Plan is built on, thus risking our whole strategic plan.

The **fourth rule** is that every strategic initiative on a roadmap must comprehensively reflect four phases. Although enablement initiatives are time-bound, it is not as simple as a start date and end date. The four stages that each strategic initiative goes through are planning, execution, adoption, and monitoring.

Our work planning for each strategic initiative will need to address the activities and deliverables in each of these four stages. We will describe the considerations for each of these stages in Principle 5. It is critical to frame the entire lifecycle of a strategic initiative on a roadmap.

Do not give in to the temptation to build obscurity and flexibility into the Enablement Roadmap to give ourselves a backdoor if execution fails. This would be selfish. Everyone is on the same side, and there is no need to avoid transparency if our organization has a strong management approach and we internalize the components of Execution Management.

Consider the following questions as guardrails to manage an effective Enablement Roadmap:

Does the Enablement Roadmap dovetail strategic initiatives across all functions and operations baseline components?

Does the Enablement Roadmap show all and only prioritized strategic initiatives?

Do each initiative's details reflect the parameters approved through strategic planning?

Does each initiative cover all four enablement execution stages – planning, execution, adoption, and monitoring?

With these rules in mind, the CEO and strategy & operations executive must develop and manage a single, comprehensive roadmap that reflects our strategic plan and all the enablement work we will do in our execution cycle. The CEO's ownership and a strategy & operations executive's independence will be necessary to dovetail our Enablement Roadmap all the way up to our corporate strategy and down to the details of the enablement initiative execution work.

Principle 4: Enablement work plans are leading indicators for enablement execution.

Our employees and colleagues are not interested in seeing magic tricks from us when we execute an enablement initiative. No one wants to be shocked or surprised by how we took an idea and got it done. Everyone prefers a well-defined path with absolutely no surprises on when and what will happen. To successfully translate an enablement initiative into incremental maturity of our management approach and value engine, we must execute with transparency and predictability.

As our working environments become more digitized and employees increasingly work remotely, the need to create transparency and predictability around execution will increase exponentially. Just like operations baseline execution, we want to manage our enablement initiatives with similar predictability and transparency using leading indicators. Well-defined **Enablement Work Plans** achieve this.

> **Things to Remember: Enablement Work Plans**
>
> Enablement Work Plans are detailed steps that frame the comprehensive execution of a strategic initiative.

Let's cover the success factors to include in enablement work plans because work plans are often poorly created, rendering them non-executable and unmeasurable. We should intend for our work plans and associated elements to create accountability for the enablement initiative owner and other resources involved.

Success factor 1: Milestones.

Strategic initiatives are significant, impactful efforts that span weeks or months. All stakeholders must have visibility into progress throughout.

However, we cannot expect every stakeholder to pay attention to every execution detail. So, we must choose a few tangible checkpoints along the way to demonstrate progress. These are our milestones. We must articulate each milestone to limit misinterpretation of its intent and ensure accountability.

All organizational stakeholders must understand that enablement initiatives do not progress linearly. As an illustrative example, if we are rebranding our company and need to rework our entire website, the externally facing website will remain unchanged until we transition to the steady state. But there are many checkpoints along the way, such as alignment on brand themes, current webpage rationalization, new content inventory, content creation, etc., that can be used as milestones. Such milestones form the first level of leading indicators to demonstrate progress.

Consider the following questions to develop effective milestones for an enablement work plan:

Is the strategic initiative broken down into five to eight reasonable interim checkpoints we can use as milestones?

Is each of the milestones articulated effectively to ensure downstream accountability?

Success factor 2: Deliverables.

Milestones should be meaningful. How do we know if we met a milestone, especially if enablement initiatives do not progress linearly and most outcomes are only observable at the end? We all want to trust each other, but after three dozen companies, I am confident that accountability only exists in environments where individuals are actually held accountable. Accountability for each milestone implies creating evidence to demonstrate the achievement of the milestone. Deliverables are evidence in a documented format that shows the stakeholders that we genuinely met the milestone.

The correlation between internalizing the importance of deliverables and the level of accountability is uncanny.

Deliverables are a fantastic way to drive accountability and ensure that we have made the progress we have set ourselves or others have set us. We must become comfortable with the reality that we are in a professional environment regardless of how early-stage our growing company is and be comfortable asking others, "don't tell me; show me!" Talking our way through our accomplishments is too squishy to be considered effective management. I have always found myself stretching the extra distance in terms of quality, completeness, or timeliness if I set myself a formal deliverable as a requirement to complete a milestone. The same goes with people that report to me.

Consider the following questions to frame effective deliverables for milestones:

Does every milestone have a tangible and verifiable output that demonstrates the milestone has been achieved?

Are deliverables for each milestone incremental to previous milestones to ensure the intent of these milestones is being met?

Success factor 3: Actionable steps.

Milestones are also outcomes, just interim outcomes. We need to frame the actions we need to take to achieve the milestones and the overarching steady state. These are the portions of work that need to be completed by various parties. One of the most important aspects of a work plan is that it is actionable. As simple as this sounds, it is a pervasive failure point. So, always frame every action step with an active verb such as 'prepare,' 'review,' 'schedule,' 'send,' etc. This helps us to close our eyes and imagine ourselves executing.

Additionally, it is important to ensure that each action step is reasonably easy to accomplish by one person in a reasonable time window. This is important because if multiple people are involved in an action step, it implies hand-offs between them, and those details would be lost in our work plan if we combined those actions. The same hand-off principle we covered for process design applies to enablement efforts. Hand-offs are the most common failure point in execution.

Incrementally, suppose one person is working on a single step for an extended time. In that case, it is unclear whether they could perform this step faster or whether they made progress in the interim. It is optimal to break up such work into smaller action steps. Do not shy away from details because execution goes wrong in the details.

> **Consider the following questions to frame effective action steps to chart a path to milestones and deliverables:**
>
> *Will we be able to achieve the milestones and the overarching steady state if we complete the action steps and take no other actions?*
>
> *Does every step in our action plan start with a verb?*
>
> *Can each step be completed in a reasonable period, say 4 hours or 8 hours?*

Success factor 4: Single point of accountability.

Accountability requires a single owner. Without ambiguity, every action step must have one name expected to execute on that step. For example, even if an action step is to conduct a meeting to review a design element associated with the enablement initiative, a single owner must ensure that the meeting is a success regardless of the number of attendees.

Additionally, accountability also requires time constraints. Every milestone and action step must have unambiguous timelines that are realistic and ensure forward momentum. Avoid the tendency to pad the timeframes.

Although this is an elementary success factor to internalize, work plans often leave out names of individuals and realistic timeframes. Not everyone is comfortable with accountability.

> **Consider the following questions to assess accountability level in enablement work plans:**
>
> *Does each action step have a single owner who will execute its original intent?*
>
> *Does each action step have an accountability timeframe?*

Success factor 5: Hand-offs.

Lastly, work plans will fail if they have gaps that stall progress. Moving from one action step to the next must feel like passing the ball in a free-flowing soccer game. If the steps in a work plan are disjointed where one doesn't lead to the next and hand-offs are missing, then our execution is in jeopardy. As a simple rule of thumb, consider whether subsequent action steps with different owners clearly articulate how responsibilities are transitioned between those owners. Our cross-functional strategy & operations executive must review enablement work plans for all strategic initiatives and assess whether this success factor and others are incorporated.

Consider the following question to evaluate work plans for hand-offs:

Does every action step seamlessly lead to the next one in a logical flow?

Building these five success factors into enablement work plans is paramount in creating transparency and predictability for strategic initiatives during execution.

Principle 5: Manage all strategic initiatives across four stages.

Now that we have framed the success factors for enablement work planning, let's cover the four stages that every enablement initiative must include. Regardless of scope, we can frame an enablement initiative in four necessary stages: 1) Work Planning & Alignment, 2) Design & Build, 3) Rollout & Adoption, 4) Monitoring. Infographic E.5 shows the minimal considerations to plan and execute an impactful enablement initiative.

The four stages are not a linear progression from one to the next; rather, they are overlapping and incrementally progressive stages. Including the concepts in these four stages will ensure comprehensive and impactful enablement work plans and execution.

Stage 1: Work planning & alignment.

Creating the work plans that we discussed in the last principle takes time and mindshare. Before the enablement initiative owner starts working on the details, we must allocate time to build a work plan and socialize it for

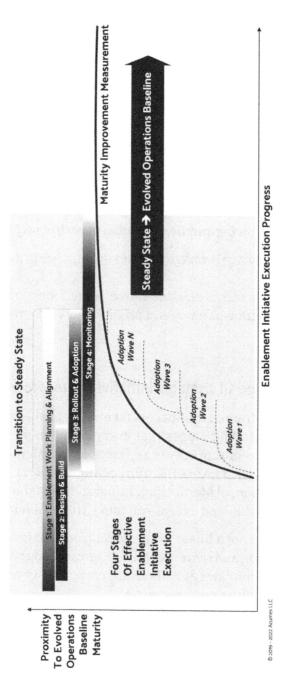

Infographic E.5 – Effective strategic initiative execution principles

alignment. The strategy & operations executive and the initiative owner must align on the details of each work plan with internal stakeholders before we adjourn strategic planning. The next opportunity to revisit this topic could be an administration group meeting a month later when 10% of a yearly execution cycle has already passed.

So, set aside time upfront and consider the work plan itself as a deliverable. As with strategic planning, work planning is also not a one-and-done effort. Enablement work plans are living tools that allow us to manage an entire initiative. As we learn new information, it is important to improve our work plan to reflect the reality of the path forward. They are our leading indicators, and without an accurate plan, we have no way of knowing where we are headed, and we cannot hold ourselves or others accountable with outdated plans.

Stage 2: Design & build.

As the name suggests, the second stage covers the solutioning aspects of the enablement initiative. Enablement initiatives will not have the desired impact if they do not follow a problem-solving mentality. If we execute with a ready-fire attitude, we will likely miss the essence of the steady state we desire.

Like our market problem-solving discussions, one of the most common reasons enablement initiatives fail is the symptom-solving of internal gaps. Often, observable Operations Baseline Gaps that we identified during enablement planning are not the root causes. However, an effective initiative owner, supported by the strategy & operations executive, will identify the real root causes and address those.

A strong problem-solving methodology allows us to do just that. All problem-solving frameworks follow a logical and predictable pattern. We may borrow or adapt a formal framework in a way that works for us. We discussed a few options under Part C: Corporate Strategy.

We have already done the hardest part of problem-solving at this stage, articulating the steady state. Now, we need to realize that steady state. We hired specialized skills in our enablement resources to take on such problem-solving challenges in a manner that fits the problem. The specific steps to problem-solving and solution development approach will be unique to each enablement initiative, not to mention unique between companies.

From an enablement resource capacity perspective, the design and build stage will likely be the meatiest. We must plan to progress through this stage with multiple iterations of problem-solving. Work planning is only effective if it is realistic. No initiative owner will likely get to the most optimal design or build the first time around and will probably need to iterate based on feedback and questions from other stakeholders.

Stage 3: Rollout & adoption.

Once we have a solution built out, we must validate that it works. Once we iron out the kinks, we need to inject it into our value engine and management approach so that operations resources can execute at the improved maturity level. Execution of an enablement initiative is not done when we have created a solution.

First, we have to validate that our solution works in practice. We have to include steps to test and learn the effectiveness of the improvement of our operations baseline before we can say 'mission accomplished.' These responsibilities continue to sit with the enablement initiative owners.

Second, once we have confirmed the effectiveness of our solution through iterative validation, we engage our operations resources and customers for internally-focused and externally-focused initiatives, respectively.

We must convince the impacted stakeholders to embrace the maturity shift during adoption. Our work plan must include the steps to enable operations resources and external stakeholders to move to the steady state. This might consist of documentation, training, and ongoing audits to transition to the improved maturity level.

We dedicated an entire chapter to change management for this reason. We must predict the detailed steps necessary to address all our pressure valves. We must include steps that other experts need to perform to close the pressure valves to ensure clear accountability.

A 'wave mindset' is optimal for adoption. It prepares us to have incremental success instead of trying to achieve all changes overnight, which is unrealistic. We must plan the steps around how we communicate, train, and ramp behaviors to the steady state. Infographic E.5 illustrates this wave mindset to adoption.

Consider the following questions to build the 'wave mindset' into strategic initiative adoption steps:

How many adoption waves are appropriate for each initiative to reach steady state?

Are adoption waves characterized by the individuals, roles, or entities that we are impacting, or are they characterized by the scope of changes that the entire impacted group would adopt, or is it a combination of both?

Which individuals, roles, or entities will be part of each wave? What scope of changes will be part of each wave?

What specific actions need to be taken to enable each adoption wave?

If we build an effective adoption plan and execute it, we optimize our probability of success in implementing change and engraining the desired steady state into the operations baseline.

Stage 4: Monitoring.

The 'end' of our enablement initiative is not characterized by completing our work plan steps. Checking off the action steps in our work plan is a good leading indicator for enablement execution. The steps in the first three stages keep us on track. But it is meaningless without improving the maturity of the operations baseline as scoped in each initiative.

As a fourth stage, we must monitor adoption and include the measurements steps in our plan to ensure we hold ourselves accountable to achieve maturity improvements. Our steady state definition of each strategic initiative from planning already lays out the leading indicators and targets that we desire. However, we must also meticulously measure our progress through adoption and early days in the steady state.

Adoption is rarely single-directional. Remember, improvements towards desired steady state can regress after early success. The impacted stakeholders may adopt changes in the short term but then revert to past behaviors when the excitement dies down. We can make a New Year's

Resolution to say that we will exercise more and fall back into our sloppy old habits by Spring.

Incrementally, adoption can also be artificial. Depending on the maturity of our management approach, operations resources may adopt changes with a check-the-box mindset without adopting the essence of the change. For example, in our New Year's resolution, we could also get a membership to an exclusive gym and visit the spa there without exercising and yet give ourselves credit for 'going to the gym.' Adoption of enablement initiatives can cause similar unintended misbehaviors.

We must consider the essence of the impact we are driving and device measurements that address behavioral skews that the change effort might create. An unidentified or unmeasured behavior skew can become a pressure valve for our initiative.

The measurements we choose to monitor during the transition to the steady state do not have to be the same steady state leading indicators in our strategic plan. Instead, we can devise interim measurements for enablement initiatives to support our transition to the steady state, and these can be decommissioned when we are confident about adoption of the steady state. For example, we might create a metric that uses manually collected data periodically, observations through audits, or cadence-based surveys to track progress towards steady state.

Consider the following questions to build the monitoring phase of the execution work plan:

What are the success factors for each adoption wave? How will we measure these success factors? Who will measure these success factors?

What are our contingency plans if our measurements show a lack of adoption for each wave?

What are the potential behavioral skews the change effort might cause? What are the interim measurements to monitor these skews?

What thresholds must be satisfied before we can retire interim measurements?

E.3 CONNECT STRATEGY TO OPERATIONS VIA ENABLEMENT EXECUTION

The gradual docking of our monitoring measurements with the steady state leading indicators set in our Aggregate Operations Plan will signify that we successfully accomplished our maturity shift.

We must begin our execution cycle with a running start by translating our strategic plan into our Enablement Roadmap and initiative-specific enablement work plans that minimally leverage the five success factors and the four execution stages we covered.

In addition to deploying these execution management tools effectively, iterative learning must be part of our psyche. If we learn that an initiative that we had initially intended to get to steady state in three months will now take four months, update the strategic plan to assess whether the change impacts our ability to complete all approved initiatives. For example, if we had prioritized eight initiatives, this shift in execution window might mean that we can only execute six or seven initiatives holding enablement investment constant.

New information is not good or bad. It is reality. But we must revisit and update our strategic plan and trickle down the impact to our enablement work plans. We must manage our living Enablement Roadmap to reflect any revisions in our strategic plan. This allows us to collectively internalize that our new execution goal is to drive fewer enablement initiatives, which influences the organizational maturity we can drive during the execution cycle. A lower maturity will imply revision to set lower leading indicator targets in our Aggregate Operations Plan. Therefore, it is in the company's best interest to predict that we will likely hit lower lagging metrics such as revenue.

The reverse scenario might also come to pass where we overestimated the commitment to execute a strategic initiative. Our approach doesn't change; we must maintain the connectivity between our strategic plan and day-to-day activities. Otherwise, the controllability and transparency we built through our macro-evolution components will break.

Being agile through execution is not about being unplanned; it's about proactively planning and incorporating new information into our plans in a thoughtful and disciplined manner. Effective enablement work plans framed across four stages give us the leading indicators to manage all our enablement initiatives transparently and predictably.

Principle 6: Leverage systemic components to manage enablement execution.

Managing and executing enablement initiatives is a matter of discipline and objectivity. All we have to do is stay on the tracks! A system mindset pays dividends during enablement execution. If we build the systemic components that we've discussed throughout, managing enablement initiatives will be a walk in the park. Alternately, every weakness in our system is a potential failure point throughout the execution cycle.

First, manage execution using work plans. They are our easily measurable leading indicators.

Work plans for enablement initiatives are created to be followed. Work plans include names and dates. Stick to them. Stay accountable and leave deadlines unchanged, even in the case of delays. Optimize work plans only when drastic and relevant new information is available. Perpetually kicking the can down the road is a sign of accountability failure.

We can purchase one of several work management tools at a modest cost and use them to store and manage our work plans. Such a centralized document and status management tool complements a good work plan. It allows owners to track progress and every stakeholder to assess progress against actionable steps, review deliverables associated with milestones, and view measurements that demonstrate progress towards steady state.

We can measure progress by reporting on actionable steps completed as a share of the total actionable steps. We can automate escalations through a centralized review of all missed milestones. Deliverables can be stored in such platforms to support organization-wide communication or progress audits to assess completion risk. Supervisors and the strategy & operations executive can support the initiative owners by using the work plan as the single source of truth on initiatives' progress towards steady state.

Second, use our mature performance management approach to drive execution accountability. Supervisors have to map enablement initiatives to performance management expectations set for enablement resources. In a mature management approach, this linkage would be obvious. But in many growth-phase companies, this accountability structure is rarely used. That is a missed opportunity. The steady state and milestones of enablement initiatives are the performance management outcomes we must set for our enablement resources. This linkage must not fail.

Third, our four decision management tools will help us manage initiatives effectively. Effective delegation of authority allows the enablement initiative owner to leverage the key stakeholders of the initiative as the SWAT team to drive progress and decisions. Supervisors must leverage formal one-on-ones to track progress against work plans and inject coaching and issue resolution into initiative execution management. Our decision meeting cadence allows enablement initiative owners and supervisors to escalate decision requirements and critical change communications effectively. A company-wide collaboration technique supports initiative owners and their supervisors by driving a decisive, decision-focused mindset into all collaborators.

Fourth, the Pressure Valve Framework empowers the enablement owner to frame likely failure points and request help. Although the approach to address these pressure valves are included in our work plans, maintaining an additional layer of validations and communication about the possible failure points will serve us well until we reach the steady state.

Leverage all these systemic components to manage initiatives without devising individualized methods or ad hoc approaches. Execution delays, modifications to the work plans, and key decisions can all be handled through these company-wide systemic components. While we move through the four stages of the initiatives to implement change, we have to ensure that our initiative has the intended maturity impact we slated during strategic planning.

Principle 7: Harmoniously reset the initiative steady state as the new operations baseline.

Our vision of the steady state, the quality of our work plan, and the contingencies we build into our work plan determine our success until it is time for us to impact the operations baseline. Once we progress this far, it is tempting to think that we are about to 'complete' our initiative.

But we must never trivialize the complexity of the last two stages of enablement execution – rollout & adoption and monitoring. An initiative owner might get questions like "are we done yet?" which can create a desire to call initiatives 'complete' without achieving our steady state definition that dovetails with the rest of the operations baseline. If the CEO or senior executives ask such questions, it is worth assessing whether this is a pressure valve around lack of executive support. As an initiative owner, it is always good to ask ourselves, "am I doing this alone?"

Ensure that we have identified all the open pressure valves, including organizational alignment and support. Regardless of the size or scope of the initiative, there will always be open pressure valves. If we aren't actively escalating and addressing them, either our initiative doesn't have the necessary evolutionary impact, or we are blindsided to risks.

We will likely improve the maturity of multiple components of our management approach and value engine during the latter execution stages. Each enablement initiative or multiple initiatives in concert must address our operations baseline's symbiotic and intertwined nature.

Regardless of the impact on our offering, every enablement initiative will elevate our processes. When we change our process, we must consider how we leverage technology to support those processes. Incrementally, our data is just a reflection of our processes. We will trigger data collection flaws if we do not address how process changes impact our data collection. We have to address the impact of our process changes from our enablement initiative on our data, related reporting, and how we might use that data for any future analysis.

When we change our offerings or introduce new capabilities, we change how customers use our offerings or the related processes that each impacted internal role performs. If this change is small, we can enable impacted parties through training and formal one-on-one coaching.

Some enablement initiatives can significantly impact roles as we elevate processes. For example, if we add significant responsibilities to one or more roles, we change our organization design. We can't just tack on more responsibilities, especially if new skills are required. Changes to the organization design also imply that we reconsider our compensation design for that role and similar roles.

E.3 CONNECT STRATEGY TO OPERATIONS VIA ENABLEMENT EXECUTION

Enablement initiatives might even impact a management approach component across the entire company or specific roles. For instance, we might have upgraded our offering significantly, which must increase each seller's revenue expectations. Alternatively, we might have matured our organization design that changes the commission plan for all customer-facing resources.

The initiative owner must ensure that such dependencies on the management approach and value engine components are already baked into our steady state definition and execution work plans. For example, it would be a shame to identify dependencies like the need for a new role or compensation design changes during adoption. This further underlines the importance of our drill-down planning mindset from strategic planning through enablement work plans that guide us through enablement execution.

A real-world enablement effort that I led epitomizes the complexities occurring with change. As an interim customer executive, I had to create a common commercial practice called account planning, which allows customer-facing functions to manage relationships with existing customers methodically. Account planning is prevalent yet notoriously interpretive across companies. Its quality level stretches from non-existent on one end to an effective customer expectation management and revenue growth tool on the other.

I developed and rolled out tailored processes and tools to the customer-facing team and their supervisors. Then, I invested a significant amount of time around adoption through group training, Q&A sessions, one-on-one coaching, and managing the process in a hands-on manner until many individuals got the hang of it. Finally, I applied the adoption wave concept by driving early adoption only among the top customers before moving to the rest.

To monitor adoption, I set up three interim measurements.

The **first** was to assess basic adoption via reporting using a work management tool that I had incorporated into the process design that demonstrated whether we completed key process steps for specific customers. It offered a basic litmus test for adoption.

The **second** measurement was manual quality review via audits, feedback summaries, and one-on-one coaching for the first three account plans created by every operations resource. I needed to ensure that we internalized the essence of a 'good' account plan.

The **third** was a steady state leading indicator that validated ongoing process adherence for a whole quarter. This included hands-on oversight of the process by attending customer meetings where we used account plans to set expectations.

This in-depth adoption monitoring was essential to prevent regression. For example, one of the supervisors decided to take old documents and rename them as 'account plans' and said that her whole team had adopted the new process. This was a bit silly because the company never considered the practice of account planning before this strategic initiative. We caught this predictable behavioral skew through the second measurement of quality reviews.

The simple truth is that every environment has rebels. There will always be resistance movements to changes driven by enablement initiatives, whether conscious or subconscious. Therefore, it is important to monitor whether abnormal influences shift the operations in unintended directions even beyond an adoption phase.

We primarily focused this account planning enablement initiative on driving changes to the company's value engine. The processes were matured as part of this change, and that change happened during the execution cycle in various adoption waves.

The change also implied management approach evolution. The company never considered account management as a specialized skill. As a result, the company's organizational design had to evolve, leading to hiring more specialized skills and optimizing compensation design for all customer-facing roles. Changing compensation for one role often implies reassessing compensation for other roles.

Enablement execution is a challenging undertaking, and the risk of failure for every initiative is high. We can only measure success by the evolutionary shift in our operations baseline that moves us closer to our corporate strategy. Anything short of that implies we lost connectivity

E.3 CONNECT STRATEGY TO OPERATIONS VIA ENABLEMENT EXECUTION

between our strategy and operations along the way. Once we inject our maturity improvements in our operations, we enable operations resources to perform at a higher level to achieve the targets we set in our Aggregate Operations Plan.

E.4
ACHIEVE PEAK PERFORMANCE VIA TRANSPARENT AND PREDICTIVE OPERATIONS EXECUTION.

WE are in the final component of our macro-evolutionary cycle. With *The Spiral Stairway*™ in mind, this is our final stretch that frames how our operations baseline executes to create customer value in alignment with our corporate strategy and strategic plan.

No sports team ever won a season by throwing Hail Marys consistently. That is the summary theme of our final chapter. We will not achieve our strategic plan because we surprised everyone by leveraging our operations baseline to our personal desire. At best, we will be able to do that for a day, a week, a month, or a quarter.

Throughout our journey, we drilled on the concept of the system mindset to allow us to operate methodically. As a result, all our operations resources are well-enabled via our management approach and value engine. Our operations execution goal is to stay disciplined and deliver to the system we have built over past and current macro-evolution cycles.

In aggregate, if we matured our management approach and value engine to the right side of the respective maturity models, we are best served by executing our high maturity operations baseline. If our management approach and value engine are at a low maturity level, the path forward is not operating in chaos. We must depend on effective strategic enablement initiatives to mature our operations baseline as quickly as possible to support our operations execution prospects.

Executing our operations baseline is like setting off a domino. A well-designed domino is an incredibly amazing sight the moment we set it off.

But a poorly setup one will only get to the finish line if we constantly jump in and try to keep the domino moving. People call this firefighting. We could think that moments of firefighting are never predictable or avoidable. But the maturity of our operations baseline and the effectiveness with which we execute against it defines our ultimate level of firefighting.

Effective operations execution delivers to Aggregate Operations Plan.

Our strategic planning exercise set leading indicator targets for our execution cycle. We didn't set these targets to ignore them. That would be silly. If our operations execution can beat targets outlandishly, then one of two things are true:

1. *Our strategic planning targets are genuinely off;* or
2. *The strategic planning effort sandbagged the targets set for the execution cycle.*

First, if our operations are genuinely capable of beating targets significantly, our strategy and planning are off, and we don't have a firm handle on the market. Did our competitors set themselves on fire? Did the market somehow turn in our favor more than we expected?

Outperforming our own goals might feel comforting. But it should also be concerning that we aren't clear on the reasons. Most companies create marginally incremental value in the market and do not drive a holistic market disruption, which only applies to a handful of companies every decade or two. Marginal progress is predictable. If we don't understand our present trajectory, we might as well prepare for a reversal of fortune in the next execution cycle.

Additionally, if we are capable of surpassing our targets in our execution cycle, it can also create problems. Our operations baseline is a finely tuned system quantified via our Aggregate Operations Plan, where we carefully considered scale decisions. We can't just run unpredictably well in one function and expect the system to stay balanced. Imagine an execution cycle where we land twice as many new customers as expected. This is fantastic because we can have more cash coming in. But this also means we have to serve twice as many new customers as planned. Do we have the operations resources to do that? Can our offering support that unexpected influx? Does our need to be reactive stall our enablement initiatives?

Peloton, the in-home exercise solution provider, was one of the major beneficiaries of Covid lockdowns that triggered unanticipated demand for its exercise bikes and treadmills. The company's ill-conceived reaction to scale manufacturing, expecting the Covid-related demand spike to persist, eventually cost the founding CEO his job and led to company-wide lay-offs because the demand spike proved an aberration.

Even a good thing can hurt sustainable growth if it pushes our execution into chaos.

The **second** likely reason for a significant upside in operations performance is a purposeful misstatement of targets. For companies without public scrutiny, the internal team and the board must stay aligned on the goals set via strategic plan. Low-balling strategic planning targets with the sole purpose of the CEO or senior executives ensuring self-protection and showing that "we beat targets" is a sign of an immature management approach. It demonstrates a lack of trust and a poor relationship between senior executives, the employees, and the board.

Some companies even manage two or three sets of targets, which is inadvisable. One is for board visibility which is the lowest bar. A second one is for employee visibility which is the highest bar. The third and middle one is the senior executive hope. Tracking and managing one set of strategic plan targets is hard enough. Monitoring multiple targets creates a heavy burden.

A growth-phase company has too many growth impediments to have such dynamics to work with. So, let's not sandbag or skew strategic planning targets. Such behaviors thrive in a low maturity operations baseline. We can achieve the desired outcomes if they are realistic, through good design without shadow games.

The same thinking applies to public companies; we are building a holistic company that focuses on value creation, not making decisions based on external investment analyst expectations who only care about extrinsic value.

E.4 ACHIEVE PEAK PERFORMANCE VIA TRANSPARENT AND PREDICTIVE OPERATIONS EXECUTION

Our goal is to achieve our strategic planning targets via disciplined execution. Even if we are overshooting our targets unpredictably, we must stay agile and refresh our Aggregate Operations Plan proactively. We want to keep our operations baseline in balance. An unplanned good year that results in a chaotic operations execution will likely stall our growth in the near future.

With this backdrop, let's frame the principles that enable disciplined and predictable operations execution.

Principle 1: Embrace management approach and value engine as execution mandates.

Simple can be hard. At a microscopic level, operations execution usually appears easy. Unfortunately, that apparent ease drives complacency and can leave us with complexity in the form of a broken system.

The actions performed by each operations resource to keep our offering up and running or deliver value to customers might appear trivial. As a result, we might get tempted to let each of them operate as independent islands because it's easier to give individuals complete freedom. But when we have several resources executing perceivably trivial actions in a divergent manner, our overall operations will involve so many permutations of actions, decisions, and outcomes.

Similarly, each sales rep might use their own independent tactics to find and convince customers to buy our offerings. It is easier for supervisors and senior executives to allow each operations resource freedom to operate in their own way. But it gets complex quickly when they start selling into the same customers, sell to customers outside our sweet spot, or promise value that deviates from our core offerings.

Even if we start with a strong operations baseline, it can all go off the rails without discipline. Deviating from our operations baseline has enormous ramifications. If our actions do not reflect the system we set in place, we no longer know whether our system is effective because our data do not reflect our system. Remember Process-Data Symbiosis?

So, we cannot stress the importance of discipline enough.

Senior executives must demonstrate commitment to the operations baseline.

Being a senior executive demands the skills to withstand pressure to conform, see the bigger picture, and see further into the future than other employees. Most importantly, a senior executive must be objective and disciplined. Some of this is a natural skill, but most come from experience.

You might have noticed that I have been careful about using the word *leadership*. A senior executive must be a leader and lead by example to demonstrate that operations is not a free-for-all or a passion-driven subject. It is a proven science with decades of history. Every executive must internalize the operations execution principles we covered and demonstrate their commitment daily. It's not easy, but that's the price of leadership. Operations discipline will not take root if senior executives waver on their commitment to it, especially when employees who do not internalize its importance and necessity challenge it along the way.

Operations resources must focus on their skills and deliver to the operations baseline.

Understandably, every human being prefers to do things in their own way. But working for a company is a team sport. Perceived high performers may have their personal style, and they should have the ability to maintain it as long as their style doesn't conflict with our operations baseline. Effective operations baseline execution has two characteristics.

The **first** is the unwavering adherence to our management approach and value engine. Our company invested heavily in our management approach and value engine. Use it! Why reinvent the wheel or break a comprehensive foundation for our feel-good factor? All operations resources must play within our system.

Amazon has a core value that epitomizes this mindset "Have Backbone; Disagree and Commit." It is important to share our ideas and sentiments and inform everyone about what we believe in. But at a certain point, it is crucial to commit to either playing on the team or leaving the team. This applies to everyone in any company, but it is critical for operations resources because they execute against a baseline system.

E.4 ACHIEVE PEAK PERFORMANCE VIA TRANSPARENT AND PREDICTIVE OPERATIONS EXECUTION

We must resist a temptation to allow perceived top performers to circumvent our operations baseline. Strong process design does not hinder top performers. Processes need to be reproducible to be effective and strong processes help performers at all levels optimize outcomes. Senior executives and supervisors must ensure that top, mid-tier, and low performers adopt and execute processes consistently.

Adherence to the operations baseline is also necessary to ensure that perceived high performers are not hitting or exceeding their targets at everyone else's expense. Almost every sales organization in the world will have at least one example of a rogue sales rep who brings in significant revenue but is setting expectations with customers misaligned with the company's offerings. In this situation, the account managers or teams that develop and deliver our offerings find themselves cleaning up behind a perceivably high-performing sales rep. Similarly, an overzealous account manager can maintain high customer satisfaction for a short period by overpromising to customers and leaving the company at risk of losing revenue months down the line. So, adherence to our operations baseline is non-negotiable.

The **second** characteristic focuses on the specialized skills associated with the operations roles. Operations execution is not asking resources in those roles to be robots. We are just asking them to be respectful of others' skills and contributions. Every operations role demands expertise, and the resources in these roles must possess the skills and desire to leverage those skills rather than be distracted by other responsibilities.

Almost all the reasons for confusion among operations resources stem from poor organization designs with ineffective role definitions or laissez-faire and biased hiring. These put individuals with misaligned skills and incentives in the wrong roles. In addition, poor performance management approaches that do not address gaps caused by organization design and hiring challenges aggravate such situations.

Each operations role will require several experts and supervisors as our organization scales. These roles require very specific skills and experience, without which we will not be able to meet the targets we set.

For instance, we must have a formalized offering on the productization front regardless of our market. Therefore, we will need a capability management process that frames a path for issue identification, root cause problem-solving, escalation paths, prioritization, and work management. The maturity of this process allows us to set an expectations floor on how we maintain the quality of our offering. However, a role that manages our offerings will require skilled problem-solvers to translate issues to identify the root cause and manage solutions to address those root causes.

The same depth of role-specific expertise applies to every operations role. Therefore, the effectiveness of our operations baseline execution to hit the planning targets is predicated on operations resources focusing on excelling on role-specific skills and delivering to the operations baseline with discipline.

Operations supervisors must have skills to oversee adoption of the operations baseline.

Operations supervisors are probably the most difficult roles to staff effectively. These are necessary roles but also present many incongruencies that we have to deal with.

First, highly skilled operations resources are hard to acquire, and our performance and compensation management approach must incentivize and reward them exponentially well. This means we might have sales reps or designers and builders of our offering who deserve very high compensation. The complication is that the operations supervisor of such operations resources' primary skill required is to coach and guide them. This might demand a lower compensation than the highest performers in the operations resource roles.

Using the sporting world to compare, a significant share of the players on top teams makes more money than the team manager or coach. The same must happen for operations resources at a company with an effective management approach. Being a supervisor must become a skill choice instead of natural progression via promotions.

Second, a dedicated operations supervisor will have to embrace their primary responsibility to enable their team's operations skills through coaching, ongoing decision-enablement, work management, and issue resolution as framed in our operations baseline. It is tempting for operations supervisors to get distracted by enablement initiatives because they impact the work their resources perform. But there is a skill gap because operations supervisors often come from an operations execution background and don't have enablement skills and experience.

If our supervisory layer does not internalize their core responsibilities of overseeing operations and get distracted by enablement initiatives, we will struggle to maintain discipline. It is even more challenging if operations supervisors do not support enablement resources and embrace maturity shifts delivered into the operations baseline through strategic enablement initiatives.

I used to work with a sales team that struggled to follow the operations baseline. The lack of adherence to processes caused 90% of sales reps to achieve less than 60% of their achievable sales quota for multiple execution cycles. The sales executive struggled to communicate the importance of a systemic approach to selling. The sales supervisors embraced the freedom mindset and advised the sales reps to be creative. I vividly remember an anecdote, "we want our reps to do their best... we want them to go after a prospect on Monday that they might have seen in an advertisement on TV on Sunday evening..." Noble intensions! But what if two sales reps saw that same advertisement and got excited about it? This company's execution and outcomes didn't improve until the supervisor roles were optimally staffed.

Consider the following questions to assess the level of discipline among operations resources:

Do senior executives understand and embrace the company's operations baseline as the foundation for disciplined operations execution?

Are operations supervisors staffed effectively, and do they focus on their primary skill of coaching and managing day-to-day execution?

Are operations roles staffed with resources with role-specific skills and interest in disciplined execution of the operations baseline leveraging those role-specific skills?

Once we establish a disciplined mindset across all levels of operations resources, we are ready to manage with transparency.

Principle 2: Start transparent operations baseline execution with operations work planning.

We took a vow to execute to the essence of our operations baseline. But the act of doing so is not trivial. What does each day of adhering to our operations baseline look like? How will supervisors know how well each operations resource adheres to our baseline? How will supervisors know when they need to coach their resources on processes or role-specific skills? How will senior executives know how effectively each team and individual is operating?

Mature processes articulate guidelines on how we should execute each element of the process. The leading indicator targets in our Aggregate Operations Plan based on analysis of historical data and operations baseline maturity codifies expected performance. But how do we know each operations resource has adopted them?

Presenteeism was never a good proxy for effective operations management. When the corporate world went virtual during Covid-19, the limitations of presenteeism-based work management became much more exposed. Ask any executive or supervisor who manages virtual teams.

I was one of them. I took over a large team and initiated a major shift away from the historical approach of observing time people spent in the office or email activity without clarity on what each resource was actually doing.

Work planning is a necessary and straightforward concept that we introduced for enablement execution management. However, work planning applies to operations execution as well. Although work planning's purpose and basic structure remain the same, **Operations Work Plans** are very different from enablement work plans. All five success factors – **milestones, deliverables, action steps, single point of accountability**, and **hand-offs** – still apply. But the way we create and use them are very different, as illustrated in Infographic E.6.

Operations work plans mirror The Company Way processes.

Building work plans are very easy for operations baseline execution, especially compared to enablement initiatives. Operations work plans transform process definitions into actionable, shareable, and monitorable formats. As a result, we do not have to create or design anything new, which is different from enablement work plans.

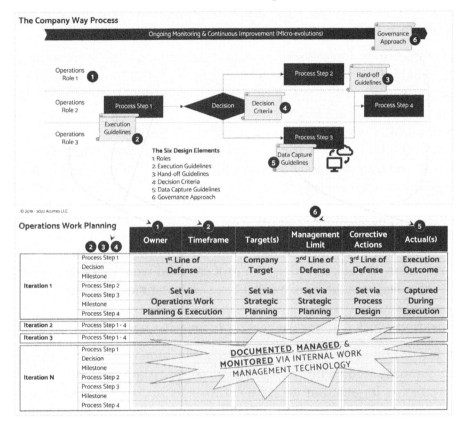

Infographic E.6 – Operations execution is predicated on a mature operations baseline

First, process steps and the detailed execution guidelines from our process design must become a work plan's action steps. **Second**, transitions between process steps and roles in our process design become the hand-offs in our operations work plan. The hand-off guidelines in our process design inform us to build any actions steps into our work plan necessary to perform a hand-off. **Third**, our milestones are the logical grouping of process steps that lead to meaningful interim outcomes. **Fourth**, our process design's execution and hand-off guidelines also articulate the appropriate deliverables for groups of process steps forming milestones.

This literal translation of our mature process design to operations work plans is our path to maintaining discipline and creating transparency. But as we are literally lifting details for work plans from our process design, you might wonder why we need them at all.

Every execution iteration of a process also requires a single point of accountability, which is our **fifth** and final success factor for work plans. Our six process design elements include the articulation of roles and critical timeframes. We must translate that into a single name and an accountability timeframe for each action step and milestone every single iteration that we perform the process. One or more operations resources in a role will execute the same processes many times over. Work plans are necessary to create accountability for every resource across every iteration.

> **Things to Remember: Operations Work Plans**
>
> **Effective operations execution management starts with optimal execution of each iteration of a process, and work plans enable it. Each operations work plan reflects a single iteration of a process.**

Operations work plans are necessary to measure operations execution.

Each iteration of a process by each resource intends to achieve the targets set using leading indicators. The governance approach of a process gives us the targets that we have set for specific steps or the process as a whole, and it must align with our Aggregate Operations Plan from strategic planning. Every iteration of a process will involve measurable performance that we have to record based on the data capture guidelines of that process, and an operations work plan allows this. Comparing the actual performance of each iteration to the targets set helps supervisors monitor the quality of each iteration of processes and tie it to the single point of accountability – the specific operations resource – performing that iteration. This is how Process-Data Symbiosis comes to life, and we capture effective operations execution data.

Operations work plans enable the operations resource to track and self-manage each iteration executed. It allows supervisors to get past managing via presenteeism and do so via the actual work being performed. Almost every company uses operations work plans for two or three of

E.4 ACHIEVE PEAK PERFORMANCE VIA TRANSPARENT AND PREDICTIVE OPERATIONS EXECUTION

the most iterated processes. However, a mature operations execution environment expands this to the entire operations baseline.

A typical example of an operations work plan is customer service teams tracking customer issue tickets. We must base the resolution of customer complaints on a strong process design. Solving customer issues will imply that we need ownership and timeline accountabilities. Each customer complaint ticket is a work plan mirroring a standard issue resolution process.

Another ubiquitous example of operations work plans is sales opportunities that almost all sales teams manage in CRM software.

Intent to manage such common processes using work planning is a good start. But it is unlikely that it moves the needle by itself because work planning, managing those plans, and monitoring them must be systemic. One-off efforts to manage common processes without organization-wide adoption of operations work plans indicate rinse-and-repeat tactics.

Usually, these efforts fall off the wagon because no operations employees want to be held more accountable than all other operations resources in the company. Senior executives will find it hard to hold one or two roles accountable via work plans and eventually increase their leniency. Even examples like sales opportunity tracking and customer service tickets will become check-the-box exercises where the individual iterations will not be based on The Company Way processes, even if they exist.

Additionally, in our balanced system mindset, if only some processes are effectively executed and managed, our operations baseline will not balance, and our system will break.

So, we must build and manage work plans for all processes in our operations baseline.

Leverage technology enablers to manage work plans.

Building the iterative execution of our operations baseline into a technology solution in this age where such options are affordable and effective is table stakes. There are many out-of-the-box platforms for the core few company processes like sales opportunities management or customer service request handling.

All technology that supports operations execution does the same thing. They have interconnected information tables and user-friendly workflows to allow users to interact with the tables. Off-the-shelf operations technologies give these tables precise names, and the columns are pre-defined with specific data types. But this precision is an illusion about the accuracy of such pre-built solutions.

Remember, operations technology always follows process. We must develop processes that fit our needs and then choose a platform to accommodate that. Often, companies live in a poor operations execution environment by attempting to use an out-of-the-box technology without a mature operations baseline or ignoring a mature operations baseline and depending too much on off-the-shelf technology. Even if a technology is sold to us by an established company with a household name, it must dovetail into our operations baseline.

Additionally, several technology solutions on the market allow us to mold tables and their columns to our needs and easily systematize our own process. We are out of excuses to manage operations work plans effectively.

For example, hiring is considered an ad hoc effort at most growth-stage companies. Recently, I instituted a robust hiring process to mature the management approach at a company because I was the most prevalent hiring executive. Early on, I managed the process via emails and spreadsheets. But as we hired more, mistakes started creeping in. There was even an instance where I mixed up two candidates, one we wanted to move forward and one we wanted to pass on.

The vital process was not operationally powerful yet. So, I built the process into the work management platform that the company used in two hours as an iterative work plan that allowed us to go through the same process with every candidate in every role. We housed all aspects of the hiring process, including negotiating stages and case studies presented by candidates, into the work plan. It transformed our hiring process into a disciplined one.

Operations technology options will only become better and easier to use. Leveraging them makes the impact of our work plans exponentially higher. The use of technology also allows us to manage and monitor work effectively without presenteeism or micro-management.

Principle 3: Monitor and manage operations predictably using three lines of defense.

Embracing our operations baseline as our day-to-day execution's religious text will help us find discipline. In addition, translating the operations baseline to work plans to manage every iteration of execution creates the transparency necessary to manage operations predictably.

If we can predict our future, we could change it if we don't like the prediction. Executing to a mature operations baseline and managing effective work plans give us three lines of defense to protect ourselves.

The first line of defense: Monitoring operations work plans identify adoption and disciplinary shortfalls.

Newton's third law of motion states that actions have equal and opposite reactions. Each execution iteration against our operations baseline is such an action. Measurable leading indicator targets we set for strategic planning are such expected reactions. We designed our mature processes to know the causal relationship between these actions and reactions.

We don't have to wait for the reactions in a mature execution environment. Instead, we know what the reactions will be if we measure the actions. So, action steps in our operations work plans offer our first line of defense on predicting our probability of achieving targets set in our Aggregate Operations Plan.

Taking sales opportunities as an example of work plans, if we effectively monitor key steps in every iteration of the opportunity process, we can predict whether we will achieve our operations targets. Essentially, all the iterations of our opportunity process execution are the only path to sell our offerings. This is a common practice that companies call sales pipeline management.

However, most companies also achieve very little predictability using opportunities tracking. How could something so common go wrong?

The fault is not with the idea itself. Instead, operations baseline immaturity or ineffective execution management is to blame. What if every sales rep has their own interpretation of what qualifies as an iteration to track?

What if the process itself isn't well-articulated where progress through various action steps is interpretive? What if there is little accountability around tracking the progress of each action step to its intent?

In a simple practical example, I once took over the management of a team that delivered the company's offerings. The level of productization was poor such that the team needed to do manual error corrections before customers could see the value. For months, customers were unhappy regularly because this manual error correction was so mind-numbing that the operations role responsible executed it very poorly. I empathized with employees in the role. But something had to change because not delivering value to customers was also untenable.

I translated the error checking portion of the process I had designed into a recurring action step in a work plan that required every resource to address errors for two hours every day. If I could get these resources to process errors for two hours each day, then I could predict that we would meet the customer's needs by the end of the month. It worked like a charm. I could predict which customers we would fail to deliver value to well before month-end by monitoring this action-step across customers.

Our first line of defense ensures that the execution follows the path it is supposed to by effectively monitoring operations work plans.

The second line of defense: Management limits enable early identification of execution shortfalls.

We can't only manage the progress of work plans, though. We expect operations resources to execute processes with quality, which are measured through leading indicators.

The execution guidelines and governance approach from process design have the targets, management limits, and breaking limits for the leading indicators to measure execution. We confirmed these during strategic planning. So, it's time to use them.

We will only use management limits and the breaking limits associated with each action step or group of action steps to manage operations. Remember, targets for a process are simply aggregate outcomes over several execution iterations. Management limits are the thresholds closest

E.4 ACHIEVE PEAK PERFORMANCE VIA TRANSPARENT AND PREDICTIVE OPERATIONS EXECUTION

to the target on both upside and downside. Crossing these limits indicates that the measurable outcomes of one iteration or several iterations of execution show a more significant aberration than we expect from the current maturity of our operations baseline.

These yellow flags triggered by management limits are our second line of defense against operations execution challenges. Breaching management limits demand supervisor involvement to bring the execution quality within that acceptable range represented by the management limits. This second line of defense is a proactive opportunity to address breakdowns at an employee-level or role-level.

Going back to my delivery team that we introduced above, what if the volume of errors were too high or if a resource just checked the box on two hours of error reviews without performing the act? Action-based work tracking is a good start, but not enough.

My second line of defense was a management limit that we must resolve every error in two business days. Setting this management limit clarified the measurable quality that we had to meet when performing the error correction daily. But it was still a leading indicator that allows corrective action before customers see problems.

Remember, effective reporting does not require attention, barring escalations. The most valuable part of reporting is to raise awareness broadly that performance is not meeting expectations when thresholds are breached. There is absolutely no reason to stare at a report for any length of time beyond a quick comparison between performance and management limits and breaking limits. Spending time looking at reports without effective management limits tells the audience no new information. Watching a stock price go up and down without any other aids only leaves us guessing when to buy or sell.

Using management limits to monitor processes is easy if we have a mature process design. It is a powerful execution management tool. It allows supervisors to sit back and focus on skills coaching and decision enablement instead of micro-management. It allows operations resources to have the breathing room to focus on using their skills instead of answering questions about progress and attending several meetings to share progress. It will enable the company to achieve significantly better operations performance. It is table stakes for *Level 5: Disciplined & Predictive* execution management.

Third line of defense: Supervisory oversight must leverage preset issue resolution paths and decision tools.

The first line of defense is trackable via work management technology because we are monitoring action-focused steps in work plans for all processes. The second line of defense is systemic monitoring using effective management limits on well-designed reports. There is no need for human intervention in a mature value engine and execution management environment for the first and second line of defense until a flag is raised. Human intervention is our third line of defense.

Once we have early awareness to address an execution gap, we can nudge outcomes in the right direction. This is where supervisors and senior executives come into operations execution management. For the third line of defense to be effective, we must ensure that the cavalry operates within our operations baseline and uses our company system. Supervisory support has to adhere to three success factors.

The **first** success factor is that supervisors and senior executives take constructive actions instead of just using the yellow flag as a stick. Asking an operations resource just to fix the problem is just shifting blame and comically incompetent. It looks good in TV shows, but it's not a handy trick in real life. Unfortunately, this stick behavior is more common than one might think because many supervisors do not have the necessary role-specific expertise, training, or maturity to manage.

Constructive corrective actions imply that the supervisor goes into a diagnosis mode. The diagnosis path will depend greatly on the company, process, metrics, and employee. This is a practical application moment for our Systems First philosophy. Rarely do breakdowns happen only because of an employee.

However, it is also important that supervisors are comfortable holding their operations resources accountable if the root cause of the flag is recurring poor execution. Confronting direct reports and holding them accountable is not easy, but supervisory roles must be filled with resources with the skill and experience to do so when necessary.

The **second** success factor is the effective use of preset escalation and corrective actions baked into our processes and reporting design. In most situations where a yellow flag occurs, the root causes are predictable, and follow-throughs are pre-defined if processes are mature.

Supervisors must demonstrate the discipline and humility to take the optimal follow-through paths. A good process design implies that a quick diagnosis would make the root cause evident and corresponding follow-through path is articulated. If supervisors have to run around and figure out how to handle every aberration as though it's the first time it has occurred, then our process design lacks maturity.

This second success factor assumes that we have mature processes just like everything else in this chapter. We must avoid supervisors and senior executives needing to repeatedly solve the same execution gaps.

But what if the root cause was unique or not considered during process design?

The **third** success factor is the effective use of our decision management tools to remediate unique root causes of operational flags. If we have mature decision management tools in place, we already have the necessary pathways to address the unplanned operations gaps.

Formal one-on-ones are the first pathway for supervisors to support issue resolution via coaching and decision-making. In addition to employees raising risks and using the opportunities to drive decisions, one-on-ones are structured opportunities for supervisors to course correct the actions of operations resources if the root cause remains within the purview of this supervisor-employee relationship. Conversely, if the root cause of an operations gap spans other stakeholders, our decision meeting cadence offers the next structured escalation path to discuss and decide on the way forward.

Does this feel bureaucratic? It's pragmatic.

If your mind is running to an instance where a customer is very unhappy and demanding immediate action, and a supervisor feels the right course of action is to have an urgent meeting with another team to remedy the situation, I understand. But this is firefighting 101. We are not leveraging any lines of defense. A screaming customer is a failure of our entire operations execution management, likely for a significant period, and likely several other components of our operations baseline. Firefighting such a scenario is akin to pushing the situation under the carpet without understanding root causes.

Our three success factors push us to embrace the discipline we need to play within our company's system. It's helping us operate predictively instead of reactively after poor outcomes have already happened.

Let's use sales opportunities as an example in this context. A common measurement for a sales opportunity is aging, which measures the fluidity of progress and keeps an eye on potential stagnation in our process.

In a simple real-life example, I set a management limit of 60 days to complete the first three milestones of an opportunity process for a sales team. This means that any stagnant opportunity in the first three milestones beyond 60 days will require supervisory intervention. In this scenario, our second line of defense works quite well. What now?

I had developed a standard third line of defense where the sales supervisor would sit down with each sales rep every month to review opportunities that aged over 60 days. We had agreed to very specific remediations based on the reason for the stagnation. This third line addressed the vast majority of stagnant opportunities allowing us to arrive at a significantly more transparent and predictable view of sales execution.

The second line of defense trigger is not intended to highlight 'bad' situations. It simply highlights an area that we must address. In a mature operations baseline, taking help through an effective third line of defense is just part of our system. Managing operations predictively implies that we have considered how we would address the escalations due to the management limit.

But we must keep an eye out for unintended distortions.

Operations execution management must always counter Hawthorne Effect.

We talked about equal and opposite reactions earlier. Well, sometimes reactions can be undesirable. Therefore, every employee, supervisor, and senior executive in an operations baseline execution environment must internalize the concept of suboptimal reactions to management and monitoring.

In any situation where we set goals, human beings tend to cut corners to meet goals. It applies to all of us. This tendency to cut corners becomes more prevalent when the gap between the goal and our ability to achieve the goal is high, or the pressure to achieve the goal is high.

When we exercise, why does our form suffer when we significantly increase the weight? Our body is cheating to meet the higher weight goal we set.

> **Things to Remember: Hawthorne Effect**
>
> **Hawthorne Effect is a simple idea that living things behave differently when observed.**

In a corporate setting, observation is a measurement of behaviors. Therefore, when a specific portion of a process is actively observed with the performers' knowledge, they are likely to change their behavior to fit the observation.

Isn't this what we want? No! We want the performer to adhere to the intent of the behavior, not just the observable portion of the behavior.

All leading indicators are only proxies for behaviors. No single metric will ever measure 100% of the intent of a behavior. Even two or three strong metrics that observe different elements of the same behavior will not be 100% conclusive. We can only get close. This means we will always leave room for the performer to intentionally or unintentionally cut corners to meet our measurement.

A well-known example of this is Wells Fargo Bank's account scandal in 2016. The company designed a great lagging indicator to report growth – the number of accounts per customer. There is nothing wrong with the metric or cross-selling to customers. However, this same metric was used for years to report the company's health in the market and assess employees' performance internally. Eventually, Wells Fargo employees felt compelled to continue to improve this metric upwards. They figured out short cuts, which included creating unnecessary accounts for unsuspecting customers because they were being measured so intently on it.

In fact, we can find this facet play out in any measurement. The greatest risk of the Hawthorne Effect comes from highly intense reporting on particular metrics for extended periods. These three factors of high intensity, a few high visibility metrics, and a long timeframe give performers' subconscious brains good reasons and time to plot for measurable success whether the real outcomes match the measurement or not.

A few years ago, I was revamping the sales operations function of a company where lead generation and conversion to sales were a struggle. Sales development representatives (SDRs) had a target number of leads to produce each month. This is a fine lagging outcome for the role, but not a good measurement for operations execution management and the second line of defense because it does not reflect the behaviors that result in the leads.

Nevertheless, the CEO had demanded that a daily report be sent to everyone highlighting the progress in lead generation by SDRs. In January, the numbers were bad, and the CEO sent a strongly worded email demanding corrective action. Amazingly, the February numbers were a complete reversal, and almost every SDR created the allotted number of leads. Powerful email, right? Not exactly!

Not even one of the leads created by the SDRs in six months converted to a customer sale. Why? The SDRs realized that they just had to schedule a meeting between a sales rep and anyone who might potentially take a meeting no matter their relevance to the buying process. So, they set many meetings with executive assistants, people in unrelated departments, or contractors at prospects who didn't have any influence. In retrospect, it was not a surprise that none of the leads closed. Who was at fault here? No one. The simple truth is that the collective group didn't understand Hawthorne Effect.

In our opportunity aging example, what if supervisors use the 60 days management limit as a stick? The sales reps will likely not log their sales opportunities unless they are sure to win quickly. This means sales reps will never trigger the management limit of 60 days because they are only logging deals that they are close to winning. However, the company will have no information about what the sales reps are working on and can't help them on leads that aren't easy wins.

E.4 ACHIEVE PEAK PERFORMANCE VIA TRANSPARENT AND PREDICTIVE OPERATIONS EXECUTION

Hawthorne Effect always creates a significant reporting risk if we do not understand it well. Supervisors and senior executives must never use measurements as a stick; measurements must be used as identifiers.

Undesired change in behavior is likely to happen when only one or two tactical and disjointed metrics are used, and they become the only method of organizational management. As a result, the impact of the Hawthorne Effect is often hidden. An experienced process designer and strategy & operations executive must own the design of leading indicators used to monitor the management approach, offerings, and processes.

Leveraging the three lines of defense allows us to predictably manage operations and ensure we can course-correct before the final outcomes are revealed when it's too late to change our fate. It also will enable supervisors and senior executives to nudge all operations resources to adhere to the intent of the operations baseline. Finally, it highlights the appropriate moments to support operations resources via coaching and decision management.

We have discussed all the permutations of when we might need to act except 'good news' or 'bad news.' Such excitement simply implies that we have triggered breaking limits on reports for one or more leading indicators.

Principle 4: Effective analyses of breaking limit triggers drive micro-evolutions.

If breaking limits are triggered, the first step is to understand why. The strategy & operations executive and analytical enablement resources need to analyze whether the deviation from the expected outcome highlighted by a breaking limit has an underlying root cause that we need to address.

If the root cause is ineffective execution of our operations baseline, senior executives and the CEO must use our three lines of defense to reinforce supervisors and operations resources to stay true to our operations baseline without succumbing to on-the-fly decisions.

Beyond execution ineffectiveness, we must understand the underlying reasons if our outcomes have breached our breaking limits positively, which is unexpected 'good news.' Is our value engine more powerful than we gave it credit for during strategic planning? Did we consciously understate our targets in our strategic plans? Were our strategic planning assumptions on scaling our operations baseline too conservative? The appropriate course of action is to stick with the execution of the operations baseline and consider these possibilities during the next macro-evolution cycle, which is only months away. Do not overreact!

Conversely, if we breach the breaking limits on the negative side, which is unexpected 'bad news,' our root cause analysis must methodically lead us forward.

One path that we cannot pursue is to deviate from our operations baseline or our strategic plan carelessly. It's worth reiterating this on every page because this tends to be a widespread reaction. It never works! It exemplifies changing lanes when stuck in traffic. That driver is just making the traffic worse and not getting anywhere faster.

If we deviate from our operations baseline, we are left with nothing but chaos. So, what do we do?

Our **first** potential root cause is a need to drive strategic improvements to our operations baseline. In this scenario, we must do nothing! Unless our strategy development and planning efforts are immature, we will likely find that the root cause is already being addressed via a currently prioritized strategic enablement initiative or an initiative we deprioritized during strategic planning. Both avenues imply that we have to wait. We live in a world of constraints, and we cannot do everything well. Our enablement resources are already busy with their defined initiatives. Changing priorities mid-cycle will lead us down *The Spiral Stairway*™.

Even if the root cause is a new strategic insight, we must still wait for the next macro-evolution cycle. One execution cycle is not a very long period. Enablement initiatives take time to drive maturity improvements. Even then, operations execution takes months to show progress in outcomes because it takes time for actions to convert to outcomes. Discipline and a cool head are paramount in execution management. Do not disrupt enablement execution.

The **second** root cause is that maturity improvements from enablement initiative execution are lagging. If one or more enablement initiatives we commissioned are behind schedule, we must adjust the Aggregate Operations Plan accordingly.

A common example of such a delay can involve the introduction of a new capability. The breaking limit breach could be the realization that lead generation resources have negligible activity to create leads for this new capability. Such a confluence of enablement initiative delay and operations execution impact must have already drawn attention from both enablement and operations resources due to the first line of defense breaches in respective work plans. Regardless, our only path forward is to improve the effectiveness of our targets, management limits, and breaking limits in our Aggregate Operations Plan in alignment with the new reality of the delayed enablement initiative execution.

Regardless of extrinsic pressure or motivations, working with realistic targets is the only path to effective execution. Even publicly traded companies refresh their prospects when conditions change significantly enough. Of course, life doesn't always pan out the way we plan. But if we don't maintain a plan, it's unlikely anything will ever pan out.

I cringe every time an executive says, "...we must see results quickly." It reveals a lack of practical experience or awareness of how to achieve better results.

Our **third** root cause of a breaking limit breach is an opportunity for tactical improvement of a small part of our operations baseline with no new investment. This pathway is our tactical micro-evolutions.

But these are also moments that we show the discipline to embrace Comparative Advantage Ecosystem mindset and allow experts to do their work. Let a process designer and analytical enablement resources tactically improve narrow components of our operations baseline using the principles we discussed under value engine while operations resources continue to focus on operations execution.

Formula 1 teams are some of the highest functioning sports teams. They design and build a car for each new season. They make tactical improvements to squeeze the last millisecond of speed out of their design during the season. But they commit all strategic redesigns of their cars for the following season.

We must embrace a similar macro-evolution and micro-evolution mindset.

Principle 5: Effective operations execution and management trigger the feedback loop for future macro-evolutions.

Our operations execution mantra embraces the enablement maturity improvements, trusts our operations baseline, and executes flawlessly using work plans and our three lines of defense. If our performance lags our leading indicators, the remediations sit in one of the topics we already discussed. We might find micro-evolution opportunities through effective analyses when breaking limits are breached. But the answer is never to go rogue and revert to Hail Mary tactics.

Focus on understanding how and why we are winning or losing without sacrificing discipline.

In the hit sci-fi novel *Ender's Game* by Orson Scott Card, the child leader, Ender Wiggin, is fighting an alien race for survival. The story has a repetitive theme around playing and learning from war games. That is akin to our macro-evolution cycles. The story has a memorable climax when humans secure a decisive victory by sacrificing moral fiber. The Colonel overseeing the battle tells the main character, Ender Wiggin, "Congratulations. You beat them and it's all over." However, our hero is devastated when he learns that his victory rested on many half-truths. How we win matters!

This is important in every aspect of life. But it's non-negotiable that we operate our company with this mentality. Our outcomes are only meaningful if it follows the operations baseline. Winning without knowing exactly why we won doesn't help us capitalize on that win.

If we have an outsized quarter of solid sales, but we achieved that without following our operations baseline, can we answer why we did so well? We cannot! We could try to find a correlation between our short-term success and some activity in our company. But correlation does not imply causality. We are more likely to confirm an incorrect bias or two through a correlation

E.4 ACHIEVE PEAK PERFORMANCE VIA TRANSPARENT AND PREDICTIVE OPERATIONS EXECUTION

analysis based on the short-term. Our data is likely too poor to analyze if we didn't execute based on our operations baseline.

The relationship between our execution and outcomes is a causal one. Success decoupled from operations often leads companies astray. Short-term success found by two or three individuals might leave us thinking that their approach is meaningful for others to follow. We might fall for recency bias that winning two or three similar customers in quick succession unexpectedly is a more meaningful trend than it really is, which might lead us to sell to similar customers who eventually cost us more to serve than the revenue we get from them.

A simple series of events at a company I worked with exemplifies challenges from such decoupling. One sales rep leveraging a personal contact landed a large customer outside the company's sweet spot. This customer directly managed residential homes they rented out across the US through their rental portal. Coincidentally, this was a good customer because they had access to data from these homes, and that data access is necessary to create customer value. But was this one deal meaningful data? No, because we decided to pursue an easily winnable customer outside our sweet spot.

The sales rep then used this opportunity to go after several other seemingly similar prospects and convinced several of them that they could capture the same value as the first company. Again, it worked – from a sales perspective!

But here was the catch – the first customer was unique; they managed real estate directly and had the data. Although the remaining customers considered themselves peers, their business models were not the same; they only invested in the properties but didn't directly manage their rentals and thus didn't have the necessary data. As a result, the post-sales value creation for these other customers was nearly impossible for the account management team. The remaining customers were left unhappy and eventually churned off. The relationship between execution and outcomes broke when the rep went after that first one-off prospect and ignored other prospects. The organizational mistake was to think there was meaning in this single decoupled success.

A similar conundrum will plague us if we experience poor outcomes. We can only know what parts of the operations baseline failed us if we execute to its intent. Otherwise, we will end up arbitrarily blaming our offerings or processes or people involved rather than objectively solving the underlying root cause.

Even in the smallest of companies, outcomes are scalable if we have a strong operations baseline and execution effectively mirrors it. One of the most successful start-ups I had the pleasure of being involved with had internalized the importance of fundamentals by the time the company had six employees. The first sales development representative had detailed scripts and call lists. By the time we hired the first sales rep, the marketing and sales engine had appropriate maturity, and the hand-offs to account management was well-defined. This company turned down sales that didn't fit the sweet spot. They maintained the sanctity of the offering in the years since. The positive outcomes at this company were based on a strong and ever-maturing operations baseline.

Be aware that there will be tempting moments when ideas and anecdotes might feel necessary to react to through our decision meeting cadence and month – or quarter-end financial reporting. Even Black Swan events like Covid-19 are not something companies must worry about because the next event will look completely different. By definition, real Black Swan events are completely unpredictable.

Companies with a strong operations baseline and the ability to execute against it can hope to navigate even such drastic events with grace; those without a strong foundation can't. It's that simple. So, as a rule of thumb, do not overreact positively or negatively to short-term outcomes. Maintain discipline!

Execution management discipline enables future strategy development and planning.

Our operations baseline must always follow our corporate strategy assessment and strategic plan because otherwise, we would never know whether our results align with our strategy. Our opportunity to redesign our operations baseline holistically comes again during the next macro-evolution cycle.

We can only chart a course for the future if we can learn from our operations execution cycle. Our actions and decisions and the market's reactions to them give us an incredible amount of data. But as we covered under value engine, data always follows a process. Therefore, our company's data is only meaningful if we follow our operations baseline.

Can we say that a specific capability is valued or not by the market if we aren't selling it as we framed in our operations baseline? Can we say that a particular capability is not valuable to a customer if we aren't teaching them how to take advantage of it as we framed in our operations baseline? Can we say that our selling process based on Buying Decision Drivers of our sweet spot is effective or not unless we live by our core values and follow our processes?

No!

If we don't execute our operations baseline, we have no valuable information, and we will be back at square 1 at the next corporate strategy development cycle. We may indulge in the same debates we did in previous years. We won't have good answers on what is working and what isn't working.

We must be disciplined and focus on delivering on promises that we made to ourselves, all employees, the board, the customers, and other external partners. If we don't, we will never know whether our strategy and planning are effective. If we don't know their effectiveness, we won't know whether we need to invest further in the strategic choices we have made or whether we should change them.

A well-managed execution cycle allows us to answer the question – *What does our next macro-evolution cycle look like?*

The next macro-evolution cycle starts with the next corporate strategy assessment around the corner.

Are you exhausted after going up one macro-evolutionary cycle of *The Spiral Stairway*™ to complete one level of maturity growth and execution?

Good! That means we are doing it right. Now, let's do it again!

Building a holistic company that focuses on sustainable growth and intrinsic value is not meant to be easy.

Align Holistic Purpose With Methods.

PEOPLE are complicated; everyone has different underlying motivations; we are all working with different sets of information. This makes our work environment seem impossible to focus on in the longer term, making our world very messy. Of course, no one intentionally plans to create a mess; but much of it is avoidable.

There is nothing called a free lunch. Either we are paying for it later, or someone else is paying on our behalf. If we reduce the number of shortcuts in our actions and decisions, messes become less likely. You are now locked and loaded to think deeper and ask more challenging questions.

I appreciate the intent behind "move fast and break things." However, it is important to move fast, improve things, and not leave a mess other people must clean up. If each of us can go to work every day focusing on how our actions and decisions lead to long-term sustainable outcomes for ourselves and other people, then our collective progress can accelerate.

I no longer look at extrinsic results of companies to understand their true prosperity. So often, those results are a story and not the reality. Instead, our five-part methodology, its components, and underlying principles give me the tools to understand any company's holistic health through everyday behaviors.

I hope you find meaning in *The Spiral Stairway*™ mindset. I hope you learned something new, and I hope you are able to make an adjustment in your work environment using these principles. Every person who jumps on the holistic company train is a victory for all of us.

I hope you use it to assess your own companies and ask hard questions. It's up to all of us to ensure that companies, including every entity that every human being works in, have a reasonable purpose and path to achieving that purpose. Not every company needs to survive or even exist. We can all choose to vacate a company that is only alive because easy money or unbalanced extrinsic motivation is coursing through its veins. We best allocate investment to a holistic purpose optimally aligned with methods to achieve that purpose.

Definitions of Fundamental Concepts.

Addressable Market	28
Aggregate Operations Plan	470
Analysis	232
Analysis vs. Reporting	236
Approver Role	320
Breaking Limit	243
Buyer Role	317
Buying Decision Driver	330
Capability	176
Capability Element Acquisition Path	348
Capability Elements	343
Chain of Controllability	412
Company	35
Company Purpose	56
Comparative Advantage Ecosystem (CAE)	76
Core Values	64
Corporate Strategy	265
Customer Groups	170
Customer Journey	170
Delegation of Authority	483
Effectiveness Vectors	344
Enablement Investment	446

Enablement Planning	390
Enablement Resources	84
Enablement Roadmap	517
Enablement Work Plans	521
Expertise	86
Externally Observable Parameters	282
Feature	175
Financial Forecasts	375
Flow Thinking	160
Formal One-on-One	121
Functions	394
Hawthorne Effect	557
Hiring	93
Holistic Company	20
Insights	233
Investment Planning	435
Lagging Indicators	239
Leading Indicators	238
Macro-evolutions	43
Management Approach	48
Management Approach Enablers	333
Management Limit	243
Market	276
Market Landscape	277
Market Problem	165

Micro-evolutions	43
Needs vs. Wants	168
Net Customer Value	161
Non-core Activities	287
Operations Baseline	41
Operations-Focused Planning	377
Operations Investment	458
Operations Planning	411
Operations Resources	83
Operations Work Plans	548
Packaging	185
Performance Management Competencies	118
Performance Management Expectations	115
Performance Management Goals	112
Performance Management Outcomes	117
Player Groups	279
Process	193
Process-Data Symbiosis	222
Productization	162
Reporting	234
Skill	88
Skill Groups	82
Steady State	440
Strategic Initiatives	391
Strategic Initiatives [Refined]	397

Strategic Trade-offs	266
Strategy and Operations Connectivity	512
Strategy-Led Planning	371
Strategy vs. Tactics	262
String of Pearls Mindset	35
Sustainable Growth Mindset	18
Sweet Spot	300
Sweet Spot [Refined]	312
Sweet Spot Rule #1	309
Sweet Spot Rule #2	310
System	36
Systems First Mantra	39
Target	241
Three Customer Roles	315
Unit Economics	410
Unvoiced Imbalances	293
Use Case	171
User Role	318
Value-Based Pricing	189
Value Engine	147
Value Engine Enablers	333
Voiced Pain Points	292

Made in the USA
Monee, IL
20 May 2022

96785947R00315